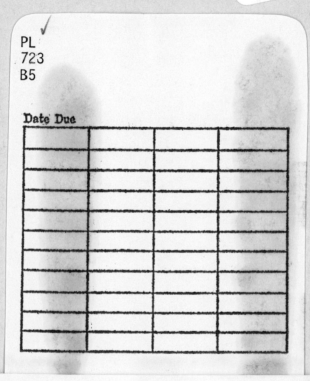

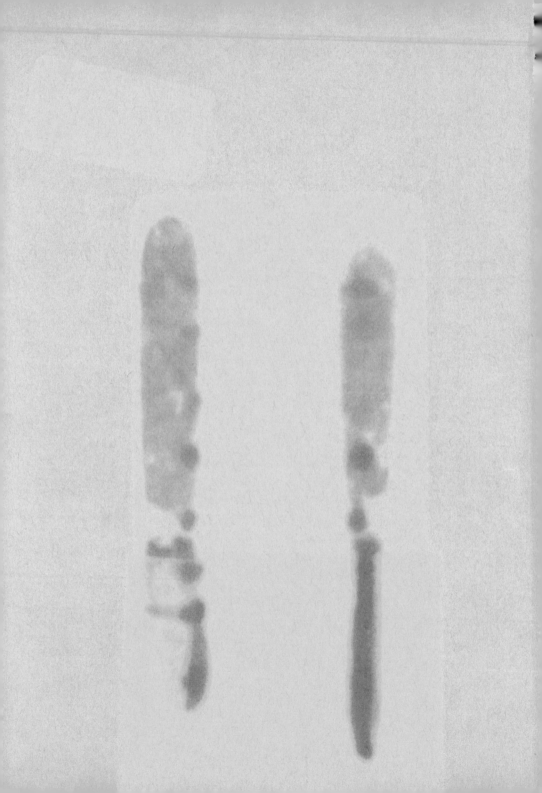

BIOGRAPHICAL
DICTIONARY
OF
JAPANESE
LITERATURE

BIOGRAPHICAL DICTIONARY OF JAPANESE LITERATURE

Sen'ichi Hisamatsu

Kodansha International Ltd.

in collaboration with the

International Society for Educational Information

Distributed in the United States by Kodansha
International/USA Ltd., through Harper & Row,
Publishers, Inc., 10 East 53rd Street, New York,
New York 10022, and in Japan by Kodansha
International Ltd., 2–12–21 Otowa, Bunkyo-ku,
Tokyo 112.

Published by Kodansha International Ltd., 2–12–21
Otowa, Bunkyo-ku, Tokyo 112 and Kodansha
International/USA Ltd., 10 East 53rd Street, New
York, New York 10022 and 44 Montgomery
Street, San Francisco, California 94104 in
collaboration with the International Society for
Educational Information, Inc., 7–8 Shintomi
2-chome, Chuo-ku, Tokyo 104. Copyright © 1976
by the International Society for Educational
Information, Inc. All rights reserved. Printed
in Japan.
LCC 75–14730 4-4-77
ISBN 0–87011–253–8
JBC 1591–784966–2361

First edition, 1976

Contents

Introduction

Surveying the development of Japanese literature from its beginnings down to the present time, one finds that its contours may be defined in terms of three criteria: the development of Japanese literature itself, the evolution of literary consciousness in Japan, and the occurrence of literary revivals. These literary revivals, which amounted to rebirths of the literature, occurred three times; applied to the periodization of the Japanese literary tradition, these criteria produce the following divisions:

Archaic Period: Asuka period to 781 (Ten'ō 1); birth of Japanese literature

Early Period: 782 (Enryaku 1) to 1155 (Kyūju 2)

Middle Period: 1156 (Hōgen 1) to 1557 (Kōji 2); first literary revival

Early Modern Period: 1558 (Eiroku 1) to 1867 (Keiō 3); second literary revival

Modern Period: 1868 (Meiji 1) to present; third literary revival

The Archaic Period, which extends to 781, saw the birth of Japanese literature. Though literature no doubt existed among the Japanese people from ancient times, the earliest written records of it date from the Asuka period, which began in 592, and it is convenient to take this as a starting point. From this period dates the *Hokekyō gishō*, a commentary by Shōtoku Taishi on the *Hokekyō* (Lotus Sutra); a manuscript of the work, said to be in his own hand, is still preserved. The *Kojiki* and *Nihon Shoki*, other works of the Archaic Period, contain material that had been handed down orally over a long period of time, but the written texts of the works are the product of the early Nara period, which began around 710. These works contain genealogies of the emperors of Japan as they were preserved in various family traditions, as well as myths, legends, and anecdotes interspersed with songs attributed to periods as far back as the mythical age of the gods.

The *Kojiki* and *Nihon Shoki*, as well as the *fudoki*, or provincial gazetteers, that were compiled around the same time, are works of narrative literature, and the songs that they contain are also essentially narrative in nature. In contrast to these, the some forty-five hundred songs contained in the *Man'yōshū*, a vast anthology compiled in the latter half of the eighth century, belong to the category of lyric poetry. Included in the anthology are the works of such outstanding poets as Kakinomoto no Hitomaro, Yamabe no Akahito, Yamanoue no Okura, and Ōtomo no Yakamochi, as well as numerous anonymous poems that appear to have been written by commoners. Japanese literature, like the literatures of so many other countries, had its beginnings in narrative and lyric poetry.

In many cases the creation of this early literature was motivated by the religious observances, work tasks, and other daily activities of the ancient Japanese, and to it they entrusted their deepest feelings. In these works of the Archaic Period, the emotional content tends to be simple and directly expressed.

The Early Period (782–1155) constitutes the four hundred some years after the capital was moved from Nara to Kyoto. In the literature of the Archaic Period, there is as yet no clear evidence of literary consciousness, but this consciousness gradually emerges in the period that followed, giving rise to a distinct set of aesthetic values. The principal concept in this system of aesthetics was that of *mono no aware*, "the sensitivity to things," as it has been translated, and though other concepts such as *okashi* (wit) and *taketakashi* (loftiness) were recognized, they were refined and modified by the prevailing emphasis upon melancholy. In poetry, the period saw the compilation of a number of imperially authorized anthologies, the first of them being the *Kokinshū*, or *Collection of Ancient and Modern Poems*, which contains poems marked by a tone of refinement and a harmony of form and content. In addition to the *waka*, the poetic form in which these works are cast, other literary forms made their appearance, such as the *monogatari* (tale), the *nikki* (diary), and the *zuihitsu* (miscellany), all devoted mainly to the expression of *aware*. Most famous of the tales is the *Genji monogatari* by Murasaki Shikibu, a lengthy work embued with a tone of refined sensitivity. By contrast, the most outstanding of the works in the *zuihitsu* form, the *Makura no sōshi*, is dominated by the ideal of *okashi*, lightness or wit. A statistical study of the language of the two works reveals that, while the *Genji monogatari* employs the word *aware* a total of 1,414 times and *okashi* 683, the word *aware* appears only 86 times in the *Makura no sōshi*, as opposed to 466 occurrences of the word *okashi*. The ideals of *aware* and *okashi* attained their highest level of expression in works such as the *Genji monogatari* and the *Makura no sōshi*, becoming increasingly conventionalized in the mannered and highly polished works of the latter part of the Early Period. Meanwhile, a new aesthetic consciousness was taking shape, creating the canons of taste that would characterize and dominate the literature of the Middle Period.

The Middle Period (1156–1557) represents the time of the first literary revival. Some might question whether such literary revivals actually occurred in the history of Japanese literature, but the present author believes that they did. Toward the end of the Early Period, for example, there was a conscious attempt to return to the spirit of the literature of the Archaic Period, the *Man'yōshū* being regarded with increasing respect, and the poet Saigyō looked to the world of nature for inspiration and fulfillment. The fact that men turned more and more to the Buddhist faith or sought to discover the meaning of life represents another aspect of the same literary revival, for as the old literature of the court nobility fell into decline, there was a search for new values and ideals. The new literature that emerged may be called both the literature of the warrior and the literature of the recluse. In such narrative works as the *Heike monogatari* or *Taiheiki*, it is the warrior and his ideals that are the focus of interest, but in the poetry of the *Shin kokinshū*, the works in *zuihitsu* form such as the *Hōjōki* or the *Tsurezuregusa*, or the Nō dramas, the figure of the recluse dominates. In the recluse literature, the ideal is designated by the term *yūgen*, mystery or profundity, which finds expression either in the overtly emotional style known as *ushin* or the more objective or transcendental style called *mushin*. One of the distinctive characteristics of the *yūgen* ideal is that it stresses a beauty that is suggestive and elliptical rather than explicit. A second characteristic is that, unlike the ideals of elegance or sublimity, it strives for a complex beauty made up of elements of quietude, ethereality, or even dryness. Again, in contrast to the ideals of *aware* and *okashi*, which embody a beauty that is emotive and sensual, works that are dominated by the *yūgen* concept have a strong philosophical tendency. This is because they are so often based upon the Buddhist doctrine of the essential oneness of all beings and a sense of the transitory nature of phenomenal existence, a fact that gives both depth as well as a tone of gloom to the literature of the period. In the *yūgen* of the poet Shinkei, there is a sense of elegance and beauty, but it is a beauty perceived by the mind, and in such statements as "nothing is more beautiful than ice" or "nothing is so rich in feeling as water," is reflected the desire to push beyond mere physical appearance to the transcendental realm of essential reality. Fixing all its attentions upon such ideals of beauty as these, the literature of the Middle Period ended its days.

The Early Modern Period (1558–1867) was the time of the second great literary revival. Though the Genroku era (1688–1704) when such writers as Bashō, Saikaku, Chikamatsu, and Keichū flourished, is generally regarded as the time when the revival took place, the beginnings of a new type of literature can already be discerned in the era of the military leaders Nobunaga and Hideyoshi that preceded it. During the Early Modern Period the country was governed by men of the military class, headed by the shoguns of the Tokugawa family, but the merchants and other townsmen, through the wealth they acquired, were often able to exercise economic domination over their nominal superiors of the warrior class. In literature as well, it was the literature of the common people, written by and for the townsmen, that dominated the scene. Poetry flourished, particularly that in the *haiku* form, and though the *haiku*'s ideal of *sabi*, an aged or worn quality, is clearly related to the Middle Period concept of *yūgen*, the philosophical tone of earlier poetry is replaced by an interest in wit and humor. The types of poetry known as *kyōka* and *senryū*, which were frankly humorous, satirical, or even scatological, are also the products of this time and reflect the lives of the common people.

Among the novels and *jōruri* (puppet theater) dramas of the period are many works belonging to the category of popular literature. The ideals of a complex and elliptical beauty cultivated in the literature of the Middle Period reappear here in such concepts as *sui* (chic), *tsū* (savoir faire), or *iki* (stylishness), but the elements of humor and vulgarity with which they are combined mark them as belonging to the literary tradition of the commoners. Even more markedly popular in tone are the *kokkeibon*, *sharebon*, and *ninjōbon*, collections of jokes and amorous tales written in a realistic manner that reflect the lives and morals of the common people. The conflict between the demands of *giri* (obligation), and *ninjō* (human feeling), a theme that is prominent in the literature of the time, likewise derives from the actual moral dilemmas faced by the common people in their daily lives. Though there are a certain number of historical dramas written for the *jōruri* and the kabuki theaters that depict the lives of the warriors, such works actually reflect the warriors' lives as seen through the eyes of the commoners. Finally, because the shogunate as a matter of governmental policy encouraged the acceptance of Confucian concepts of morality, the standard Confucian view of the didactic function of literature became, at least ostensibly, the basis for all literary activity. Such didacticism, with its professed aim of "encouraging good and punishing evil," provided the principal ingredient in the content of most novels and plays and at the same time served as a convenient device in ordering their structure.

The third literary revival took place in the Modern Period, 1868 to the present. The transition from the Early Modern to the Modern Period was marked by dramatic and far-reaching changes. These changes occurred not only in the political sphere, where a new system of government was set up, but in the cultural sphere as well, occasioned by the introduction of Western culture and learning to Japan. Aesthetics, rhetoric, sociology, psychology, and similar modern disciplines all exercised an influence on literary criticism and, at times, on the creative process of literature itself. Realism, romanticism, naturalism, and other schools of literature took shape, constituting what may be called the third literary revival in Japan.

While critics such as Tsubouchi Shōyō, Mori Ōgai, Takayama Chogyū, and Shimamura Hōgetsu sought to define the aims of the new literary revival, novelists such as Ozaki Kōyō, Kōda Rohan, Natsume Sōseki, and Shimazaki Tōson dominated the creative scene, to be succeeded in the Taishō and Shōwa eras by such well-known writers as Tanizaki Jun'ichirō, Shiga Naoya, and Kawabata Yasunari. In the field of poetry, the works of Masaoka Shiki, Yosano Akiko, Kitahara Hakushū, and Hagiwara Sakutarō are particularly noteworthy. The literature of the Modern Period, while receiving and absorbing various influences from Western culture, at the same time has its roots firmly fixed in the traditions of the past. From early times until the end of the Early Modern Period, what foreign literary influences there were entering Japan came almost entirely from China, producing a literature that was "Japanese in spirit, Chinese in technique." With the advent of the Modern Period, foreign influences began to enter the country from another direction, engendering a literature "Japanese in spirit, Western in technique," and setting off a whole new phase of creative activity.

あしひきのやまち川一つ
れもねわねやすのきり
川郎女奉和天皇一首
が君る活計武

千

つねに
情なる

了

Archaic Period

HIEDA NO ARE (dates uncertain)

He appears to have lived in the latter part of the seventh century and the early part of the eighth and is famous for having recited from memory the "imperial records" (genealogies of the rulers) and the "old words" (legends of antiquity) to the compiler of the *Kojiki*. According to the preface to the *Kojiki*, he acted as a *toneri*, or attendant, an office of rather low status, in the personal service of Emperor Temmu. The emperor, distressed at the state of confusion into which the various family genealogies and legends of the past had fallen, commanded Hieda no Are to recite what he knew of such matters so that a correct record might be compiled to be handed down to future ages. Emperor Temmu did not live to see the work completed, but his successor, Empress Gemmei, carrying on his wishes, ordered Ō no Yasumaro to listen to Hieda no Are's recitations and write them down. The result was the *Kojiki*, or *Record of Ancient Matters*, in three chapters, which was completed in 712.

Scholars disagree as to whether Hieda no Are was a man or a woman. Said to have belonged to the Sarume-no-kimi clan, which descended from the goddess Amenouzume-no-mikoto and which customarily supplied women attendants to the court, for this reason it has been suggested that Hieda no Are was in fact a woman. On the other hand, the office of *toneri* strongly suggests masculine sex, though there would seem to be no way to decide the matter definitively. In any event, the fact that, although occupying a rather insignificant post, he was assigned the difficult and important task of memorizing and reciting the genealogies of the imperial family and the legends of antiquity indicates that he must have been a person of unusual intelligence and learning and truly extraordinary powers of memorization who enjoyed the confidence of Emperor Temmu and was constantly in attendance by his side. Whether a man or a woman, he deserves to be honored and remembered for the part he played, along with Ō no Yasumaro, in the compilation of the *Kojiki*, the oldest extant work of Japanese history.

Hozumi no Miko (d. 715)

Statesman of the Asuka period. He was the fifth son of Emperor Temmu; his mother was Ōnu no Iratsume, the daughter of Soga no Akae. In 691 he was presented with a fief of five hundred households. Upon the death of Empress Jitō in the twelfth month of 702, he was appointed *sakumogari-no-miya-no-tsukasa*, director of the place of temporary interment. In 704 his fief was increased by two hundred households, and when the Chidaijōkanji Prince Osakabe died in the fifth month of the following year, he was appointed in the ninth month to succeed him in the office of *daijōkanji*, the highest ministerial post in the government. He held the post throughout the remainder of the reign of Emperor Mommu, and under the emperor's successor, Empress Gemmei, joined the Minister of the Left Isonokami no Maro and the Minister of the Right Fujiwara no Fuhito in managing affairs of state. In the first month of 715 he was promoted from the rank of *nihon* to that of *ippon* and died in the seventh month of the same year; it has been surmised that he was around fifty at the time of his death.

Four of his poems in *tanka* form are included in the *Man'yōshū*. They concern his intense and tragic love for Princess Tajima, his younger sister by a different mother, who was in residence in the palace of Prince Takechi, and his grief at her death, and give some idea of his character. Noteworthy is that entitled "Poem written by Prince Hozumi to pour out his grief as he viewed the grave of Princess Tajima from afar on a snowy day" (II: 203):

> Falling snow,
> do not fall so thickly!
> The hill of Ikai in Yonabari
> must be so cold!

In his late years he had a love affair with Ōtomo no Sakanoue no Iratsume.

Ishikawa no Iratsume (dates uncertain)

Poet of the *Man'yōshū*. Iratsume is a familiar form of address for a woman; the name Ishikawa no Iratsume appears several times in the *Man'yōshū*, but whether it refers to a single writer or several is not certain. It occurs in the following instances:

1. An Ishikawa no Iratsume who exchanged poems with the Buddhist priest Kume no Zenji in the time of Emperor Tenji (662–71).

2. An Ishikawa no Iratsume who was a lady-in-waiting and lover of Prince Ōtsu, son of Emperor Temmu and younger brother of Princess Ōku. She is famous for the poem she wrote in reply to one by the prince; her poem reads:

> Would I had been, beloved,
> The dripping dew of the hill,
> That wetted you
> While for me you waited.[1]

It has been suggested that she is the same person as the Ishikawa no Iratsume to whom Prince Hinamishi, the younger brother of Prince Ōtsu, sent a poem in a note to which the recipient is identified as Ōnago (another name for Ishikawa no Iratsume) and the Ishikawa no Iratsume who, having proposed marriage to Ōtomo no Tanushi and been refused, sent a mocking poem, which reads:

> I heard that you were
> A gallant courtier,
> Yet you refused me shelter and sent me away—
> How boorish of the gallant courtier![1]

If so, then we may conclude that Ishikawa no Iratsume's name was Ōnago. All of these poems are marked by a deliberate display of wit and are remarkable for their similarity of technique and conception. The poems sent in reply to Prince Ōtsu and Ōtomo no Tanushi are particularly close in technique and suggest very strongly that they are by the same person.

3. An Ishikawa no Iratsume who sent a rather ordinary poem to Ōtomo no Sukune and who is identical with Ishikawa no Naimyōbu, the wife of Ōtomo no Yasumaro and mother of the talented Sakanoue no Iratsume.

4. An Ishikawa no Iratsume who was the wife of Fujiwara no Sukunamaro and who wrote the following poem when he had grown cold toward her and they were living apart:

> With longings deep
> as the great sea's floor
> I trail my skirts,

---

1. Most of the *Man'yōshū* translations used here are from *The Man'yōshū*, The Nippon Gakujutsu Shinkōkai Translation, Iwanami Shoten 1940; Columbia University Press 1965.

> pacing back and forth through
> the village of Sugawara.

The poem has been praised for its boldness and breadth of conception, unusual in poems by women of the time.

Jimmu Tennō

Legendary first emperor of Japan. Accounts of Jimmu Tennō are found in two early works of history and legend, the *Kojiki* and *Nihon Shoki*. Jimmu is a posthumous name assigned to him during the Nara period; according to the accounts in the works mentioned above, his name was Kamu Yamato Iware-hiko-no-mikoto and he was the son of Ugaya Fuki Aezu-no-mikoto and the great-grandson of Ninigi-no-mikoto. He is said to have left his native land of Hyūga in Kyushu and advanced eastward along the Inland Sea, landing at Naniwa; he marched overland but was driven back by a local leader named Nagasune-hiko at Mt. Ikoma. Taking to the sea once more, he proceeded to Kumano at the end of the Kii Peninsula, from whence he made his way north through the mountains to Yoshino and thence to the region of Yamato. He conquered the powerful local leaders, overthrew Nagasune-hiko, and, after pacifying the Yamato area, became the first emperor of Japan at Kashiwara on the first day of the year 660 B.C. He is reported to have passed away at the age of 127. According to archaeological evidence, Japanese society in the seventh century B.C. was still in a very primitive state of development, and there is, needless to say, no evidence to suggest that any such supreme ruler existed or carried out the activities described above. It has been surmised that the legend of Jimmu Tennō's eastern expedition was created in the early days of the growth of the Yamato court, tracing the origin of the imperial family to the far-off region of Hyūga in order to emphasize the importance and inevitability of ties between Kyushu and the area of central Japan.

Examining the accounts of Jimmu Tennō in the *Kojiki* and *Nihon Shoki*, one finds that both works stress his importance as the first sovereign and founder of the Japanese nation, and present portraits of him that are clearly closer to myth than to history. If one considers him purely as a literary figure, however, the portraits of him that emerge in the two works differ considerably. The *Kojiki* presents him less as a deified ruler than as a human hero, during the eastern expedition cheerfully sharing the same living conditions as the brave men under his command, composing battle songs and love songs (*Kojiki* 17/20) and otherwise conducting himself like the typical hero of an epic poem. In the account of him in the *Nihon Shoki*, however, the epic or romantic quality gives way to an emphasis upon political qualities, and he is presented as a wise and foresighted leader of a sovereign nation. These differences that mark the treatment of the figure of Jimmu Tennō in the *Kojiki* and *Nihon Shoki* may be said to reflect basic differences in the nature of the two works as a whole.

Jitō Tennō (d. 702)

Forty-first sovereign of Japan. She was the second daughter of Emperor Tenji; her personal name was Unonosasara no Himemiko. Her mother was the daughter of Soga no Ishikawamaro. At the age of twelve she became the consort of Prince Ōama, the future Emperor Temmu, and bore him a son, Prince Kusakabe. During the Jinshin civil disturbance, in which Prince Ōama and his forces clashed with those of the sovereign, she constantly assisted her husband, and in 674, after the disturbance had ended and her husband had ascended the throne, she was made empress. During the reign of Emperor Temmu, she continued to take an active part in affairs of state, and after his demise in 686, she exercised the actual power of rule. Her son, the heir apparent Prince Kusakabe, died in 689 at the age of twenty-seven, and the following year she herself ascended the throne, being known posthumously as Empress Jitō. In the eleventh year of her reign she ceded the throne to her grandson Emperor Mommu, but continued for the following five years to supervise affairs of state until her death in 702.

She is said to have been a woman of great talent and dignity. Carrying on the efforts of her husband, Emperor Temmu, she worked to extend and bring to completion the *ritsuryō*, or bureaucratic system of government, and brought stability and prosperity to the aristocratic society of the time. Her reign, during which Kakinomoto no Hitomaro flourished, represents one of the greatest ages of Japanese poetry. In particular, the frequent progresses and outings that the empress made to such places as Yoshino, Kii, and Ise served greatly to foster and inspire the poetic efforts of the various nobles and officials who accompanied her. Furthermore, the empress herself composed poems, the *Man'yōshū* preserving two *chōka* and four *tanka* from her hand. They have an air of grandeur and at the same time a sensitivity that is characteristically feminine, and in style seem peculiarly appropriate for an absolute monarch who reigned at a time when the bureaucratic state system was brought to completion. The following poem is representative of her finest work, and indeed of the finest work of the period as a whole, and is widely known among Japanese readers because of its inclusion in the famous anthologies of later ages, the *Shin kokinshū* and *Ogura hyakunin isshu* (I: 28):

> Spring has passed away
> And summer is come;
> Look where white clothes are spread in the sun
> On the heavenly hill of Kagu!

Also famous and indicative of her great talent are the *chōka* and *tanka* written after the death of Emperor Temmu and giving expression to her grief.

JOMEI TENNŌ (593–641; r. 629–641)

Thirty-fourth sovereign of Japan. He was the son of Prince Osaka-hikobito Ōe, the son of Emperor Bidatsu; his mother was Princess Nukade-hime; his name was Prince Tamura or Okinaga-tarashi-hi Hironuka. After the death of Empress Suiko, the high minister Soga no Emishi, disregarding the empress's dying instructions to set up Prince Yamashiro no Ōe, son of Crown Prince Shōtoku, as ruler, forcibly placed Prince Tamura on the throne. He became ruler in 629 and the following year took Princess Takara as his consort. In the tenth month of the same year he moved the capital to the Asuka Okamoto Palace in Yamato. During his reign the power of Soga no Emishi and his son Iruka increased with dramatic rapidity. Two of Emperor Jomei's poems are preserved in the *Man'yōshū*. The first, number two in chapter one, is the famous poem that begins:

> Countless are the mountains in Yamato,
> But perfect is the heavenly hill of Kagu.

Grand in conception, it belongs to the type known as *kunimi*, "land-viewing poems," and represents a first step in the transition from such poems to true landscape poetry. The other, number 1511 in chapter eight, which reads

> The stag of the Ogura Mountain
> That cries when evening comes,
> Cries not tonight—
> Is it that he sleeps?

displays a feeling of tender concern for the deer. His consort later reigned as Empress Saimei, and from their union were born the future emperors Tenji and Temmu and Empress Hashihito, the consort of Emperor Kōtoku.

Kakinomoto no Hitomaro (dates uncertain)

Though he is generally acknowledged to be the greatest of the poets represented in the *Man'yōshū*, no information concerning him is preserved in any text other than the anthology, and the date and place of his birth and death are unknown. He was active at the courts of Empress Jitō (687–96) and Emperor Mommu (697–707) and seems to have died around the age of fifty, shortly before the capital was moved to Nara in 710. The Kakinomoto family for generations lived in the region of Ichinomoto south of Nara, and presumably Hitomaro also grew up in this area. He was probably still a child at the time of the Jinshin civil disturbance, but later reached the age when he could enter the service of Crown Prince Kusakabe. In 689, when the prince died, he seems to have transferred to the service of Prince Takechi. At later dates he held other court offices and also spent some time as an official in the provinces. It appears that he was very closely associated with the courts of Empress Jitō and Emperor Mommu and served as a kind of court poet, accompanying the ruler on outings and hunting trips and composing poems to commemorate such occasions, as well as the deaths of members of the imperial family. Thus he is known to have accompanied the sovereign on a visit to the province of Kii, and also seems to have made trips as an official to the detached palace at Yoshino, the province of Sanuki in Shikoku, and elsewhere. In his later years he was appointed to office in the province of Iwami and presumably died there.

His official rank was very low, being below that of the Sixth Rank, and it is uncertain what sort of post he held during the time he served in the provinces. From the poems mentioning his wife, it is clear that he was married at least twice. His first wife, whose name is unknown, was a court lady and died sometime before Hitomaro. She was a woman of great talent and wrote excellent poetry, much of it in the form of exchanges of poems between herself and Hitomaro. It would seem that they had one or more children. In his later years, when he was living in Iwami, Hitomaro married again, this time to a woman named Yonami no Otome, who also wrote poetry.

Among the numerous poems preserved in the *Man'yōshū* attributed to Hitomaro there is a certain number of works of doubtful authenticity, and it is therefore impossible to say exactly how many of his poems are extant. Among the works that can be attributed with certainty to him are twenty *chōka* and seventy *tanka*, and if the works contained in the so-called Hitomaro Collection are added, the total number is considerable. It is clear that by the time of the compilation of the *Man'yōshū* he was already recognized as a poet of the highest rank. His works display an unusual breadth of subject matter, dealing, as mentioned above, with state functions of the court and imperial family but also including songs of parting, love songs, songs descriptive of travel, etc. He employed all the three poetic forms in existence at the time and excelled in the *chōka* and *sedōka*, raising them to their highest level of development. He made skillful use of the various rhetorical devices that had been developed in the songs and poetry of the past, employing pillow-words, parallelism, introductory phrases, assonance, etc., as well as experimenting with new devices of his own invention. His work is thus both conventional and creative at the same time. Products of a superlative natural talent that reflect the flourishing aristocratic society of the Asuka period, his poems possess an elegance and nobility of diction and an intensity of feeling that place them in the highest rank of works in the Japanese language. There is probably no other figure in all of Japanese culture who has been so deeply and consistently revered from the century of his lifetime down to the present. Already, some fifty years after his death, Ōtomo no Yakamochi was speaking of him with the highest respect, and Ki no Tsurayuki in the preface to the *Kokinshū* dubbed him *kasei*, "Saint of Poetry." From that time on he became an object of popular adulation, and in Heian times a ceremony known as *Hitomaro eigu* was performed in which incense, flowers, and poems were offered before his portrait. His work has continued to the present day to exert a profound influence upon the growth and direction of Japanese poetry, and he continues to be recognized as the greatest poet the literature has so far produced.

KARU NO HITSUGI-NO-MIKO (dates uncertain)

Kinashi no Karu no Hitsugi-no-miko, Crown Prince Karu, was the heir apparent of the nineteenth sovereign Emperor Ingyō; his mother was the consort Empress Oshisaka no Ōnakatsu-hime. According to the *Kojiki*, after the demise of Emperor Ingyō he committed incest with his sister by the same mother, Karu no Ōiratsume, and thereby lost the support of the people of the time. He was attacked and seized by the soldiers of Prince Anaho (later Emperor Ankō) and banished to Iyo. According to this account, both he and his sister committed suicide. The version of the incident in the *Nihon Shoki*, however, places it during the time when Emperor Ingyō was still alive. It records that Ōiratsume was banished to Iyo and states that, after Emperor Ingyō had passed away, the crown prince was defeated in a struggle over the succession with Prince Anaho and committed suicide. Nine poems attributed to Prince Karu are recorded in the *Kojiki*, three in the *Nihon Shoki*, one in the *Kinkafu*, and one in chapter thirteen of the *Man'yōshū*. The poems in the *Kojiki* constitute a superb series of love songs, giving expression to the wild joy and passion of the prince's love for his sister, his pledges of fidelity and attempts to comfort her after he had been seized and was about to be banished to Iyo, and to the other aspects of their tragic and fatal infatuation. But the form and style of the various poems are a mixture of early and later elements, and notes are appended to them designating them as *shirage-uta*, *hinaburi*, *amataburi*, or *yomiuta*, terms that pertain to early song forms, suggesting that the poems are in fact a kind of song cycle or story in ballad form. In any event, it is very doubtful that they are really the work of Crown Prince Karu.

Karu no Ōiratsume (dates unknown)

She was a daughter of Emperor Ingyō (412–454) and is renowned for the songs attributed to her. She is said to have fallen in love with her elder brother Karu no Hitsugi-no-miko (Crown Prince Karu) and was accordingly punished.

The *Kojiki* account of the love affair reports that Prince Karu relinquished his position as heir apparent and was banished to Iyo on the island of Shikoku, but the account in the *Nihon Shoki* makes Princess Karu the one who was banished. Both the *Kojiki* and the *Nihon Shoki* record love poems exchanged by the pair, though the texts of the songs differ in the two works. The songs are highly passionate in nature and outstanding as examples of early Japanese poetry. The following, by Karu no Ōiratsume, is from the *Kojiki*:

> Aine of the
> summer grasses,
> don't tread on the oyster shells
> along its shore—
> wait and come to me when it's light!

Kasa no Iratsume (Otome) (dates uncertain)

Poet of the middle Nara period. Nothing is known of her outside of her works in the *Man'yōshū*. Twenty-nine poems in *tanka* form by her are preserved in the anthology, all of them love songs addressed to Ōtomo no Yakamochi, and it is surmised that she had an affair with him during his youthful years before he left the capital to take up duties in the provinces. However, because two of her poems in chapter four indicate that they were written "after we had parted," it is probable that the affair did not last very long. Outside of this, nothing whatever is known of her, including whether she was related in any way to Kasa no Kanamura. Because the *Man'yōshū* contains only two poems by Ōtomo no Yakamochi written in response to her love poems, it may be supposed that her love was not returned with any great enthusiasm, and indeed her poems as a whole are imbued with a deep sense of longing and despair. In technique her poems are characterized by the frequent use of rhetorical devices such as pillow-words and introductory phrases, while in theme they depict the various aspects of love and convey an impression of gentle but passionate feminity. Their melancholy music has touched the hearts of readers over the centuries and caused her to be regarded as one of the finest women poets in the history of Japanese literature.

The following are representative of her best works (IV: 600, 602):

> Oh how steadily I love you—
> you who awe me
> like the thunderous waves
> that lash the seacoast of Ise!

> More sad thoughts crowd into my mind
> when evening comes; for then
> appears your phantom shape—
> speaking as I have known you speak.

Kasa no Kanamura (dates uncertain)

Nothing is known of his life outside of what can be learned from the poems preserved in the *Man'yōshū*, but it is certain that he was born in the early part of the Nara period and seems therefore to have been a contemporary of Yamabe no Akahito. He appears to have lived in Nara and to have been a minor official at the courts of Empress Genshō (715–23) and Emperor Shōmu (724–48). He served as a court poet and left a number of works written when he accompanied the sovereign on various outings. These include journeys to relatively nearby spots such as Yoshino, Naniwa,

Harima, and Yamashiro, as well as more distant journeys to the region in Ōmi north of Lake Biwa or the province of Echizen. Because of the large number of his poems and their position in the anthology, it is possible to surmise that he was looked upon as a more important poet than Yamabe no Akahito at the time when the *Man'yōshū* was compiled.

The works that are indisputably his number eight *chōka* and twelve *tanka*, and if the poems in the so-called Kanamura Collection are added, it brings the total to forty-five poems. It has been customary in the past to describe his works as formalistic, conventional, and lacking in creativity. But at a time when few poets could still handle the *chōka* form with any degree of skill, he left a relatively large number of works in that form and probably deserves to be more highly regarded. He seems to have thought of himself specifically as a court poet and to have concentrated upon expressing the emotions occasioned by the various journeys he made in that capacity, and his works thus have a slightly different tone and spirit, not found in previous poetry. In skill and manner of expression, many of his works come close to rivaling those of Kakinomoto no Hitomaro. Among his finest works are the lament written in 715 on the death of Prince Shiki and the poems written on the occasion of his visit to Mt. Shiotsu in Ōmi.

Kɪ no Iratsume (dates uncertain)

Poet of the middle Nara period. A note appended to an early manuscript of the *Man'yōshū* records that her personal name was Ojika, that she was the daughter of Ki no Kahito, and the wife of Aki no Ōkimi (Prince Aki). It would appear that the note had already been appended to the manuscript some time before the middle of the Heian period. Her father, Kahito, is represented in the *Man'yōshū* by two *tanka* and one *sedōka*, and the *Shoku Nihongi* mentions him in several places, indicating that he was an official in the reign of Emperor Shōmu (724–48).

Her poems are found in chapters four and eight of the *Man'yōshū* and total twelve in number. Chapter four contains three poems entitled "Ki no Iratsume's Songs of Jealousy," which suggest that her husband's love for her in time cooled and that the couple parted. In addition, her works contain five love poems sent to Ōtomo no Yakamochi. Since his replies to them appear only in chapters four and eight, which preserve the works of his early period, it would seem that the affair between him and Ki no Iratsume took place in his youth, sometime after she had separated from her husband. Again, the order in which the poems of the chapter are arranged suggests that the affair took place somewhat after the love affair between Yakamochi and Kasa no Iratsume, poems relating to which are also preserved in the *Man'yōshū*.

Her works, one may say, are characterized first of all by cleverness, and whatever sincerity they may possess is likely to be hidden by artifice. One finds in them none of the passion and gentleness that mark the love poems of Kasa no Iratsume, but rather a tone that is almost shrill and harsh. Nevertheless, in terms of dexterity and mastery of technique, she deserves to be ranked as one of the most outstanding women poets of the *Man'yōshū*.

Nakatomi no Yakamori (dates uncertain)

Poet of the Nara period, the fourth period into which the works of the *Man'yōshū* are divided. Nothing is known of his life outside of what is recorded in chapter fifteen of the *Man'yōshū* and in two entries in the *Shoku Nihongi*. Because of his affair with Sano no Chigami no Otome, an attendant in the *kurabe*, an office attached to the Bureau of the Princess Imperial Deputy at the Great Shrine of Ise, he was banished to the province of Echizen. The women attached to the Bureau of the Princess Imperial Deputy were forbidden to have any relations with men, and presumably Yakamori was punished for having violated this prohibition. He was not pardoned at the time of the general amnesty in 740, but in 763 he was granted the court rank of Junior Fifth Rank Lower Grade, so presumably he received pardon sometime during that interval.

The poems by him recorded in chapter fifteen of the *Man'yōshū* are grouped together with those by Sano no Chigami to form a single series of sixty-three works in the *sōmonka*, or "inquiry and answer," genre, which in the *Man'yōshū* is usually employed for love poems. The series contains forty poems by Yakamori and twenty-three by Sano no Chigami. The last seven of Yakamori's poems, however, bear the title, "Pouring Out My Feelings in Relation to the Flowers and Birds," and are in the nature of soliloquies; hence they should be considered as separate from the poems that he exchanged with Sano no Chigami. With the exception of the poems composed immediately after being sentenced to banishment, as he journeyed along his way, and immediately after reaching his place of banishment, as well as the seven poems mentioned above, all of Yakamori's poems are descriptions of his love for Sano no Chigami. His poems are generally regarded as somewhat inferior to hers, though it does not appear that his love was any less sincere than that of the lady. On the contrary, their rather casual manner of expression would seem to conceal a passion that is as intense and deeply moving as that more openly revealed by Sano no Chigami. As a writer of love poetry, he holds a place of unique importance among the male poets who flourished in the Tempyō era (729–48).

Nukada-no-ōkimi (dates uncertain)

Poet of the *Man'yōshū*; she was active during the reigns of emperors Tenji and Temmu (661–86). Much about her life remains a mystery, the only references to her being found in the *Man'yōshū* and the chapter pertaining to Emperor Temmu in the *Nihon Shoki*. From these sources one learns that she was the daughter of Prince Kagami, though little is known of him either. She became a favorite of Prince Ōama, the future Emperor Temmu, bearing him a daughter named Princess Toochi. At some later date, she was summoned to the palace of Prince Naka no Ōe, the older brother of Prince Ōama and the the future Emperor Tenji. The move was probably forced upon her against her will and would seem to have taken place around 660. The *Man yōshū* contains a spirited poem (I: 8) composed at Nigitazu in the province of Iyo written in 661, when she accompanied the expedition led by Empress Saimei that had set out to attack the state of Silla in Korea, and it is likely that at this time she was already a part of Prince Naka no Ōe's entourage. The poem that she wrote in 667 on the occasion of the removal of the capital to Ōtsu in the province of Ōmi and the poems that she exchanged with Prince Ōama in 668 when he was hunting at Gamono are particularly famous. Meanwhile, Prince Naka no Ōe had officially ascended the throne and reigned until his death in 671. The following year, the so-called Jinshin civil war broke out, a confrontation between the forces of Prince Ōama and those of Prince Ōtomo, the son and heir of Emperor Tenji.

Princess Nukada's position at this time must have been extremely difficult: she was a friend and former favorite of Prince Ōama, but at the same time her daughter Princess Toochi had become the consort of Prince Ōtomo and had borne him a son, Prince Kadono. However, it seems certain that both she and her daughter sided with the forces of Prince Ōama, who emerged the victor and ascended the throne to become Emperor Temmu. Princess Toochi died in 678, but it is clear that Princess Nukada lived considerably beyond that date, since two poems of hers are preserved that were written during the reign of Empress Jitō (687–96). From what can be determined of the dating of her works, they appear to have been composed over an interval of about thirty years.

The *Man'yōshū* contains two *chōka* and nine *tanka* attributed to her, though some of these are of doubtful authenticity. Her most outstanding works are probably the poem composed at Nigitazu, mentioned above, and the *chōka* describing Mt. Miwa, which was written on the occasion of her journey to Ōmi. The former poem reads as follows:

> While at Nigitazu we await the moon
> to put our ships to sea,
> with the moon the tide has risen;
> now let us embark!

Her poems are marked by charm, loftiness of tone, and technical skill. The deftness with which intensity of feeling and beauty of expression are balanced in her works entitles her to be ranked among the leading poets of the *Man'yōshū*.

Ōku no Himemiko (661–701)

Her father was Emperor Temmu and her mother Princess Ōta, the daughter of Emperor Tenji. She was the elder sister of Ōtsu-no-miko, Prince Ōtsu. In 661, Empress Saimei set off by ship at the head of a military force to attack the state of Silla in Korea. When the ship had proceeded as far as the Sea of Ōku in the province of Bizen, Princess Ōta gave birth to a daughter. According to the *Nihon Shoki*, which records the event, the child was therefore named Princess Ōku. Her mother died when the child was very young. At the age of thirteen she was appointed as *saigū*, or vestal virgin, of the Grand Shrine of Ise, and the following year proceeded to Ise to take up her duties. She remained there for the following thirteen years, or until 686, when she was twenty-six. Late in this year her father, Emperor Temmu, passed away, and some twenty days or more after his decease Prince Ōtsu, Princess Ōku's younger brother, was accused of plotting treason and was put to death. It is said that shortly before the treason plot was discovered, he paid a visit in secret to his sister in Ise. After the death of the prince, Princess Ōku was relieved of her duties in Ise and returned to the capital, a fact that she refers to in the poems she composed lamenting the fate of her brother, but nothing is known of her whereabouts from that time until her death in 701 at the age of forty.

The *Man'yōshū* contains six poems in *tanka* form by her, all having to do with the fate of her brother and marked by a tone of intense grief. The downfall of Prince Ōtsu was probably the result of machinations on the part of rival contenders for power, who resented his position as a likely successor to the throne. The death of her only brother certainly represented a cruel blow to Princess Ōku, whose tender love for him and anguish over his fate are poignantly expressed in her poems. Particularly noteworthy is the poem written when she took leave of her brother in Ise (II: 105):

> To speed my brother
> parting for Yamato,
> in the deep of night I stood
> till wet with the dew of dawn.

Equally moving is the poem written as she gazed from a distance toward Mt. Futagami, where her brother was interred (II: 165):

> From tomorrow ever
> shall I regard as brother
> the twin-peaked mountain of Futagami—
> I, daughter of man!

Both works are among the most famous and beautiful poems of the ancient period and remain as moving today as in the time of their composition.

Ō no Yasumaro (d. 723)

He is famous as the compiler of the *Kojiki*. In 704 he was awarded the court rank of Junior Fifth Rank Lower Grade. In the ninth month of 711, Empress Gemmei commanded him to compile a record of the succession of rulers and the accounts of the past as they were recited to him by a retainer named Hieda no Are (q.v.). The work was finished and presented to the throne in the first month of 712. It is in three chapters and is known as the *Kojiki*, or *Record of Ancient Matters*. In 715 Yasumaro was promoted to the Junior Fourth Rank Lower Grade and the following year was appointed as *uji-no-chōja*, or leader of his clan. In 720 he was among those chosen to join with Prince Toneri in compiling the *Nihon Shoki*, or *Chronicles of Japan*.

The *Kojiki* is the oldest extant book in Japan and, along with the *Nihon Shoki*, stands as one of the great historical classics of the Japanese tradition. The first chapter consists entirely of myths dealing with the creation of heaven and earth and the age of the gods, while the second and third chapters record the reigns of the various rulers of Japan from Emperor Jimmu, the legendary founder of the imperial line, down to the reign of Empress Suiko, which ended in 628. The narrative, while dealing with historical matters, possesses considerable literary interest, displaying the rich imaginative powers of the men of ancient times and abounding in human warmth and earthiness. The culture of the Nara period, when the work was written, was deeply influenced by the culture of China and Korea; Chinese characters were employed for all kinds of writing, and all official documents were written in the Chinese language. As a result, all books compiled during the period, such as the *Kojiki* and the *Man'yōshū*, employed Chinese characters, even though the language recorded in them was in part Japanese, while others such as the *Nihon Shoki* were written in the Chinese language.

The preface to the *Kojiki* is written in excellent classical Chinese, indicating that Ō no Yasumaro was perfectly capable of writing in that language when he wished. But he apparently felt that it was too difficult and forced to try to record in the Chinese language the various legends and accounts that had been handed down in Japanese. In the body of the work, therefore, he used a combination of the Japanese and Chinese languages, often employing Chinese characters to represent the sounds of the Japanese language and taking care to add notes so as to make clear the proper reading and meaning of the text. In the case of the numerous songs that he recorded in the text, he employed Chinese characters purely for their phonetic value, using one character to express each syllable of the original, a procedure that in later centuries lead to the invention of the Japanese syllabary. It is clear that Yasumaro thus exerted every effort to record and preserve the form of the early language, a fact that has made his work of enormous value in the study of early Japanese.

Ōtomo no Ikenushi (dates uncertain)

Poet of the Nara period. Also known as Ōtomo no Sukune, he is listed as having held the position of *jō*, or provincial official, in Etchū in Tempyō 18 (746), at the time when Ōtomo no Yakamochi was appointed as governor of Etchū. In the third month of Tempyō 21 he held a similar position in the province of Echizen. In 753 he was recalled to the capital to take the position of *sakyō-shōshin*. The *Shoku nihongi* in its account of the revolt planned by Tachibana no Naramaro lists his name among the fellow conspirators of Naramaro, though it is not clear what punishment he received.

In chapter eight of the *Man'yōshū*, in the section containing miscellaneous poems of autumn, there is a poem by him that was written at a banquet held by Tachibana no Naramaro; chapter seventeen contains thirteen *tanka* and four *chōka* by him, along with a preface and poem in Chinese in seven-character form on a late spring outing; and chapter eighteen contains nine *tanka* by him. Chapters seventeen and eighteen, it should be noted, also contain poems exchanged between Ōtomo no Yakamochi and Ikenushi as well as lengthy letters exchanged between the two. Two more of Ikenushi's poems are found in chapter twenty. All of his poems were written at banquets or exchanged with his friend Yakamochi; they are thus the product of social relationships and, rather than revealing the emotions of the writer himself, they are designed for the most part to please the persons to whom they were addressed and to offer a display of wit. Both the distinctive nature of Ikenushi's poetry, as well as its shortcomings, may be said to have their source in this fact.

Ōtomo no Tabito (665–731)

One of the best-known poets whose works are represented by the *Man'yōshū*, he was the eldest son of the Dainagon (Counselor) Ōtomo no Yasumaro and the father of the equally famous poet Ōtomo no Yakamochi. The Ōtomo family was renowned for its military prowess, reaching the height of its power under Ōtomo no Kanamura in the early part of the sixth century. Because of miscalculations in its policy toward Korea, however, the family lost all of its real power to the Mononobe family, while in government position it was soon surpassed by the Fujiwara family. Thus, by Tabito's time, though highly distinguished in name, the fortunes of the family were clearly in decline.

Tabito held a series of posts, such as General of the Left and *chūnagon*. In the third month of 720, when the Hayato peoples of southern Kyushu revolted, he was given the imperial credentials making him a general and was sent to put them down. Having accomplished his mission, he returned to the capital in the eighth month of the same year. Around 725 or 726, when he was in his early sixties, he was appointed *Dazai-no-sochi*, or head of the Dazaifu, the government office in northern Kyushu. In 730, when he was sixty-five, he was appointed *dainagon* and recalled to the capital, an event that, like his earlier appointment to the post in Kyushu, is mentioned in the *Man'yōshū*. The following year he was given the court rank of Junior Second Rank and he died in the seventh month of the same year.

Nearly all of his extant poetry was written during the closing years of his life when he was in Kyushu or after he had returned from his period of service there, and accordingly much of it is set in Kyushu. While carrying out his official duties as head of the Dazaifu, he maintained a close relationship with the poet and governor of Chikuzen, Yamanoue no Okura. He also gathered about him a group of outstanding scholars and poets from the region, creating and serving as the leader of a Kyushu poetry circle worthy to rival the one that flourished at the time in Nara. In 730 Tabito held a plum blossom banquet at his home at which all the cultured persons of Kyushu gathered and competed in displays of literary talent.

The *Man'yōshū* preserves over eighty poems in Japanese by Tabito, while the *Kaifūsō* contains one poem in Chinese by him, and a few other writings and prose pieces from his hand are also extant. His works include the various laments and pieces of reminiscence that he wrote after the death of his beloved wife in 728, poems expressing his feelings of homesickness when he was living in Kyushu, laments on old age, and the famous series of poems in praise of wine. Tabito belongs to the third period of poets represented in the *Man'yōshū*. He was clearly a highly intelligent and cultured man, learned in many fields and particularly well versed in Chinese literature. His works reveal him as a man of basically mild and sunny disposition who possessed a natural gift for lyricism. This does not mean, however, that he was an optimist pure and simple. His works, which give sincere and open expression to the feelings of his heart, at the same time frankly and without reserve confess the numerous sorrows that he encountered in the course of his various experiences. Among his most famous works is the following poem, which was written in reply to condolences he had received on his wife's death (V: 793):

> Now that I am brought to know
> the vanity of human life,
> sadness bows me down
> deeper than ever.

The following is the first in the series of poems in praise of saké (III: 338):

> Instead of wasting thoughts on unavailing things,
> it would seem wiser
> to drink a cup of raw saké.

The fondness for Japanese poetry that Tabito developed in his later years was inherited and carried on by his son Yakamochi and probably inspired him to undertake the compilation of a collection of poetry, since he is believed to have been one of the persons responsible for the compiling of the *Man'yōshū*.

Ōtomo no Yakamochi (716–785?)

One of the most important poets represented in the *Man'yōshū*, it is probable that he also played a part in the compilation of the anthology. The eldest son of Ōtomo no Tabito, he was born into a family that for some time had been distinguished for its military prowess. When he was around ten or eleven, his father was appointed head of the government office in Kyushu. The young boy, one may surmise, was much influenced by the circle of literary friends such as Yamanoue no Okura and others who gathered around his father in Kyushu and began to take an interest in the writing of poetry in Japanese and Chinese. He returned to the capital with his father, who died in 731, and in time entered upon an official career, being appointed as an *udoneri*, or officer in the imperial bodyguard.

At this period in his life, he seems to have exchanged love poems with a large number of women. In 746 he was appointed governor of Etchū, but his years in that post were often unhappy ones. He was much saddened by the death of his younger brother Fumimochi and suffered a serious illness that nearly cost him his life. At best, his period of service in the province was marked by loneliness and longing for the capital, to which he was finally able to return in 751. He was at first appointed as *shōnagon*, and later attached to the *hyōbushō*, or Ministry of Military Affairs, but was once more appointed as a provincial governor, this time to the province of Inaba, and dispatched from the capital. Around this period, Tachibana no Moroe, a close friend of Yakamochi, fell from power, and Moroe's son Tachibana no Naramaro was discovered to be plotting revolt, events that placed the Ōtomo family in a difficult position. It is not surprising, therefore, that Yakamochi, as head of the family, composed a poem entitled "Admonition to His Clansmen," in which he called for circumspection.

The latest poem preserved in the *Man'yōshū* is one by Yakamochi written in the first month of 755, and the facts pertaining to the remainder of his life must hence be gleaned from other sources. According to historical accounts, he was appointed to a post in the *nakatsukasashō*, or Ministry of Central Affairs, but because of suspected involvement in the revolt of Emi no Oshikatsu in 764, he was appointed governor of Satsuma and in effect exiled to Kyushu. He eventually returned to office in the capital, holding the post of Steward to the Crown Prince, but was deprived of office once more in 781 because of his part in the revolt of Hikami no Kawatsugu. Fortunately, he was able to overcome this setback as well and in time held such offices as *chūnagon* and Commander-in-chief of the Eastern Expeditionary Force. His closing years were relatively quiet ones, and he died in the eighth month of

785 at an age close to seventy. His often trouble-filled life had hardly come to a close, however, when, because his distant relatives were involved in the assassination of Fujiwara no Tanetsugu at Nagaoka, he was posthumously deprived of his office and rank. It is said that, as a result of the affair, his body remained unburied for some twenty days after his death. In 806 he was finally granted a posthumous pardon, thus bringing to an end the sad affair.

Yakamochi is the most important poet of the latter part of the *Man'yōshū* period, the anthology preserving 46 poems in *chōka* form, 426 *tanka*, and one *sedōka* from his hand. Though he does not seem to have possessed the kind of natural genius that marked Kakinomoto no Hitomaro, he succeeded in moving beyond the sentimentalism of his youthful works and gradually created a poetic world that is marked by lucidity and delicate observation, with a particularly penetrating and refined sensitivity to the world of nature. Stylistically, he thus represents a transitional stage between the robust manner of the earlier poets and the highly refined style of the Heian period, and it is probably this forward-looking quality in his work that is of greatest historical significance.

He is also important for the role that he is presumed to have played as one of the compilers of the *Man'yōshū*. The anthology, which is in twenty *kan* (chapters), contains forty-five hundred poems written over a period of some 440 years and representing the work of several hundred poets. Nearly every class in society is represented, from emperors to beggars and prostitutes, while the geographical provenance of the works ranges from Kyushu in the west to the northeastern regions of Honshu. The anthology is thus marked by a wealth and variety unmatched in later collections of poetry. The literary and historical value of the anthology is inestimable, and it has exerted a powerful influence upon the development of Japanese poetry in later times. Though it is written in an extremely difficult system, which employs Chinese characters at times for their meaning and at other times for their sound, and could be read only with great difficulty as early as the beginning of the Heian period, there have been numerous scholars in later ages who have devoted themselves to the task of studying and deciphering the text. Thus it has continued through the centuries since the time of its compilation to be admired as one of the greatest classics of Japanese literature.

Ōtsu-no-miko (663–686)

He was the third son of Emperor Temmu. His mother was Princess Ōta, a daughter of Emperor Tenji, and he was thus a younger brother of Princess Ōku. At the time of the Jinshin civil war, which broke out upon the death of Emperor Tenji in 671, the prince, at the age of ten, in company with his brother Prince Takechi, left the capital at Ōmi and made his way to the camp of his father, who shortly after became emperor. In 683, at the age of twenty-one, he was for the first time allowed to take part in affairs of state. In the first month of 685, when various ranks were assigned to the members of the imperial family and the various court officials, the prince was given the rank of Pure Great Second Rank. This placed him above the other imperial princes and second only to the crown prince, an indication of the great favor he enjoyed with his father. Emperor Temmu, however, passed away in the ninth month of the same year, and in the early part of the tenth month, barely more than twenty days after his demise, Prince Ōtsu was accused of plotting treason and was put to death. He was twenty-three, or, according to Japanese and Chinese style reckoning, twenty-four at the time of his death. According to the account in the *Nihon Shoki*, his consort, Princess Yamanobe, barefoot and with her hair in disarray, hastened to his side and joined him in death. He is also said to have paid a visit in secret to his sister Princess Ōku in Ise shortly before being charged with treason, though why he visited his sister at that critical time is uncertain. He was buried atop a small hill called Mt. Futagami, where what is said to be his grave is still visible today. The prince's aunt, his mother's younger sister and the consort of Emperor Temmu, apparently felt that he was a threat to her son Prince Kusakabe, the heir apparent, and therefore she and her supporters joined together to have him done away with. She herself then ascended the throne as Empress Jitō.

Prince Ōtsu was a person of unusual capability and candor, talented in the writing of poetry in both Japanese and Chinese and widely loved and admired. He shared his father's heroic disposition and was said to have been a particular favorite with his grandfather Emperor Tenji. Because of his outstanding character and ability, his tragic end aroused wide sympathy and sorrow among the people of the time. The *Kaifūsō* contains four of his poems in Chinese, and the *Man'yōshū* four Japanese poems in *tanka* form, a small number of works but all of high quality. Particularly noteworthy is the *tanka* composed just before his death, one of the most famous and moving works of early Japanese poetry (III: 416):

> Today, taking my last sight of the mallards
> crying on the pond of Iware,
> must I vanish into the clouds.

Saimei Tennō (594–661; r. 642–45, 655–61)

Thirty-fifth and thirty-seventh sovereign of Japan. Her name was Ame no Toyo Takara Ikashi-hi Tarashi-hime-no-mikoto, or Princess Takara; her father was Prince Chinu, a grandson of Emperor Bidatsu, and her mother was Princess Kibi. At first she married Prince Takamuku and gave birth to Prince Aya; later she became the consort of Emperor Jomei, giving birth to Prince Naka no Ōe (Emperor Tenji), Prince Ōama (Emperor Temmu), and Empress Hashihito, the consort of Emperor Kōtoku. After the death of Emperor Jomei, she ascended the throne, and during this period she is referred to as Empress Kōgyoku. She resided first in the Oharida Palace, but later moved to the Asuka Itabuki Palace. It was a time when the members of the Soga family were at the height of their power, but when they were overthrown in 645 by Prince Naka no Ōe in the move that instituted the Taika period, the empress abdicated in favor of her younger brother Prince Kaku, who became Emperor Kōtoku. On his death, she once more ascended the throne, being known this time as Empress Saimei, and resided in the Nochi no Asuka Okamoto Palace. Following on the period of the Taika Reform, it was a time when the nation faced numerous internal and external problems, but the empress worked vigorously during the years from 658 to 660 to solve them, sending Abe no Hirafu on an expedition against the Ezo people of the north and taking other measures. In 661 she led an army on an expedition to assist the state of Paekche in Korea, but died of illness on the way at the Asakura Palace in Kyushu.

Five poems of hers are extant (nos. 116–121 in the *Man'yōshū*), all of them recorded in the *Nihon Shoki*, beginning with the famous lament for her eight-year-old grandson Prince Takeru, which reads:

> On the Hill of Omure
> In Imaki—
> If but a cloud
> Arose, plain to be seen,
> Why should I lament?[1]

Though there is some doubt about the authenticity of such works attributed to early figures, the poem is marked by great pathos and lyric beauty. In recent years, as a result of the researches of Omodaka Hisataka, scholars have also come to regard poems numbers 4, 7, 8, 10, 11, 12, 485, and 487 of the *Man'yōshū* as works of Empress Saimei. Though some doubtful points still remain to be solved in these attributions, the atmosphere of these

---

1. W. G. Aston, *Nihongi*, p. 253.

poems in no way conflicts with that found in the poems on the death of Prince Takeru and strongly suggests that they are all from the same hand. Empress Saimei may thus be said to be the first major lyric poet in the history of Japanese literature.

Sakanoue no Iratsume (dates uncertain)

Poet of the middle Nara period. She was the daughter of the Dainagon (Chief Counsellor) Ōtomo no Yasumaro and a younger half-sister of the poet Ōtomo no Tabito. In her youth she enjoyed favor with Prince Hozumi, the fifth son of Emperor Temmu, but after the prince's death in 715 she married Fujiwara no Maro, the fourth son of Fujiwara no Fuhito. Her husband, however, fell victim to the smallpox epidemic of 737, after which she married Ōtomo no Sukunamaro and gave birth to two daughters known as Sakanoue no Ōiratsume and Sakanoue no Otoiratsume respectively. The former in time became the wife of Ōtomo no Yakamochi, the son of Ōtomo no Tabito, and Sakanoue no Iratsume thus became Yakamochi's mother-in-law as well as aunt. When the wife of her elder brother Tabito died in Kyushu, she journeyed there to look out for Tabito's children, and after Tabito's death she seems to have played an important role as a kind of supervisor of clan affairs, working to promote harmony among the various branches of the Ōtomo family, conducting family sacrifices, and inspecting the family's estates.

Her works consist of seventy-seven *tanka*, six *chōka*, and one *sedōka*, a total of eighty-four poems, composed over a period of some twenty years or more. Because of the relatively large number of her works and the fact that they represent all three major poetic forms of the time, she deserves to be regarded as one of the most important poets of the *Man'yōshū*, though the large number of her works preserved may in part be due to the fact that she was closely associated with Ōtomo no Yakamochi, who is regarded as one of the compilers of the anthology. At the same time, her works display a wide variety of themes and moods and give evidence of a rich talent and sensitivity. It is easy to imagine, therefore, that she played a large part in helping Yakamochi to mature both as a person and as a poet.

Her poetic style is on the whole rather intellectual and ornate and includes imitations of the songs of antiquity. Though her works have generally been looked upon as somewhat stereotyped, it is clear that she could handle a large variety of themes with great finesse, and many of her poems abound with a wealth of sentiment and a freshness and delicacy of feeling.

She deserves, in fact, to be recognized as among the leading poets of the *Man'yōshū.*

Sano no Chigami no Otome (dates uncertain)

Poet of the early eighth century, or the fourth and last period into which the works of the *Man'yōshū* are divided. She served as an attendant in the *kurabe,* an office attached to the *saigūryō,* Bureau of the Princess Imperial Deputy, at the Great Shrine of Ise. Such attendants were persons of rather low social position, being chosen from among the lesser female attendants of the palace. In spite of her humble station, she ranks as one of the most important women poets of the *Man'yōshū* because of the works by her included in chapter fifteen of the anthology, love songs exchanged between her and Nakatomi no Yakamori. The poems were written when Yakamori was in banishment in the region of Ajima in the province of Echizen. Presumably he was banished because of his affair with Sano no Chigami, the women attached to the Bureau of the Ise Shrine being forbidden to have any relations with men, though very little is known about Yakamori and many aspects of the incident are unclear. In 763, however, Yakamori was granted the court rank of Junior Fifth Rank Lower Grade, so his offense had apparently been pardoned by that time.

The series of love poems recorded in the *Man'yōshū* begins with a poem by Sano no Chigami expressing the grief occasioned by her parting from Yakamori, and consists of sixty-three poems, of which twenty-three are by Sano no Chigami. The opening poem (XV: 3724) reads as follows:

> O for a fire from heaven
> to haul, fold and burn up
> the long-stretched road you go!

The passionate impulsiveness of her works and the purity and intensity of the love expressed in them make them profoundly moving. Though at times somewhat hyperbolic in expression, they are superior to the poems of Yakamori that were written in response to them and indeed rank among the most sensitive and deeply felt works in the anthology.

Shiki-no-miko (d. 716)

He was the seventh son of Emperor Tenji and the father of Emperor

Kōnin. In later times he was sometimes referred to as Kasuga-no-miya Tennō or Tawara Tennō. The notable *Man'yōshū* poet Yuhara no Ōkimi (Prince Yuhara) was his second son. Very little is known of his life, though the *Nihon Shoki* and *Shoku Nihongi* contain a few references to him. From these texts one learns that he was given a fief of two hundred households in the time of Emperor Temmu; in 703 he was made an imperial prince of the fourth rank; in 708 his fief was increased by two hundred households; in 715 he was advanced to the second rank; and the following year he died. It would appear, therefore, that he was active as a poet for a period of around sixteen years, most of it when the court was located in the Palace of Fujiwara.

Only six poems by him are preserved in the *Man'yōshū*, but all are marked by a strongly individual style. A contemporary of Kakinomoto no Hitomaro, he shows a tendency toward greater inventiveness than Hitomaro, and his works are on the whole characterized by freshness of feeling and a lucid, flowing style. The following poem in particular is looked upon as his masterpiece and one of the finest works in the *Man'yōshū* (VIII: 1418):

> Above the cascade tumbling down the rocks
> the bracken sprouts and burgeons on the hill—
> ah, the happy spring is come!

Shōmu Tennō (701–756)

The forty-fifth ruler of Japan, he was the eldest son of Emperor Mommu; his mother was Miyako, a daughter of Fujiwara no Fuhito. His personal name was Obito-no-miko. His consort was also a daughter of Fujiwara no Fuhito, Asukabe-hime, better known as Empress Kōmyō. When his father passed away in 707, the prince was only six years old, and his grandmother, Empress Gemmei, therefore ascended the throne to rule in his place until he was of age. After a reign of seven years she relinquished the throne to her daughter Empress Genshō, the prince's aunt. The prince was designated heir apparent in 714, when he was thirteen, and in 724 he at last ascended the throne, his aunt having abdicated in his favor. Both Emperor Shōmu and his consort Empress Kōmyō were devout Buddhists. The emperor ordered that an official monastery (*kokubun-ji*) and an official nunnery (*kokubun-niji*) be set up in each province, founded the great temple of Tōdai-ji in Nara to supervise their administration, and began work on the casting of the great image of the Buddha to be enshrined in the Tōdai-ji. He also worked to improve the effectiveness of the government, actively encouraged the spread of Chinese culture and institutions, and created an era renowned for its art and learning, customarily referred to in art history as the Tempyō era. In 749, at the age of forty-eight, he relinquished the throne to his daughter Empress Kōken and entered the Buddhist clergy, adopting the religious name Shōman.

The emperor's poems are preserved in the *Man'yōshū* and consist of one *chōka* and ten *tanka*. All are lofty in tone and have an air of grandeur befitting the works of a great ruler, though at the same time they tend toward conventionality. The poems preserved in chapter six of the anthology, which were written at a farewell banquet for the envoy to China, are considered the emperor's finest works and indeed possess a grandeur of expression seldom matched in the poetic works of later rulers of Japan.

SHŌTOKU TAISHI (574–622)

He was the second son of Emperor Yōmei; his mother was Empress Anahobe-no-hashibito no Himemiko. The prince's personal name was Umayado or Toyotomimi, and he is also referred to as Prince Kami-no-miya. In 593, when he was nineteen, he became regent for his aunt Empress Suiko, who was reigning as sovereign, exerting his efforts in attending to domestic and foreign affairs of state. In 603 he established a system of twelve cap-ranks for court officials and the following year proclaimed the famous Seventeen Article Constitution, which laid down principles of government. In 607 he dispatched Ono no Imoko as an envoy to the court of the Sui dynasty in China, establishing official relations with China and working to promote the introduction of continental culture. He was particularly zealous in his efforts to encourage the spread of Buddhism and to this end founded the famous Shitennō-ji and Hōryū-ji temples. He also undertook the compilation of the first Japanese historical works, texts dealing with the history of the imperial house and the country as a whole. Unfortunately, the works were all burned in the civil disturbance that accompanied the Taika Reform in 645.

There are several poetic works attributed to Prince Shōtoku. The *Nihon Shoki* records a *chōka* that he is said to have composed when he saw a starving man at Kataoka. He is reported to have given the man food and drink and presented him with his own robe. Chapter three of the *Man'yōshū* contains a poem expressing the prince's feelings of pity on seeing a dead man at Mt. Tatsuta. Both poems seem to be designed to demonstrate the prince's great virtue and are probably part of the body of legendary material that grew up around his name after his death. In addition, one poem attributed to the prince is found in a work called *Jōgū Shōtoku Hōō teisetsu* and two in a work called *Shōtoku Taishi denryaku*. But these in places duplicate the *Kunishinubi-uta*, ("Songs of Longing for Home") recorded in the *Kojiki* and attributed to Yamato Takeru-no-mikoto. Presumably they are early ballads that came to be attributed to Prince Shōtoku. Three works in Chinese are attributed to the prince; these are *gisho*, or commentaries, on three Buddhist sutras, the Lotus Sutra, the Vimalakīrti Nirdeśa, and the Sutra of Queen Śrīmālā. The *Jōgū Shōtoku Hōō teisetsu*, mentioned above, is a compilation of various records pertaining to the prince. The date of compilation is unknown, but from the fact that it does not reflect a knowledge of the accounts of the prince found in the *Kojiki* and *Nihon Shoki*, it was presumably compiled before those works. After the death of the prince, a large body of legendary material seems to have grown up around his name, and this work in all likelihood represents an early compilation of such material. Though the prince died at the age of forty-eight, the governmental ideals that he had been working toward were eventually realized in the Taika Reform of 645. The role played by the prince in the political and cultural advancement of ancient Japan was of incalculable importance, and he has continued down to the present to be one of the most highly revered figures in all of Japanese history.

TAJIMA NO HIMEMIKO (d. 708)

Her father was Emperor Temmu, her mother Hikami no Iratsume, a daughter of Fujiwara no Kamatari. The heading to one of her poems (114) preserved in chapter two of the *Man'yōshū* reveals that she lived for a time in the palace of her half-brother Prince Takechi, but it appears that she developed a violent passion for another of her half-brothers, Prince Hozumi, also a son of Emperor Temmu. In 690, the year after the death of the heir apparent Prince Kusakabe, Prince Takechi was appointed *dajōdaijin* (prime minister) and played an important role in state affairs until his death in 696, and it would appear likely that this was the period during which Princess Tajima lived in his palace. The heading to poem 116 in the same chapter reveals that her clandestine relationship with Prince Hozumi had been discovered. At that time the prince had received an imperial command to proceed to the Sūfuku-ji, a temple at Shiga in Ōmi. The intention probably was to separate the lovers, but Princess Tajima, in a poem filled with passionate longing, declares her intention of setting out in pursuit of him. No reply to her poem by the prince has been preserved, and it is not known how the unhappy love affair ended. In 705, in the reign of Emperor Mommu, Prince Hozumi became prime minister and took an active role in political affairs. In the sixth month of 708 Princess Tajima died. Sometime after, probably in the winter of the following year, Prince Hozumi composed a poem (203) describing his feelings of grief as he gazed from a distance at the sight of snow falling upon the gravemound of the princess, an indication that he still thought of her with deep affection.

Three poems in *tanka* form by Princess Tajima are preserved in chapter two, all outstanding works having to do with her passionate and pathetic love for Prince Hozumi. Like the poems relating to the execution of Prince Ōtsu, these works are clearly inspired by real and intensely moving experiences in the personal life of the writer and for that reason have a special power to touch the heart of the reader. One other poem in *tanka* form by the princess is preserved in chapter eight of the anthology.

Takechi-no-miko (654–696)

He was the eldest son of Emperor Temmu; his mother was Munakata-no-kimi Amako no Iratsume. He was only eighteen at the time of the Jinshin civil war in 672, but he managed to escape from the Ōtsu Palace in Ōmi and make his way to his father's camp, where he was appointed a general and played an active part in winning victory for his father's cause. In 690, the year after the death of the heir apparent Prince Kusakabe, he was appointed *dajōdaijin* (prime minister) and took a very active part in governmental affairs during the reign of Empress Jitō. He enjoyed great favor, being assigned to the court rank of Pure Broad First Rank, and was given the revenue from a fief of five thousand households. He lived in a splendid mansion at the foot of Mt. Kagu and was said to have been one of the most highly respected leaders of the time. His wife was Princess Minabe, a daughter of Emperor Tenji, and his sons Nagaya-no-ō and Suzuka-no-ō both played an active part in the political and cultural life of the Nara period.

Only three poems by the prince are preserved in the *Man'yōshū*, laments in *tanka* form written on the death of Princess Toichi. He is said to have resembled his father, being a man of gallant and upright disposition. The lament written in *chōka* form by Kakinomoto no Hitomaro on the prince's death, which runs to 149 lines, is the longest poem in the *Man'yōshū* and one of the very finest.

Tanabe no Sakimaro (dates uncertain)

Like Ōtomo no Yakamochi, he is a poet of the late *Man'yōshū* period. Nothing is known of him outside of what can be determined from the *Man'yōshū*. From information in chapter eighteen of the anthology, it is known that in the third month of 748 he acted as messenger for the Minister of the Left Tachibana no Moroe, traveling to the province of Etchū and calling upon Ōtomo no Yakamochi, at that time the governor of the province. Sakimaro at the time held a post as a secretary in the *miki-no-tsukasa*, the office in charge of brewing saké for the imperial table. Sakimaro stayed with Yakamochi for four days, from the 23rd to the 26th of the month, accompanying him on an outing to Lake Fuse, and seems to have been treated very generously. It is also known that he exchanged poems with Yakamochi. From this it would appear that, although Sakimaro held a relatively low official position, he was very well received by Yakamochi, partly because he was a retainer of Tachibana no Moroe, with whom Yakamochi was allied in an attempt to oppose the power of the Fujiwara family, and also because, like them, he was a distinguished poet. It is also known from poems in chapters six and nine that he made occasional journeys to the palaces in Kuni and Naniwa and composed poems to celebrate the trips, while the poem written when he crossed the Ashigara Pass, which lies between the provinces of Sagami and Suruga, indicates that he traveled rather widely about the country. He can perhaps best be considered as a kind of court poet in the tradition of Kakinomoto no Hitomaro and Yamabe no Akihito, who, like him, held relatively low official positions but in their works celebrated the activities of the court.

Forty-four poems by Sakimaro have been preserved, ten *chōka* and thirty-four *tanka*. Twenty-one of the latter, however, are *hanka* (envoys appended to the *chōka*), and therefore he is best regarded as a poet who worked mainly in the *chōka* form. His poems are largely descriptive in nature and have a rather plain and matter-of-fact tone to them, with little evidence of deep emotional involvement. They are conspicuous for their use of rhetorical devices such as parallelism and pillow-words and have often been criticized for their excessive attention to surface ornament.

Temmu Tennō (d. 686)

The fortieth sovereign of Japan, his father was Emperor Jomei and his mother Empress Kōgyoku. He was a younger brother of Emperor Tenji and Princess Hashibito, the consort of Emperor Kōtoku. In his youth he was known as Ōama-no-miko, or Prince Ōama, and in 667 was appointed as heir apparent to his elder brother Emperor Tenji. But in 671, shortly before Emperor Tenji's death, he perceived what his brother's true wishes were, and accordingly shaved his head and retired to Mt. Yoshino to live a religious life. After Emperor Tenji's death, the emperor's son Prince Ōtomo ascended the throne, but hostility quickly developed between the new ruler, whose capital was at Ōtsu in Ōmi, and the forces supporting Prince Ōama. In time a military confrontation ensued, ending in victory for Prince Ōama; from the cyclical designation for the year in which it occurred, 672, it is known as the Jinshin civil war. After the conclusion of the fighting, he returned to the province of Yamato and established the capital at the Kiyomihara Palace in Asuka, reigning there for the succeeding fifteen years. He worked diligently to put the laws and regulations into order and to fix the system of court ranks and also initiated the task of compiling a national history. In this way he did much to strengthen the position of the imperial family and to raise it to a position of eminence. Authorities disagree concerning his age at the time of his death in 686, some placing it at sixty-four, others at around fifty-six. The *Nihon Shoki* describes him as being of "outstanding heroism and god-like valor." It is clear that he was a man of great wisdom and force of character who from his early years inspired trust in those about him and who contributed greatly toward the growth and stabilization of the *ritsuryō*, or bureaucratic form of government.

Emperor Temmu appears to have been a skilled poet, though only one *chōka* and three *tanka* of his are preserved in the *Man'yōshū*. All of these, however, are characterized by a loftiness of tone and a distinctively masculine air. Particularly famous because of the circumstances surrounding it is the poem that he wrote in his youthful years in reply to a poem from Princess Nukada. Princess Nukada, an outstanding poet of the *Man'yōshū*, had been a favorite of Emperor Temmu when he was still a prince and had borne him a daughter, but later she was summoned to enter the harem of Emperor Temmu's elder brother Emperor Tenji. The prince's poem, written when he was on a hunting trip to Gamōno, describes how he still feels attracted to her, although she has now become "the wife of another."

The centralized government and cultured aristocratic society that characterized Emperor Temmu's reign were carried on and brought to even higher development through the efforts of his successor, Empress Jitō, formerly his consort, and the other members of his lineage. His reign marks the first great flourishing of Japanese poetry, as the works preserved in the *Man'yōshū* clearly demonstrate, and in many other ways as well his influence upon the growth of the arts was profound and far-reaching.

Tenji Tennō (d. 671)

The thirty-eighth sovereign of Japan, he was the son of Emperor Jomei and the older brother of Emperor Temmu and Princess Hashibito, the consort of Emperor Kōtoku. In his youth he was known first by the title Kazuragi-no-miko and later as Naka no Ōe. Angered by the overweening power of the Soga family, he plotted with Nakatomi no Kamatari and in 645 succeeded in overthrowing them. He then carried out the so-called Taika reforms, which laid the foundation for a centralized bureaucratic form of government modeled on that of China. In 667 he moved his residence to the Ōtsu Palace in the province of Ōmi and the following year officially ascended the throne, but he died three years later, in 671, before he had had time to consolidate the power of his new capital at Ōtsu. According to some theories, he was forty-five at the time of his death, according to others fifty-two or fifty-seven. He seems to have been a man of unusual forcefulness who was determined to carry out radical social and governmental changes, while the severity with which he dealt with Prince Arima, the son of his uncle Emperor Kōtoku, suggests a strain of cruelty in his character. He was also a skillful poet, his extant works being marked by a kind of old-fashioned gentleness and grandeur quite in contrast to the impression conveyed by his political activities. The *Man'yōshū* contains only four works that can reliably be attributed to his hand, including the well-known *chōka* dealing with the legend of the Three Hills, providing a very limited basis upon which to judge his accomplishment as a poet. The following work, noteworthy as one of the earliest and finest attempts to depict the natural scene in poetry, will give some indication of his talent (I:15):

> Over the sea's
> bright bannered clouds
> the setting sunlight plays:
> the moon tonight—
> how clearly it will shine!

Also well known is the relationship between Emperor Tenji and Nukada-no-ōkimi, which is alluded to in her poems. One of the outstanding women poets of the *Man'yōshū*, she was originally a favorite of Emperor Tenji's younger brother, who later became Emperor Temmu, but later was summoned by Emperor Tenji and made a member of his harem.

Yamabe no Akahito (dates uncertain)

One of the most important poets of the *Man'yōshū*, he was active in the middle Nara period, particularly in the Tempyō era (729–49). He seems to have been an official of very low rank, since neither the *Man'yōshū* nor any of the historical texts of the period make any mention of his office or court rank. Since so many of his poems were written when he was accompanying the ruler on journeys and outings and are recorded alongside those of men like Kasa no Kanamura and Kurumamochi no Chitose, it would appear that, like them, he served as a kind of court poet in the entourage of Emperor Shōmu.

The *Man'yōshū* contains thirteen *chōka* and thirty-seven *tanka* from his hand. With the exception of three poems of lament for the dead, all his works are devoted to descriptions of the natural world, most composed when he was attending the sovereign on journeys to Mt. Yoshino or the province of Kii or on journeys of his own. His *chōka* are unexceptionable from a technical point of view and lacking in a sense of realism. His *tanka*, however, are highly realistic, and it is generally conceded that this was where his genius lay. He seems to have observed the natural world with great care and to have been extremely sensitive to its most subtle changes. In his descriptions, he shows extraordinary skill in perceiving the beauties and delights of nature and depicting them in a highly graphic manner, as may be seen from the following two well-known works (VI: 924, 925):

> Oh, the voices of the birds
> that sing so noisily in the treetops
> of the Kisa Mountain of Yoshino,
> breaking the silence of the vale!

> Now the jet-black night deepens;
> and on the beautiful river beach,
> where grow the *hisagi* trees,
> the sanderlings cry ceaselessly.

It is generally agreed that no poet of early times exceeds Yamabe no Akahito in the skill with which he depicts natural scenes. And in the way in which he excludes all sentiment from his work and confines himself to a purely objective rendering of the sights before him, he is unique in the history of Japanese poetry.

The delicacy, refinement, and technical skill of Akahito's style had a profound influence upon the poets of the Heian period and led Ki no Tsurayuki to write in his preface to the *Kokinshū* that "one cannot place Hitomaro above Akahito, or Akahito beneath Hitomaro." Since Tsurayuki had earlier accorded Kakinomoto no Hitomaro the highest possible praise by declaring him to be the "Saint of Poetry," it has become customary in Japan to honor both Hitomaro and Akahito as the greatest geniuses of the poetic tradition. In recent years the school of modern *tanka* that originated with Masaoka Shiki has valued Akahito very highly because of his objective descriptions of the natural world, and Akahito's influence is particularly evident in the poetry and writings on poetic theory of Shimaki Akahiko and others.

YAMANOUE NO OKURA (dates uncertain)

One of the most important poets of the *Man'yōshū*, he appears to have lived around 660 to 733. Since he did not come from a family of particular eminence, it is probable that he spent a long time studying and attempting to make his way ahead in the world. In 702, when he was over forty, he was appointed as a member of an official embassy to the T'ang court in China. It is not certain just when he returned to Japan, though in all probability he remained in China for two or perhaps even three or more years. On his return to Japan he was first appointed governor of Hōki and later was made tutor to the crown prince, the future Emperor Shōmu. In 726, when he was around sixty-six, he was appointed governor of Chikuzen in Kyushu. It was about the time when Ōtomo no Tabito was appointed to head the government office in Kyushu known as the Dazaifu, which means that Yamanoue no Okura was a subordinate of Ōtomo no Tabito. As may be seen from the works preserved in chapter five of the *Man'yōshū*, both men were very active in the writing of poetry at this time, though their respective works contrast in many ways. Having completed his tour of duty, Yamanoue no Okura returned to the capital in 732 and appears to have died the following year.

The *Man'yōshū* contains ten *chōka*, one *sedōka*, and fifty-one *tanka* by Okura, while chapter sixteen of the anthology contains a series of ten poems entitled "Poems of the Fisher-Folk of Shiga in the Province of Chikuzen," which is also believed to be from his hand. Finally, the anthology records two poems in Chinese and a few prose pieces in Chinese composed by him. From information contained in the original notes of the *Man'yōshū*, it is known that he compiled an anthology known as the *Ruijū karin* ("Forest of Classified Verse"), though the work is no longer extant. Most of his works appear to have been composed after he took up the position of governor of Chikuzen.

Both the number and the quality of his works make him one of the most noteworthy poets of the *Man'yōshū*. The social and financial hardships he underwent and his worries over health and domestic affairs, as well as his extensive knowledge of Chinese literature and culture, combine to produce a style and tone unlike that of any other writer represented in the anthology. His works, when compared with those of his illustrious predecessor Kakinomoto no Hitomaro or of his contemporaries such as Yamabe no Akahito or Ōtomo no Tabito, are markedly more personal in tone and tend to deal with the experiences of everyday life. As one of his best-known works, "Thinking of Children," suggests, many of his poems deal with his love for his wife and his children, while others treat such themes as old age, sickness, and poverty. Indeed, his single most famous work is undoubtedly that entitled "A Dialogue on Poverty." While so many other poets of the period were content simply to sing of the beauties of nature, the joys and sorrows of love, or other elegant or refined themes, Okura wrote works that are economic or political in theme or that deal with the hardships and harsh realities of life, and for this reason he holds a place of unique importance in the history of Japanese literature. The following two poems (V: 803; VI: 978), the latter written on the occasion of his sickness, are particularly famous:

> What use to me
> silver, gold and jewels?
> No treasure can surpass children!

> Should I, a man, die in vain
> with no renown—no name
> spoken of for ten thousand ages?

Yamato Takeru-no-mikoto

Legendary hero of ancient times. He was the son of Emperor Keikō and Inabi no Iratsume of Harima. According to the account in the *Kojiki*, Emperor Keikō, displeased that his son Ōusu-no-mikoto did not appear at the morning and evening meals, ordered his younger son Ousu-no-mikoto (Yamato Takeru) to reprimand his elder brother. Ousu thereupon seized his elder brother and crushed him to death with his hands. The emperor, alarmed by such fierce behavior, dispatched Ousu on an expedition against Kumaso Takeru, the leader of the Kumaso people of Kyushu. Ousu, donning clothes given to him by his aunt Yamato-hime and disguising himself as a woman, made his way into the banquet of the Kumaso and stabbed Kumaso

Takeru. Before he died, Takeru, admiring the bravery of the prince, presented him with the name Yamato Takeru, or Brave Man of Yamato, and Ousu was thereafter known as Yamato Takeru. When he returned to the capital in Yamato, Emperor Keikō immediately sent him on an expedition against the eastern region. On his departure he received from his aunt Yamato-hime a sword called Kusanagi and a pouch. He made his way east, subduing the gods of the mountains and rivers as he proceeded, until he reached the province of Sagami, but there he was attacked by the governor, who lured him into a moor and set fire to the grass. With the aid of his sword and flints that he found in the pouch, he was able to cut down the grass, set a backfire, and thus escape. He proceeded by boat across the sea of Hashiri-mizu, where he encountered a violent storm, but his wife Ototachibana-hime threw herself into the water and thereby calmed the waves. The prince ascended the slope of Ashigara and sighed three times, exclaiming "Alas, my wife!" which is the origin of the name Azuma (my wife) used to designate the eastern provinces. In time he returned to the province of Owari, where he exchanged love songs with Miyazu-hime and then set off to conquer the god of Mt. Ibuki but, stricken by the poisonous vapors of the mountain, he fell ill. He made his way to Nobono in Ise, where he composed *kuni-shinobiuta*, or songs of longing for one's native land, and there died. After his death his soul turned into a white bird called *yahiroshiro-dori* and flew away.

Yamato Takeru is pictured in this account in the *Kojiki* as a romantic hero who was afflicted with a tragic fate. In the corresponding passage in the *Nihon Shoki*, however, which is written in Chinese, the legend is characterized by Chinese modes of expression and does not mention the prince's attacks on Kumaso Takeru or Izumo Takeru; it lacks the romantic atmosphere of the *Kojiki* version and instead has been given political and ideological overtones. The *Kojiki* narrative, with its long and short songs that serve to give expression to the prince's inner thoughts and feelings, in fact constitutes an early example of the *uta-monogatari* (poem-tale), a genre that was to become very important in later Japanese literature. In addition to these accounts, scattered references to the Yamato Takeru legend are found in the *Hitachi fudoki* and other local gazetteers, usually in passages explaining the origin of place names. These were no doubt inserted out of a desire to link the name of the hero of ancient times with the writer's own locality, which could be conveniently done by picturing the prince as having passed that way in the course of his various expeditions. The prince's name has also from early times been associated with the *renga*, or linked verse, form, which is sometimes called *Tsukubadō*. This association springs from the fact that the prince and an old man named Mihitaki no Okina were said to have composed a kind of *renga* or exchange of songs beginning "Niihari Tsukuba." It is clear from these facts that Yamato Takeru was widely loved and admired as a hero of ancient times, and his legend and the songs attributed to him constitute one of the most beautiful and moving passages in legendary accounts of the ancient period.

YUHARA-NO-ŌKIMI (dates uncertain)

Poet of the early Nara period. He was the second son of Prince Shiki, the seventh son of Emperor Tenji. Prince Shiki is famous for the poem that begins "Above the cascade tumbling down the rocks" and other works in the *Man'yōshū*, and Prince Yuhara carried on his father's style, working to endow it with even greater elegance and charm.

Though almost nothing is known of his life, the *Man'yōshū* preserves nineteen poems in *tanka* form from his hand. The chapters that record his works are all those that appear to have some connection with Ōtomo no Yakamochi, and it would seem that Prince Yuhara, though of an older generation than Yakamochi, was one of the poets belonging to Yakamochi's circle. In many ways his works represent a transition between the style of the third period of the *Man'yōshū* represented by Yamanoue no Okura and Yamabe no Akahito and the fourth period represented by Ōtomo no Yakamochi. His poetry is marked by gentleness and simplicity, and though it shows a certain tendency toward mannerism and preoccupation with technical finesse, these faults are not offensively conspicuous, as they were to become in the poetry of the age that followed. His best-known work is the following, a poem that is regarded as one of the finest in the anthology (III: 375):

> On the pool of the River of Natsumi
> that flows through Yoshino
> the wild ducks are crying—
> in the shade of the mountains.

Though the poem lacks the old-fashioned elegance found in the poem on the tumbling cascade by Prince Yuhara's father, Prince Shiki, it exploits to the fullest, through the skillful repetition of *ka* and *no* syllables in the original, the musical beauty of the Japanese language. In mood many of Prince Yuhara's works resemble those of Ōtomo no Yakamochi.

しぬそゝるねゝよ

ゝ引共随意

ゆみひ

Early Period

A<small>KAZOME</small> E<small>MON</small> (dates uncertain)

Poet of the middle Heian period. Regarded as the daughter of Akazome Tokimochi, she was said in fact to have been the child by her mother's former marriage to Taira no Kanemori; the name Emon derives from Tokimochi's official title. She became the wife of Ōe no Masahira, a professor of the state university, and gave birth to a son named Takachika and a daughter named Kō no Jijū. Ōe no Masafusa was her great-grandson.

She served as a lady-in-waiting to Rinshi, the wife of Fujiwara no Michinaga, and also seems to have been in the service of the latter's daughter, Jōtōmon-in. Some time after she held these positions, her husband, Masahira, was appointed governor of the province of Owari, and she accompanied him to his post, later also accompanying him when he was appointed governor of Tamba; he died in 1012 at his post in Tamba. Her son Takachika carried on an affair with the daughter of Ōe no Masamune, the younger sister of Izumi Shikibu, and through this connection she had occasion to exchange poems with Izumi Shikibu. Her daughter Kō no Jijū served in the household of Fujiwara no Michinaga and later became the wife of Takashina no Naritomi. Emon lived at least until the time of the birth of her great-grandson Masafusa in 1041, since there is a poem that mentions her sewing a set of robes for him. In later life she entered the Buddhist clergy, ending her days as a nun.

Her reputation as a poet was already well established in her lifetime, and she and Izumi Shikibu were referred to as the two women poetic geniuses of the time. In contrast to Izumi Shikibu's impassioned style, her works display a gentle and moderate tone and include many poems descriptive of motherly love and the grief that she experienced on the death of her husband. Over ninety of her poems are included in the *Shūishū* and other officially sponsored anthologies, as well as some twenty poems in the *Shisenshū*. She is included among the Five Poetic Geniuses of the Pear Court and the Thirty-six Poetic Geniuses of the Early Period. There is a collection of her works entitled *Akazome Emon shū* as well as a travel diary, the *Owari kikō*. It has also been claimed that she authored the work called the *Eiga monogatari*, but as yet there is insufficient evidence to support the attribution.

Ariwara no Narihira (825–880)

Poet of the early Heian period. He was the fifth son of Prince Abo, a son of Emperor Heizei; his mother, Princess Ito, was the daughter of Emperor Kammu. He and his elder brother Yukihira were presented by the emperor with the surname Ariwara and removed from the register of the imperial family, a procedure often resorted to to prevent the imperial family from growing too large. At the age of fifty-two he was appointed *ukon'e-no-gon-no-chūjō*, or lieutenant-general of the right palace guard, and is often referred to as Zai no Chūjō or Zaigo no Chūjō, *zai* being the Sino-Japanese reading of the character for *ari* in his surname.

Almost nothing is known of his life, but he appears to have been ambitious and talented, at least in the field of poetry; it is probable that, like many other learned and capable members of the court nobility, he found his efforts at advancement blocked by the dominance of the powerful Fujiwara family. From early times he was famous as the model of the courtly lover, and numerous legends surround his name. The work known as the *Ise monogatari (Tales of Ise)*, a narrative interspersed with poems, records many of these legends of Narihira's romantic adventures.

Ki no Tsurayuki, the compiler of the *Kokinshū*, designates him as one of the Six Poetic Geniuses, and in his preface to the anthology speaks of Narihira's poetry as "overflowing in heart, lacking in words, like withered flowers that have lost their color but leave their scent behind." As this remark suggests, Narihira's poems are passionate in nature and seem to have been written with great conviction, but they do not seek to give full and complete expression to the ideas underlying them. Nevertheless, because of their purity of feeling and the expression they give to the beauty of love and the true nature of the human heart, his poems were highly prized by the members of the Heian aristocracy as models of court poetry.

Eighty-seven of his poems are preserved in the imperial anthologies, beginning with the thirty recorded in the *Kokinshū*, and ten more are to be found in privately compiled anthologies; a collection of his works exists entitled *Narihira shū*.

Fujiwara no Akisue (1055–1123)

Poet of the late Heian period. His father was Fujiwara no Takatsune, his mother Ju'nii Chikako, the wet nurse of Emperor Shirakawa. He became the adopted son of Fujiwara no Sanesue and hence took the name Akisue. After serving as the governor of various provinces, he was appointed *suri-no-daibu* and is hence referred to as Rokujō Suri-no-Daibu. He enjoyed great favor with Retired Emperor Shirakawa, and was also on very close terms with Minamoto no Toshiyori. In 1119 he gathered together a large group of poets to pay reverence to a statue of Kakinomoto no Hitomaro, the great poet of the *Man'yōshū*, in a ceremony known as *Hitomaro eigu*, and at that time he recommended that Toshiyori be the first to present a poetic offering and treated him with great respect.

Akisue from an early age demonstrated outstanding talent in poetry and often served as a judge in poetry matches. His son Akisuke, his grandsons Kiyosuke and Kenshō, and others of his descendants were noted as poets and critics of poetry, and he is honored as the founder of the Rokujō family school of poetry. His poetry may be described as mild and temperate in tone. Forty-eight of his poems are preserved in the *Goshūishū* and other official anthologies and in such private anthologies as the *Goyōshū*, *Shoku shikashū*, and others. There is a collection of his works entitled *Rokujō Suri-no-Daibu no shū*.

Fujiwara no Akisuke (1090–1155)

Poet of the late Heian period. He was the third son of Fujiwara no Akisue, the founder of the Rokujō family school of poetry, and the father of Kiyosuke. In 1141 he was simultaneously appointed to the three posts of *sakyō-no-daibu*, *chūgū-no-suke*, and acting governor of the province of Ōmi. He carried on the traditions of the Rokujō family in poetry and took part in a number of poetry matches. In 1144 he was commanded by Retired Emperor Sutoku to compile the anthology known as the *Shikashū*, a task that he completed in 1151.

His poetry, like that of his father, is neither markedly old-fashioned nor modern in tone, but is characterized by moderation; intellectual and analytical in approach, it aims for elegance and lucidity of style. As a result, his works give the impression of being somewhat austere and restricted in scope. At the same time, however, he was capable of appreciating works that employed a highly individualistic or romantic style quite different from his own, as demonstrated by the fact that he included in the *Shikashū* seventeen poems by the eccentric Sone no Yoshitada, as well as sixteen poems by Izumi Shikibu. Fourteen of his poems are found in the *Kin'yōshū* and seventy more in other official anthologies, and a number are also included in private anthologies. His works are collected under the title *Sakyō-no-Daibu Akisuke-kyō no shū.*

Fujiwara no Kintō (966–1041)

Poet of the middle Heian period. His father was Kampaku Fujiwara no Yoritada, his mother was the daughter of the Nakatsukasa-kyō Yoshiakira Shinnō, and he was married to the daughter of Akihira Shinnō; he thus belonged to the highest ranks of the nobility and grew up in surroundings of affluence and culture. In 1009 he was appointed *gon-no-dainagon* and was promoted to the Senior Second Rank, but though the son of an illustrious family, the latter part of his career in office did not always proceed smoothly; others around him advanced more rapidly, and he was never appointed to a top ministerial post, facts that caused him considerable dissatisfaction. In 1024, at the age of fifty-eight, he resigned from office, became a Buddhist monk, and lived a life of retirement at Nagatani in the hills north of Kyoto.

Kintō held office at a time when Fujiwara no Michinaga was at the height of his power, when the consorts of Emperor Ichijō, Teishi and Shoshi, vied to outdo each other in beauty and had in their service such famous women writers as Sei Shōnagon, Murasaki Shikibu, and Izumi Shikibu, making it one of the most brilliant periods in all Japanese literature. Kintō, with his aristocratic background and wide learning and his remarkable ability in music and the writing of poetry in Chinese and Japanese, regarded at the time as the highest forms of art, held a position of unrivaled authority in the artistic world. Contemporary works such as the *Midō Kampaku-ki*, *Murasaki Shikibu nikki*, and *Makura no sōshi* give some idea of his way of life and the respect he enjoyed among the members of the court, and a number of anecdotes concerning him are recorded in the *Kōdanshō*, *Eiga monogatari*, *Ōkagami*, *Fukurozōshi*, and other works.

The contribution that he made to literature is a large one. He compiled a work entitled the *Wakan rōeishū*, which contains some eight hundred poems or parts of poems in Chinese and Japanese drawn from various collections and selected on the basis of their suitability for recitation; the work was highly regarded at the time, being widely read and used as a text for calligraphy practice, and its contents had an enormous effect upon such literary forms of later periods as the *gunkimono* (war tales), *enkyoku* (banquet songs), and the Nō and puppet dramas. In addition, he compiled the *Sanjūrokuninsen*, a selection from the works of thirty-six poets, who became known as the Thirty-six Poetic Geniuses, and wrote a work on poetics called the *Shinsen zuinō*, which is one of the most important statements on literary theory to come out of the middle Heian period. He is thought to have been the compiler of the officially sponsored anthology known as the *Shūishū*, and some ninety of his poems are included in official anthologies; in addition, there is a collection of his works called the *Saki-no-Dainagon Kintō-kyō shū*. His poems are typical of the period when the Fujiwara family was at the height of its power, clever in presentation and homey in theme; all of his poems deal with aspects of his daily life and show no inclination to indulge in private thoughts or poetic meditations. His poetic theories carry on and develop the line of thought expressed by Ki no Tsurayuki in his Preface to the *Kokinshū*, stressing the importance of form and suggestiveness and laying the foundation for the type of poetry later to be found in the *Shin kokinshū*. He produced other works such as the *Shinsō hishō*, *Kingyokushū*, and *Waka kuhon*, making a contribution to the history of Japanese poetics that is of primary importance.

Fujiwara no Kiyosuke (1104–1177)

Poet and critic of the late Heian period. He was the son of Fujiwara no Akisuke. For a long time he served as an official to the empress of the ruler of two reigns back and did not advance in office as rapidly as his younger brother Shigeie; he seems to have held the rank of *san'mi*, though the facts are uncertain. He played an important part in carrying on the traditions of the Rokujō family school of poetry, opposing Fujiwara no Shunzei, the principal exponent of the Sanjō family school. At the time when his father, Akisuke, was compiling the anthology known as the *Shikashū*, some kind of disharmony seems to have arisen between father and son; not only did Akisuke not heed any of his son's opinions, but he failed to include even one of his son's poems in the anthology, a fact that is said to have caused Kiyosuke considerable dissatisfaction. Kiyosuke then compiled an anthology of his own entitled the *Shoku shikashū*, intending to present it to Retired Emperor Nijō, but the latter passed away before the work was completed.

According to the *Mumyōshō* of Kamo no Chōmei, Kiyosuke was a man of rather intolerant disposition and disliked having anyone contradict his views. He took up a stand in direct opposition to Shunzei in all matters of poetic theory and practice. His poems are inferior to those of Shunzei, but he was a devoted scholar and worked to develop and refine the style typical of the Rokujō school, contributing more as a critic and theorist of poetry than as a poet. He wrote explications and commentaries on the imperial anthologies, examined the practices followed in the compilation of anthologies and the holding of poetry matches, compiled biographies of poets, and attempted to work out principles of poetic theory and criticism, producing studies of the classics of poetic literature that are based on careful and thorough examination of the source materials. His scholarship is highly praised by Kampaku Fujiwara no Kanezane in his diary, the *Gyokuyō*. Kiyosuke's poetry tends to be rather intellectual in nature and on the whole is lacking in poetic feeling.

His most important works on poetics are the *Fukurozōshi*, *Ōgishō*, and *Waka shogakushō*, and in addition he produced commentaries and annotations to the various imperial anthologies and to such other works as the *Ise monogatari* and *Yamato monogatari*. Many of his poems are included in imperial anthologies, and there is also a collection of his works entitled *Kiyosuke Ason shū*.

FUJIWARA NO MICHITOSHI (1047–1099)

Poet of the late Heian period. He was the second son of Dazai-no-daini Fujiwara no Tsunehira; his mother was the daughter of Shōnagon Hino no Ienari. His elder brother Michimune was governor of Wakasa. In 1059 he was appointed to the court rank of Junior Fifth Rank Lower Grade, and after serving as *kurōdo-no-tō* and *sangi*, he was in 1094 appointed *gon chūnagon* Junior Second Rank and *jibu-kyō*, or head of the ministry of the interior. Michitoshi's elder brother Michimune never advanced beyond the status of a provincial governor, but he was a very enthusiastic follower of the art of poetry, and it may be surmised that he exercised a considerable influence over his younger brother. Michitoshi's younger sister served as an attendant to Emperor Shirakawa, enjoying great favor with him, and as a result Michitoshi also seems to have been well looked upon by the emperor. In 1075 he was ordered by the emperor to compile the anthology known as the *Goshūishū*, a task he completed in 1086. The most prominent personage in poetry circles of the time was Minamoto no Tsunenobu, a man who surpassed Michitoshi in both popularity and ability, and it was generally thought that he was the one who should have been appointed to compile the anthology. But because Michitoshi, a young man of only twenty-eight, was chosen instead, there was criticism voiced against the *Goshūishū* from many quarters, and about the same time that the anthology was completed, Minamoto no Tsunenobu wrote a work entitled *Nan goshūishū*, or "Objections to the *Goshūishū*," in which he expressed his disapproval. However, the Japanese preface to the *Goshūishū* is conceded to be second only to that written by Ki no Tsurayuki for the *Kokinshū*, and Michitoshi had great confidence in his own ability. In order to make his position clear, he wrote a work entitled *Goshūi mondō*, or "Questions and Answers on the *Goshūishū*," fragments of which still exist, in which he attempted to answer Tsunenobu's objections. While he was in the process of compiling the anthology, he continued to be active as a participant and judge in poetry matches and carried on similar activities after the anthology was completed. As a critic he followed Fujiwara no Kintō in placing great emphasis upon the qualities of *jō* (emotional content) and *sugata* (form). His own poetic style is rather intellectual, keeping sentiment and mood under careful control and displaying flashes of ego and an attitude of willfulness, elements that lend it an air of novelty. Twenty-seven of his poems are preserved in the *Goshūishū* and other anthologies, and there was probably a separate collection of his works, though no such text is extant now.

Fujiwara no Mototoshi (d. 1142)

Poet in Japanese and Chinese and critic of poetry in the late Heian period. His father was Udaijin (Minister of the Right) Fujiwara no Toshiie; his mother was the daughter of Takashina no Yorinari. A descendant of the illustrious Fujiwara no Michinaga, he came from a highly distinguished family, and his brothers all rose to prominent positions, but for reasons that are unclear Mototoshi never advanced beyond the court rank of Junior Fifth Rank Upper Grade and the post of *saemon-no-suke*, or second in charge of the palace guard. He seems to have devoted all his energies to writing and theorizing about *waka* poetry and in 1138 he entered the Buddhist priesthood, taking the religious name Kakushun. His critical writings display considerable erudition, and according to what is recorded concerning him in the *Mumyōshō* of Kamo no Chōmei and other works, he appears to have been a rather haughty man who took great pride in his learning.

As a poet and critic, he opposed the new trends advocated by his contemporary Minamoto no Toshiyori, taking the stand of a classicist and defending the traditions of the past. Though he wrote *kanshi* (poetry in Chinese), he left no particularly distinguished works in that medium, and it may be said as a whole that he is more important as a critic than as a creative poet.

Over one hundred of his poems in Japanese are preserved in the *Kin'yōshū* and other officially sponsored anthologies, and there is a collection of his works entitled *Mototoshi shū*. He was at times called upon to act as a judge in poetry matches, acting in that capacity at the *Naidaijin no Ie* contest in 1118 and the *Akisuke no Ie* contest in 1134, and he compiled an anthology entitled the *Shinsen rōeishū*, which has been preserved. When he was eighty-four, Fujiwara no Shunzei requested to become his disciple, and his influence on the latter in the area of poetic theory is considerable.

FUNYA NO YASUHIDE (dates uncertain)

Poet of the early Heian period, he is numbered among the so-called Six Poetic Geniuses. He was descended from Prince Naga, a son of Emperor Temmu; his father, Funya no Muneyuki, held the office of *nuidono-no-suke*, second in charge of the office in charge of needlework. He held posts as a lesser provincial official in Mikawa and Yamato and in 879 was appointed to the same post his father had held, that of *nuidono-no-suke*. His name is listed among the participants in the *Koresada no Miko no Ie* poetry match, so it would appear that he lived until around the Ninna (885–89) and Kampyō (889–98) eras. Few of his works have been preserved, the most important ones being the five poems contained in the *Kokinshū*. These suggest that his style was rather intellectual and that he excelled in works marked by wit and technical dexterity. Ki no Tsurayuki writes of him in the Japanese preface to the *Kokinshū* as follows: "Funya no Yasuhide is very skillful with words, but the style does not fit the content, and the effect is like that of a tradesman trying to wear fancy clothes." Almost nothing is known of his life, though he appears to have been acquainted with the famous poetess Ono no Ko- machi, and the story of how he invited her to visit Mikawa when he was serving as a provincial official there is well known.

GOSHIRAKAWA TENNŌ (1127–1192)

Seventy-seventh sovereign of Japan. Named Masahito, he was the fourth son of Emperor Toba; his mother was Taikenmon-in Shōshi, the daughter of Dainagon Fujiwara no Kinzane. He ascended the throne in 1155 at the age of twenty-eight and abdicated after three years of rule, handling affairs of state as a *jōkō*, or retired sovereign. In 1169 he entered the Buddhist clergy. Living in a turbulent age—which saw the Hōgen and Heiji uprisings, the flourishing and downfall of the Taira family, and the rise to power of the Minamoto—

he proved himself to be a forceful ruler, both as a reigning emperor and as a retired sovereign exercising power from behind the scenes.

In his private life he displayed a particular interest in the arts. In addition to being a skilled flute player, he excelled in the various types of singing known as *imayō*, *shōmyō*, *saibara*, etc. Just how great was his enthusiasm for *imayō* can be judged from a passage in chapter ten of the *Ryōjin hishō kudenshū*, an anthology of *imayō* that he compiled over a period of years, in which he records his views on *imayō* singing, describes his own experiences with the art, and relates the motives that led him to the compilation of the anthology. At the palace or at various temples, he frequently held gatherings devoted to the performance of *eikyoku*, a general term for *imayō*, *kagura*, *saibara*, and other types of song, music, recitation, and displays of artistic skill popular at the time, and he acted as teacher to a number of distinguished performers, creating through his efforts what may be called the golden age of the *eikyoku*. The anthologies he compiled, the *Ryōjin hishō* and *Ryōjin hishō kudenshū*, provide invaluable materials for the study of the *imayō* and hold a place of special importance in the history of Japanese songs. Finally, mention should be made of the *Nenjū gyōji emaki*, a scroll painting in sixty scrolls that Goshirakawa commissioned Fujiwara no Mitsunaga and others to execute. Though only nineteen scrolls of a later copy of the work are still extant, they provide valuable information on the year-round activities of the court and the lives and customs of the residents of the capital in late Heian times.

A work entitled the *Eikyokushū* has also been attributed to him, and fifteen of his poems are preserved in the *Senzaishū* and other anthologies.

Ise (dates uncertain)

Poet of the early Heian period. She was active during the reigns of emperors Uda and Daigo (889–930); one theory maintains that she died in 939. She was a descendant of the Kita (North) branch of the Fujiwara family, and her grandfather Fujiwara no Iemune is well known as the founder of the Hōkai-ji in Hino, a temple of great importance in the history of Japanese art. Her father, Fujiwara no Tsugukage, was appointed to such posts as governor of Ise and governor of Yamato, being a member of the *zuryō*, the provincial governor class that produced so many women of literary talent at this time. Her uncle Hirokage and her cousin Shigetoki both held the post of *daigaku-no-kami*, or director of the imperial university, and her father was a graduate of the literature course of the university. Thus she seems to have grown up in an atmosphere permeated with learning and literature. She served first as a lady-in-waiting to Empress Onshi, the consort of Emperor Uda, and came to be called Ise because her father held the title of governor of Ise. After an unhappy love affair with the empress's elder brother Fuji-wara no Nakahira, she seems to have spurned the attentions of several would-be lovers while continuing to serve in the palace. After some years, she gained favor with Emperor Uda and bore him a son, but the boy died at the age of seven. At some later date she attracted the notice of Emperor Uda's fourth son, Prince Atsuyoshi, and bore him a daughter named Naka-tsukasa. The prince, however, died in 930, and the remainder of her life is a mystery. From these facts it may be surmised that she was a woman of beauty and charm who attracted considerable attention at court, but who for that very reason was destined to a life marked by continual changes of for-tune.

As a poet she ranks beside Ono no Komachi among the outstanding women contributors to the *Kokinshū*. She was chosen to take part in the poetry match held in 913 known as the *Teiji-no-in utaawase*, participating alongside such eminent poets as Ki no Tsurayuki and Ōshikōchi no Mitsune, and in other ways enjoyed a degree of recognition not held by any of the other women poets of the time. Her works, cast in the highly refined style typical of the *Kokinshū*, display a carefully controlled passion and a mastery of technique, though the latter quality at times leads her into an excessive concern with rhetoric and form. A total of 180 of her poems are preserved in officially sponsored anthologies, beginning with twenty-two in the *Kokinshū*. They are especially prominent in the *Gosenshū*, which includes sixty-nine of her poems, making her second only to Ki no Tsurayuki in number of poems included. This will give some indication of how important a writer she was regarded to be at the time. There is a collection of her works entitled *Ise shū*, and she is numbered among the so-called Thirty-six Poetic Geniuses.

Izumi Shikibu (b. ca. 976)

Poet of the middle Heian period. Her father was Ōe no Masamune, gover-nor of the province of Echizen; her mother was said to be the daughter of Taira no Yasuhira, though the facts are uncertain. It would appear that around the age of twenty she married Tachibana no Michisada, the governor of Izumi, and hence came to be called Izumi Shikibu. She bore a daughter by Michisada, known in history as Ko-Shikibu, but separated from her husband and returned to the capital, where she carried on an affair with Danjō-no-miya Tametaka, the third son of Retired Emperor Reizei. He died at the untimely age of twenty-five, whereupon she began an affair with his younger brother Sochi-no-miya Atsumichi, as she relates in her diary, the *Izumi Shikibu nikki.* Her affair with Sochi-no-miya seems to have been the most intense and passionate of her whole life, and when he died at the age of twenty-six, she gave expression to her profound grief in some 120 poems preserved in the *Izumi Shikibu zokushū.* She was summoned to the palace by Fujiwara no Michinaga and served as a lady-in-waiting to Empress Shōshi, where she became a companion of Murasaki Shikibu, who from some time in the past had been in the service of the empress. Later she married again, this time to Fujiwara no Yasumasa, and accompanied him when he was assigned to the post of governor of Tango, a fact alluded to in the famous poem by her daughter included in the *Hyakunin isshu.* Death deprived her of her beloved daughter, and her marriage to Yasumasa does not seem to have proceeded harmoniously, though little is known about her closing years. A woman of great beauty and poetic talent who abandoned herself to the dictates of her passions, it is hardly surprising that she became the inspiration for numerous legends in later ages.

Her poems, as might be expected, are filled with intense feeling and, breaking away from the conventionalized tone of the poetry of the *Kokinshū,* achieve a freedom of expression that was novel to the poetic world of middle Heian times. In addition to poems giving expression to passionate abandon and sensual charm, she also wrote works marked by a deeply mediative and religious tone, and her lyric gift was of the highest order, assuring to her works a place of prime importance in the history of Japanese poetry. A large number of poems have been preserved in the collections entitled *Izumi Shikibu shū* and *Izumi Shikibu zokushū.*

Jōjin Azari no Haha (dates uncertain)

Writer of the middle Heian period. She would appear to have been born around 989, and since the work she wrote entitled *Jōjin Azari no haha no shū* records events that took place as late as 1073, it would appear that she lived to be about eighty-five. Although there is no clear evidence, it has been speculated that her father was Toshikata, the son of Minamoto no Takaakira. The identity of her husband is likewise uncertain, though he was perhaps Yoshikata, the son of a poet named Fujiwara no Sanekata, who was well known at the time. She bore him two sons, but he died when she was around the age of thirty, and she was left to raise her sons alone; in time she placed them both in the Buddhist clergy. The elder eventually rose to the rank of *risshi* and resided at the Ninna-ji in Kyoto; the younger, who entered the priesthood at the age of six, became a monk of the Tendai sect and, known as Jōjin Azari, was highly regarded at the time. At the age of fifty-nine he requested permission to visit Sung China. Two years later he made the journey and won prominence on the continent as an outstanding religious leader. He died in China in 1081.

The *Jōjin Azari no haha no shū*, in two chapters, was written after Jōjin's mother, then over eighty, first learned of her son's determination to go to China, and gives expression to the sorrow his parting occasioned. It contains 174 poems in *waka* form and one *chōka*, and has traditionally been treated as a collection of poems. The prose passages that are interspersed with the poems, however, go far beyond the brief *kotobagaki*, or introductions, that are customarily found in such works and give it more the character of a *nikki*, or diary. The work covers a period of seven years around the time of her son's departure for China and is permeated by the aged woman's feelings of grief and expressions of intense maternal affection. The last entry deals with events of the fifth month of 1073, and it appears likely that the author died shortly after, dreaming of her son far away on the continent.

Keikai (dates uncertain)

Buddhist priest of the early Heian period. He is the author of a work in three chapters entitled *Nihonkoku gempō zen'aku reiiki*, or "Account of the Miraculous Ways in which Good and Evil are Rewarded in the Land of Japan," more often referred to by the abbreviated title *Nihon reiiki*.

Under the heading of each chapter is a notation saying that the chapter was written by "the priest Keikai of the Yakushi-ji in the western sector of Nara," and hence it is known that he was affiliated with the Yakushi-ji, but beyond this very little can be determined about his life. There is, however, a section in the third chapter that appears to be autobiographical in nature; it suggests that the author did not enter the clergy until his middle years and that he had for a long time before this taken a great interest in both religious and secular literature.

The *Nihon reiiki* is the earliest collection of Buddhist tales in Japan and, as the author states in his preface, was influenced by such Chinese collections of tales as the *Ming-pao-chi* and the *Pan-jo yen-chi*. The author states that, saddened by the state of the world, he undertook the writing of the work because he felt that the only hope for remedy lay in the Buddhist doctrine of retribution. The numerous tales in the book, presented as accounts of actual historical fact, tell of the various ways in which deeds of good or evil are recompensed, either in this world or the world hereafter. The work is written in Chinese but served as the inspiration for later collections of tales in Japanese such as the *Konjaku monogatari*. His name is sometimes read Kyōkai, and the title of the work he wrote *Nihon ryō ki*.

KENREIMON-IN NO UKYŌ-NO-DAIBU (b. ca. 1157)

Poet of the late Heian period. Her father was Fujiwara no Koreyuki, a descendant of the famous calligrapher Fujiwara no Kōzei and a member of a family distinguished for generations for skill in calligraphy. Her mother, known as Nun Yūgiri, was the daughter of Ōmiwa no Motomasa, a well-known *gagaku* musician, and Ukyō-no-daibu herself was skilled in playing the *sō*, a stringed instrument. In 1173, when she was around sixteen, she became a lady-in-waiting to Tokuko (later called Kenreimon-in), the consort of Emperor Takakura and daughter of Taira no Kiyomori. It was around this time that she began the love affair with Taira no Sukemori, second son of Shigemori, which was to fill her lifetime with sadness. In 1185, after Sukemori's death in the battle of Dan-no-ura, she joined her elder brother in residing in the monks' quarters of the Hōjō-ji temple at Kujō Kawara in Kyoto, but in 1195, when she was past forty, she once again became a lady-in-waiting, this time to Emperor Gotoba, who retired shortly afterward, and remained in service for the following twenty or more years. In 1234, when Fujiwara no Teika was compiling the anthology known as the *Shin chokusen-shū*, he asked Ukyō-no-daibu for copies of her poems; she presented him with the collection entitled *Kenreimon-in no Ukyō-no-daibu shū*. It is believed that she died around the Jōei (1232–34) era.

The *Kenreimon-in no Ukyō-no-daibu shū* contains some three hundred poems prefaced by lengthy introductions, which give the work something of the character of a diary. These introductions, or *kotobagaki*, describe the circumstances leading to the composition of the various poems and record the author's fond memories. The poems dealing with the author's love affair with Sukemori and her intense grief after his death, along with their introductions, constitute the heart of the collection. The lengthy prose passages are skillfully balanced by the emotionally charged poems, the whole creating an effect of great beauty and pathos. The style of her poems is simple and lucid and, at a time when there was a strong tendency to indulge in wordplays and other rhetorical flourishes, is remarkable for its directness.

Often as
I've sung of the moon,
the night's deep sadness
I feel for the first time
tonight.

KENSHŌ (ca. 1130—ca. 1210)

Poet and critic of the late Heian period. He was of the Fujiwara family and was also called Suke-no-kimi; he was the adopted son of Fujiwara no Akisuke and one of the most important figures in the Rokujō family school of poetry and poetic criticism founded by Akisuke's father Akisue. It is said that he was already composing *waka* by the age of eleven. In his youth he entered the monastery on Mt. Hiei to practice religious austerities. After returning to the capital, he was treated with special favor by Shukaku Hōshinnō, the second son of Emperor Goshirakawa and head of the Ninna-ji in Omuro, and at Shukaku's request wrote various works on poetics. He also took part in numerous poetry matches and at times acted as a judge. It has been said that as a poet he was inferior to Kiyosuke, the son of his foster father, but excelled Kiyosuke in scholarship. Be that as it may, he and Kiyosuke, as well as the other members of the family, worked together to establish the principles of the Rokujō school, opposing the principles and practices of the poets of the Mikohidari family such as Fujiwara no Shunzei and his son Teika. The famous document entitled *Roppyakuban chinjō*, in which Akisuke complained of the judgments handed down by Shunzei in the poetry contest known as the *Roppyakuban utaawase*, is a classic statement of the differences of poetic theory that characterized the two families.

Kenshō's poems tend to be overintellectual and lacking in feeling, but they display a mastery of old-fashioned diction and a profound knowledge of the poetic tradition. This is hardly surprising, since he excelled in scholarship and placed great emphasis upon the importance of a thorough knowledge of the works of the past. He was unparalleled as a writer of commentaries, producing annotations to the *Kokinshū, Shūishū, Goshūishū, Kin'yōshu, Shikashū, Sambokushū,* and others, as well as works dealing with Kakinomoto no Hitomaro and other poets of the *Man'yōshū,* and his *Shūchūshō* is one of the most important works of poetic criticism and explication to come out of the period. His passion for scholarship was unrivaled, and the great Edo period scholar of Japanese literature Keichū acknowledged a profound debt to his work. Some sixty of his poems have been preserved, about half in official anthologies and the other half in privately compiled works. It would appear that a collection of his works existed at one time, though no such text is extant today.

Ki no Tomonori (late ninth century)

Poet of the early Heian period. According to the *Kishi keizu*, a genealogy of the Ki family, Tomonori was the son of Ki no Aritomo and a cousin of Ki no Tsurayuki. From the *Gosenshū* it is learned that, having passed the age of forty without attaining public office, he appealed to the Minister of the Left Fujiwara no Shihei for assistance. In 897 he became a local official in the province of Tosa, the following year was made a *shō-naiki*, or junior secretary, of the *nakatsukasa-shō*, and in 904 advanced to the post of senior secretary. In 905 he was ordered to join with his cousin Ki no Tsurayuki and others in compiling the *Kokinshū*. Presumably he was by this time well along in years; chapter sixteen of the *Kokinshū* contains poems by Ki no Tsurayuki and Mibu no Tadamine written on the death of Tomonori, and it would therefore appear that he died while the anthology was in the process of compilation. In addition it is known that he took part in such famous poetry matches as the *Kampyō no ontoki Kisai-no-miya no utaawase* and the *Koresada Shinnōke no utaawase*, and that he was asked by Koretaka Shinnō to present the poems that Tomonori's father had written during his lifetime. Since he was chosen as one of the compilers of the *Kokinshū*, there is no doubt that he was regarded as a poet of considerable importance, but his works, especially when compared with those of Ki no Tsurayuki and Ōshikōchi no Mitsune, appear somewhat mediocre in quality.

His poems are noteworthy principally for their warmth and sincerity of feeling and their lucidity of style. Poetic fashion at the time placed great emphasis upon wit and verbal cleverness, often to the point of becoming contrived, but Tomonori's works are relatively simple and direct in expression. Sixty-four of his poems are preserved in imperial anthologies, beginning with the *Kokinshū*, and there is also a collection of his works entitled *Tomonori shū*.

Ki no Tsurayuki (ca. 868–945 or 946)

Poet of the early Heian period. The son of Ki no Mochiyuki, he applied himself to the study of Chinese verse and prose, studies that had been traditional in the Ki family, as well as mastering the techniques of *waka*, taking part in such famous poetry matches as the *Kampyō no ontoki Kisai-no-miya no utaawase*, the *Koresada Shinnōke no utaawase*, and others and displaying great literary talent. In the fourth month of 905, when he was serving as head of the *goshodokoro* (palace library), he was commanded by the emperor to join with Ōshikōchi no Mitsune, Mibu no Tadamine, and others in compiling an anthology of Japanese poetry under imperial auspices. After some period of time, the group produced the *Kokinshū*, or *Collection of Ancient and Modern Japanese Poems*, in twenty chapters and presented it to the throne; it was preceded by a famous Preface written by Tsurayuki in the *kana* syllabary, which is the first major piece of literary criticism in Japanese and which, along with Tsurayuki's poems included in the anthology, marks him as the foremost figure in the poetic world of the time. In 907 he was appointed to the posts of *naizen* and *tenzen*, offices having to do with the preparation of the imperial meals, and he was chosen to accompany Retired Emperor Uda on an outing to the Ōi River west of Kyoto, contributing nine poems in Japanese and a preface to commemorate the occasion. After holding various other posts in the capital, he was appointed in 930 as governor of the province of Tosa in the island of Shikoku, serving in that position for five years before returning to the capital. During this period he was commanded by the ruler to compile a selection of the most outstanding poems in the *Kokinshū*, a commission that resulted in the *Shinsen wakashū*, or *New Selection of Japanese Poems*, and after returning to the capital he wrote the famous *Tosa nikki*, or *Tosa Diary*, describing the journey back to Kyoto.

By 940 he had advanced to a position that allowed him to enter the palace itself, and in 945 he was appointed *moku no gon no kami*, an office having to do with the repair and upkeep of the palace, but he died shortly afterward around the age of eighty. From the point of view of official position he was hardly distinguished, the posts he held in his lifetime being all of a relatively insignificant nature, but in literary matters, particularly those concerning the composition of poetry in Japanese, he commanded an authority that brought prime ministers and high officials knocking at his gate in search of counsel. It was an authority founded upon his profound knowledge and understanding of Japanese and Chinese literature, his remarkable ability as a writer and critic, the creativeness of his innovations in the field of *kana* literature, and the sincerity and uprightness of his character.

Tsurayuki has been looked up to by later ages as one of the fathers of Japanese poetry, not only because of the skill of his own compositions, but perhaps even more so because of the fame of his Preface to the *Kokinshū*. Beginning with the statement, "The poetry of Japan has its roots in the human heart and flourishes in the countless leaves of words," it has served as a foundation for later statements on the nature and ideals of Japanese poetry as well as a model of *kana* prose. His poetry tends to be rather intellectual in tone, highly polished in diction, and marked by wit and verbal cleverness, being in these respects typical of the new style of Japanese poetry represented in the *Kokinshū*, though at times his interest in word play results in works that are excessively rhetorical and mannered. The *Tosa Diary* was one of the earliest works of that genre to be written in the Japanese syllabary, Chinese having earlier been the medium for such prose works, and it served as a point of departure for numerous later works in Japanese, not only in the diary form, but in the novel and other forms as well; at the same time it stands as a masterpiece in its own right because of its content and beauty of expression.

Four hundred fifty of Tsurayuki's poems have been preserved in imperial anthologies, over a hundred in the *Kokinshū* alone, while some fifty or more are to be found in privately compiled anthologies. In addition, his works include the *Tsurayuki shū*, the works mentioned above, the Preface to the *Shinsen wakashū*, the *Ōigawa gyōkō wakajo*, and others. He is numbered among the so-called Thirty-six Poetic Geniuses.

> My longings unbearable,
> I went to see my love—
> the winter night's
> river wind
> so cold the plovers cried.

Kisen Hōshi (dates uncertain)

Poet of the early Heian period. Almost nothing is known of his life. He is also known as Daigo Hōshi, and it has been suggested that he was 1) a descendant of Emperor Kammu; 2) a descendant of Tachibana no Moroe; and 3) the son of Ki no Natora; and some have even suggested that Kisen was the religious name assumed by Emperor Seiwa when he retired and entered the priesthood. All that is known for certain is that he lived in the province of Yamashiro sometime around the Kōnin era (810–24), that he was a priest of the Shingon sect residing at Mt. Daigo, and that he later retired to a hut in the mountains around Uji and lived the life of a recluse.

He is numbered among the Six Poetic Geniuses, being mentioned by Ki no Tsurayuki in the Preface to the *Kokinshū*. There Tsurayuki quotes the poem by Kisen,

> My hut is southeast of the capital—
> Thus I live in peace,
> though men call these
> the hills of sorrow.

which depends for much of its effect on the play on the placename "Uji" and the word "sorrow" (*uki*), and the word *shika*, meaning "thus" or "deer," and adds a comment that indicates Kisen's poems were little known at the time the *Kokinshū* was compiled. Another of his poems is quoted by Kenshō Hōshi in his *Kokinshū jochū*, and a third, religious in nature, is found in the *Jukashū*.

With regard to the style of Kisen's poetry, Tsurayuki in his Preface remarks, "It is subtle in language and vague throughout, like an autumn moon dimmed by dawn clouds."

There is also a work on poetics attributed to Kisen and entitled the *Kisen-shiki*, which was said to have been compiled at the command of Emperor Kōkō.

KŪKAI (774–835)

Buddhist priest of the early Heian period. He was born in the province of Sanuki in Shikoku; his father was of the Saeki family, his mother of the Ato family; as a child he was named Mana. At first he studied the Confucian texts but later journeyed to Nara and received instruction in the doctrines pertaining to the Bodhisattva Ākāśagarbha (Japanese: Kokūzō) from a priest named Kinsō Sōzu. He became a student in the state university, specializing in *myōgyō*, the study of the Confucian Classics, and about this time seems to have determined to devote his life to Buddhism. It was also around this time that he traveled about the provinces of Awa and Tosa in Shikoku practicing various religious austerities. At the age of nineteen he shaved his head and took the religious name Kyōkai and several years later received formal ordination at the Tōdai-ji in Nara and changed his name to Kūkai. In 804, at the age of thirty, he accompanied the Japanese envoy and his party to China, journeying to Ch'ang-an and receiving instruction in the mysteries of the Shingon sect of Buddhism from Abbot Hui-kuo of the Ch'ing-lung-ssu and others. Having won the approval and admiration of his master, he returned to Japan in 806, charged with the mission of introducing the Shingon teachings to his native country. He brought back with him from China a number of Buddhist scriptures and religious articles, as well as collections of Chinese poetry and works on poetics. On his return, he was given permission to propagate the teachings of Shingon, and in 816 founded a temple known as the Kongōbu-ji on top of Mt. Kōya in the province of Kii. In 823 he was invited to the capital to head the newly founded Kyōō-gokoku-ji, popularly known as Tō-ji, where he conducted prayers for the safety of the nation and worked to spread the teachings of Shingon. He was advanced to the ecclesiatical rank of *daisōzu*, and in 828 founded a school known as the Shugeishuchi-in for the instruction of sons of the common people. Having lived to see the Shingon sect firmly established in fact as well as name, he passed away on Mt. Kōya in 835. After his death he was promoted to the rank of *daisōjō* and was given the posthumous name Kōbō Daishi.

Like his slightly older contemporary Saichō, Kūkai labored to establish and propagate Buddhism as the national faith of Japan. Of special significance among his achievements was the founding of the Shugeishuchi-in. Institutions of higher learning were at the time restricted in enrollment to the aristocracy, but Kūkai's dream was to provide an opportunity for education to the sons of the common people as well, offering instruction to monks and laymen alike and teaching both religious and secular literature, and in this way creating a new class of intellectual leaders in the nation. In addition to his importance as a religious leader, he was a man of great artistic and literary talent and contributed substantially to the development of Japanese literature. His *Bunkyō hifuron*, a work on Chinese poetics and literary criticism, served as a model for later writers of Chinese verse and prose in Japan and even exercised an influence on the later development of poetry in Japanese. He himself was a skilled writer of Chinese verse, as may be seen from his works preserved in the *Henjō hakki shōryō shū*, and he has also left several poems in Japanese. His doctrinal works did much for the advancement of Buddhist studies in Japan and include such important texts as the *Sangō shiiki* and the *Himitsu mandara jūjūshinron*. Finally, he was celebrated as a calligrapher, being numbered among the Sampitsu, Three Masters of Calligraphy, of the period, the other two being Emperor Saga and Tachibana no Hayanari. The piece known as the *Fūshinchō* is a particularly renowned example of his skill as a calligrapher.

Because of his numerous achievements and the vital role that he played in the religious and cultural life of the nation, Kūkai has continued down to the present day to inspire feelings of intense admiration and personal devotion in the hearts of his countrymen, and numerous legends have grown up around his name. There is hardly a region of Japan that does not revere the good works of Kōbō Daishi and claim to have received some special benefit or blessing from him.

MIBU NO TADAMINE (dates uncertain)

Poet of the early Heian period. He was the son of Mibu no Yasutsuna and the father of Tadami. Judging from the dates of his works, he seems to have lived until the latter part of the Engi era (901–23).

At first he served as an attendant to the General of the Right Fujiwara no Sadakuni, but in the fifth year of Engi (905) he was appointed a minor official in the Imperial Guards of the Right. Later he advanced to the post of *shōgen*, or secretary, in the Imperial Guards of the Left. As a poet he is known to have taken part in such famous poetry matches as the *Kampyō no ontoki Kisai-no-miya* contest and the *Koresada Shinnōke* contest. In 905 he was among the four men commanded by the emperor to compile the anthology known as the *Kokin wakashū* or *Kokinshū*, the *Collection of Ancient and Modern Poems*, but he appears to have been the lowest in rank among the four compilers and was probably already quite old. In 907 he participated in the famous imperial outing to the Ōi River west of Kyoto and submitted poems on the occasion. He wrote a preface to the collection of the poems composed on the outing, as did Ki no Tsurayuki. He is known to have exchanged poems with Ki no Tsurayuki and Ōshikōchi no Mitsune and with Ariwara no Shigeharu, a son of the famous poet Ariwara no Narihira. His poetic style is very restrained and marked by a mild and gentle lyricism. A total of over eighty poems from his hand have been preserved, thirty-four of them in the *Kokinshū*. He wrote a work on poetic theory entitled the *Tadamine jittai*, which, judging from the fact that it is referred to in the *Ōgishō*, the *Waka genzai shomoku*, and other works, was very highly regarded in Heian times. There is a collection of his works entitled the *Tadamine shū*.

MICHITSUNA NO HAHA (937?–995)

Known to history only as Michitsuna no Haha ("Mother of Michitsuna"), she is renowned as a poet and author of the *Kagerō nikki (Gossamer Diary)*. Her father is Fujiwara no Tomoyasu, governor of Ise and a graduate of the literature course of the state university. Her mother was said to have been the daughter of Minamoto no Mitomu, a *gyōbu-no-daisuke* (official in the Ministry of Justice). The well-known poet Fujiwara no Nagatō appears to have been her younger brother, while the elder sister of the famous woman writer Sei Shōnagon was the wife of one of her elder half-brothers. In addition, it would seem that one of her sisters was the mother of another eminent woman writer, Takasuke no Musume, author of the *Sarashina nikki*, and her grandson Michikoto was also a renowned poet. She was thus connected in one way or another to a number of important literary figures and undoubtedly exercised some degree of influence upon them.

She was reported to have been one of the three most beautiful women of the time, and in addition was gifted with great poetic talent. She was undoubtedly one of the outstanding young women of the aristocracy of the period, and in time became the second wife of Fujiwara no Kaneie, a distinguished aristocrat of the period who eventually rose to the highest office in the government, that of *sesshō-kampaku*. She bore him a son named Michitsuna. The *Kagerō nikki* is a record of the events in her life over a period of some twenty-one years beginning sometime between 972 and 976. Though called a *nikki* (diary), it is more in the nature of an autobiography or work of reflective literature dealing with about half of the author's life. It begins with Kaneie's proposal of marriage and describes the marriage itself and the birth of Michitsuna, recording in a highly realistic manner the emotions of love, jealousy, loneliness, joy, resignation, and maternal affection that the stormy course of her marriage aroused. The work is important not only because it is the first of a series of major works in diary form by women writers, but also because it is the earliest prose work in the *monogatari*, or tale, form that departs from the fantasy of such previous works and introduces a note of unadorned realism. It thus exercised a profound influence upon the growth and direction of the literature by women writers of the time, a literature that reached its culmination in *The Tale of Genji*. The absolute sincerity with which the writer presents her account, permitting herself no compromise or obfuscation, and the frankness of her revelations of emotional turmoil cannot fail to move the reader even today.

She was famous in her time as a poet, being described in the *Ōkagami*, a fictionalized work of history dealing with the period, as a writer "of extraordinary skill in the art of *waka*." In the second year of the Anna era (969), when she was around thirty-three years old, she was requested to write a poem for a poem screen for the Minister of the Left Koichijō, an indication that she had by this time gained recognition as a writer of genuine stature. The *Shūishū* and other imperially sponsored anthologies contain thirty-six of her poems, and her works are also found in such privately compiled anthologies as the *Chōnōshū*, *Kingyokushū*, and *Korai fūteishō*.

Minamoto no Shitagou (911–983)

He was the decendant of Emperor Saga and the son of Minamoto no

Kozoru, who held the office of *sama-no-tō* (head of one of the offices in charge of the imperial stables). He lost both parents at an early age and remained a student until the age of forty-two. In 953 he completed the literature course at the state university and three years later embarked upon an official career, holding such posts as *kageyushi*, *kurōdo* in the household of the crown prince, governor of Izumi, and governor of Noto. As a member of the Minamoto family he suffered under the dictatorial power of the Fujiwara family, who virtually controlled the government at this time, and was prevented from rising to a position of importance. He gave vent to his frustration on frequent occasions in both his Japanese poetry and Chinese poetry and prose, and indeed this attitude of complaint and discontent over his lot is one of the principal characteristics of the poems found in his collected works, the *Minamoto no Shitagou shū*. At the same time he stands with his contemporary Sone no Yoshitada as the center of a group of poets who wrote works about the experiences of their daily lives, particularly those that were difficult and trying. In spite of his lack of success in official life, however, Shitagou was recognized as one of the outstanding poets and literary figures of the time and, as one of the group known as the Nashi-tsubo-no-go'nin (Five Men of the Pear Garden), was chosen to help in compiling the *Gosenshū*, and also devoted much time and energy to the exegesis of the *Man'yōshū*. He participated frequently in meetings and matches for the composition of poetry in Japanese and Chinese, produced *byōbu-uta* (folding-screen poems) at the request of members of the imperial family, and frequented the homes of many persons of high position and power. At the command of Princess Kinshi, the fourth daughter of Emperor Daigo, he compiled the *Wamyō ruijūshō*, a dictionary of Chinese and Japanese words arranged by categories, which was completed sometime during the Shōhei era (931–38).

Because of his literary talent and wide knowledge of Japanese and Chinese literature, he is often alleged to be the author of such anonymous prose works as the *Taketori monogatari*, the *Utsubo monogatari*, and the *Ochikubo monogatari*. The *Shūishū* and other imperially sponsored anthologies contain fifty-one of his poems, and a series of poems dealing with the names of horses known as the *Minamoto no Shitagou uma no ke na no awase* has also been handed down. As mentioned earlier, his Japanese poems are collected in a·work known as the *Minamoto no Shitagou shū*, and his poems and prose works in Chinese are to be found in such anthologies as the *Fusōshū* and the *Honchō monzui*.

Minamoto no Takakuni (1004–1077)

The third head of the "Daigo Genji," a branch of the Minamoto family descended from the Emperor Daigo. His grandfather Takaakira, who received the family name of Minamoto, became an ordinary subject and rose to the rank of Minister of the Left; he was also a scholar who wrote a work on court practice and ceremonial entitled *Saigūki*, but he became involved in a dispute with the Fujiwara family concerning the placing of the crown prince on the throne and was sent into virtual exile as governor of the Kyushu area (*Dazai-no-gon-no-sochi*). His son Toshikata (Takakuni's father) strove to restore the family's fortunes and eventually rose to the rank of *gon-dainagon*.

Takakuni, Toshikata's second son, was a favorite of Kampaku Fujiwara no Yorimichi; he became one of Yorimichi's closest advisors and, like his father before him, rose to the rank of *gon-dainagon*. In his youth he showed great industriousness in performing his official duties, but he also had a devouring curiosity, a love of collecting things, and a gift for conversation. In later years, after he had retired from official service and retired to Uji near Kyoto, he would often, apparently, hail wayfarers as they passed by and ask them for any unusual tales they had heard in the provinces. It seems, thus, that he was the kind of man with both the capability and personality required to compile a large collection of popular tales such as the *Konjaku monogatari*. He was referred to popularly as Uji Dainagon because of the location of the villa to which he retired. Thus he is considered to be the author of the collection known as *Uji Dainagon monogatari* and in a sense the original author of the *Konjaku monogatari*, the most celebrated of the collections of popular didactic tales, since the *Uji Dainagon monogatari* is said to have provided the model for the *Konjaku monogatari*. He also wrote *An'yōshō*, a work on Pure Land Buddhism, and his poems are included in the *Goshūishū*, *Senzaishū*, *Shin kokinshū*, and other anthologies.

Minamoto no Toshiyori (d. 1129)

Poet of the late Heian period. He was the third son of Minamoto no Tsunenobu; his mother was the daughter of Minamoto no Sadasuke, who held the title of governor of Tosa. After holding such posts as *sakyō-no-gon-daibu*, he was in 1105 appointed *moku-no-kami*, or head of the construction office in the Imperial Household Ministry. In court rank he advanced as high as Junior Fourth Rank Upper Grade. In 1094, when his father was appointed to the post of *Dazai-no-gon-no-sochi* in Kyushu, he accompanied his father to Tsukushi, where the Dazaifu was located, but returned to the capital after his father's death. He seems to have retired from official duties around 1111 and afterwards to have lived a rather lonely life, but he made at least two trips to Ise before his death. On the occasion of his departure for the second trip in 1122 he was appointed to a post in the *Saigū* (Office of the Imperial Deputy to the Great Shrine of Ise). The following year, when the deputy, who was always a princess of the imperial family, concluded her term of office, he accompanied her back to the capital. In 1124 he was commanded by Retired Emperor Shirakawa to compile an official anthology of poetry. The result was the *Kin'yōshū*, which, after various revisions, was finally approved by the emperor in 1127, when it was presented to him for the third time. Two years later Retired Emperor Shirakawa died, and Toshiyori likewise died within the same year at the age of seventy-four.

Toshiyori was the most accomplished poet of the period represented by the *Kin'yōshū*. He was the leader of the more progressive group of poets, standing in opposition to his contemporary Fujiwara no Mototoshi, the leader of the conservative poets. He took over his father's poetic style and worked to develop it further, a style marked by an air of freedom and freshness and rich in poetic fancy. In compiling the *Kin'yōshū*, he concentrated upon descriptive pieces that departed from the old traditions handed down from *Kokinshū* times and were vivid in imagery and novel in tone. The anthology thus stands as a representative of the newer and more progressive trends of the times, which sought in both conception and diction to break away from the conventions and cliches of the past and to move in the direction of greater freedom.

Some two hundred of Toshiyori's poems are preserved in the *Kin'yōshū* and other imperial anthologies. He was also active as a participant and judge in poetry matches and wrote works in the *renga*, or linked verse, form. He seems to have been a man of genial and tolerant personality and was highly respected by such men as the Rokujō Suri-no-daibu Fujiwara no Akisue and others. In addition, the celebrated poet Fujiwara no Shunzei, though officially a disciple of the conservative leader Fujiwara no Mototoshi, was greatly attracted by Toshiyori's style. Toshiyori was also much admired in later times and thus came to exercise an important influence upon the development of Japanese poetry.

Though Toshiyori's later years were ones of relative privation, he never ceased to enjoy high acclaim as a poet. A work on poetic theory entitled the *Toshiyori zuinō* has from early times been widely attributed to him. He himself compiled a collection of his works entitled the *Samboku kikashū*, an excellent selection that demonstrates his vitality and great breadth of interest and serves as a fitting summation of his artistic career.

Minamoto no Tsunenobu (1016–1097)

Poet of the late Heian period. He was also known as Katsura no Dainagon, because his home was in the village of Katsura west of Kyoto, and Sochi no Dainagon because of the last office he held. He was the son of Minamoto no Michikata and the father of Minamoto no Toshiyori. He served at court from the reign of Emperor Goichijō to that of Emperor Horikawa, but in 1095 was assigned the post of *Dazai-no-gon-no-sochi*, vice-governor of the Dazaifu government office in Kyushu. He journeyed to Kyushu to take up his duties but died shortly after at the age of eighty-one. His son Toshiyori went to Kyushu to conduct the funeral.

Tsunenobu was a man of wide learning who excelled in the art of poetry and was also skilled in music. In 1078, when Fujiwara no Michitoshi completed compiling the official anthology entitled *Goshūishū*, Tsunenobu wrote a work criticizing the anthology entitled *Nan goshūishū*. While the *Goshūishū* includes many works by women poets and favors a lyric style, Tsunenobu emphasized the importance of descriptive poetry that is fresh in feeling and theme and he himself wrote many poems depicting the countryside. Developing directions earlier explored by Sone no Yoshitada, he thus succeeded in opening up a new strain in Japanese poetry. The *Gotoba-in gokuden*, a compilation of critical comments by Retired Emperor Gotoba, rates him highly as a poet. He served as judge for the poetry contest known as the *Kayain utaawase*. His extant works include *Dainagon Tsunenobu kashū* and *Tsunenobu-kyō no ki*. The following is an example of his descriptive poetry:

> As evening comes,
> it sweeps the rice stalks
> in fields by the gate—
> the autumn wind that blows over
> my reed-thatched hut.

Minamoto no Yorimasa (1104–1180)

He was a descendant of Minamoto no Yorimitsu and the son of Minamoto no Nakamasa, who held the post of *hyōgo-no-kami*, head of the arsenal. He began his career as a *hōgandai*, an official in the household of Retired Emperor Shirakawa, and after serving as a *kurōdo* he advanced to the post that his father had held, that of *hyōgo-no-kami*. He served under a total of eight sovereigns, from Retired Emperor Shirakawa to Emperor Takakura, and was granted *shōden*, or permission to enter the upper part of the imperial palace. In 1178 he was advanced to the court rank of Junior Third Rank, and the following year he entered the Buddhist priesthood, thereafter being known as Gen San'mi Nyūdō, the Religious Adherent Minamoto of the Third Rank. During the Hōgen civil war he supported the government forces and aided the members of the Taira family, and during the Heiji civil war, which occurred shortly after, he opposed Minamoto no Yoshitomo and sided with Taira no Kiyomori. Later, however, he found himself increasingly frustrated by the dictatorial power of the Taira family. Finally in 1180, when he was seventy-six years of age, he felt he could endure the situation no longer and he joined with Prince Mochihito in an attempt to overthrow the Taira family, acting as the leader of the Minamoto forces. His army was defeated at Uji, however, and he committed suicide near the site of the battle. He is famous for the legend, recorded in the *Heike monogatari* and elsewhere, of how he shot down the *nue*, a monster bird that was menacing the imperial palace. His daughter, known as Nijōin Sanuki, became well known as a poet in the early part of the Kamakura period.

In addition to being a figure of political importance, Yorimasa is counted among the finest poets of the late Heian period, and although he cannot compare with his contemporary Saigyō, he has left many works that are widely admired. In addition, as a poet belonging to a warrior rather than to a court noble family, he ranks beside Minamoto no Sanetomo. Kamo no Chōmei in his *Mumyōshō* remarks: "My teacher Shun'e used to say, 'Lord Yorimasa is a truly outstanding poet. He immerses himself in poetry until it penetrates to the innermost recesses of his heart and never allows himself to forget it.' " From this and other indications, it would appear that Yorimasa was much admired by Shun'e and others such as Fujiwara no Shunzei. His works show quite a different style from that of most of the works of the *Kin'yōshū* and the *Shikashū*, the imperial anthologies that were compiled in his time, and at times display a depth and rare beauty that foreshadows the style of Shunzei and other poets of the *Shin kokinshū*. The *Shikashū* and other imperial anthologies contain sixty of his poems, and there is a separate collection of his works known as the *Yorimasa shū*.

MURASAKI SHIKIBU (dates uncertain)

Writer of the middle Heian period. She is renowned as the author of the *Genji monogatari*, or *The Tale of Genji*. There are various theories concerning her dates, the most plausible of which would make her twenty-nine years of age in 1008 and place her death somewhere between the ages of thirty-six and thirty-eight. She came from an eminent family that descended from

Fujiwara no Yoshikado, the sixth son of the illustrious Fujiwara no Fuyu-
tsugu. Her father, Fujiwara no Tametoki, was highly versed in Confucian
studies and wrote poetry in both Japanese and Chinese, though he seems to
have been admired more for the latter; a number of his poems and other
works in Chinese are preserved in the *Honchō resiō*. Her mother was the
daughter of Fujiwara no Tamenobu. Many persons on both her father's and
mother's side of the family were known for their talents as poets and literary
figures, and her elder brother Nobunori was a poet of repute. Because her
father held the post of *shikibu-no-jō*, she was at first known as Tō no Shikibu,
Tō being the Sino-Japanese pronunciation of the first character in her surname Fujiwara; later, however, she came to be called Murasaki Shikibu. Her
real name is unknown. She seems to have been a highly precocious child and
from an early age began receiving an education at home. She was well read
in Chinese as well as Japanese works, particularly the famous historical
work known as the *Shih chi (Records of the Historian)* and the *Po-shih wen-
chi*, collected writings of the poet Po Chü-i, and at some later date acquired
a considerable knowledge of Buddhist literature. In addition, she was talented in calligraphy, painting, and the musical instrument known as the koto.
In her diary, the *Murasaki Shikibu nikki*, she records how her father used to
lament that she had not been born a boy. In 996, when she was around
eighteen, she journeyed to Echizen, where her father had been appointed to
serve as governor, returning to the capital about a year later. Around the
age of twenty or twenty-one she married Fujiwara no Nobutaka, who was
probably about forty-seven at the time. Shortly after, she bore a daughter
named Kenshi, later better known as Daini no San'mi, but the following year
her husband died. For a while in her grief she apparently considered becoming a Buddhist nun; at least it seems apparent that the love she felt for her
departed husband and her little daughter set her to thinking deeply on the
problem of human happiness, particularly that of a woman, and that around
this time she began work on her masterpiece, *The Tale of Genji*. By the time
she entered service in the palace five of six years later, a fairly large portion
of the work was probably completed, and at least by around 1008 it had
begun to be fairly widely circulated and read. It was probably as a result of
the fame gained from her writing that, when she was around the age of
twenty-nine, she was made a lady-in-waiting to Shōshi, the daughter of
Fujiwara no Michinaga and consort of Emperor Ichijō. In her diary she
describes the favor and respect she enjoyed from the members of the imperial
family and nobles and courtiers, as well as the jealousies that such favor
aroused. She also depicts the lavish and colorful life of the court and the
details of its less glamorous side, which her keen eyes were careful to

observe. After the death of Emperor Ichijō in 1011, she continued in the service of Shōshi, but the last definite mention of her we have is in 1013, when she was probably thirty-five. Shortly after, her elder brother and also her friend of many years Koshōshō no Kimi both died, and she probably followed them not long after.

The Tale of Genji, written almost a thousand years ago, is the world's earliest novel and one of the longest. Its artistry and position in the history of literature have been the subject of comment by countless Japanese writers in the past, and in recent years by foreign scholars as well. The magnitude of its conception, the subtlety of its psychological insights, the combination of a generally romantic approach with a wealth of realistic and closely observed detail, and the beauty of its tone and style qualify it to rank as the undisputed masterpiece of all Japanese literature. The influence that it exerted upon later writers has been enormous, but though it was often imitated, it has never been equaled.

In addition to *The Tale of Genji* and the diary mentioned above, a collection of poems entitled the *Murasaki Shikibu shū* has been preserved, and a number of her poems are included in imperial anthologies.

Nakatsukasa (dates uncertain)

Poet of the middle Heian period. Her father was Atsuyoshi Shinnō, also known as Nakatsukasa-kyō, and later Shikibu-kyō, the son of Emperor Uda; her mother was the famous poetess Lady Ise. Her personal name is unknown, the name Nakatsukasa deriving from one of the posts her father held. Judging from the fact that the *Gosenshū* contains an exchange of poems between her and Ki no Tsurayuki and her collected works contains a poem written in 979 when Minamoto no Shitagou was appointed governor of Noto, and taking into consideration what is known of her father's career, it may be surmised that she was born during the Engi era (901–22) and probably lived to the age of sixty or more.

She was married to Minamoto no Saneakira, but she appears also to have had affairs with Motonaga Shinnō, Tsuneakira Shinnō, Taira no Kaneki, and Ono-no-miya no Saneyori. From her mother she inherited a talent in poetry and the playing of the koto, and she was one of the outstanding women poets of the time. From a notation in the *Shūishū* it is known that she had a daughter; according to the *Motosukeshū*, the girl was referred to as *chūnagon*.

Nakatsukasa's poetry is marked by a gentle subjectivity and is rich in lyric beauty. Sixty-one of her poems are preserved in the *Gosenshū* and other imperially sponsored anthologies, and it is apparent that she took an active part in the poetry contest held at the imperial palace in 960 and in other contests. Her collected works bears the title *Nakatsukasa shū*. She is numbered maong the Thirty-six Poetic Geniuses.

Ōe no Masafusa (1041–1111)

Late Heian period poet and scholar of Chinese. The great-grandson of Ōe no Masahira, he was a child prodigy, beginning to read at the age of three and becoming conversant with such difficult Chinese historical works at the *Shih chi* and *Han shu* by the time he was seven. At fifteen he had already completed his studies at the state university, thereafter holding a series of posts in the government until, at twenty-eight, he was simultaneously appointed to the offices of *kurōdo*, *saemon-no-gon-no-suke*, and *ushōben*, a recognition of his extraordinary ability that won him both fame and the envy of his contemporaries. He continued to advance until, at the age of fifty-two, he was appointed *gon-no-chūnagon*, one of the highest positions in the government. Two years later he was also made head of the Dazaifu, the government office in Kyushu, and the following year proceeded to Kyushu, where he won acclaim for his administration of the affairs of the island and also initiated the festival at the Anraku-ji in honor of the scholar-statesman Sugawara no Michizane. At the age of seventy he was appointed head of the *ōkura-shō* (Ministry of Finance), but he died the same year.

He was first of all admired for his scholarship, but he was also distinguished as a writer of Chinese verse, being highly praised by the head of the university Fujiwara no Akihira, Minamoto no Morofusa, and others. His poems in Japanese recorded in the *Shikashū* employ a brilliant style that foreshadows the famous *yōembi*, or style of ethereal beauty, later developed by Fujiwara no Teika, while in the poems preserved in the *Gō-no-sochi shū* he employs phrases borrowed from the works of the *Man'yōshū*. He was a man of upright and unbending temperament and was said on several occasions to have admonished the ruler to his face. He was well known as a collector of books, housing his library in a building named the Sensōden, but it was destroyed by fire in the fourth month of 1153.

He wrote voluminously, among his works being the *Zoku-honchō ōjōden*, *Gōke shidai*, *Gō-no-sochi shū*, and others.

Ōe no Masahira (952–1012)

Middle Heian period poet and scholar of Chinese. He received instruction from his grandfather Ōe no Koretoki and carried on the traditions of the family, which was noted for its devotion to scholarship. He showed a fondness for learning from his early years, and at the age of eight began composing poetry in Chinese. At twenty-three he became a student in the state university, specializing in literature and history, and was awarded the *shūsai* degree. At the age of thirty-one he was appointed as a *kebiishi* in the office of the *kebiishi-no-chō*, an unusual honor that startled the people of the time. At thirty-seven he was made a professor of the university and later was appointed special lecturer to Emperor Ichijō, instructing him in the *Book of Odes*, *Book of Documents*, *Book of Rites*, *Lao Tzu*, *Wen hsüan*, and other important works of Chinese literature. Subsequently he held such posts as *tōgū gakushi*, *shikibu tayū*, and governor of Tamba.

His writings in Chinese are collected in a work called the *Gōrihōshū*, and his poems in Chinese are also preserved in such works as the *Honchō monzui* and *Honchō reisō*; the *Goshūishū* and other anthologies preserve twelve poems by him in Japanese; there is also a collection of his writings entitled the *Ōe no Masahira Ason shū*. An examination of his writings reveals that he was of more importance as a scholar than as a poet, his poetic works being rather old-fashioned and pedantic in tone and lacking in literary interest. However, the fact that, though he was a Confucian and specialist in Chinese studies, he also chose to write poetry in Japanese as well, makes him a rather unusual figure for the time, in this respect resembling his famous great-grandson Ōe no Masafusa. His wife, a woman of both beauty and talent, was the famous *waka* poet Akazome Emon.

Ono no Komachi (dates uncertain)

Poet of the early Heian period. Though she is numbered by Ki no Tsurayuki, the compiler of the *Kokinshū*, among the Six Poetic Geniuses, the only woman included in the group, very little is known for certain about her. Some accounts make her the granddaughter of Ono no Takamura, others the daughter of a *gunji* (district head) of the province of Dewa named Ono no Yoshizane, and both the Jōgan (859–77) and Shōwa (834–48) eras have been named as her period of greatest activity. It has been suggested that Komachi is not a proper name but a general appellation often applied to the *uneme* (ladies-in-waiting), girls chosen from among the daughters of district heads or persons of similar rank to serve in the palace, as seen in the similar names Sanjō no Machi and Mikuni no Machi. Another theory is that her elder sister was a lady-in-waiting named Ono no Machi, and that when the younger sister took service in the palace, she was referred to as Ko-Machi, "Little Machi." Numerous locations throughout the country have been claimed as her place of birth and death, a fact that also suggests that there was a multiplicity of Komachis. A work known as the *Tamatsukuri Komachi sōsui sho* describes her as a woman of great beauty who was lovingly reared by her parents and, filled with dreams of the glory that might be hers if she could become the consort of the ruler, repeatedly turned down offers of marriage. Later, when her beauty had faded, she was obliged to become the wife of a hunter, to whom she bore a son, but death in time deprived her of both husband and son, and she was forced to end her days as a beggar wandering the roads. Such accounts are of dubious reliability and may be no more than the embroideries of later legend, but the existence of Komachi as a historical personage is beyond doubt.

When one turns to her works themselves, one finds that she exchanged poems with such eminent literary figures as Funya no Yasuhide, Sōjō Henjō, Ariwara no Narihira, and others, and very likely carried on love affairs with some of them; the collection of her poems known as the *Komachi shū* certainly suggests that she had an affair with a person or persons of high social rank. It also reveals that she composed poems praying for rain on imperial command. It is probable that the Komachi legend grew up through a process of accretion over a considerable period of time, emphasizing the themes of feminine beauty and the waywardness of fate, and when her story was taken up in such Nō dramas as *Sotoba Komachi* and *Sekidera Komachi*, a further element of religious mystery was added to the figure of the court lady and poet.

Ono no Komachi's poetry is characterized by gentle elegance combined with an underlying passion and forcefulness and is especially noted for the skill with which it employs metaphors, *kakekotoba* (multiple entendres), and other intricacies of language. Her love poems, which explore the psychological subtleties of the romantic passion, set the style for later works on the subject and have won for her a place of unique importance in the development of the love poetry of the Heian court. The *Kokinshū* contains seventeen of her poems, and later official anthologies bring the total to over sixty, while five more have been preserved in private anthologies. In addition, there is a scattering of poems that legend attributes to her hand.

Ono no Takamura (802–852)

Early Heian period poet and scholar of Chinese. He was a descendant of Ono no Imoko, who in 607 became the first Japanese envoy to the Chinese court; his father, Minemori, advanced to the post of *sangi* (counselor) and, being a master of Chinese verse and prose, was chosen to be one of the compilers of the *Ryōunshū*, the first imperially sponsored anthology of Chinese verse by Japanese writers. At the age of nineteen Takamura was enrolled as a student in the state university, specializing in the study of literature and history, and at twenty-eight became an official in the *kurōdo-dokoro*, an office in charge of palace affairs. In 834 he was chosen to act as assistant envoy on a mission to the Chinese court, but because the mission was headed by Fujiwara no Tsunetsugu, an official under whom he did not care to serve, he excused himself from the assignment on grounds of illness and instead wrote a poem entitled "Song of the Western March" in which he criticized the sending of such missions to China. As a result he incurred the anger of Retired Emperor Saga and was banished to the island of Oki. At this time he composed a poem entitled "Song of Exile," which attracted considerable attention, though unfortunately the text has not been preserved. Seven years later, he was pardoned and recalled to the capital, where he once more advanced in government service until he had reached the post of *sangi*. He was referred to as Ya Saishō or Ya Shōkō, *ya* being the Sino-Japanese reading of the character for *no* in his surname.

From an early age he won acclaim for his wide learning and unusual talent and seems to have been a man of warm and poetic temperament. His literary works were highly praised, and he enjoyed great personal favor with the ruler. He was especially distinguished as a writer of Chinese verse, and Retired Emperor Saga was said to [have valued his works as highly as those of the celebrated Chinese poet Po Chü-i. He was also a noted calligrapher.

Not many of his poetic works have survived, though twelve poems in *waka* form are preserved in the *Kokinshū* and other officially sponsored anthologies, and six more in anthologies that were privately compiled, while his extant poems in Chinese are to be found in the *Keikokushū*, *Wakan rōeishū*, *Fusōshū*, and other works. There is also a work in the *monogatari* (tale) form entitled *Ono no Takamura shū*, but it is the product of later times.

Ōshikōchi no Mitsune (dates uncertain)

Poet of the early Heian period. Along with Ki no Tsurayuki, he was one of the outstanding poets of the period of the compilation of the *Kokinshū*. He held only minor posts in the government, a fact about which he at times complains in his poetry. However, he was recognized as the equal to Tsurayuki in poetic talent, and in 905 was ordered to join with Tsurayuki, his nephew Tomonori, and others in compiling the *Kokinshū*, the first imperially sponsored anthology of Japanese poetry. He is listed as a participant in the *Kampyō no ontoki Kisai-no-miya no utaawase* and other famous poetry matches, and was particularly skilled at composing poems for screens. In the autumn of 907 he was chosen to accompany Retired Emperor Uda on an outing to the Ōi River west of Kyoto, and contributed a poem on the occasion. He was on close terms with Ki no Tsurayuki, and the poems that they exchanged in the course of their friendship have been preserved. Once he was asked by Emperor Daigo why the half-moon is called *yumihari* ("bow-shaped"), whereupon he immediately replied with the following impromptu poem:

> Why is the shining moon
> likened to a bow?
> Because its rays
> enter [pierce][1] the mountainside.

According to the *Yamato monogatari* and *Ōkagami*, which record the anecdote, he was much praised for the skill and aptness of his reply. He also wrote many congratulatory pieces on imperial command, *daiei* (poems composed in place of another person), and poems for screens, as mentioned above, serving, like Ki no Tsurayuki, as a poet for the court and winning wide recognition for his outstanding skill in poetic composition.

Though some of his poems are marked by the kind of intellectualizing found often in the poetry of the *Kokinshū*, others express a gentle love for mankind and the world of nature, and his landscape poems are particularly noteworthy. About two hundred of his poems are preserved in the *Kokinshū* and other imperial anthologies, and some thirty in anthologies privately compiled. A collection of his works exists, entitled the *Mitsune shū*.

Ōtomo no Kuronushi (dates uncertain)

Poet of the early Heian period. He is also called Shiga no Kuronushi. He probably lived around the Jōgan (859–77) and Engi (901–23) eras. It has been suggested that he was perhaps a descendant of Prince Ōtomo, who

---

1. *Iru*, a homophone for the verb *iru*, to shoot or pierce with an arrow.

became Emperor Kōbun. It is said that he owned the land on which the Onjō-ji (or Mii-dera) in the province of Ōmi was built, but he memorialized the throne and obtained permission to convert it into an auxiliary temple of the Enryaku-ji on Mt. Hiei. It has been surmised that he was also an *ommyōshi*, or expert in the Chinese yin-yang system of cosmology and divination, and an official under the *shingihaku*, the chief minister in charge of offerings to the gods.

He composed poems on the occasion of the banquet held in celebration of the imperial accession at the beginning of the Ninna era (885–89), on the occasion of the poetry contest known as the *Ninna no ontoki Miyasundokoroke no utaawase*, and on the occasion of the outing to Ishiyama-dera made by Teiji-in (Emperor Uda). Three of his poems are preserved in the *Kokinshū*, three in the *Gosenshū*, and four in other works.

Because he was mentioned by Ki no Tsurayuki in the Preface to the *Kokinshū*, he is counted among the so-called Six Poetic Geniuses. Tsurayuki writes of him, "His ideas are engaging but his style is crude; it is as though a peasant from the mountains with a load of firewood on his back were to be found resting in the shade of a blossoming tree." This would seem to indicate that Tsurayuki found his style somewhat too plain or rustic.

He is deified under the title of Kuronushi Myōjin of Shiga.

SAGA TENNŌ (786–842)

Fifty-second sovereign of Japan. He was the second son of Emperor Kammu and a younger brother of Emperor Heizei; his mother was Fujiwara no Otomuro. In his youth he was known as Kamino Shinnō. He showed a fondness for learning from an early age and was widely read in the Confucian Classics, histories, and other important works of Chinese literature. He came to the throne in 809, and the following year faced a challenge to his power in the so-called Kusuko disorder, a plot by Fujiwara no Kusuko, the favorite concubine of Emperor Heizei, and her older brother Nakanari to restore Emperor Heizei to the throne. The plot was discovered, however, and order restored. Emperor Saga instituted various changes in the governmental system, setting up the *kurōdo-dokoro*, an office directly under the emperor that handled confidential documents and suits, the *kebiishi*, or capital police, and other organs. He also attempted to emulate the Chinese ideal of the sage ruler who leads and reforms his people through learning and the arts. The great Buddhist leaders Saichō and Kūkai were active during his reign and enjoyed his favor and support. He also fixed the form for the various rituals and court ceremonies carried out throughout the year, encouraging the adoption and spread of Chinese culture. In 813 he ordered the *Shinsen shōji roku* or ("New Compilation of the Register of Families") to be drawn up, and during his reign such important histories and legal works as the *Nihon kōki, Kōnin kyakushiki,* and *Ryō-no-gige* were compiled. In addition, he sponsored the compilation of the anthologies of verse in Chinese known as the *Ryōunshū* and *Bunka shūreishū,* which included many of his own compositions, thus acting as leader of the cultural life of the nation and contributing to the advancement of literature. In addition to being a skilled writer of Chinese verse, he was famed as a calligrapher, and is numbered as one of the Sampitsu, Three Masters of Calligraphy, of the period, the other two being Kūkai and Tachibana no Hayanari.

Sanuki no Suke (dates uncertain)

Poet of the late Heian period. Her name was Chōshi; she was the daughter of the poet Fujiwara no Akitsuna, who was known by the title Sanuki Nyūdō. She would appear to have been born around 1079, since it is known that she was around forty in 1119. Her elder sister Iyo no San'mi Kenshi and her elder brother Arisuke both wrote poetry, and their names are recorded in officially compiled anthologies. In 1100 she became a lady-in-waiting to Emperor Horikawa, and the following year was assigned the rank of *suke* or *tenji.* In 1107 Emperor Horikawa died, but she continued to serve as *suke* under Emperor Toba for the following ten years. Around 1118 she developed some kind of mental disorder, however, and retired from service the following year. Nothing is known of her after that.

She has left a diary known as the *Sanuki no Suke nikki,* which covers the period from the sixth month of Kashō 2 (1107) to the twelfth month of Tennin 1 (1108), a period of a year and one-half. It is in two chapters, the first describing the period from the outbreak of Emperor Horikawa's illness until his death, the second recording reminiscences of the deceased ruler and describing the author's first year of service under his successor. The work focuses around the death of the sovereign and is remarkable for the fact that the author displays not so much respect for the young ruler as an attitude of deep and intimate affection. The tone of the work, as might be expected, is one of intense and pervading sorrow and melancholy, but at the same time it creates a strikingly warm and human portrait of the emperor, something that is very rare in Japanese literature, especially that of the Heian period. Twenty-three poems in *waka* form are included in the diary, ten of them by the author herself, and one of her poems is included in the *Shin chokusenshū*.

Sei Shōnagon (dates uncertain)

Poet and writer of the middle Heian period. Her father was Kiyohara no Motosuke, one of the compilers of the *Gosenshū*, and her great-grandfather Fukayabu was also a celebrated poet. She was thus born into a highly cultured family and grew up in fortunate surroundings, receiving an education in the literature and culture of both Japan and China. Her personal name is unknown; the name Sei Shōnagon, by which she is customarily referred to, is made up of the Sino-Japanese reading of the character for *kiyo* in her surname Kiyohara, plus the court title *shōnagon*. Likewise, little is known of her life for certain, but from her writings and the genealogy of the Kiyohara family it would appear that she first married Tachibana no Norimitsu, gave birth to a son named Norinaga, but separated from her husband shortly afterward. She probably entered service as a lady-in-waiting in 993, attending Teishi, the consort of Emperor Ichijō and daughter of Kampaku Fujiwara no Michitaka. She seems to have been on very intimate terms with the empress, and the atmosphere at court gave her an ideal opportunity to display her remarkable knowledge of things Japanese and Chinese and her ready wit, making her the center of attraction in the women's quarters. But after the death of Michitaka in 995, the empress's fortunes declined rapidly and, deprived of her backers at court, she was reduced to unhappy circumstances and died without recovering favor. Sei Shōnagon accordingly retired from service and in time became the wife of the governor of Settsu Province, Fujiwara no Muneyo. It is known that she had a daughter named Koma no Myōbu, presumably by this marriage, but after the death of her husband she lived a life of loneliness and is said eventually to have become a Buddhist nun. She probably died at Tsukinowa, the place in Kyoto where her father, Motosuke, had his residence.

Because of her learning and extraordinary literary talent, Sei Shōnagon ranks with Murasaki Shikibu, the author of *The Tale of Genji*, as one of the foremost women writers of the Heian period. Her work, the *Makura no sōshi (Pillow Book)*, written in the early eleventh century, a time when the *monogatari*, or tale, form was at the height of its popularity, became the model for a new literary genre known as the *zuihitsu* (miscellany). It is made up of some three hundred entries dealing with the beauties of nature and happenings in the world of human affairs, particularly those connected with the outings, ceremonies, and romantic intrigues of the court. In it the author displays the keen wit and intelligence for which she was apparently famous, and the work is distinguished throughout for its closeness of observation and wealth and aptness of expression.

Sei Shōnagon was also a prolific poet, and though not many of her works have survived, some thirty poems that appear to be from her hand are preserved in the *Sei Shōnagon shū*, sixteen in the *Makura no sōshi*, fourteen in officially compiled anthologies, and a few others in such works as the *Kintō shū* (collected works of the poet Fujiwara no Kintō), and the *Izumi Shikibu shū*. In style she clearly owes a debt to her father, Motosuke, and her poems are characterized by the same air of intellect and spontaneity found in the *Makura no sōshi*. In spite of the interest of her poetry, however, it has generally been agreed that her genius found its fullest and most striking expression in prose, and it is the *Makura no sōshi* that entitles her to a place of importance in the history of world literature.

Shikishi Naishinnō (d. 1201)

Poet of the late Heian period. She was the daughter of Retired Emperor Goshirakawa; her mother was Takakura San'mi Seishi, the daughter of Dainagon Fujiwara no Suenari; she was thus a sibling of Shukaku Hōshinnō, Prince Mochihito, and Impumon-in. In 1159, when she was probably around nine, she was appointed as *saiin* (priestess) of the Kamo Shrine in Kyoto, a position she resigned in 1169, around the time when her father entered the Buddhist clergy, because of illness. Her exact movements after that are difficult to determine, but because it was the period of the great struggle between the Taira and Minamoto families, in which her uncle Sutoku-in, her elder brother Prince Mochihito, her nephew Emperor Antoku, and others of her immediate family were one after the other entangled and brought to grief, her later years can hardly have been peaceful ones. In 1197, because she was suspected of having been involved in a plot led by the Kurōdo Tachibana no Kanenaka, she became a Buddhist nun, and in 1200 she took as her adopted son the future Juntoku-in, the grandson of her younger brother Takakura-in, who was at the time an infant of three, but the illness from which she had been suffering for some time worsened and she died shortly after. Something of the quiet years of her life as a nun can be determined from the *Ienaga nikki*, a diary covering the years 1196 to 1207 by Minamoto no Ienaga, and her last days are described in Fujiwara no Teika's famous diary, the *Meigetsuki*.

The princess devoted herself to poetry throughout her life and was the outstanding woman poet of her time. She was on very close terms with Fujiwara no Shunzei and his son Teika, and at her request Shunzei wrote his famous statement on poetics entitled *Korai fūteishō*. Her poetry is marked by delicacy, grace, and a feminine tone; the expression of feelings of sorrow and the rapt contemplation of the world of man and nature are themes that run throughout her work. Her poems are included in the *Senzaishū* and other imperial anthologies, forty-nine of them in the *Shin kokinshū* alone, and there is also a collection of her works entitled *Shikishi Naishinnō shū*.

> Mountains so deep
> I didn't know it was spring—
> By the pine door
> drip-dripping,
> bright drops of melted snow.

SHUN'E (b. 1113)

Poet of the late Heian period. His father was Minamoto no Toshiyori, compiler of the *Kin'yōshū*, recognized authority on Japanese poetry, and an innovator in matters of poetic style; his mother was the daughter of Moku-nosuke no Atsutaka. He began the study of poetry under his father, but the latter died when Shun'e was sixteen; around this time he entered the Tōdai-ji in Nara and became a monk. As a poet he first appears as a participant in the poetry match referred to as the *Kiyosuke Asonke no utaawase* held by Fujiwara no Kiyosuke in 1160; thereafter he participated frequently in poetry matches and was widely praised for his literary ability. At his house in the Shirakawa section of Kyoto, which he named the Karin'en ("Poetry Forest Garden"), he held monthly poetry meetings and other gatherings, and these in time led to the formation of a type of literary society. The association, which attracted such outstanding figures as Minamoto no Yorimasa and Kamo no Chōmei, appears to have been characterized by an atmosphere of warmth and informality that took no note of differences of sex or social position; it continued to be active up until the time of Shun'e's death. His late years correspond to the period when the dominance of the Rokujō family in the poetic world was giving way to that of its rival Mikohidari family, but Shun'e associated freely with both groups and was on friendly terms with all the outstanding poets of the time.

The *Mumyōshō*, a work by his disciple Kamo no Chōmei, here and there records Shun'e's remarks and views on poetry, and from it we learn that he advocated a rather simple and uncontrived approach to poetry, emphasizing the primary importance of expression and asserting that the *waka* should be allowed to develop naturally and with the utmost degree of freedom. His own poetry conveys a feeling of perfect ease, combining mild sentiment with a freshness and purity of expression. Some eighty-four of his poems are preserved in official anthologies, and there is a collection of his works originally entitled *Rin'yō wakashū* but now referred to as the *Shun'e Hōshishū*.

Sōjō Henjō (816–890)

Poet of the early Heian period. His name before entering the priesthood was Yoshimine no Munesada, and he is also known by the names Ryō Sōjō and Kazan Sōjō; he was a grandson of Emperor Kammu and the son of Dainagon Yoshimine no Yasuyo. He had two sons, who both became Buddhist monks and are known as Sosei and Yusei. He enjoyed great favor with Emperor Nimmyō and in 844 was assigned to the *kurōdo-dokoro*, an office having to do with the administration of the palace. He later held such posts as *sahyōe-no-suke* (assistant to the guard of the left) and governor of the province of Bitchū, and in 849 was made head of the *kurōdo-dokoro*. On the death of Emperor Nimmyō in the following year, he entered the monastery on Mt. Hiei and became a member of the clergy under the religious name Henjō. A somewhat fictionalized account of his entry into the priesthood is found in the *Yamato monogatari*, a work of the tenth century. Sometime around the Jōgan era (859–77), he founded a temple called the Genkei-ji at Kazan near Kyoto, assuming the position of head priest. He was treated with great favor and reverence by Emperor Kōkō, who presented him with 153 *chō* of unused land and later promoted him to the highest ecclesiastical rank, that of *sōjō*, often translated in English as bishop. His seventieth birthday was celebrated at the Jijūden, one of the halls of the imperial palace, and the following year he was assigned the revenue from one hundred households and permitted to enter the grounds of the palace in a hand-drawn carriage. The *Zokuhonchō ōjōden* records how he employed his spiritual powers to overcome a *tengu* demon who was causing trouble, a story that suggests he commanded great respect as a religious leader.

Sōjō Henjō is famous as one of the Six Poetic Geniuses mentioned by Ki no Tsurayuki in his Preface to the *Kokinshū*. Tsurayuki says of his works that "they mere the formal requirements of poetry but are lacking in truth, resembling mere paintings of beautiful women that stir the heart of the beholder to no effect." Tsurayuki would seem to be saying that, although

Henjō's poetry possesses outward beauty and elegance, it is deficient in inner sincerity, though in fact Henjō wrote poems expressing sorrow that impress one as being filled with deep feeling. Again, in the *Gosenshū* is recorded an exchange of romantic poems between Henjō and Ono no Komachi, which reveals the lighter and more unconventional side of his character. Sixteen of his poems are included in the *Kokinshū* and about twenty in other official anthologies, and there is also a collection of his works entitled *Henjō shū*.

SONE NO YOSHITADA (dates uncertain)

Poet of the middle Heian period. Nothing is known of his parentage. Since he served at one time as a *jō*, or lesser official, under the governor of the province of Tango, he came to be called So Tango no Jō, So Tango, or simply So Tan. The *Shin senzaishū* and *Fubokushū* contain poems by him that were written at a poetry contest held in the imperial palace in the second year of Kanna (986), but this is the only clear evidence extant by which to date his career. As a man he was said to have been arrogant and eccentric in his ways, saying and doing things that were quite at variance with normal codes of behavior, and he was often treated with contempt by the members of the court aristocracy. Among the various anecdotes concerning him, which are recorded in the *Konjaku monogatari*, *Ōkagami*, and other works, is one that tells of an outing held by Retired Emperor En'yū at Funaoka, a hill in the northern part of Kyoto, in 985. Kiyohara no Motosuke, Taira no Kanemori, and other eminent poets were in attendance, seated respectfully on their mats, when Yoshitada appeared, wearing a shabby hunting costume. Asked why he had come to the gathering when he had not been invited, he replied that he had heard that poets were invited and considered himself in no way inferior to the ones he saw seated around him. According to the accounts, he had to be dragged by the collar and forcibly ejected from the meeting.

Whatever his character may have been, it is important to note that he was the first poet to attempt to break away from the conventions of the so-called *Kokinshū* style that prevailed at the time, and the innovations he introduced were carried on and extended by such later poets as Minamoto no Tsunenobu and his son Toshiyori. Yoshitada's innovations were confined to the sphere of diction and phrasing and did not extend to matters of content or overall tone, but he treated a wide variety of subjects in his poetry, and his vocabulary is unusually rich. To capture the subject with the greatest possible fidelity he employed a variety of adjectives, colloquialisms, old-fashioned words, and other types of diction that departed from the usual poetic canons of taste, and yet he possessed the kind of unfailing literary instinct that allowed him to combine such disparate elements in a single poem without creating an effect of disharmony. From the fact that eighty-nine of his poems are included in the *Shūishū* and other officially sponsored anthologies, it is evident that his poetry was highly regarded. Though he may have been despised and mistreated as a person, his abilities as a poet were amply recognized. He stands out as one of the most distinctive of all Heian poets. His works have been collected under the title *So Tan shū*.

Sugawara no Michizane (845–903)

Early Heian period scholar of Chinese. The third son of Sugawara no Kore-yoshi, at the age of twenty-five he became a *monjōshō*, or student in the state university specializing in literature and history. After holding various posts, he was appointed a professor of the university in 877; he was the third member of his family in succession to hold that position, his grandfather Kiyokimi and his father having also been professors. He enjoyed the favor of Emperor Uda and at the age of forty-six was appointed head of the *kurōdo-dokoro*, an office in charge of palace affairs, and thereafter advanced with a rapidity all but unprecedented for one of his scholarly background. In 894 he was chosen to head a mission to the T'ang court in China, but he submitted a memorial pointing out the internal disorder and decay into which the T'ang rule had fallen and recommending that the mission be abandoned; his advice was accepted, and thus ended the practice of sending regular diplomatic missions to the mainland that had begun in the Nara period. In 899 he was appointed Minister of the Right, but in 901 he fell victim to the slanders of the members of the Fujiwara family and was appointed *Dazai-no-gon-no-sochi*, or head of the administrative office at Dazaifu in Kyushu; the appointment was nominal, for in fact he was being condemned to banishment. He died two years later at his place of exile in Kyushu.

Michizane was one of the most distinguished scholars of Chinese of the period, compiling a work on Japanese history entitled the *Ruijū kokushi* and taking part in the compilation of the *Sandai jitsuroku*. He was a highly accomplished writer of Chinese verse and prose, his works being preserved in the *Kanke bunsō* and *Kanke kōsō*, and his poems in Chinese are also included in the *Fusōshū* and *Honchō monzui*. His Chinese poems are marked by deep feeling and great facility and grace of expression; the works that date from the time in his youth when he served as governor of the province of Sanuki in Shikoku and from his last years, both periods of hardship and sorrow, are particularly powerful.

He also wrote poetry in Japanese, thirty-four of his poems in *waka* form being preserved in the *Sandaishū*, *Shin kokinshū*, *Shoku kokinshū*, and other anthologies. In addition, he is said to have been the compiler of the *Kanke man'yōshū* (or *Shinsen man'yōshū*), an anthology that records the poems from the *Kampyō no ontoki Kisai-no-miya no utaawase*; the poems are written in *man'yōgana*, and to each is appended a poem in Chinese in seven-character *chüeh-chü*, or quatrain form, which repeats the gist of the Japanese poem. The work is important because, while it reflects the passion for Chinese verse that had dominated the literary world of the early Heian, it also marks the revival of interest in Japanese verse that was taking place at the time and that led to the increasing frequency of *utaawase*, poetry contests.

After his death, Michizane was deified as Temman Tenjin, feared because it was believed that his angry spirit would seek revenge for the injustice he had suffered and honored because of his literary and scholarly accomplishments. Regarded as the patron god of learning, his cult spread throughout the country, and the shrines dedicated to him continue to flourish today.

T AIRA NO KANEMORI (d. 990)

Poet of the middle Heian period. He was the son of Prince Atsuyuki, the great-grandson of Emperor Kōkō; in 950 he was removed from the register of the imperial family and given the surname Taira. He was said to have been the father of the poetess Akazome Emon. He was active around the Tenryaku era (947–57), and is especially famous for the following incident that occurred at a poetry contest in the imperial palace in the fourth year of Tentoku (960). Writing on the theme of hidden love, Kanemori, a member of the team of the right, produced the poem *Shinoburedo iro ni idenikeri waga koi wa; mono ya omou to hito no tou made*[1] to match one on the same subject by Mibu no Tadami of the team of the left, which reads *Koi su chō; waga na wa madaki tachinikeri; hito shirezu koso omoisomeshika.*[2] The judge, unable to decide which of the two was superior, looked to Emperor Murakami, who was presiding at the gathering; the emperor said nothing, but repeated Kanemori's poem over to himself and the judge accordingly declared Kanemori the winner. He is said to have performed a dance of gratitude before withdrawing from the ruler's presence. In 979 he was assigned to the post of governor of Suruga, and in 985 at the time of Retired Emperor En'yū's outing on the Day of the Rat, he contributed the topic and preface for the poems to be composed on the occasion. He was thus active as a court poet of the time, though the criticism has been made that his poems stick too slavishly to the subject assigned him and are lacking in style. Eighty-three of his poems are preserved in official anthologies, beginning with the thirty-eight poems in the *Shūishū,* and there is also a collection of his works entitled *Kanemori shū.* He is included among the so-called Thirty-six Poetic Geniuses.

1   Try as I did to hide it
      it's begun to show—
      this love of mine
      till people ask,
      who's in your thoughts.

(by Taira no Kanemori)

2   He's in love!
      Already
      the word spreads abroad,
      though when I first fell in love
      no one was aware.

(by Mibu no Tadami)

Takasue no Musume (b. 1008)

Writer of the middle Heian period. She was a descendant of Sugawara no Michizane and a daughter of Sugawara no Takasue. Her mother was the daughter of Fujiwara no Tomoyasu. Her father held positions as *suke,* or assistant governor, of the provinces of Kazusa and Hitachi. She spent her childhood in Kazusa, where her father was serving as an official, and in 1020, when his period of office expired, she journeyed back to the capital in Kyoto by way of the Tōkaidō. When she was around the age of thirty-one, she entered service in the palace, but shortly after left to marry Tachibana no Toshimichi. Toshimichi was assigned to a post in the province of Shinano, but later returned to the capital and died in 1058. Two years later, around the age of fifty-three, she wrote the work for which she is famous, the *Sarashina nikki,* or *Sarashina Diary.* The date of her death is unknown.

The *Sarashina Diary* begins with an account of her journey from Kazusa to Kyoto, records her fondness for such works of literature as *The Tale of Genji,* her experiences in service in the palace, her marriage and the death of her husband, and her lonely life in the years that followed. In her youth she was much attracted to the figure of Ukifune, one of the heroines of *The*

Tale of Genji, but in her diary we see these early fancies and romantic dreams giving way before the realities of life, in time to be followed by a growing religiosity and concern with the affairs of the other world. The beauty and subtlety with which the diary delineates this process of spiritual growth and change marks it as one of the finest works of early Japanese literature.

Tsunenobu no Haha (eleventh century)

Poet of the late Heian period; the exact dates of her life are unknown. She was the daughter of Minamoto no Kunimori, the wife of Mimbukyō (Minister of the Interior) Minamoto no Michikata, and the mother of the well-known poet Minamoto no Tsunenobu. Tsunenobu died in 1097 at the age of eighty-one and was one of the most outstanding poets of the late Heian. A collection of his mother's poems exists under the title *Tsunenobu-kyō haha no shū*. The text of it found in the *Gunsho ruijū* contains fourteen poems, prefaced by lengthy prose introductions that give information on the circumstances of their composition. According to these introductions, the fact that Tsunenobu excelled in *eikyoku*—the various types of singing that were popular in middle and late Heian times—was due to the instruction given him in them by his mother. It would appear, therefore, that she was a woman of great literary and artistic talent. Her poetry is not strikingly original but is marked by vividness of impression, as may be seen in the following example:

> Has the dawn come?
> Through rifts in the mist
> over river shallows
> one can see the sleeves
> of persons in the distance.

Middle Period

A<small>BUTSU-NI</small> (d. 1283)

Poet and writer of the middle Kamakura period. She is commonly known by her religious name Abutsu-ni, the Nun Abutsu. Her family name is unknown, but around the time when she was in the service of Ankamon-in, the empress of Retired Emperor Juntoku, she was referred to as Shijō or Uemon-no-suke. Around the age of thirty she became the second wife of Fujiwara no Tameie, the son and heir of the famous poet Fujiwara no Teika. She appears to have borne him three sons, one of whom, Tamesuke, became the founder of the Reizei branch of the Fujiwara family and of the school of poetry associated with it. She had been married once before her marriage to Tameie, it would appear, and had two sons from this earlier union. In 1275, when Tameie died at the age of seventy-seven, she took the vows of a nun and assumed the name Abutsu. At that time Tameuji, Tameie's eldest son by his first wife, was already fifty-three years old, while Abutsu's son Tamesuke was only twelve. A quarrel broke out between the two half-brothers and their supporters over the ownership of a Fujiwara estate called the Hoso-kawa-shō in the province of Harima in present-day Hyōgo Prefecture. Abutsu, determined to fight for her son's rights, decided to journey to Kamakura and submit the dispute to the shogunate for a legal decision. She made the journey in the tenth month of 1277 and kept a diary of the trip, which is known as the *Izayoi nikki*. It describes the circumstances that led her to undertake the journey and the progress of the journey itself, and contains close to ninety poems in *waka* form interspersed through the text. Elegant and refined in style, the work reveals the writer's remarkable taste and learning as well as her intense love and concern for her children. After three years of waiting, however, the lawsuit remained unsettled, and she returned to Kyoto in 1280, where she died three years later. Thirty years after her death, the suit was finally decided in favor of her son Tamesuke.

Judging from her words and actions, Abutsu was a woman of strong character. She was a distinguished poet, and close to fifty of her works are included in the *Shoku kokinshū* and other imperially sponsored anthologies. Her poems reflect the highly conventionalized style of the time, however, and are rather stilted in diction and lacking in freshness of feeling. In addition to the diary, several other works such as the *Utatane no ki* and the *Yoru no tsuru* are attributed to her.

Asayama Bontō (ca. 1349–1427)

Renga poet of the early Muromachi period. He was in the personal service of Shogun Ashikaga Yoshimitsu, but became a Buddhist monk sometime after the age of forty. He studied *renga* with Nijō Yoshimoto and is represented in the *Ishiyama Hyakuin renga* meeting. The greatest master of the late thirteenth and early fourteenth centuries, he is represented by his collections *Sode-no-shita shū*, *Chōtan shō*, *Bontō renga awase*, and *Bontō anshu hentō sho*. He studied *waka* with Reizei Tamehide and penetrated to the essence of the *renga* form, yet maintained an aescetic's state of mind.

Asukai Masatsune (1170–1221)

Poet of the early Kamakura period. He was the fifth son of the Gyōbu-kyō Fujiwara no Yoritsune; he held the rank of *jusan'mi* and the post of *sangi*, or counsellor of the *dajōkan*. He studied the writing of Japanese poetry under Fujiwara no Shunzei and his son Teika, and in 1205 was chosen, along with Teika and others, to be one of the compilers of the officially sponsored anthology known as the *Shin kokinshū*. Twenty-two of his poems are included in this anthology, as well as twenty in the *Shin chokusenshū*, all characterized by technical elegance and beauty. There is a collection of his works entitled *Asukai shū*. He was skilled in *kemari*, a kind of football played at the court since ancient times, and his descendants specialized in these two arts of poetry and *kemari*, honoring him as the founder of the Asukai school.

His most famous poem is probably that included in the *Hyakunin isshu*, which describes peasant women fulling cloth for winter clothes in a village at the foot of Mt. Yoshino:

> On Mount Yoshino,
> autumn wind;

night deepens in the old village
where cold comes the sound of fulling mallets.

Azuma (Tō) Tsuneyori (1401–1494)

Poet and great-grandson of Chiba-no-suke Taira no Tsunetane. The name
Azuma, which means "east," was derived from the fact that Tsunetane's son
Taneyori was lord of a manor in the east, in the province of Shimōsa.
Taneyori, a pupil of Fujiwara no Teika, is said to have been skillful at
composing verse, and his grandson Taneyuki marrried the daughter of Nijō
Tameie, which led to his becoming a pupil of Tameie; from then on until the
time of Tsuneyori, successive generations of the family are represented in
the imperial anthologies. Tsuneyori's father, Masuyuki, associated with such
literary figures as Ryōshun, Shōtetsu, and Asukai Masayo, the family as a
whole showing a concern for literary matters unusual in a samurai family.
Tsuneyori became acquainted with Shōtetsu via his father; he heard
Shōtetsu's theories, and their influence was pronounced in his verse from
around the age of forty, but he himself attached more importance to Akitaka,
who carried on the traditions of the orthodox Nijō school, and became a
pupil of Akitaka. At the age of fifty he succeeded his father as head of the
Azuma family and became Lord of Shimotsuke. Shortly after this, an
internal dispute within the Chiba family led to his moving eastward at the
command of the shogunate and taking up residence in the eastern manor.
This period is believed to have marked the full maturity of his poetic
activity. During the disturbances following the Ōnin war, he lost his
territories in the province of Mino and wrote a poem lamenting the loss;
this poem, it is said, came into the hands of the man responsible, who was
moved to such sympathy that he promptly returned the land in question. On
retiring from his position as head of the family, he went to Kyoto, and
thereafter his relationship with his pupil Iio Sōgi became still closer. He held
that the ideal model for the poet was the *Kokinshū*; he began studies of this
anthology and transmitted to Sōgi his views on its interpretation—views
that, under the name of *Kokin-denju*, became a verbal tradition of learning
handed on personally from master to pupil. He subsequently became an
instructor in the art of poetry, frequenting the residences of such illustrious
figures as Konoe Masaie, Sanjō Kimiatsu, and Shogun Yoshihisa. He
composed poems mostly on given themes, and his verse lacked the originality to distinguish it clearly from the general style of the Nijō school, though
there is an experienced mastery in the ease with which he handled his

distinguished style and melody. His works include *Tō yashū kikigaki*, *Tō yashū shōsoku*, and *Tō yashū kashū*.

Ben no Naishi (dates uncertain)

Poet of the Kamakura period. More properly known as Gofukakusa-in Ben no Naishi, she was the granddaughter of Fujiwara no Takanobu and the daughter of Nobuzane, both famous poets and portrait painters. She and her older sisters Shōshō no Naishi and Sōhekimon-in no Shōshō were also distinguished poets. Little is known of her life, most of which was spent as a lady-in-waiting in the palace, but a work called the *Suia gammoku* by Ton'a mentions that in her old age, when she had become a nun and was living at a place called Ōki north of Sakamoto on the west shore of Lake Biwa, she composed a poem at a banquet held by Retired Emperor Kameyama to celebrate the Tanabata Festival. Poems by her are included in the *Genson sanjūrokunin shika*, a work compiled in 1276, and it would appear that her period of service at court extended approximately from 1246, when Emperor Gofukakusa was still on the throne, to around 1259, the last year of Gofukakusa's reign.

It is clear that her poetic talent was recognized in her own time, since forty-six of her poems are included in the *Shoku gosenshū* and other official anthologies, and others are to be found in privately compiled collections, and her name is listed among the participants at various poetry matches held at the court. She has left a work in diary form entitled *Ben no Naishi nikki*, which consists mainly of poems arranged chronologically and prefaced by *kotobagaki*, or notations describing the circumstances of their composition. The work covers a period of seven years and deals with life at court; it is noteworthy in that, unlike the sorrow-laden diaries of most women writers from Heian times and on, it is marked by cheerfulness and youthful vigor, and was probably composed during her younger years.

Chikako (or Shinshi) (dates uncertain)

Poet of the late Kamakura period. She was of the Minamoto family and was known as Jusammi Chikako; the name Chikako may also be read Shinshi. Belonging to the branch of the Minamoto (Genji) family known as the Murakami-Genji, she was the daughter of Dainagon (Great Counselor) Minamoto no Morochika, grandfather of the famous Kitabatake Chikafusa, and the sister of Shōkeimon-in Ichijō.

She participated in various poetry matches of the Kyōgoku school such as the *Sanjūban utaawase* held in 1289 and the *Sendō gojūban utaawase* held in 1303. Fifty-four of her poems are included in the *Shin gosenshū* and other anthologies, and she is particularly well represented in the *Gyokuyōshū*, which accords her recognition as an outstanding poet by including thirty of her works. She later came to be known by the title Mimbu-kyō San'mi and, gaining favor with Emperor Godaigo, bore him a son named Morinaga Shinnō, who later became famous in the history of the period.

The following is an example of her poetry:

> While distant peaks
> on the far side
> catch the setting sun,
> pines on these shaded slopes
> darken into evening.

DŌGEN (1200–1253)

Zen monk of the early Kamakura period, later regarded as the founder of the Sōtō branch of the Zen sect. His father was Naidaijin Kuga no Michichika, his mother the daughter of Sesshō-daijin Fujiwara no Motofusa. He was orphaned at an early age and, impressed with the transitory nature of human life, determined to enter the priesthood. At the age of twelve he entered the monastery on Mt. Hiei, the headquarters of the Tendai sect, and the following year became a disciple of the leader of the sect, Kōen Sōjō, shaving his head and devoting himself to the study of Buddhist doctrine. But by the time he had reached the age of seventeen he found himself with deep misgivings concerning the exoteric and esoteric versions of the doctrine taught at the monastery and decided to seek the truth in the Busshin, or Zen, sect, becoming a disciple of Eisai, a master of the Rinzai branch of the Zen sect who resided at the Kennin-ji in Kyoto. After Eisai's death, Dōgen placed himself under Eisai's disciple Meizen, and in 1223, when he was twenty-three, he accompanied Meizen in a journey to Sung China. There he continued his search for the true Way of the Buddha, traveling about from one temple to another; finally, under the master Ju-ching of Mt. T'ien-t'ung he achieved Enlightenment and returned to Japan in 1227.

After his return he resided for a time at the Kennin-ji and later moved to the An'yō-in in Fukakusa. In 1233 he founded a temple called Hōrin-ji on the site of the old Gokuraku-ji near Kyoto, and the same year wrote a work called the *Fuka zazengi*. His fame soon spread abroad, and the number of his disciples increased greatly. In 1243, when the monks of Mt. Hiei were working to stir up ill feeling against him, he accepted an invitation from Hatano Yoshishige to take up residence in the Daibutsu-ji in the province of Echizen, and in 1246 the name of the temple was changed to Eihei-ji. In time it was to become the headquarters of the Sōtō branch of the Zen sect.

In 1247 Dōgen journeyed to Kamakura at the request of Hōjō Tokiyori, *shikken* (regent) of the Kamakura shogunate. Tokiyori intended to found a new temple, appoint Dōgen as its head, and thus insure that the latter would remain in Kamakura permanently, but Dōgen adamantly declined and the following year returned to Eihei-ji. In 1250 he was presented by Emperor Gosaga with a *shie* (purple robe), a mark of high distinction conferred by the ruler since 1249 upon eminent members of the clergy; once more he firmly declined, and though he was eventually obliged to accept the robe, it is said that he put it away and never once wore it. Around the summer of 1252 he fell ill, and the following year, returning to Kyoto, he handed over his preaching mat to his disciple Ejō and died at the age of fifty-three.

In his teachings Dōgen attacked the concept of *mappō*, or "the latter days of the Buddhist law," a doctrine very popular at the time, which held that the world had entered a period of degeneracy and that individuals could no longer gain salvation by their own efforts. Instead, he stressed the importance of acquiring a faith that would transcend time and circumstance and penetrate to the eternal truth of the Dharma. He also opposed the syncretic tendencies of the time, which attempted to view the three religions of Confucianism, Buddhism, and Taoism as essentially one, and emphasized the necessity for purity of religious faith. He rejected all striving for worldly fame or profit and scorned the authority of the court nobles and warrior aristocrats, concentrating all of his energies upon the pursuit of the Way of Zen.

Dōgen wrote many works, including the *Fuka zazengi* mentioned above, the *Gakudō yōjinshū, Eihei seiki, Eihei kōroku, Kōmyōzō sammi*, and others, but most important are the sermons and explications that he wrote in Japanese over the years after his return from China until his death, which after his death were compiled in a work ninety-five chapters in length entitled the *Shōbō genzō*. In closeness of reasoning, acuity, and depth of understanding the work is unparalleled in the writings of Japanese Buddhism and holds a place of unique importance in the history of Japanese thought. Also of great value in the understanding of Dōgen's thought is the collection of conversations with Dōgen recorded by his disciple Ejō under the title *Shōbō genzō zuimonki*.

Eifuku (Yōfuku) Mon-in (1271–1342)

Poet of the late Kamakura and Northern and Southern Courts periods. Her father was Saionji Sanekane. At the age of seventeen she became Chūgū, the consort of the Emperor Fushimi. Upon the emperor's abdication she was given the title of Eifuku Mon-in and at the age of forty-five became a nun. Along with Retired Emperor Fushimi she studied poetry with Kyōgoku Tamekane and developed a characteristic verse style of her own. The *waka* included in the *Gyokuyō shū* and *Fūga shū* show her style at its most characteristic. Typical is the following poem:

> Rays of the late sun
> that shone for a while
> over the cherry blossoms
> now, before it has even set,
> have all lost their light.

As the work suggests, her style is characterized by freedom and novelty in the choice of words, by the suggestion of the passage of time within the description of a scene, by the interplay of light and shadow, and by the use of color and realistically descriptive effects.

Fujiwara no Ietaka (1158–1237)

Poet of the early Kamakura period. He was the son of Chūnagon (Middle Counselor) Fujiwara no Mitsutaka. From an early age he studied the art of *waka* with the celebrated poet Fujiwara no Shunzei, and at the age of thirty he had five of his poems accepted for inclusion in the *Senzaishū*, an anthology compiled by Shunzei on imperial command. Ietaka continued to give increasing evidence of his artistic talent and enjoyed particular favor with Retired Emperor Gotoba, who took a deep interest in matters pertaining to the art of Japanese poetry. At this time Ietaka and Fujiwara no Teika were the two most outstanding figures in the poetic world. In 1201, at the age of forty-three, Ietaka, along with Teika and others, was chosen to compile an anthology under imperial auspices, a task to which he devoted great energy and which resulted in the famous *Shin kokinshū*, or "New Collection of Ancient and Modern Poems." During the following ten years or more he occupied himself in the service of Retired Emperor Gotoba, and in 1206 was appointed to the office of *kunai-kyō* (minister of the imperial household). In the so-called Jōkyū disturbance of 1221, Retired Emperor

Gotoba was exiled to the island of Oki, and Ietaka's fortunes likewise declined dramatically. In the years that followed, however, he managed to exchange poems and letters with the exiled sovereign and never ceased to display his loyalty and devotion to his former lord and patron. In 1236 he left secular life and entered the priesthood and died the following year at the age of seventy-nine.

Ietaka's poems are noted for their rich lyricism and tone of freshness and novelty. Around the period when he was engaged in the compilation of the *Shin kokinshū* he composed his most elegant and strikingly beautiful works, while in his late years his poetry takes on a keenly personal and realistic tone. In the *Shin chokusenshū*, an official anthology compiled by Fujiwara no Teika, he is represented by forty-three poems, the largest number of any poet in the anthology. He is noted for his prolificacy, legend reporting that he composed some sixty thousand poems in the course of his long lifetime. There is a collection of his works entitled the *Minishū*, while a total of 282 of his poems is preserved in the *Senzaishū* and other official anthologies. The following poem is among his most famous:

> On hills where
> the first red leaves are falling,
> wet by evening showers,
> the lone deer
> must be crying.

Fujiwara no Shunzei (1114–1204)

Poet of the late Heian and early Kamakura periods. His father, Toshitada, was also a poet, and Shunzei started composing poems at an early age, taking part in poem-making parties when he was only seventeen or eighteen and becoming a close friend of Saigyō. When he was twenty-three, he became a pupil of Fujiwara no Mototoshi, a conservative poet who attached great importance to tradition, with the intention of studying poetics in earnest. However, it was the progressive and intensely creative poet Minamoto no Toshiyori to whom, from an early age, his own verse was most indebted. He had a close acquaintance not only with verse but with such Heian period romances as the *Tales of Ise* and *The Tale of Genji*. By the time he was twenty-six, he was producing such symbolic works as the poem

> As evening comes,
> autumn wind from the meadows

strikes with a chill;
quails cry
in the village of Fukakusa.

in which he displays the combination of heartfelt lyricism and a sense of the profound mystery of the natural world that was to characterize his verse. The Hōgen war that broke out when he was forty-two and the downfall of the Taira clan that occurred when he was around seventy both heightened his sense of the impermanence of all things, influencing his outlook and giving a new dimension to his verse. The anthology *Shika shū* compiled around 1151–52, contains only one of his poems, but from then on his reputation increased steadily, and he established a position for himself as judge at poetry contests and leader of the world of poetry. During this period, when he was sixty-three, he suffered a serious illness and took Buddhist vows, assuming the Buddhist name of Shakua. In 1178 at the request of the Hōshinnō (Cloistered Prince) Shūkaku, chief abbot of the Ninna-ji temple, he compiled a collection of his own verse entitled *Chōshū eisō* in three books. He also acted as editor of the *Senzaishū*, an anthology completed in 1187–88, which is famous for containing more pieces by Minamoto no Toshiyori than by his own teacher Fujiwara no Mototoshi.

Shunzei's art is seen at its most profound and mature in the work that followed the *Senzaishū*, beginning around the time when he was seventy and including such works as *Gosha hyakushu*, *In hyakushu*, and the hundred verses in the *Sengohyakuban utaawase*. He also did valuable work in educating the leading poets of the age of the *Shin kokinshū*, among them his own son Fujiwara no Teika. In 1197, when he was eighty-three, he wrote a two-chapter dissertation on verse entitled *Korai fūtai shō* at the request of Princess Shikishi. It consists mainly of Shunzei's views on the art of verse-making and the history of the *waka*, discoursing with a breadth of outlook that gives it an epoch-making place in the history of poetic criticism in Japan. Besides its sense of history, it is notable for citing *yūgen* as representing the highest contemporary ideal of beauty and the ideal for the *waka*.

Fujiwara no Tameie (1198–1275)

Poet of the middle Kamakura period; son of Fujiwara no Teika. A youthful preoccupation with *kemari*, (the sedate version of football still occasionally performed at the imperial court) at the expense of verse-making distressed his father, Teika, but from the time of the Shōkyū war on, he began to apply himself assiduously to the life of the poet, composing the *Tameie-kyō senshū*

("One Thousand Verses by Lord Tameie"), it is said, within the space of five days. He gradually came to see himself as successor to the Mikohidari school and occupied an increasingly important place in the world of poetry, including that of the court, presenting his own best work at official gatherings as well as holding "one hundred verse" parties and *renga* parties at his own residence. In 1251, he compiled an anthology, the *Shoku gosenshū*, at the command of Retired Emperor Gosaga. In 1259, he was commanded to compile a *Shoku kokinshū*, but a number of poets who objected to Tameie's style intervened, and it was finally presented to the retired emperor in 1265 under the names of four poets including Tameie. Tameie's style, as exemplified by the poem

> Distant hills
> in the breaking dawn—
> their cherries
> must have opened in one night:
> cloaked in white clouds!

tends to be lacking in emotion, yet his verse has geniality and absence of anything forced and, though plain, is well-turned. He was the leading poet of the Nijō school style of verse.

Towards the end of his life, he was deeply devoted to his wife Anka Mon-in Shijō (Abutsu-ni) and to Tamesuke, the child she bore him (ancestor of the Reizei family), thereby laying the seeds of a famous inheritance dispute between Tamesuke and Tameuji, his eldest son by his legal wife. The *Tameie shū* is a collection of his verse, and the *Eika ittai* contains his views on the theory of poetry. He also produced commentaries on the *Kokinshū* and *Gosenshū* and was well versed in *The Tale of Genji*.

Fujiwara no (Kyōgoku) Tamekane (1254–1333)

Poet of the late Kamakura period. He was a member of the Kyōgoku branch of the Fujiwara family, and is usually known as Kyōgoku Tamekane or Irie Tamekane. He entered the priesthood late in life and was known first as Rengaku and later as Jōkan. His father was Fujiwara no Tamenori, the third son of Fujiwara no Tameie and a descendant of the famous poets Shunzei and Teika, and thus grew up in a family distinguished for its mastery of the art of poetry.

After the death of Tameie in 1275, his sons Tameuji, Tamenori, and Tamesuke became heads of the Nijō, Kyōgoku, and Reizei branches of the family respectively. But disputes over property rights led to feelings of enmity and rivalry among the three houses, which were carried on by their descendants, while each house or branch constituted a separate school of poetry that claimed to be the sole heir and preserver of the poetic traditions of the family.

Tamekane, the head of the Kyōgoku branch of the family in late Kamakura times, tended to side with Tamesuke of the Reizei branch and with his mother, the nun Abutsu, which brought him into open opposition with Tameyo, the head of the Nijō branch at the time. In poetic matters as well, the Kyōgoku and Reizei schools were in sympathy and worked to develop a new poetic style known as the Gyokuyō style, from the anthology in which it is best represented, the *Gyokuyōshū*. In the sphere of politics, Tamekane enjoyed the patronage of Emperor Gofukakusa, who belonged to the Jimyō-in line of the imperial family, while his rival Tameyo was patronized by Emperor Kameyama of the Daikaku-ji line. According to an arrangement of the time, the rulers, most of whom reigned for fairly brief periods, were chosen alternately from first one line and then the other, which meant that Tamekane and Tameyo were destined to frequent reversals of fortune, one enjoying favor while the other went into a period of temporary eclipse. Thus the Nijō and Kyōgoku families stood in opposition to one another both in political affiliation and in matters of poetic theory and practice.

Tamekane was awarded noble rank at the age of two, and by the time he was sixteen had advanced to the court rank of Junior Fourth Rank. Around this time he began studying the art of poetry under the guidance of his grandfather Tameie, but his grandfather died when he was twenty-one, and his father died three years later. By this time he held two official posts, that of middle commander of the right and vice-governor of Tosa, and was taking part in the composition of so-called hundred-poem collections at court. But because rulers belonging to the Daikaku-ji line were on the throne at the time, Tamekane was unable to play a very important part either in political or poetic affairs and was obliged to suffer considerable frustration and disappointment. In 1287, however, Emperor Fushimi of the Jimyō-in line ascended the throne, and in the three or four years succeeding, Tamekane rose dramatically in position until in 1291, at the age of thirty-seven, he was appointed to the Senior Third Rank with the post of *gon-chūnagon* (acting middle counselor).

In 1293 Tamekane, along with Nijō Tameyo, Asukai Masaari, and Rokujō Takahiro, were commanded to compile an anthology under imperial auspices, but because of differences of opinion between Tamekane and Tameyo, the project was abandoned. Meanwhile Tamekane gained wide respect as a result of his activities as a judge in poetry matches, but in 1298 he became the object of slander because of certain political policies that he was pursuing and was exiled to the island of Sado, Emperor Fushimi abdicating the throne on the same occasion.

He was finally pardoned in 1303 and allowed to return to the capital, but it was the reign of Emperor Gonijō and Tameyo was in favor, having been commanded by the ruler to compile the anthology known as the *Shin gosenshū*. In 1308 Emperor Hanazono of the Jimyō-in line came to the throne, and his father, Retired Emperor Fushimi, took charge of affairs of state, and as a result Tamekane was once more treated with great favor and advanced to the post of *gon-no-dainagon* (acting great counselor). His views on poetry were also highly respected, and in 1312 at the command of the retired emperor he undertook single-handed to compile the anthology known as the *Gyokuyōshū*. Both the plan and execution of the anthology aroused severe criticism from the members of the Nijō school, and the dispute between Tamekane and Tameyo increased in intensity, until in 1310 they drew up the *Enkyō ryōkyō sochinjō* ("Enkyō era petition setting forth the positions of their two lordships") in which they expounded their respective views. The Nijō school's criticisms of the *Gyokuyōshū* were also aired in other works such as the *Kaen rensho kotogaki* and the *Nomori no kagami*.

When the *Gyokuyōshū* was completed in 1313, Retired Emperor Fushimi entered the priesthood, and Tamekane followed him in taking the same step. In 1316, when Tamekane was sixty-two, however, he had a falling out with Saionji Sanekane, a benefactor from his youthful years, and was once more ordered into exile, this time to the province of Tosa in Shikoku. He was never permitted to return to the capital and died at the age of seventy-eight in the province of Izumi south of present-day Osaka.

His views on poetry are set forth mainly in the *Tamekanekyō wakashō* and the *Enkyō ryōkyō sochinjō*. Essentially he favored the kind of direct and open expression of emotion typical of the *Man'yōshū*, while at the same time approving of the style and technique of the *Shin kokinshū*, his ideal being a type of poetry that would combine these two elements in a natural and harmonious fashion. He placed highest emphasis upon the emotional sincerity of the poem, urged greater freedom of language, and valued realism and simplicity over considerations of form and technique. In his own work he observed closely the changes in the natural and human worlds and sought to capture the vivid emotions that they aroused and to grasp the true essence of man and nature.

His style represents a conscious attack upon tradition, attempting to destroy the image of the *waka* as something invariably elegant and refined and substituting instead accuracy and precision of observation, subtlety of emotional expression, and a tendency toward constructivism or formal symmetry in his more lyrical works, all characteristics that are typical of the works contained in the *Gyokuyōshū*.

The following is an example of his poetry:

> Along the fringes
> of those mountains
> where the sudden storm passed,
> flashing in farewell—
> streaks of intermittent lightning.

Fujiwara no Tameuji (1222–1286)

Poet of the middle Kamakura period. He belonged to the Nijō branch of the Fujiwara family; his religious name was Kakua. He was the eldest son of Fujiwara no Tameie, who in turn was the second son of the famous poet Fujiwara no Teika. He thus grew up in a family steeped in the traditions of Japanese poetry and devoted himself to that art, becoming the founder of the so-called Nijō school and exercising great influence in the poetic world of the time.

Around the age of thirty he was appointed to the office of *sangi* (consultant), and served for a number of years in that capacity with distinction. Later he rose to the office of *dainagon* (great counselor), being known as Reizei Dainagon. In 1285, when he held the rank of Senior Second Rank *gon-no-dainagon*, he retired from official life, entered the Buddhist priesthood, and died the following year.

His earliest known poem was written sometime between the ages of twelve and sixteen, when, as *sashōshō* (lesser commander of the left) he passed the Shirakawa Barrier on his way to visit his maternal grandfather Utsunomiya Renshō. In 1243, at the age of twenty-one he took part in the Kawai Yashiro poetry match, and many of his poems from this period and after are preserved. His poems are also found in the hundred-poem collections known as the *Mitsutoshi kanjin kechiengyō kyakushū* of 1245 and the *Hōji ninen hyakushū* of 1248, as well as in the privately compiled anthology *Mandaishū* and the official anthology *Shoku gosenshū*.

In 1259, at the age of thirty-seven, he paid a second visit to the Utsunomiya family and compiled a private family anthology consisting mainly of their works and entitled the *Shin wakashū*. Following this, he contributed to a number of hundred-poem collections such as those composed in 1261, 1263, and 1278, and the seven-hundred-poem collection of the Shirakawa Palace of 1265. His most notable achievement, however, was the compilation of the anthology known as the *Shoku shūishū*, which he undertook at the command of Retired Emperor Kameyama in 1276 and completed two years later, and which includes twenty-one of his own poems.

His poems are also included in the imperial anthologies *Shoku kokinshū*, *Shin gosenshū*, *Gyokuyōshū*, *Shoku senzaishū*, *Shoku goshūishū*, *Fūgashū*, *Shin senzaishū*, *Shin shūishū*, *Shin goshūishū*, and *Shin zoku kokinshū*, and twenty-five *renga* verses by him are preserved in the *Tsukubashū*.

His poetic style is conservative and faithfully reflects that of his father, Tameie, possessing no outstanding characteristics of its own but being marked in general by grace and delicacy. In comparison to the later poets of the Nijō school, he wrote a rather larger number of descriptive pieces, and his poems are relatively free in construction and show attempts to incorporate *renga* techniques.

Tameuji, as is well known, became involved in a dispute with his step-mother, the nun Abutsu (q.v.), over the property rights to the Hosokawa estate in the province of Harima that had been in the family for some generations, which led to discord between him and his half-brother Tame-suke, and he also quarreled with his younger full brother Tamenori. As a result, the Nijō family and school of poetry split into three rival branches, the Nijō branch headed by Tameuji, the Kyōgoku branch headed by Tame-nori, and the Reizei branch headed by Tamesuke, a fact that has greatly complicated the history and development of *waka* in succeeding centuries. There is a collection of Tameuji's works entitled *Dainagon Tameuji-kyō shū*, which is preserved in chapter seven of the *Katsura-no-miya-bon sōsho*.

The following is an example of his poetry:

> Touched by dew and frost
> the late rice ripens,
> and in the makeshift shed
> the wind from the hills
> blows cold.

Fujiwara no (Nijō) Tameyo (1251–1338)

Poet of the late Kamakura period. He belonged to the Nijō branch of the Fujiwara family, a branch and school of poetry also known as the Mikohi-dari-ke; his religious name was Myōshaku. His father was Tameuji, the grandson of the famous compiler of the *Shin kokinshū* Fujiwara no Teika and the founder of the Nijō school of poetry.

Tameyo was born at a time when the fortunes of the Nijō family were at their height. He was granted a noble title at the age of one and by the age of eleven had advanced to the court rank of Junior Fourth Rank and the post of Middle Commander of the Left. He himself records that he first began to study the art of poetry at the age of fourteen, and by the time he was around twenty he was already taking part in poetry gatherings at court. He served under Emperor Gouda, who belonged to the Daikaku-ji line, one of the two branches of the imperial family that, according to the agreement of the time, took turns in succeeding to the throne, the other branch being known as the Jimyō-in line. In 1278, when Tameyo was twenty-eight, he was appointed *kurōdo-no-tō*, or head of the archives, and in 1283 he was made a *sangi*, consultant, and took an active part in government affairs. In 1286, however, his father, Tameuji, died, and the following year, with the abdication of Emperor Gouda, Emperor Fushimi came to the throne, a member of the Jimyō-in line. As a result, Tameyo was replaced in importance and imperial favor by Fujiwara no Tamekane of the rival Kyōgoku line of the family. Furthermore, although Emperor Fushimi abdicated after eleven years, he was succeeded by his son, Emperor Gofushimi, and the Jimyō-in line thus held the throne for a period of some fourteen or fifteen years, during which Tameyo's political fortunes fell to a low ebb. In 1293 Emperor Fushimi ordered Nijō Tameyo, Kyōgoku Tamekane, Asukai Masaari, and Rokujō Takahiro to compile an anthology of poetry, but because of differences of opinion between Tameyo and Tamekane, the project was never completed.

In 1301, when Emperor Gofushimi abdicated and Emperor Gonijō of the Daikaku-ji line came to the throne, Tameyo's fortunes rose once more and he soon became extremely active in poetry circles. In 1303 he finished compiling the *Shin gosenshū*, an anthology that he compiled single-handed at the command of Retired Emperor Gouda. He was a constant visitor to the palace and rose to the position of *mimbu-kyō*, minister of the interior. In 1308, however, a ruler of the Jimyō-in line once more came to the throne; for the following ten years Tameyo's fortunes again ebbed, and he resigned his official position. Meanwhile the opposition between him and Kyōgoku Tamekane over matters of poetic theory and practice continued to grow more intense, until in 1310, the third year of the Enkyō era, the two men set forth their respective positions in a work entitled the *Enkyō ryōkyo sochinjō* ("Enkyō era petition setting forth the positions of their two lordships").

In 1318 Emperor Godaigo of the Daikaku-ji line ascended the throne, and Tameyo, now sixty-seven, enjoyed favor once more, being looked upon as the leading elder figure of the poetic world. In 1319 he was ordered to compile an official anthology, the result being the *Shoku senzaishū*, completed a few years later. In 1326, at the age of seventy-five, he wrote a work entitled the *Waka teikunshō* in which he expounded his theories of poetic composition. During the following years, until he entered the priesthood at the age of seventy-nine, he enjoyed his period of greatest acclaim. His daughter Tameko became a cubine of Emperor Godaigo.

There is no extant collection of Tameyo's works, but the *Shoku senzaishū* contains thirty-three of his poems, the *Shoku goshūishū* twenty, the *Shin senzaishū* forty-two, and the *Shin shūishū* twenty-four, while others are to be found in the *Gyokuyōshū*, *Fūgashū*, *Shin goshūishū*, and *Shin zoku kokinshū*, making a total of 171 poems. In addition to these poems preserved in official anthologies, others are to be found in such works as the *Kagen hyakushu* and *Kameyamadono nanahyakushu*.

As a poet Tameyo was a conservative and traditionalist, concerned only with preserving and carrying on the style associated with the Nijō school, and his works tend toward flatness and monotony. In his descriptive pieces, however, he often shows considerable skill in capturing in realistic manner the subtle and momentary changes of the natural world. The following is an example of his work:

> Sky still deep in
> darkness of night,
> the edges of the mountain
> whiten with the sheen
> of fallen snow.

Fujiwara no Teika (1162–1241)

Poet of the early Kamakura period. His father was Fujiwara no Shunzei (Toshinari) and his mother Kaga, a lady-in-waiting to Bifukumon-in, the empress of Emperor Toba. Taking after his father, who was one of the most celebrated poets of the time, he began to write at an early age and gained recognition of his unusual talent through the *Shogaku hyakushu*, written when he was seventeen, and the *Horikawa hyakushu*, written the following year. The *Senzaishū*, an official anthology completed in 1187, includes eight of his poems, an impressive number for someone of his youth, albeit his father, Shunzei, was the compiler of the anthology. From the age of twenty-four he became a retainer in the household of Sesshō-kampaku (Regent-Chancellor) Kujō Kanezane and had occasion to become acquainted with such prominent poets of the time as Jien and Fujiwara no Yoshitsune and to play a lively part in poetic activities. The Kujō family, however, lost much of its power and influence to the rival group led by Minamoto no Michichika, and as a result Teika remained relatively poor and did not advance in official position.

In 1200, when he was thirty-eight, he was allowed to take part in a poetry match sponsored by Retired Emperor Gotoba and known as the *Shōji shodo hyakushu*. His performance was so highly rated that on the very same day he was granted *shōden*, the privilege of entering the palace, and was launched upon a brilliant career as a court poet. In another poetry match held the following year and known as the *Sengohyakuban utaawase* he was active both as a participant and a judge, and in 1201 he was appointed as a *yoriudo*, official in the *wakadokoro* (Office of Japanese Poetry), which Retired Emperor Gotoba had revived. Following this, he was chosen to be one of the compilers of the *Shin kokinshū*, one of the most important and influential of all official anthologies, and in fact acted as the leader and driving force behind its completion. In 1211, when he was forty-nine, he was awarded the court rank of Junior Third Rank, and the following year advanced to the position of *mimbu-kyō*, or minister of the interior. But from the time of his activities as a compiler of the *Shin kokinshū* his relations with Retired Emperor Gotoba, who commissioned the anthology, had begun to worsen, perhaps because of disagreement over poetic matters, and in 1220 he was informed by Emperor Gotoba that he would no longer be welcome in the latter's presence.

With the so-called Jōkyū disturbance of 1221 the political situation changed drastically and Retired Emperor Gotoba was exiled to the island of Oki. Because of the patronage and protection that Teika enjoyed from his wife's relatives of the Saionji family, he was able to advance to the rank of Senior Second Rank and the post of *gon-no-chūnagon* (acting middle counselor). Finally, at the age of seventy-one, he entered the priesthood, taking the religious name Myōjō. He continued to remain very active in poetic affairs, however, gathering together various collections of poems to present to the ruler and in 1235 compiling singlehanded the official anthology known as the *Shin chokusenshū*. He died six years later at the age of seventy-nine.

Teika took over and developed the poetic style of his father Shunzei, placing emphasis upon emotional content and striving, through the use of richly symbolic language, to create an atmosphere of mystery and ethereal beauty. According to legend, when he was composing poetry, he would adjust his robes, open the sliding doors on the south side of the room and, seating himself in the center of the room, gaze far off at the sky as he pondered over his verses. The *Shin kokinshū* and other imperial anthologies contain a total of 465 works from his hand, and there is also a separate collection of his works entitled *Shūi gusō*. In addition, he wrote works on poetic theory such as the *Kindai shūka, Eika taigai,* and *Maigetsushō*. In his later years he devoted much time to the preparation of commentaries and collated editions of earlier works of Japanese literature, copying out the texts in his own hand, and in this way made a contribution quite as important as that which he made through his poems and works on poetic theory. The standard editions of many such well-known classics as the *Genji monogatari, Tosa nikki,* and *Sarashina nikki* are based upon these texts that Teika edited and wrote out by hand. He kept a diary called the *Meigetsuki*, written in Chinese and covering the fifty-six-year period from 1180 to 1235, and though there are many gaps and uncertainties in the present text, it provides an invaluable source of information for the history and social background of this troubled period. One of his most famous poems, representative of his youthful style of mystery and dreamlike beauty, is the following. The notes that follow it will perhaps give some suggestion of the rich symbolism typical of so many of his works:

> A spring night's dream—
> as its floating bridge
> melts away,
> from the peaks parting,
> banks of clouds in the sky.

"Spring night's dream"—suggestive of brevity, particularly the brevity of worldly glory.

"Floating bridge"—suggestive of "The Floating Bridge of Dreams," the last chapter of *The Tale of Genji* and hence of the romantic and old-fashioned world of the *Genji*.

"From the peaks parting, banks of clouds"—suggestive of an old Chinese legend of an amorous encounter between a mortal ruler and a mountain goddess; as the goddess took her leave, she said, "At dawn I am the morning clouds."

Fushimi Tennō (1265–1317)

Ninety-second sovereign of Japan and poet of the late Kamakura period. Even during his days as crown prince he would often engage his attendants in discussions on the *Kokinshū* or *The Tale of Genji* and other literary topics, and he was fond of reading the *Man'yōshū*. He bestowed favors on Kyōgoku Tamekane, a progressive poet of the day, and studied the writing of verse with him. He himself wrote a great deal of verse and is believed also to have had a hand in the compilation of the *Gyokuyōshū* anthology. The surviving verse in his own writing—strips of paper from his collection of verse referred to as *Hirosawa-gire*—are prized as specimens of calligraphy; scattered among many different collections, they account for a total of more than two thousand well-known verses in all. In imperial anthologies, he has a total of 294 verses, notably the 93 verses in the *Gyokuyōshū*, while 530 more verses are included in *On hyakushu* ("One Hundred Imperial Verses") and other collections. A typical example of his poetry is:

> Distant peaks,
> till now faintly seen,
> fade from view:
> as evening falls, white fog
> at the mountain's base.

As this shows, his style is basically graphic, but it is sweet, sentimental realism and lacks the individuality of Tamekane's work. His achievement lies, rather, in his patronage of Tamekane and the part he played as a leading figure in the compilation of the *Gyokuyōshū*.

Godaigo Tennō (1288–1339)

The ninety-sixth sovereign of Japan; his personal name was Takaharu. He was the second son of Emperor Gouda and, being a member of the Daikaku-ji line of succession, was raised in an atomosphere of intense rivalry with the members of the Jimyō-in line. In 1318 he succeeded Emperor Hanazono, beginning a reign that was to last twenty-one years. When he first came to the throne, power was still in the hands of the *insei*, or cloister government, of Retired Emperor Gouda, but from 1321 on Emperor Godaigo was able to rule in person. He selected such talented officials as Yoshida Sadafusa, Kitabatake Chikafusa, Hino Suketomo, and Hino Toshimoto to assist him, encouraged learning and the military arts, reestablished the *kirokusho* (Records Office), and attended to law suits, introducing various reforms in government affairs.

Perceiving that the military clans were beginning to lose faith in the power of the Kamakura shogunate, he laid plans to overthrow the shogunate and restore power to the throne, but twice, in the Shōchū disturbance of 1324 and the Genkō disturbance of 1331, his plans were discovered. He was exiled to the island of Oki, but succeeded in escaping and making his way back to Honshu in 1333. The same year the Kamakura shogunate was overthrown and Emperor Godaigo headed a new government in Kyoto and set about instituting the measures known as the Kemmu Restoration. But he attempted to employ both courtiers and military leaders in his new regime, which resulted in disharmony between the two groups, and the military families were particularly disgruntled over the way in which their demands for reallocation of fiefs and estates were met. In 1335 Ashikaga Takauji raised the standard of revolt in the Kantō area, and after only two years of existence the Kemmu Restoration government was overthrown. In 1336, under strong pressure from Ashikaga Takauji, peace was for a time restored, but shortly afterward Emperor Godaigo fled from Kyoto south to Mt. Yoshino in Yamato, where he set up the so-called Southern Court in rivalry with the Northern Court, that of the emperor established by Takauji in Kyoto. Emperor Godaigo worked vigorously to bring about the restoration of his rule, but circumstances were against him, and he faced growing disappointment and, in time, illness. In 1339 he abdicated in favor of his son Prince Yoshinaga, who is known posthumously as Emperor Murakami, and the following day passed away in the palace on Mt. Yoshino.

He was well read in history and the writings of the Chu Hsi school of Neo-Confucianism, and was also an excellent poet, his works being included in such anthologies as the *Shin'yōshū*, *Shin senzaishū*, *Shin shūishū*, and *Shin goshūishū*. He wrote two works entitled *Kemmu nenjū gyōji* and *Kemmu nitchū gyōji*, which reveal the ideals that motivated his attempts to restore imperial rule. The following two poems, both written at Mt. Yoshino, which is famous for its cherry blossoms, convey the mood of loneliness and despair that filled his later years:

> In this place too
> bloom cherries
> like those of the palace,
> though I think of it
> as a mere makeshift lodging.

> A melancholy season
> even in the capital,
> and here where clouds never lift,
> the depths of Yoshino
> in the fifth month rains—

Gomurakami Tennō (1328–1368)

The second emperor of the Southern Court and ninety-seventh sovereign of Japan, son of Emperor Godaigo and Ano Renshi (Shintaiken Mon-in). Born during the troubled times of the Northern and Southern Courts, he grew up from earliest childhood in an atmosphere of martial readiness. In 1333 he went to the province of Mutsu with Chikabatake Akiie in his service. In the fifth month of the following year he was officially made an imperial prince and, under the temporary restoration of imperial power effected by Emperor Godaigo, quelled the Tōhoku districts. In 1335 and again in 1337 he went to Kyoto with the aim of defeating Ashikaga Takauji. Following his accession in 1339, he made his headquarters in Yoshino, whence he made several unsuccessful attempts to reestablish himself and his court in Kyoto. He faced increasing hardship and disappointment, being forced to move to Anou, to the Kanshin-ji temple in Kawachi, to Sumiyoshi, and to other places in turn. His poems are included in the imperial anthology of the Southern Court entitled *Shin'yōshū*; they number one hundred, more than those of any other poet represented. Evidence in the anthology indicates that Emperor Gomurakami intended to select an imperial anthology himself, and it seems likely that this anthology was compiled by Prince Munenaga, his younger brother. One of his poems reads:

> O god of
> Iwashimizu,
> look in pity
> on my heart
> as I live in hiding.

Gotoba Jōkō (1180–1239)

Eighty-second sovereign of Japan and poet of the early Kamakura period. He came to the throne in 1183, the year in which the Taira forces fled from Kyoto with the infant Emperor Antoku, but in 1198 gave up the throne in order to rule from retirement, from which time on he gathered about him the poets of the day and engaged in energetic activity in the world of poetry. In 1201, he revived the old *wakadokoro* (Bureau of Poetry), and more than one hundred poets—counting only those whose names are known today—joined its ranks. He also organized many "one hundred-verse" meetings, poetry parties, and poetry contests, the finest fruits of which are embodied in the *Shin kokinshū* anthology. The two poets whom the retired emperor especially favored are Saigyō and Fujiwara no Shunzei. He commanded six established poets of the day, including Fujiwara no Teika, Fujiwara no Ietaka, and Jakuren, to compile an anthology of *waka* dating from ancient times onward. He himself carefully selected from the poems they gathered together and added new selections of his own, so that it was not until nine years later, in 1210, that the anthology, entitled the *Shin kokinshū*, reached approximately the form in which it is now known. Thirty-three of the emperor's poems are included, one of the most famous verses being:

> Softly, it seems,
> spring has come
> to the sky at last—
> over the heavenly hill of Kagu[1]
> the mists trail.

In 1221, he attempted to rally armed forces against the Hōjō government in Kamakura, but failed and was exiled to the island of Oki; the episode is referred to by historians as the Shōkyū disturbance. Lonely in exile, he set about revising the *Shin kokinshū* again, and around 1235–36 produced the "Oki version," in which the original collection, numbering close to two thousand verses, is reduced to somewhat over sixteen hundred. During the years spent on Oki, the element of personal emotion becomes more pronounced in his work, as might be expected; one of the verses in his *Entō hyakushu* ("Hundred Poems from a Distant Isle") reads as follows:

> The sorrow of one
> at the limit
> of cares he cannot flee—
> lamenting all the while,
> I still go on.

He died on the island after eighteen years of exile. Among Gotoba's extant works is the *Gotoba-in onkuden*, which contains his theories on poetry and criticism of contemporary poets.

Hanazono Tennō (1297–1348)

Ninety-fifth sovereign of Japan; poet of the late Kamakura period; second son of Emperor Fushimi. Well versed in both Japanese and Chinese studies, he had a profound acquaintance with Buddhism and with Zen in particular. He

---

1. A hill in the Nara plain that was said to have descended from heaven.

was a skilled calligrapher and artist, while in the field of *waka* he shared his father's preference for the style of Kyōgoku Tamekane and throughout his life worked for the development of the school. *Hanazono-in Tennō shinki*, the emperor's personally kept journal, of which more than forty chapters survive, contains a large number of entries concerning poetry or discussing the characters of poets such as Nijō Tametoki and Nijō Tamekane. The *Fūgashū*, an imperial anthology completed near the end of the emperor's life, was compiled by Emperor Kōgon, but it is certain that the guiding hand was that of Emperor Hanazono, and the introductions to the anthology in Japanese and Chinese are also by Hanazono. His verse, like that of Emperor Fushimi, is marked by its precise imagery and its Zen overtones.

Hōnen (1133–1212)

Priest and founder of the Jōdo sect of Buddhism. When he was nine his father, Uruma no Tokikumi, who was *ōryōshi* (military governor) of Mimasaka was killed, and he entered the priesthood in accordance with his father's last wishes. At the age of fourteen he went to study the teachings of the Tendai sect with Kōen, a high-ranking priest of the Mt. Hiei monastery, and at the age of seventeen continued his studies with Eikū of the same monastery, acquiring a reputation as the most gifted young monk there. However, he soon became dissatisfied with the doctrinal studies that characterized the Tendai and Shingon sects of Esoteric Buddhism at the time. A reading of a commentary on the *Kammuryō-kyō* sutra (one of the three Pure Land sutras, containing an account of the Buddha Amida [Amitābha] and the glories of his Paradise) by Shan-tao, a celebrated monk of T'ang China, convinced him that it was possible to obtain salvation merely by the repetition of the invocation of Amida (*Namu Amida Butsu*) without the performance of other religious practices. In 1175, at the age of forty-two, he founded the Jōdo (Pure Land) sect of Japanese Buddhism.

He subsequently took up residence at Ōtani in Kyoto, and came to number among his disciples not only samurai and commoners but aristocrats such as Kujō Kanezane, so that his teachings enjoyed a great vogue. This prompted attempts by the forces of traditional Buddhism to suppress the new faith, and when someone claiming to be one of Hōnen's followers caused trouble and an appeal was made to the court, a ban was imposed on the practice of invoking Amida. Hōnen himself, then seventy-four, was given the lay name of Fujii Motohiko and banished to Tosa. He was pardoned in 1211 and returned to Ōtani in Kyoto, where a disciple set down on paper his famous *Ichimai kishōmon*, containing the essence of the Pure Land teachings. The following year, however, he fell ill and died.

He is believed to have been a highly learned man, but personally he was modest and generous towards others; it seems more likely that he rose above mere scholarship and dwelt on an exalted level of pure faith. All who met him and received instruction from him were captivated by his greatness, and the number of persons who at least claimed to be his disciples or followers was extremely great. A large number of books are attributed to him, but few exist in his own hand, and most of them are believed to have been written by his pupils. Some fifty-odd years after his death his disciple Ryōe gathered them together and compiled from them the two works known as *Wago tōroku* and *Kango tōroku*.

Ichijō Kanera (Kaneyoshi) (1402–1481)

Poet and classical scholar of the mid Muromachi period. His father was Kampaku Ichijō Tsunetsugu, and Nijō Yoshimoto, *sesshō* and *kampaku*, was his grandfather. He became Minister of the Interior at the age of nineteen, Minister of the Right at the age of twenty-two, and *sesshō* (regent) and *dajōdaijin* (prime minister) at thirty. At forty-five, he became *kampaku* and *uji-no-chōja* (head of the Fujiwara family) and the title *junkō* was also used of him. His career and the positions he held give a good idea of his personal ability and social status. Following the Ōnin war, he took refuge in Nara and became a Buddhist monk at the age of seventy-one. Despite civil war and old age, his enthusiasm for scholarship did not flag, and it was in 1472 that he completed his thirty-volume book *Kachō yojō*, a study with commentary on *The Tale of Genji*. He wrote many other works on the classics, including *Genji monogatari toshitate*, *Genji wahi shō*, *Ise monogatari guken shō*, and *Kokinshū dōmō shō*, and *Karin ryōzai shū*, a work of poetic criticism. In addition to these, he wrote other works ranging over many different fields: *Bummei ittōki* and *Shōdanchiyō* on the art of government; *Sayo no nezame* on women; and *Kuji kongen* on ancient rituals and practices. He was not very distinguished as a poet, but he was a good critic and scholar of verse and had an extraordinary knowledge of ancient rituals and practices; his intellectual outlook, combined with a deep familiarity with the Japanese classics and a knowledge of both Buddhist and Confucian teachings, made him one of the foremost cultural leaders of his time.

Ikkyū Sōjun (1394–1481)

Zen priest and writer of Chinese poetry of the middle Muromachi period. His childhood name was Shūken, and he is also known by his literary names Kyōun, Mukei, etc. His mother, a member of the Fujiwara family, entered the women's quarters of the palace and enjoyed great favor with Emperor Gokomatsu, but later she withdrew and shortly after gave birth to Ikkyū. When he was five, he was placed in a temple called Ankoku-ji, and at twelve he began to study the composition of verse in Chinese under Boki-tsuhan of Higashiyama in Kyoto, producing works that attracted wide attention; by the time he was fourteen or fifteen he had become recognized as a full-fledged poet. In 1410 he went to study under Seisō of the Hōdō-ji, receiving instruction in various works of sacred and secular literature, and later he studied under Iken-ō of the Saikon-ji, a follower of the Kanzan or Myōshin-ji branch of Rinzai Zen. After Iken-ō's death, he went to the Zenkō-an in the province of Ōmi to study under Sōdon and at the age of twenty-four was assigned the name Ikkyū by his teacher. Following the death of Sōdon, he moved about to various temples in Izumi, Nara, and the Kyoto and Osaka area. In 1474, when he was eighty, he received an imperial order to become head of the Daitoku-ji in Kyoto, and he died there in 1481 at the age of eighty-seven.

Ikkyū was said to have been of very eccentric character; in daily life he behaved very kindly toward persons of noble and humble station alike, was beloved by children, and showed great fondness for birds; but in matters pertaining to religion he was severe and unrelenting, denouncing the lack of discipline that characterized the Zen sect at that time, and even going so far as to burn the religious books and records that had been handed down to him from his teachers. There are many other anecdotes that illustrate his violent opposition to the vulgarity and abuses of the period, including one that describes how he went on a hunger strike when one of the monks of the Daitoku-ji was put into prison. From his early days he displayed great literary talent in the writing of poetry and prose in Chinese and Japanese, and his works are characterized by freedom of language and originality of ideas. In addition, he was a skilled painter, producing figure paintings, landscapes, and works depicting flowers and birds. Integrity of character, artistic sense, and a scorn for the petty conventions of the world are themes that run throughout his works and the numerous anecdotes that surround the life of this unusual man. His writings are collected in the *Kyōunshū, Jikaishū, Bukkigun,* and other works.

Imagawa Ryōshun (1326-?)

Poet of the early Muromachi period. His original name was Imagawa Sadayo. His family was a branch of the Ashikagas. He studied *waka* under Fujiwara no Tamemoto and later became a pupil of Reizei Tamehide. He also studied *renga* with Gusai and Nijō Yoshimoto. As a general of the shogunate forces he took part in the battle of Tōji and the attack on Yoshino, and his name occurs frequently in the celebrated martial romance *Taiheiki*. In 1367 he took his place in the inner circle of the Muromachi shogunate, but upon the death of the Shogun Yoshiakira in the same year, he became a Buddhist monk, taking the name Ryōshun. The forces of the Southern Court were strong in Kyushu, so Ryōshun was made commissioner for the island with the task of preventing any rising. He embodied his account of his journey to Kyushu in a work entitled *Michiyukiburi* (1371). He served as commissioner for Kyushu for twenty-five years in all. He wrote *Shitakusa*, based on an exchange with Nijō Yoshimoto concerning the *renga*, and *Kaishi-shiki*, which deals with old forms of making *waka* and *renga*. In 1395 he was relieved of his post and sent to Tōtōmi. He made up for his political downfall by engaging in vigorous literary activity during his last years, devoting himself particularly to preserving and encouraging the poetics of the Reizei school. He produced many works on poetics, among them *Wakadokoro e fushin jōjō*, *Benyōshō*, and *Rakusho roken*. In *Nan Taiheiki* (1402) he describes the traditions of the Imagawa family and defends the position he took at the time of the Ōei war.

Inawashiro Kensai (1452-1510)

Master of *waka* and *renga* poetry of the middle Muromachi period. He was a native of Aizu in eastern Japan; his original surname was Minamoto, and he went under various literary names such as Kōkansai and Sōembō.

In the early part of the Bummei era (1469-87) he studied *renga* under Shinkei, who was living in the Kantō area at the time. He also studied *waka* under Gyōe and was permitted to receive the *Kokin-denju*, a series of explanations of words and phrases in the *Kokinshū* that was guarded in secret by certain schools of poetry of the time and passed on only to select disciples.

Around 1476 he left the Kantō area and journeyed to the capital, and in 1486 he changed his name from Sōshun to Kensai. At the unusually young age of thirty-seven he was appointed to succeed Sōgi as head of the government office in charge of *renga*. In 1495 he joined with Sōgi in compiling an anthology of *renga* known as the *Shinsen Tsukubashū*, and indeed he and Sōgi may be said to have been the leaders of the *renga* world of the time. He was given the ecclesiastical rank of *hōkyō*, it being the custom at this time to honor outstanding artists, literary men, etc. with such titles.

In 1501 he left the capital and returned to the Kantō region. He was living in retirement at a place near Shirakawa when, in the following year, he received word that Sōgi had died at Hakone while on a journey. He composed a poem in *chōka* form to express his grief. Around 1504 he fell ill and went to Koga in an attempt to regain his health, but he died not many years after at the age of fifty-eight.

He left a number of works on poetry and poetic theory such as the *Shinkei Sōzu teikin, Renga entokushō, Wakakusayama, Baikunshū*, and *Keikandō*. It is clear that in his theories on poetry he was very strongly influenced by Shinkei. Other works by him include the *Usuhanazakura, Kensai zōdan, Sono no chiri*, and *Renga honshiki*. The following is an example of his *renga*; in the last section, the rays of the moon are imagined to be reflected in the dew on the oak and camellia.

> Though we call it autumn,
> its rays are now those
> of a winter moon

> Yet the rays of the moon
> are ever the same

> Wet with dew, they shine alike—
> the white oak on the ridge,
> the jeweled camellia.

JAKUREN (1139?–1202)

Poet of the early Kamakura period. His lay name was Fujiwara no Sadanaga. His father was Fujiwara no Shunkai, younger (some say elder) brother of Fujiwara no Shunzei, but around 1150 he was adopted by his uncle Shunzei. He served at court for a while, but later gave up his position as Shunzei's adopted son and took Buddhist vows around 1172.

His activities as a poet begin with the *Taira no Tsunemorike utaawase* (poetry contest at the residence of Taira no Tsunemori) in 1167. Around this time, Fujiwara no Akisuke and Fujiwara no Kiyosuke of the Rokujō school were actively joining hands with the Taira family, which had recently come to power. Before long, Jakuren was able to take part with Shunzei in poetry parties for professional poets and established a place for himself in their world. After he became a monk, he frequently traveled about the provinces performing religious austerities, but at the same time managed to continue his activities as a poet in the capital. At a poetry contest, the *roppyakuban utaawase* held at the residence of Fujiwara no Yoshitsune during the period of the compiling of the *Shin kokinshū* anthology, Jakuren, as representative of the new style of the Mikohidari school, had a famous argument on poetics with Kenshō, representative of the old-style Rokujō school.

His verse is collected in the *Jakuren Hōshi shū*. Two famous poems included in this are:

> Though I do not know
> where the dwindling spring
> is headed,
> rafts of firewood on the Uji
> slip off into the mist.

> Drops from the sudden shower
> have yet to dry
> on the evergreen leaves
> when mists begin to rise up
> in the autumn evening.

He was one of the central figures in the group of poets that gathered around Retired Emperor Gotoba and was among those chosen to compile the *Shin kokinshū* anthology, but died before the task was completed.

Jien (1155–1225)

Poet and writer of historical treatises of the early Kamakura period. Following his death he was given the posthumous name of Jichin. A son of Kampaku Fujiwara no Tadamichi, at the age of ten he began studies with Cloistered Prince Kakkai. He took Buddhist vows at twelve, changing his name first to Dōkai and then, around the age of twenty-six, to Jien. He carried out the practice known as *sennichi-nyūdō* (shutting oneself up in a temple for one thousand days to pursue religious activities) at the Mudō-ji temple on Mt. Hiei and had a hand in the management of many temples, at the same time engaging in political activity to assist his elder brother Kujō Kanezane, which brought him into contact with Minamoto no Yoritomo. At the age of thirty-seven he became head of the Tendai sect of Buddhism, a post that he held four times before he was sixty, reaching the rank of archbishop (*daisōjō*).

He first began writing *waka* when he was around nineteen and became friendly with Saigyō, who was then near the end of his life. Later, he was part of the poetry-writing group gathered at the home of his nephew Fujiwara no Yoshitsune, which included such poets as Fujiwara no Shunzei and Fujiwara no Teika. Around 1200, when Retired Emperor Gotoba began to promote large-scale poetry events, Jien figured prominently as poet or adviser, taking part in many poetry contests, poetry-making parties, "hundred-verse" parties, and the like. He has ninety-two verses—more than any other poet apart from Saigyō—in the *Shin kokinshū*.

Since, unlike Shunzei or Teika, he did not have an intense awareness of tradition, his verse is free and lively, written purely for the pleasure of writing; his collection *Shūgyoku shū* contains some commonplace pieces but also many that give elegiac expression to his thoughts on life. A typical example is the poem

> If only I could show you—
> piled up snows
> all melted away,
> little birds calling branch to branch—
> this scene in spring!

Finding himself unable to cooperate in the plan of Retired Emperor Gotoba to overthrow the shogunate, Jien began to ponder deeply on the fluctuations of the political situation and started writing a history of Japan based on his own firmly held ideals. The result was the six-chapter *Gukanshō*, completed in 1220, in which he discusses the forces underlying and the principles guiding history from the time of Emperor Jimmu up to the 1220s. The Shōkyū war gave him a shock from which he did not recover, and he was a semi-invalid from then until his death in retirement.

JōBEN (d. 1356)

Priest-poet of the period of the Northern and Southern Courts. He was a native of Kyoto and the father of Kyōun (Keiun), also a poet and priest, but his family and personal name are unknown, and little is recorded of his life. He is said to have entered the Buddhist monastery on Mt. Hiei and to have attained the highest ecclesiastical rank, that of *hōin*. In his late years he became known for his ability as a poet.

In matters of poetry he was a disciple of Nijō Tameyo, and in 1315, around the age of fifty-eight, he participated with Tameyo, Tamefuji, Ton'a, Kyōun and others in the composition of the *Hana jusshu yosegaki*. Around the end of the Kamakura period (1333) he received from Tameyo the interpretations that were handed down in secret in the Nijō school concerning the *Sandaishū*, the first three of the imperially sponsored anthologies—*Kokinshū*, *Gosenshū*, and *Shūishū*. From evidence in the *Sōanshū*, it is known that he went to Tsukushi in Kyushu sometime around the Karyaku era (1326–29), and when he was around the age of eighty he produced a commentary on the *Kokinshū* entitled *Kokin shūchū*. In 1344 he was among the poets who, at the encouragement of Ashikaga Takauji and his brother Tadayoshi, contributed to the *Kōya-san Kongōsammai-in nōkyō waka*, but after that nothing further is known of him.

While he was still living, he had one *zōka*, or miscellaneous poem, selected for inclusion in the imperially sponsored *Shoku senzaishū* and one love poem in the *Shoku goshūishū*, and he was numbered, along with Kenkō, Ton'a, and Keiun, as one of the so-called Waka Shitennō, Four Heavenly Kings of Japanese Poetry, though he scarcely equals the other members of the group. One of his best-known poems is the following:

> On leaves of the reeds
> rising from the ice
> in the inlet
> evening frost rustles;
> bay winds are blowing.

Because of the poem, he came to be known by the nickname of Ashi-no-ha-no-Jōben or "Jōben of the reed leaves." He seems to have written a relatively small number of works, and few of them have been handed down, though those that exist display a fine feeling of depth and mystery.

Jōō (1502–1555)

Poet and master of the tea ceremony of the late Muromachi period. His family name was Takeno. Starting life as a merchant in Sakai, he was later appointed lord of Inaba. At the age of thirty he became a Buddhist monk and took the name Jōō. He studied the tea ceremony with Sōri, Sōgo, and Sōchin, the *waka* with Sanjōnishi Sanetaka, incense with Shino Shōshoku, and Zen with Tairin Sōtō. In his late years he had a tea room built at Shijō in Kyoto and invited the tea adepts of Kyoto and Sakai to the tea ceremonies that he held in it. He became known as a tea master in the line of Murata Jukō and Torii Insetsu; among his pupils he numbered such outstanding exponents of the tea ceremony as Tsuda Sōkyū, Imai Sōkyū, and Sen no Rikyū from Sakai, and his collection of teabowls included many celebrated pieces. He was responsible for various innovations; for instance, he still further simplified the tea ceremony held in a four-and-one-half-mat room of rustic simplicity, making rooms of only three or two-and-one-half mats, and he is important as a link between Murata Jukō and Sen no Rikyū.

JUNTOKU-IN (1197–1242)

Eighty-fourth sovereign of Japan and poet of the Kamakura period; son of Emperor Gotoba. Coming to the throne in 1210, he reached maturity at a time when the circle of poets that had formed around Retired Emperor Gotoba was at the height of its activity, and started composing verse at the age of fourteen. He selected a collection of his own verse entitled *Juntoku-in gyoshū* and asked Retired Emperor Gotoba and Fujiwara no Teika to pass judgement on it. He also planned a massive compilation of the best of poetic criticism since ancient times, which resulted in the six-chapter *Yakumo mishō*, and was responsible for another work, *Kimpi mishō*, which dealt with practices and systems at the court since ancient times. In 1221 he relinquished the throne in favor of Emperor Chūkyō and together with Retired Emperor Gotoba plotted the overthrow of the Hojō government in Kamakura. When their armed rising (known as the Shōkyū disturbance) failed, he was exiled to the island of Sado. Even on that distant island, he continued to write verse enthusiastically until his death and produced a collection entitled *Juntoku-in on-hyakushu*, which includes appraisals by Gotoba and Teika. One of his best-known verses is:

> In the palace
> ferns reach out
> for the old eaves,
> but the past, though we reach for it,
> is too far away.

(The poem plays on the noun *shinobu*, a kind of low spreading fern, and the verb *shinobu*, "to long for.")

Kakimon-in (dates uncertain)

Poet of the period of the Northern and Southern Courts. She was a concubine of Emperor Gomurakami and, it has been surmised, the mother of emperors Chōkei and Gokameyama. Her name is not known for certain, though some accounts give it as Shōshi. She is described by some sources as the daughter of Konoe no Tsunetada, by others as the daughter of Ichijō Tsunemichi or Nijō Moromoto, though the last would seem to be correct. After the demise of Emperor Gomurakami, she was given the title Kakimon-in and shaved her head and became a Buddhist nun. Around 1377, at the request of Munenaga Shinnō, she presented a collection of her poems in one volume entitled *Kakimon-in shū*. An early manuscript of the work exists in the possession of the Maeda family, and the text is also included in the *Gunsho ruijū*. The poems by her found in the *Shin'yōshū* were all taken from this collection.

Kamo no Chōmei (1155–1216)

Poet of the early Kamakura period. He was the second son of Chōkei, priest of the Shimogamo Shrine, but lost his father at the age of seventeen or eighteen, whereupon he gave up the family vocation and devoted himself to artistic pursuits and training as the fancy took him. He studied *waka* with the monk Shun'e of the Rokujō Minamoto school and the *biwa* (a lutelike instrument) with Nakahara Yūan. Thanks to his natural gifts and hard work, by the time he was in his thirties he had become the leading poet of the Rokujō Minamoto school (Shun'e was now dead). Before long, he was discovered by Retired Emperor Gotoba and was accorded treatment quite unusual for a poet who was outside the court, being appointed a judge in the Bureau of *Waka*, which the retired emperor had established. For three years Chōmei devoted himself to untiring service at the court of Gotoba, and his poetic gifts also won recognition, but finally he took Buddhist vows and became a monk. It was an inevitable step, perhaps, for one who had always been a hermit-poet by nature.

Leaving court, he at once established himself in a hermitage at a beautiful spot overlooking the Uji River, where he spent an easy life as a recluse, his own master, composing verse and playing the *biwa*. Around 1209, he wrote a work on the theory of poetry entitled *Mumyōshō*, in which he sets down the theories of his teacher Shun'e as well as episodes concerning poets that he had heard of or witnessed, stories of poetry parties, and an account of the Mikohidari and Rokujō schools. His lasting fame, however, derives from his

Hōjōki (completed around 1212), in which he describes, from a Buddhist standpoint, various great natural disasters that he himself experienced, dwells on the unpleasantness and undependability of life in the city, and gives an account of his own search, via life in his hermitage, for tranquillity and freedom from care. The *Hōjōki* was later to serve as a model for Matsuo Bashō's *Genjūan no ki*. Chōmei also wrote the *Hosshin shū*, a collection of Buddhist tales.

KAN'AMI (1333–1384)

Nō actor and playwright of the period of the Northern and Southern Courts. His name was Yūzaki Kiyotsugu and he was born into the Yamada Sarugaku family of Iga Province; his childhood name was Miyomaru, but later in life he entered the priesthood and took the religious name Kan'ami. At first he formed a theatrical troup at Obata in Iga, but in his middle years he moved his troop to the village of Yūzaki in Yamato, forming the Yūzaki-za. Eventually his reputation as an artist attracted attention in Kyoto, and from around the Ōan era (1368–75) he began to make trips to Kyoto from time to time, giving performances of *sarugaku* at shrines and at the same time presenting dramatic entertainments of the type known as *kanjin-nō*, or benefit performances, which were open to the general public and soon won him great popularity. One such performance in particular, given at Imagumano in Kyoto in 1374, when he was forty-one, attracted the attention of Shogun Ashikaga Yoshimitsu, who was so deeply impressed by the high level of Kan'ami's art that he thereafter lavished his patronage on the actor. Under these fortunate circumstances, Kan'ami was able to continue his work, raising the *sarugaku* to a new artistic level and laying the foundations for the Nō drama as it is known today. He thus stands as one of the most important figures in the history of the Nō and of Japanese literature in general. He was not only an actor of superb talent but a playwright as well, working to refine the *sarugaku* pieces, incorporating the better elements from the *dengaku*, a dramatic form that had originally derived from harvest songs and dances, and skillfully fashioning these and other ingredients into dramatic texts of great literary beauty. To accompany these texts he created a new kind of music and dance, borrowing from the type of dance performances known as *kusemai* that were popular among the people of the period. His son Zeami was also a highly gifted actor and playwright and he carried on and brought to perfection the new art form that his father had created. According to information found in the papers of Zeami, Kan'ami was the author of the plays entitled *Komachi, Ji'nen koji, Shii no shōshō,* and others, and the *Nihyakuban yōkyoku mokuroku* attributes to him a number of other plays such as *Shirahige, Hanagatami, Matsukaze, Makiginu, Hyakuman, Tsuru,* and others.

KEIUN (Kyōun) (dates uncertain)

Priest and poet of the period of the Northern and Southern Courts. He would appear to have been born around 1293, the first year of the Einin era. The son of the eminent priest-poet Jōben, he studied the art of poetry under his father and in time entered the priesthood himself, taking the religious name Keiun, which may also be pronounced Kyōun.

He first made his appearance on the poetic scene in 1315 when, along with his father, he joined with a group of poets centering around Nijō Tameyo in composing a work called the *Hana jusshu yosegaki.* He soon gained recognition for his ability as a poet and was customarily allowed the honor of attending formal poetry matches. Later he came to be regarded as an important member of the Nijō school of poetry. It is not clear what his activities were during the troubled times of the Kemmu Restoration, but around the age of fifty-two or fifty-three he occupied, along with Ton'a, a place of great importance in the poetic world. Sometime around this time he took up residence in the Shōren-in, an important temple of the Tendai sect in Kyoto, which was customarily headed by a prince of the imperial family, and in his late years he was honored with the highest ecclesiastical rank, that of *hōin.* He was often requested by Nijō Yoshimoto and other persons of great eminence to appraise and suggest improvements in their poetry, but he seems to have felt dissatisfaction with the poetic group that centered about Ton'a and refused to allow any of his poems to be included in the two official anthologies compiled by members of that group, the *Shin senzaishū* and the *Shin shūishū.* His poems are, however, included in the *Kōya-san Kongōsammai-in nōkyō waka* sponsored by Ashikaga Tadayoshi, in the *Fūgashū,* an imperial anthology compiled in 1345, in the *Kinrai fūtaishō* of Nijō Yoshimoto, and in other works. He was ranked along with Jōben, Ton'a, and Kenkō as one of the Waka Shitennō, or Four Heavenly Kings of Japanese Poetry. He carried on the traditions of the Nijō school, which means that his poetry is conservative and carefully avoids innovation, but his works have been admired for their graveness and tone of poignant loneliness. He appears to have died around the age of seventy or more.

One of his most famous poems is the following:

> My hut on the mountain,
> the evening lark
> rises up from the fields below,
> yet I seem to hear his voice
> drifting down.

From the word *susono* ("fields below") used in the poem, he came to be known as Susono no Keiun. His poems are collected in the *Kyōun Hōin shū*, *Jōben narabini Kyōun kashū*, and *Kyōun Hōin hyakushu*.

KITABATAKE CHIKAFUSA (1293–1354)

Poet and politician of the Northern and Southern Courts period. Son of Dainagon Moroshige, he served at court and became a trusted minister of Emperor Godaigo, but in 1330 became a Buddhist monk out of a sense of responsibility for the early death of Prince Tokinaga, whom he had brought up himself. The following year the Genkō rising occurred, and he returned to office and accompanied his eldest son, Akiie, when he went to take up the post of Lord of Mutsu to which he had been appointed with the emperor's son Prince Norinaga as his superior. Subsequently Akiie was killed doing battle with Ashikaga Takauji, who had risen against the court. Chikafusa set sail from Ise together with Prince Norinaga and Prince Munenaga, but they encountered a storm and were driven ashore separately. Prince Norinaga went to Yoshino, where he succeeded Godaigo, becoming Emperor Gomurakami. It was for this emperor, who was only eleven, that Chikafusa wrote his famous historical work *Jinnō shōtōki*. He later returned to Yoshino and took command of the Southern Court's forces against Ashikaga Takauji, who was fighting for the Northern Court, and he was accorded treatment worthy of an imperial personage. He died at the age of sixty-one.

The poems that he composed as a member of the Nijō school, showing his tragic fate, are embodied in two collections, the *Shin'yōshū* and the *Rikashū*.

The *Jinnō shōtōki* in six chapters starts by explaining why Japan is the country of the gods, the origins of the country's name, its place in the world, the special nature of the national polity, and the aims of the work. Next, it deals with the formation of heaven and earth, the birth of the Japanese islands, and the myths from Amaterasu Ōmikami to Ugayafukiaezu-no-mikoto. It also gives a chronological list of the successive emperors, with accounts of their actions, seeking to establish through historical fact the legitimacy of the Southern Court. The work has considerable merit as literature, both in the author's deeply felt descriptions of various important episodes in the nation's history and in the well-reasoned way in which he discusses certain questions.

KŌGON-IN (1313–1364)

The first emperor of the Northern Court, eldest son of Emperor Gofushimi. In 1326, with the beginning of the dispute to the throne between what were to become known as the Northern and Southern Courts, he became crown prince to Emperor Godaigo. In 1331 the Genkō war broke out, and he was placed on the throne by Hōjō Takatoki. In 1333, with the fall of the Hōjōs, he was forced to abdicate and went into retirement. In 1336, at the request of Ashikaga Takauji, his young brother, Emperor Kōmyō, ascended the throne, and from then until 1351 Kōgon wielded actual power as a "retired emperor." In 1352, Emperor Gomurakami abolished the Northern Court and took Kōgon and his followers into captivity at the headquarters of the Southern Court. During this period Kōgon became a Zen monk. In 1357 he returned to Fushimi and resided at the Kōgon-in. He subsequently set up his own temple at the foot of the hills near Shūzan in Tamba, where he spent the last years of his life. Known as the Jōshōkō-ji, it is the site of his tomb. He was well versed in all kinds of learning, Chinese and Japanese, Confucian and Buddhist alike, and his surviving writings include personal journals. He was also an excellent poet, and many scholars believe that the *Fūgashū*, an imperial anthology of the Southern Court, the selection of which has traditionally been ascribed to Retired Emperor Hanazono, was in fact the work of Kōgon. The anthology contains thirty poems by Kōgon himself, while the next imperial anthology, the *Shin senzaishū*, contains more than twenty, and the *Shin shūishū* fifteen. Stylistically he follows the Kyōgoku school, one of the Three Schools of *waka* verse, which was officially adopted by the Northern Court, and he was an admirer of Kyōgoku Tamekane, whose outlook was especially progressive for his time.

KOMPARU ZENCHIKU (1405–1468)

Nō actor and playwright of the middle Muromachi period. His name was Shichirō Ujinobu; Zenchiku is his religious name. He was associated with the Emaiza, the oldest and most distinguished of the Yamato *sarugaku* troops, and worked to solidify the standing of the Komparu family school of Nō, serving in effect as its virtual founder. He was the son of Komparu

Yasaburō but was adopted as the heir of Bishaōjirō, the head of the main branch of the Komparu family, and married the daughter of the famous playwright and actor Zeami. He received instruction in the Nō drama from Zeami and Zeami's son and heir Motomasa, working diligently to master and carry on their teachings. Zeami appears to have recognized his talent and held great hopes for his future, and chose to spend the remainder of his life in Zenchiku's household when he returned to Kyoto in his late years after a period of banishment to the island of Sado.

Zenchiku was in a position to benefit from Zeami's teachings at a time when the latter's art had reached its period of fullest maturity and as a result was able to effect a revolution in the Komparu style. Zeami for his part, after the death of his son Motomasa, seems to have felt that Zenchiku was a more conscientious and orthodox transmitter of his art than was On'ami of the Kanze school. Zenchiku, whose activities were centered in the Nara area, did not perhaps enjoy such great success as On'ami, who was active in Kyoto, yet at the same time Ichijō Kanera, who held the position of *kampaku* (regent), went so far as to characterize Zenchiku as "a true master of modern times."

Zenchiku is second only to Zeami in importance as a writer of critical works on the Nō, his writings of this nature including *Shidō yōshō*, *Rokurin ichiro*, and *Shūgyoku tokka*. He also wrote over twenty plays, among them such distinguished works as *Saigyō-zakura* and *Ugetsu*. He was clearly a man of considerable learning and literary talent and associated on intimate terms with such eminent statesmen and monks of the time as Ichijō Kanera and Ikkyū Sōjun.

Kōun (Nagachika) (d. 1429)

Poet and scholar of the Northern and Southern Courts and the early Muromachi periods. The exact date of his birth is unknown. He was a member of the Fujiwara family and went by the literary name Kōun. His father, Fujiwara Iekata, was an official of the Southern Court and rose to the position of *naidaijin* (interior minister), but died at the age of thirty-six. Nagachika appears to have been born at the residence of the Southern Court on Mt. Yoshino sometime during the early part of the Shōhei era (1346–69). Both his grandfather and father were talented poets of the Nijō school, and Nagachika was trained at home in the art of poetry. He also studied in his youth under Prince Munenaga, a son of Emperor Godaigo and a distinguished poet. In 1376 he was made a *monjō hakase*, or Doctor of Letters, and compiled an anthology of poetry called the *Kōun senshū*. He also appears to have assisted Prince Munenaga in the compilation of the anthology known as the *Shin'yōshū*, a task that was completed in 1381. In 1389 he rose to the position of *naidaijin*, but in 1392, when peace was brought about between the Northern and Southern Courts, he accompanied Emperor Gokameyama to Kyoto and immediately thereafter entered the Buddhist priesthood. He would appear to have been around forty at the time. He became a disciple of Sankō Kokushi and lived in retirement in Shirakawa in the northeastern suburbs of Kyoto but in 1408 moved to a residence he called the Kōun-an at the foot of Higashiyama, and later to the Zensei-in within the compound of the Nanzen-ji. The same year, he wrote a work entitled *Kōun kuden*, in which he set forth his personal views on poetry. At this time death had removed from the literary scene such earlier luminaries as Ton'a and Nijō Yoshimoto, and poetry was in a period of decline. Nagachika was looked up to as one of the few remaining figures of true artistic stature and was invariably invited to act as a judge in poetry matches. He continued to reside in Kyoto until 1428, when he moved to a temple called the Kōun-ji in the province of Tōtōmi, and died there the following year.

In addition to his achievements as a poet, he produced textual studies and exegetical works on *The Tale of Genji*. He also wrote a work entitled *Yamato katakana katakire gige* in which he traced the origin and development of the *hiragana* and *katakana* syllabaries, discussed the Chinese characters from which they derived, and studied Japanese phonology. The earliest work of its kind, it exercised a profound influence upon Edo period studies of the syllabaries.

Kyūsei (1284–1378)

Renga poet of the late Kamakura and Northern and Southern Courts periods. He studied *renga* with Zenna, the great forerunner of the noncourtly school of poets, and was the driving force behind the vogue enjoyed by the *renga* during the Northern and Southern Courts period. During his thirties he is said to have composed one thousand verses in honor of the gods before the Kitano Shrine, and a *hokku* he wrote at that time runs:

> The clear night
> with its wind and moonlight
> wears on.

but nothing is known of his life for a period of twenty years after this. He suddenly reappears, at the age of fifty-five, as author of part of a *renga* composed at the home of Toki Yoritō in 1339. Thereafter he became active as a *renga* poet: he became friendly with Nijō Yoshimoto and from then on was one of the leading figures in the world of *renga*, winning great favor both among the court nobles and the samurai.

His influence is strong in *Hekiren shō* and *Renri hishō*, and *Ōan shinshiki*, in which he and Yoshimoto collaborated, providing a model for *renga* for centuries to come. He also cooperated in the compilation of the *Tsukubashū*, the first imperially recognized anthology of *renga*. He died at the age of ninety-four, and was revered thereafter as the first master of the art of the *renga*. With his aptness in linking verses, the distinction of his tone, his freshness, he combines the best qualities of both the *haiku* and the *waka*, providing an ideal model of what the *renga* should be.

Mujū (1226–1312)

Compiler of collections of popular tales during the middle Kamakura period. He is said to have been a descendant of Kajiwara Kagetoki. He became a monk at the age of seventeen and traveled to Kamakura, Kyoto, and Nara studying various aspects of Buddhist teaching and practice. At the Tōfuku-ji temple in Kyoto, he is said to have been initiated into the Tendai tradition of Esoteric Buddhism by the celebrated priest Shōitsu Kokushi (Ben'en). Ben'en, who propounded such new theories as the blending of Zen Buddhism and Esoteric Buddhism and the essential identity of the three teachings of Buddhism, Confucianism, and Shinto, exerted a strong influence on Mujū. From 1263 onward, Mujū devoted himself mainly to the instruction of the common people and published a number of collections such as *Shasekishū*, *Shōzaishū*, and *Zōdanshū* before his death at the age of eighty-six. The title of *Shasekishū*, which means "Grains of Sand and Stones Collection," is intended to suggest the moral that grasping after money is like collecting grains of sand and that amassing precious gems is like picking up stones and polishing them. The tales are set down just as he remembered them, the aim being to make the ordinary people realize the laws of causation, escape from the cycle of birth and death, and thereby enter nirvana. The whole work, which extends to five chapters, is a mixture of abstract Buddhist doctrines and crude popular tales.

Munenaga Shinnō (Prince Munenaga) (1318–1385)

Poet of the Northern and Southern Courts period. Son of Emperor Godaigo, he became head (*zasu*) of the Tendai sect of Buddhism in 1330. Following the Genkō war he was exiled to Sanuki. Later he returned to secular life and spent nearly forty years as a general on the side of the Southern Court, working to open up the province of Shinano and other parts of the Chūbu district. In 1374 he returned to Yoshino, the headquarters of the Southern Court, and gathered nine hundred poems that he had written in the meantime in a collection entitled *Rikashū*. He became one of the leading figures in the world of poetry at the Southern Court during the Tenju era (1375–81) in the reign of Emperor Chōkei and was a judge at the poetry contest *Nanchō gohyakuban utaawase*. In 1381, along with Kōun and others he set about compiling the anthology *Shin'yōshū*, which was later adopted as an imperial anthology. His poetic style is basically that of the Nijō school, plain and elegant, but many of his poems give poignant expression to the feelings of the warrior doing battle far from home. Typical of his work are the following two poems:

> To think—
> I, who never so much as handled
> the catalpa bow,
> from now on
> must keep it ever by my side!

> Wild geese northward homing,
> why do they hurry so?
> Do they not know the hills of home
> hold no such memories
> for them as for me?

Musō Soseki (1275–1351)

Zen monk of the late Kamakura period. He was born in Ise and raised in the province of Kai, entering the priesthood at the age of eight. At first he studied the doctrines of the Tendai and Shingon sects, but later turned to Zen and took instruction under a Chinese master named I-shan I-ning (Japanese: Ichizan Ichinei) and Kōhō Kennichi, becoming the Dharma heir of the latter. Although he does not seem to have had any desire to associate himself with the men in power at the time, his warm and tolerant disposition and profound learning attracted the attention of such political leaders as Hōjō Sadatoki, Emperor Godaigo, Ashikaga Takauji and his brother Tadayoshi, and emperors Kōgon and Kōmyō of the Northern Court. Three times during his lifetime he was honored as a *kokushi* (national master), with the titles Musō, Shōkaku, and Shinsō, and after his death the Ashikaga shoguns continued to pay him respect, honoring him four more times with the title of *kokushi*, until he became known as the National Master of Seven Reigns. He was twice the head of the Nanzen-ji in Kyoto and founded the Erin-ji in Kai, the Rinsen-ji in Kyoto, and other temples. He persuaded Ashikaga Takauji to establish a temple and pagoda in each of the provinces of the country to pray for the souls of those who had been killed in battle and also prevailed upon him to found the Tenryū-ji in the western suburbs of Kyoto, a temple dedicated to the repose of the soul of Emperor Godaigo, of which Musō Soseki became the first head. He had many eminent disciples, such as Gidō Shūshin, Zekkai Chūshin, and others who became leaders of the great Zen temples of Kyoto and Kamakura. All were men of learning and skilled writers of Chinese verse and prose, and occupy a prominent place in the literary movement known as *Gozan bungaku*.

In addition to his activities as a religious leader, Musō Soseki played an important role in attempts to reconcile the differencies between Takauji and his brother Tadayoshi and to negotiate a settlement in the disagreement between the Northern and Southern Courts. He was also a lover of nature and constructed beautiful gardens in such temples as the Eihō-ji at Kokeizan in the province of Mino and the Saihō-ji in Kyoto, making an important contribution to the development of Zen style landscape gardening. A profound scholar of Zen learning, he was also skilled in writing Chinese verse and Japanese *waka* and *renga*; his *waka* are included in the *Shin senzaishū* and other collections, and his *renga* are found in the *Tsukubashū*. His writings include a work on the principles of Zen, which he wrote in simple Japanese at the request of Ashikaga Tadayoshi, entitled *Muchū mondō*, as well as the *Rinsen-ji kakun*, *Musō hōgo*, *Musō Kokushi wakashū*, and others.

Myōe (1173–1232)

Early Kamakura period Buddhist scholar and priest of the Kegon sect. His family name was Itō; he is often referred to by his posthumous name, Kōben. He was born in the district of Arita in the province of Kii of a samurai family, but lost both his parents at an early age. At the age of eight he entered the Jingo-ji, a temple at Mt. Takao northwest of Kyoto, and studied under the eminent priest Mongaku. At the age of fifteen he formally entered the priesthood under the direction of another eminent priest, Jōgaku. At the Tōdai-ji in Nara he received instruction in the *Gusokukai*, the 250 precepts that a monk of the rank of *biku* is required to observe, and studied the *Kusharon*, an important work of Buddhist philosophy. He then returned to Kyoto and studied the scriptural interpretations of the Shingon sect at the Ninna-ji, and the *Kegon gokyōshō*, a work on the teachings of the Kegon sect, under Keiga of the Kegon-in. At the age of seventeen he received instruction in the *Bukkyō jūhachidō* from Jōgaku, and the following year instruction in the *Kongōkai* from Kyōnen. Later he journeyed to the Tōdai-ji once more to receive instruction in the scriptural interpretations of the Kegon sect. Thus his youth was marked by intense study and the observation of strict rules of discipline.

In the autumn of 1195, in his twenty-second year, he left Jingo-ji and embarked upon a journey through the province of Kii. He lived for a time in a rude hut on Mt. Shiragami and later in a similar hut on Mt. Ikadachi, practicing austerities and offering prayers before a statue of Śākyamuni.

In 1206, at the age of thirty-three, he was presented by Retired Emperor Gotoba with a plot of land at Toganoo, near his old temple of Jingo-ji in Takao, where he restored an earlier temple and named it Kōzan-ji. By this time he was becoming known far and wide for his piety and learning. He seldom stayed long in one place, however, but traveled about, building huts on the tops of mountains, which he called *rennyadai*, "forest platforms," where he would spend day and night sitting in mediation or reciting scriptures. Later he returned to Toganoo, where he built a hut that he called the Sekisui-in, living there for a time in retirement, but later moved to various other locations in Kamo and Toganoo. Finally, at the age of fifty-one, he settled in a hut on Mt. Ryōga back of the Kōzan-ji at Toganoo, where he sat in meditation and practiced concentration. At this time he composed a number of poems in Japanese and also lectured on the *Bommō bosatsu kaibon*, a text describing the ten major and forty-eight minor commandments set forth in the *Bommō-kyō*, as well as on other works, but he collapsed from the effects of severe fasting and, after giving parting instructions to his disciples, died at the age of fifty-nine.

Myōe is generally known as a representative of the Nara sects of Buddhism and particularly as a restorer of the Kegon sect, though he chose to live the life of a hermit-saint, refusing to accept any ecclesiastical rank or office. Nevertheless, it is said that in his later years he was very highly respected by many members of the court and the nobility. In the great emphasis he put upon faith, he may be said to represent in its purest form the Buddhism typical of the early Kamakura period. He did his very best to understand and carry out the teachings of Śākyamuni and, in the spirit of a bodhisattva, to assist all other beings to attain salvation. He devoted his entire life to carrying out the practices of Buddhism as he understood them, displaying the utmost intensity of devotion and never once deviating from his goal.

Many of his Japanese poems in *waka* form are marked by a tone of innocence and freedom and are written in language that is very easy to understand, though others deal with doctrinal matters and present greater difficulties in interpretation. The *Shin chokusenshū* and other imperially sponsored anthologies contain a total of twenty-two poems from his hand. The following is an example of his poetry:

> From clouds coming forth
> to keep me company,
> the winter moon:
> the wind—how it stings!
> the snow—how cold it is!

His numerous writings include the *Saijaron* in three chapters, the *Kegon yuishin gishaku* in two chapters, the *Yume no ki, Myōe shōnin wakashū*, and over forty other titles.

Myōkū (dates uncertain)

Priest of the Tendai sect in the Kamakura period. He is noted as a composer of *enkyoku*, "banquet songs," a type of musical entertainment popular among the warriors and aristocracy of Kamakura and Muromachi times. Very little is known of his life, but it would appear that he was born around the beginning of the Kangen era (1243). There is rather strong evidence to suggest that Myōkū may be identical with another well-known composer of *enkyoku* named Gekkō, and if this is true, it would mean that Myōkū was still alive in the third year of the Bumpo era (1319) and hence lived to be close to eighty or more.

Myōkū is famous both as the originator of the *enkyoku* form and the one who did most to collect and preserve works in the form. He composed both lyrics and musical settings and is responsible for compiling nearly all the collections of *enkyoku* that have been handed down. Though something like the *enkyoku* may already have been in existence in his time, he invested it with new interest and worked to develop it as a serious art form, an achievement for which he deserves due recognition.

At present a total of 175 *enkyoku* have been preserved in nine collections and seventeen folios. Of these nine collections, the four collections compiled in 1301 and entitled *Enkyokushū, Enkyokushō, Shinkyokushō*, and *Kyūhakushū*, and the *Shūkashū* compiled in 1306, all appear to be the work of Myōkū. The *Shūkashō* compiled in 1314, and the *Besshi tsuikakyoku* and *Gyokurin'en* compiled in 1319 appear to have been compiled by Gekkō, though, as stated above, these two persons may in fact be identical. Of particular importance are the one hundred songs contained in the first four compilations mentioned above. Of these, about eighty are the work of Myōkū, and most of the remainder by Gekkō, with two or three attributed to other composers.

Another work compiled by Myōkū entitled *Sen'yō mokuroku* has been preserved. It consists of Myōkū's prefaces to the first four compilations mentioned above and to the *Shūkashū*, as well as tables of contents of all the compilations listed above.

Nakatsukasa no Naishi (dates uncertain)

Poet and diarist of the late Kamakura period. She was the daughter of a courtier who served as head of the *Kunaishō*, the Department of the Imperial Household; she herself was a lady-in-waiting to Emperor Fushimi and held a post in the *naishi-no-tsukasa*. She was a talented writer of poetry, and two of her works are included in the *Gyokuyō wakashū*. She left a diary, known as the *Nakatsukasa no Naishi nikki*, which covers a period of some thirteen years from 1280, when the future Emperor Fushimi was still heir apparent, until 1292, when the author's illness led her to leave the service of the emperor and retire to her own home. The diary is concerned mainly with the affairs of the court and records the feelings and reactions of a woman of the palace to the turbulent political events of the period and the more intimate occurrences of her private life. It would appear that she wrote the diary late in life, when she was already an old woman and was suffering from illness.

Nichiren (1222–1282)

Buddhist monk and founder of the Nichiren sect in the middle Kamakura period. He was born in the province of Awa, in present-day Chiba Prefecture. He entered the priesthood at the age of eleven, and at seventeen shaved his head and became a monk in the monastery of Mt. Hiei, the headquarters of the Tendai sect, devoting himself to the study of Buddhist doctrine. In time he arrived at the conviction that the foundation of all Tendai teaching had originally been the *Hokekyō* (Lotus Sutra), though this sutra had come to be neglected in the Tendai sect, as well as in the Shingon, Ritsu, Zen, and Amidist sects, which he felt had fallen into erroneous ways as a result. He therefore determined to devote all his energies to upholding and propagating the teachings of the Lotus Sutra, devising the so-called seven-character *daimoku* (mantra) *Namu Myōhō Rengekyō*, "Homage to the Lotus of the Wonderful Law," which he repeated and taught his followers to repeat, thus founding a new sect of Buddhism known as the Nichiren sect. He declared that the nation was suffering from endless natural disasters and social upheavals precisely because it failed to observe the teachings of the Lotus and predicted that Japan would suffer the even greater disaster of foreign invasion if it did not quickly abandon its erroneous ways and return to the Lotus, writing a work entitled the *Risshō ankokuron* in which he expressed these ideas and urged that steps be taken to protect the nation from foreign enemies and inner turmoil. His attacks upon other sects of Buddhism and his self-assertiveness, however, only aroused the animosity of the Kamakura shogunate. Later when, as though in fulfillment of his prophecies, the Mongols attempted to invade Japan, he once again urged the shogunate to reconsider his advice, but, having incurred the enmity of the other Buddhist sects, he found himself faced with increasing difficulties and was finally banished to the island of Sado. There he continued to be more active than ever, devoting himself to preaching and writing. He was pardoned and permitted to return to Kamakura in 1274, but he rejected all offers to make peace with the other sects and instead retired to Mt. Minobu in the province of Kai. In time, weakened by his long years of hardship and struggle, he fell ill and left his mountain retreat, taking up residence in the province of Musashi, where he died in 1282 at the age of sixty.

Nichiren was a highly prolific writer, over a hundred works from his hand being extant. Among these, the *Risshō ankokuron* already mentioned and a similar work of political nature, the *Shugo kokkaron*, are written in Chinese, employing an elegant and highly formal style marked by the frequent use of parallel phrases. In other works written in Japanese, such as the *Minobusan gosho* and *Shuju onfurumai gosho*, however, he employs a pure and simple style almost devoid of parallelisms; the latter in particular is a masterpiece of literary style, imbued throughout with a spirit of elevation and intensity that is the reflection of Nichiren's passionate religious faith. Other works of importance among his numerous writings are the *Kanshin honzonshō*, *Kaimokushō*, and *Senjishō*.

Nijō Yoshimoto (1320–1388)

Waka and *renga* poet of the Northern and Southern Courts period. He served Emperor Godaigo together with his father, Kampaku Michihira, who was also a poet with a deep interest in *renga*, but following the Kemmu Restoration he served Retired Emperor Kōgon and five other emperors of the Northern Court and was four times *kampaku, dajōdaijin*, and *sesshō*. He was also on close terms with successive Ashikaga shoguns and was extremely active politically. However, he is far more noteworthy for the works he wrote with the aim of reviving various court rituals and ceremonies and preserving traditions of art and learning and for his role as a leader in the cultural field, especially the fields of *waka* and *renga*. A work on ceremonial is *Hyakuryō kun'yō shō*, while court ritual is described in *Jōji ni'nen onmari no ki*, and there is reason to believe that he is also the author of *Masu-kagami*. He studied *waka* with Ton'a of the Nijō school and took part in both official and private poetry parties as well as writing works of poetic criticism such as *Gumon kenchū* and *Kinrai fūtai shō*. *Mochizake utaawase*, a collection from a contest of humorous verse (*kyōka*) shows the lighter side of his character, while *Kojima no kuchizusami*, an account of a journey accompanying the emperor to the province of Mino, shows the richness of his use of language.

Nevertheless, it is the *renga* that lies at the heart of his literary activities. He took up the *renga*, under his father's influence, while he was in his teens and showed an almost eccentric preoccupation with the form right through until the last years of his life. Around the age of twenty he studied with the *renga* poet Kyūsei and was only twenty-five when he wrote an organized treatise on the form entitled *Hekirenshō*. In 1356 he compiled the anthology *Tsukubashū*, the first quasi-imperial anthology of *renga*, and in 1372 drew up *Ōan shinshiki*, a new set of rules for the composition of *renga*. Both these major undertakings, which were achieved with the cooperation of Kyūsei, helped establish the literary respectability of the *renga* and became authoritative works for later ages. He also wrote a large number of other works such as *Tsukuba mondō* on the theory of the *renga*, in which he stressed the blending of the element of amusement proper to the *renga* and the classical poetic profundity that came from the *waka* and thus showed a direction for the *renga* to develop. A well-known *hokku* by Yoshimoto is:

> Though the sun has set,
> on red leaves still remaining
> an evening glow.

Reizei Tamehide (d. 1372)

Poet of the late Kamakura period. He was a member of the Reizei branch of the Fujiwara family; his religious name was Shūtaku. He was the second son of Reizei Tamesuke, the founder of the Reizei line and school of poetry, but because his elder brother Tameshige died at an early age, he became the head of the family.

In the troubles accompanying the Kemmu Restoration, he was deprived of his lands, but in the ninth month of the third year of the Kemmu era (1336) he accompanied the military leader Ashikaga Takauji on a visit to the Sumiyoshi Shrine and presented poems to celebrate the occasion and in 1344 he was among the poets participating in the *Kōya-san Kongōsammai-in butsumyō waka*, contributing a set of one hundred poems entitled *Jōwa hyakushu*. Along with Nijō Tamemoto and Ōgimachi Kinkage, he was chosen to act as a *yoriudo*, or official in charge of selecting poems, in preparation for the compilation of the anthology known as the *Fūgashū*.

In 1350 he participated in the *Gen'e tsuitō waka*. He was also invited to participate in the *Embun hyakushu*, but he declined, perhaps because he was on bad terms with Nijō Tamesada at this time and the *Embun hyakushu* was largely dominated by members of the Nijō school. It is certainly significant that the *Shin senzaishū*, an official anthology compiled by Nijō Tamesada, does not contain a single poem by Reizei Tamehide.

After the death of Tamesada in 1360, however, Tamehide established friendly relations with Tamesada's cousin Nijō Tameaki, arranged for his own eldest son, Tamekuni, to become the adopted son of Tameaki, and as a result gained a position of greater importance in poetry circles of the time. From 1364 on he acted as teacher in the art of poetry to Shogun Ashikaga Yoshiakira. He was dispatched by Sesshō Nijō Yoshimoto to act as Yoshimoto's envoy and journey to Fujisawa to call on the monk Yūa, and he also held discussions on the history and theory of poetry with Ashikaga Motouji, the *Kantō kanryō*, or governor of the eastern regions. In addition, he was invited from time to time to take part in poetry meetings held by the court in Kyoto, and in fact, both in reputation and actual influence, was the most prominent personage in the poetic world of the period.

Perhaps because he was not of very robust constitution, he did not advance very rapidly in official position, though from 1362 on he held the court rank of Junior Second Rank and the office of *chūnagon* (middle counselor). His eldest grandson, Tamemasa, succeeded him as head of the Reizei family when he died in 1372 around the age of seventy or more.

Tamehide received instruction in poetry from his father, Tamesuke, and was rather liberal in his views, believing that, of the so-called ten styles of *waka* poetry, one should be free to choose the style that fits one's own personality best. He placed great emphasis upon tone and emotional content and particularly admired the style of Sone no Yoshitada and the poets of the *Shin kokinshū*, displaying great taste and intelligence in his critical views. His works are preserved in such official anthologies as the *Fūgashū* and *Shin shūi-shū*, private anthologies such as the *Goyōshū*, and other works such as the *Shin Tamatsushima utaawase, Nenjūgyōji utaawase*, and *Tamehide, Tametsuna, Tamehisa eiwaka*, and in various works by Imagawa Ryōshun. His works include a large number of descriptive pieces that are remarkable for their acute sensitivity. He was trusted and confided in by such prominent persons of the time as Ashikaga Yoshiakira and Nijō Yoshimoto and was widely respected even by followers of the rival Nijō school of poetry such as Kenkō and Ton'a. His disciples included Imagawa Ryōshun and the *renga* or linked-verse poet Bontōan. The following is an example of his poetry:

> "Once the fifth month arrives . . ."
> I thought,
> but alas, I have yet to hear
> the voice
> of the cuckoo.

Rᴇɪᴢᴇɪ Tᴀᴍᴇsᴜᴋᴇ (1263–1328)

Poet of the late Kamakura period; son of Fujiwara no Tameie and Abutsu-ni; founder of the Reizei family. At court, he rose to the position of Senior Second Rank and the post of *gon-chūnagon*. This was the period of rivalry between the Nijō and Kyōgoku schools of verse; Tamesuke was at first influenced by Kyōgoku Tamekane, but gradually developed an independent style of his own. He spent a large part of his time in the Kantō district, where he gave instruction in poetry to the samurai.

A collection of his verse is entitled *Gon-Chūnagon Tamesuke-kyō shū*, (or *Fujigayatsu waka shū*), and he also compiled the anthologies *Shūi fūtaishū* and *Ryūfū waka shō*. He also seems to have had a hand in drawing up *Fuji-ga-yatsu shikimoku*, a collection of conventions for writing *renga*, and made many transcriptions of the classics in his own hand.

Saigyō (1118–1190)

Poet and priest of the late Heian and early Kamakura period. His name before he entered the priesthood was Satō Norikiyo, and he later went by the religious names En'i and Saigyō.

At an early age he was given the office of *sahyōe-no-jō*, lieutenant of the imperial guards of the left, and served as a *hokumen no bushi*, or guard, in the palace of Retired Emperor Toba. It would appear that during his youth he became an expert in the arts of war. As a writer of Japanese poetry, he displayed great admiration for Minamoto no Toshiyori and counted among his poet friends Fujiwara no Shunzei.

He entered the priesthood at the age of twenty-two. Various motives have been suggested for this step, among them disappointment in a love affair with a lady of noble station and disillusionment with the political situation of the time, and his works in fact include passionate love poems and outspoken reflections. It would appear, however, that from an early age he had desired to embrace the religious life, and for the remainder of his years he devoted himself to the practice of Buddhism and the writing of poetry.

For a while after entering the priesthood, he lived in various temples and humble retreats in the vicinity of the capital. The poetry of this period is deeply imbued with romantic spirit and a devotion to beauty. At the age of twenty-nine he appears to have set off on the first of many journeys to northern Japan. At other periods he seems to have spent much time in the vicinity of Mt. Kōya, the headquarters of the Shingon sect of Buddhism to which he belonged. He joined with Jakuchō and other priests of the time in forming a poetry circle, and many of his outstanding poems of this period are preserved in the *Kikigaki zanshū*. Before long, he became involved with poetry circles in the capital as well, exchanging poems with Jakuren, Jien, and other young poets belonging to the group centered about Fujiwara no Shunzei. At the age of sixty-one he compiled a collection of his life works entitled *Sankashū*.

In 1180, when fighting broke out between the Taira and Minamoto clans, Saigyō moved his residence to Ise. There he conducted poetry contests with the Shinto priests of the Ise Shrine and acted as a teacher in the writing of poetry. A record of his remarks on poetry at that time has been preserved under the title *Saigyō shōnin danshō*. In his late years he enjoyed great acclaim and developed a distinct and highly matured style of his own. The *Shin kokinshū*, an imperially sponsored anthology compiled shortly after his death, contains ninety-four of his poems, making him the best-represented poet in the anthology, and his works also exercised a profound influence upon Matsuo Bashō, the great *haiku* poet of the seventeenth century. The following examples are representative of his work:

> If only there were
> someone else
> willing to bear this loneliness—
> side by side we'd build our huts
> for winter in a mountain village.

> Did I ever think
> in old age
> I'd cross it once again?
> So long I've lived,
> Saya-Between-the-Hills![1]

Sanjōnishi Sanetaka (1455–1537)

Poet of the late Muromachi period. A gentle and sincere courtier, he won the confidence of emperors Gotsuchimikado and Gokashiwabara and played an important role in shoring up the economy of the imperial household and restoring the old rituals at the court; this, together with his work in promoting the study of Japanese literature and history, won him respect as the leading cultural figure of the day. In 1506, when he had attained the post of minister of the interior, he retired from public service and in 1516 took Buddhist vows. The remaining twenty years until his death at the age of eighty-two were devoted to cultural and religious activities.

He studied *waka* with Asukai Masachika and left two collections of verse, *Setsugyokushū* and *Chōsetsushū*, as well as a verse-diary, *Saishōsō* a product of his old age. He also wrote many *renga*, and cooperated with Sōgi and others in the compilation of the *Shinsen Tsukubashū*, a *renga* anthology. Outstanding among his achievements were the guidance he gave to Sōgi and others, his literary commentaries such as the *Genji monogatari sairyūshō* and *Man'yōshū ichiyōshō*, his work in gathering together, transcribing, and examining the authenticity of varying versions of classical works that had been scattered during the Ōnin war, and the laying of the foundations for the movement to revive interest in the Japanese classics. He was also well versed in such Chinese classics as the *Book of Changes*, *Shih chi*, and *Han shu* and listened to lectures on the verse of Tu Fu and other Chinese poets, promoting the

---

1. A long winding road up over the mountains in present-day Shizuoka Prefecture.

tendency for a blending of *waka* and Chinese verse styles. He is also known as a competent calligrapher, and made several transcriptions of *The Tale of Genji*. The journal *Sanetaka-kō ki*, which he kept from the age of twenty until he was eighty-one, provides invaluable information not only for the historian but also for the student of the history of medieval literature.

Sнiнкеі (1406–1475)

Poet of *waka* and *renga* in the middle Muromachi period. He became head priest of the Jūjūshin-in temple in Kyoto and attained the rank of *gon-daisōzu* (acting bishop). He became a pupil of Shōtetsu, a poet of the Reizei school. He studied *renga* with Takayama Sōzei, but he had a special admiration for Asayama Bontō. From sometime around the age of forty he was an established *renga* poet and by his fifties he had become the central figure in the world of contemporary *renga*. In 1463 he wrote *Sasamegoto* and frequently took part in poetry gatherings held at the homes of distinguished figures of the day. Around this time he wrote the first letter of the collection *Tokorodokoro hentō* and produced a volume of poems selected by himself and entitled *Shin gyokushū*. Just before the outbreak of the Ōnin war he left Kyoto and went to Ise, and later went on to Musashi in the Kantō district, where he spent the closing years of his life. During these years he produced the second and third letters of *Tokorodokoro hentō*, works on the art of *renga* such as *Shiyōshō*, and collections of verse and commentaries on his own work such as *Renga hyakku-zuke* and *Shibakusa no uchi iwahashi*. In 1469 he participated along with Sōgi in *Kawagoe senku*, a *renga* meeting sponsored by Ōta Dōshin. He also served as a judge at poetry contests held in Edo Castle. He wrote *Oi no kurigoto*, as well as many collections of *renga* and *waka*.

His *waka* have an individuality beneath their surface purity and grace, but his most significant work is in his *renga*, his special qualities being especially apparent in those profoundly suggestive verses in which he applies the traditions of the *Shin kokinshū* to the world of the *renga* and in those grave verses in which he embodies his profound observation of human life. His writing on the art of the *renga* ranks with Zeami's writing on the Nō as one of the twin peaks of artistic criticism of medieval Japan, and he had a profound influence on *renga* poets of the following generation such as Sōgi and Inawashiro Kensai.

Shinran (1173-1262)

Buddhist monk and founder of the Jōdo Shinshū sect in the early Kamakura period. He was born in Kyoto, the son of Hino Arinori, a high official in the office of the empress dowager. He was orphaned at an early age and at eight shaved his head and entered the religious life, becoming a disciple of Jien and taking the name Han'en. Later he entered the monastery on Mt. Hiei, spending some twenty years studying Buddhism and practicing religious austerities. Failing to gain enlightenment, he left the mountain and at the age of thirty became a disciple of Hōnen, the proponent of the Amidist doctrines of the Jōdo (Pure Land) sect. Changing his name to Shakkū, he became a fervent follower of Jōdo, practicing the *nembutsu*, or ritual intoning of the name of the Buddha Amida, which characterized the sect. In 1207 the older sects of Buddhism launched a vigorous movement for the suppression of the practitioners of the *nembutsu*, and Hōnen and his disciples were condemned to punishment. Shinran was forced to return to lay life, being given the name Fujii Yoshinobu, and was exiled to the province of Echigo.

The change in environment and way of life brought about in him a profound spiritual revolution. He no longer concerned himself with such outward distinctions as priest and layman, but gave himself up wholly to spiritual endeavor, taking a wife and calling himself Gutoku, the Stupid Priest. In 1211 he was pardoned and around this time changed his name to Shinran. He did not return to Kyoto immediately, however, but spent some ten years in the province of Hitachi in the east, continuing his studies of Jōdo and preaching, mainly among the farmers and members of the lower samurai class. At the same time he wrote a work in six chapters entitled the *Kyōgyō shinshō* in which he set forth his teachings and in time founded the Jōdo Shinshū, or True Sect of Jōdo, which he conceived of as a faith specifically intended for the common people. After traveling about the Kantō region, he returned to Kyoto, but did not take up any fixed residence, living, it is said, a life of great poverty. He gave all his effort to writing doctrinal works, at the same time dispatching letters of encouragement and direction to his followers in the eastern provinces, expanding upon the teachings of his master Hōnen, and extending the faith in new directions. His teachings had a great influence upon the men of his time, particularly his emphasis upon the need for absolute reliance upon the saving power of the Buddha Amida and that even the evilest of men may be saved through such reliance.

In 1272, not long after his death at the age of eighty-nine, his descendant Kakunyo founded a temple at Higashiyama in Kyoto called the Hongan-ji, which became the head temple of the Jōdo Shinshū sect.

Shinran's writings include the *Kyōgyō shinshō* mentioned above, as well as the *Sanjō wasan, Jōgai wasan, Yuishinshō bun'i, Jōdo bunrui jūshō, Gutōsho,* and others.

S{HŪA} (dates uncertain)

Renga poet of the early Muromachi period. He was a disciple of Kyūsei and, along with his teacher and Nijō Yoshimoto, is counted as one of the Sanken, Three Worthies, of the *renga* world. In spite of this fact, very little is known of his life. In 1355 he participated in the composition of the *senku* (thousand-verse) *renga* at the Nijō Palace, and twenty-two verses by him are included in the *Tsukubashū,* a *renga* anthology compiled in 1356. In the second month of the fifth year of Ōan (1372) he composed a *dokugin hyakuin,* or poem of "a hundred links by a single poet." He also assisted Nijō Yoshimoto in formulating the rules for *renga* composition. At one point he was invited to journey to Kyushu by Imagawa Sadayo (Ryōshun), who was serving as *tandai* (military governor) of the island at the time, an invitation that he accepted. He was also ordered to add critical comments to the poems written by Shogun Ashikaga Yoshimitsu. His style enjoyed great popularity at the time, and after the death of his teacher, Kyūsei, he was looked upon as the greatest living master of *renga* composition. He thus seems to have been active for a period of some twenty or more years beginning in 1355, and died probably in 1376 or 1377.

Following the fashion of the day, he worked to develop his own style of verses or links, striving to concentrate the greatest amount of beauty and depth within the compass of a single verse and exploiting to the fullest the felicities and technical devices typical of *waka* poetry.

S{ŌGI} (1421–1502)

Renga poet of the middle Muromachi period. He first became interested in *renga* around the age of thirty and studied with Takayama Sōzei, Shinkei, and Senjun. He also studied *waka* with Asukai Eiga and ancient matters with Ichijō Kaneyoshi (Kanera) and his son. Little is known of his youth, but he was winning recognition by around the time he was forty. To avoid the fighting during the Ōnin war, he spent eight years in various parts of the Kantō district, during which time he wrote two works on the theory of the *renga* entitled *Chōroku bumi* and *Azuma mondō* and improved his own poetic prowess to the point where he was represented alongside Shinkei in Ōta Dōshin's *Kawagoe senku*. At the age of fifty he received the *Kokin-denju*, special instruction in the art of the *Kokinshū*, from Tō no Tsuneyori, and wrote a work entitled *Kokinshū ryōdo monjo*. This, together with *Mishima senku*, a series of one thousand *renga* composed in Mishima entirely by himself, established his position as a classical scholar and *renga* poet. Returning to Kyoto in 1473, he lived in a residence known as Shugyoku-an and devoted himself to the writing of verse. The work he produced included a first collection of his own verse, *Wasuregusa*, a second collection entitled *Wakuraba*, *Chikurin shō*, a selection of verses by seven wise senior poets, and *Oi no sugami*, a commentary on selected verses from the *Chikurin shō*. He gave lectures on such classics as *Kokinshū*, *Ise monogatari*, and *Genji monogatari*, and passed on the *Kokin-denju* (secret, orally transmitted traditions concerning interpretation of some parts of the *Kokinshū*) to Sanjōnishi Sanetaka, Shogun Yoshihisa, Prince Kunitaka, and such noted samurai as the Uesugi family (lords of Echigo), and the Ōuchi family (lords of Suō). At the age of sixty-seven he produced his chief work, *Minase sangin hyakuin*, and was appointed *Kitano kaisho renga bugyō* (the highest official rank available to a *renga* poet). At the age of seventy-four, he completed a major undertaking, the compilation of the *Shinsen tsukubashū*, and compiled a third collection of his own verse, entitled *Shitagusa*.

He was one of the leading figures in the culture that flourished during the rule of Shogun Ashikaga Yoshimitsu, an expert not only in poetry but in Shintoism, Chinese verse, calligraphy, and the appreciation of incense (there were even playful references in verse to his beard, which was perpetually soaked with the fragrance of incense). A thoroughly mature, well-rounded personality, he did invaluable work in preserving and propagating the national traditions of literature and beauty during an age of civil war and cultural impoverishment. The technical dexterity with language that he learned from Sōzei and the profound understanding of life that he acquired from Shinkei blend in his work and show the *renga* form at its finest.

Sōson Shinnō (Prince Munetaka) (1242–1274)

Poet of the middle Kamakura period. Eldest son of Emperor Gosaga, he was made shogun at the age of ten by the Kamakura shogunate and held the post for fifteen years, but in 1266 was relieved of the title under suspicion of insurgency and returned to Kyoto. From then on he led a melancholy life until the death of his father, Retired Emperor Gosaga, in 1272, when he became a Buddhist monk. He himself died two years later at the age of thirty-two.

Some thirty-one hundred of the prince's poems are extant, including the *Keigyokushū* collection. Most of the poems were composed to a given theme, but the sincerity of feeling is patent, and the straightforwardness and plainness of his style (some of his verse recalls the *Man'yōshū*) gives it great distinction among the other verse of the day. The work composed following his return to Kyoto betrays his strong feeling of anguish at having been wrongly suspected. He is an interesting figure, similar to Minamoto no Sanetomo, as a young Kamakura shogun who was also a poet.

TAKAYAMA SŌZEI (?–1455)

Renga poet of the middle Muromachi period. Originally a samurai in the service of the powerful Yamana family, he studied *waka* with Shōtetsu and *renga* with Asayama Bontō. At the time of Bontō's death, he was already living the life of a recluse on Mt. Kōya, and the following year he wrote *Shoshin guei shū*, in which he set down the poetic theories of his teacher. He subsequently went to Kyoto, where he participated in various *renga*-making gatherings, the results being embodied in *Kitano manku, Tsuki senku, Yuki senku*, and other collections. In 1448, he was elected *Kitano kaisho renga bugyō*, the highest honor in the world of *renga* at the time, and thenceforth applied himself to revising the rules governing the writing of *renga*, contributing to the compilation of Ichijō Kanera's *Shinshiki kon'an*. His style follows the tradition of the *renga* proper, and he attracted attention for the skill with which he could respond to a preceding couplet or triplet and his fondness for apt, artistic turns of phrase. Many of his verses are included in Sōgi's *Chikurin shō*. He also wrote many studies of the *renga* form, such as *Kokin rendan shū*.

TAMEKO (dates uncertain)

Poet of the late Kamakura period. She appears to have been born around 1250. She was the daughter of Fujiwara no Tamenori, the grandson of Teika, third son of Tameie, and founder of the Kyōgoku family school of poetry. She was the elder sister of the poet Kyōgoku Tamekane. She was commonly referred to as Junii Tameko.

She spent all her life as a lady-in-waiting at the Jimyō-in court, at first attending Ōmiya-in, the mother of emperors Gofukakusa and Kameyama, and being known by the title Gon-no-Chūnagon (Acting Middle Counselor). Later she served Fushimi-in and Eifukumon-in, consorts of Emperor Fushimi, and came to be called Tō-no-Dainagon (Fujiwara Great Counselor). By 1299 she had risen to the office of *naishi-no-suke*, the second highest post in the *naishi-no-tsukasa*, the bureau in charge of women of the palace.

As representatives of the Kyōgoku school, she and her younger brother Tamekane were called upon to act as poetry companions to Fushimi-in and Eifukumon-in. Tameko was also a regular participant in poetry matches of the Kyōgoku school, such as that held in the fifth year of Einin (1297), and in her later years often served as a judge at such matches. That over half the poets of the Kyōgoku school were women was due to the very active role that Tameko and Eifukumon-in played as leaders of the school. Tameko also assisted her brother Tamekane in compiling the imperially sponsored anthology known as the *Gyokuyōshū* and worked to promote her brother's views on poetry.

The *Shin gosenshū*, completed in 1303, is the earliest imperial anthology to contain any of her works. She is one of the most important poets of the *Gyokuyōshū*, being represented by a total of sixty-four poems, while thirty-nine of her poems appear in the *Fūgashū*. A separate collection of her works entitled the *Tō-no-Dainagon norisukeshū* has been handed down, but it contains only sixty-three poems.

In depth and breadth of subject her poetry cannot match that of her brother Tamekane, but her works have a kind of tension about them that resembles that found in her brother's poetry. She excels in descriptive pieces, demonstrating an acute observation of the natural world.

There are many things about Tameko's life and career that are unknown. Around the time when her brother Tamekane was exiled to Sado in 1298, her name ceases to appear in any of the records of the period, and it seems likely that, like her brother, she lived a life marked by frequent reversals of fortune and had her full share of bitter experiences.

The following two poems will perhaps convey something of the nature of her work:

> Old fallen leaves
> withered and piled up,
> and on top of them
> anew, the hue

of red maple leaves scattering.

Bank on bank of clouds,
and where they part,
from openings come forth
stars to herald
the dawn.

Ton'a (1289–1372)

Poet of the late Kamakura and Northern and Southern Courts periods. Around the age of twenty he retired to monasteries on Mt. Hiei and Mt. Kōya to devote himself to religious practice and later became a pupil of the priest Jōa at the Kinren-ji temple, becoming a member of the Ji sect of Japanese Buddhism. He gradually became well known as a poet-priest of the school of Nijō Tameyo, contributing to the *Hana jusshu yosegaki* (a collection containing ten poems about flowers from each of various poets) compiled by Tameyo and making his first appearance in an anthology, the *Shoku senzaishū*. He appears in almost all subsequent anthologies, and is counted as one of the Waka Shitennō, or Four Heavenly Kings of Japanese Poetry, all of them pupils of Tameyo. After Emperor Godaigo moved his court to Yoshino, the Nijō school fell into obscurity, but Ton'a found favor with the brothers Takauji (the first Ashikaga shogun) and Tadayoshi and was chosen to compose the *Kōya-san Kongōsammai-in nōkyō waka*, which greatly increased his fame as a poet. He also aided Fujiwara no Tamesada in the compilation of the *Shin senzaishū* anthology.

With his wide learning and his affable and unaffected personality, he found favor with court nobles and samurai alike; his views on verse were moderate, stressing a harmony of feeling and words, his ideal being the style of the Nijō school. The poets of the Muromachi period looked on him as a respected model, and he was revered by such celebrated later scholars as Motoori Norinaga. His work includes a collection of verse, *Sōanshū*, a work on poetic theory, *Seia shō*, and *Gumon kenchū*, a collection of answers he gave to questions by Nijō Yoshimoto. One of his most celebrated poems is:

Snipes that slept
in paddies under the moon
fly up
from the frozen surface
into the sky of dawn.

Yoshida Kenkō (1283–1350)

Poet and essayist of the late Kamakura and early Muromachi periods. His real name was Urabe Kaneyoshi, but because he lived in the Yoshida area of Kyoto, he came to be called Yoshida Kaneyoshi. When he entered the Buddhist priesthood, he continued to use the name Kaneyoshi, but pronounced the two characters with which it is written according to the Sino-Japanese reading Kenkō. The Urabe family were hereditarily attached to the Yoshida Shinto Shrine in Kyoto and were members of the low aristocracy.

Although there are many points about Kenkō's life that remain unclear, it is certain that in his youth he served at court. Sometime in his early thirties he entered the priesthood, living in seclusion in Yamashina near Kyoto. He is also known to have traveled to Kamakura and to have lived on Mt. Hiei for a time. His later years coincided with a period of violent political and social change, but he continued to be active as a poet, in time gaining recognition as one of the Waka Shitennō, or Four Heavenly Kings of Japanese Poetry, of the era. It is surmised that he wrote his famous *Tsurezuregusa* (*Essays in Idleness*) when he was around forty-six or forty-seven. In his last years he is said to have lived at Narabigaoka in the western suburbs of Kyoto.

Kenkō was a man of wide learning, well read in both Japanese and Chinese literature and an authority on the traditional ceremonies and usages of the court. In addition to being an excellent poet, he was also recognized as one of the most cultured and refined persons of the time. His poetry reflects the simple and rather conservative style associated with the Nijō school. Sixteen of his poems are included in officially compiled anthologies, and there is also a collection of his works entitled the *Kenkō Hōshi shū*. The *Tsurezuregusa* is made up of some 240 brief paragraphs, some dealing with Buddhism, Japanese poetry and the other arts, the traditional customs of the past, and contemporary events, other presenting descriptions of the beauties of nature or advice on how to get along in the world. The work richly reflects the erudition, poetic sensitivity, and refined taste of the author and expresses particular respect for the professional artist and the seeker after truth. Its style represents a judicious mixture of native Japanese elements and words and phrases borrowed from Chinese. The work, in fact, has long been looked upon not only as a masterpiece of the medieval period but as the finest example of the *zuihitsu* (miscellany) form in all of Japanese literature.

ZEAMI (1363–1443/45)

Nō actor and playwright of the middle Muromachi period. His name was Yūzaki Saemon Tayū Motokiyo and as a child he was called Fujiwakamaru. He was commonly called Kanze Saburō. Zeami is a religious name he took later in life, when he was also known as Shiō. His father was the famous Nō actor Kan'ami of the Sarugaku Kanze theater in Yamato.

In 1374 Kan'ami won the admiration of Shogun Ashikaga Yoshimitsu for the superb artistry he displayed at a Nō performance at Imakumano in Kyoto. At the time, Zeami, then known as Fujiwakamaru, was an attractive boy of eleven who likewise won the shogun's admiration and thereafter was treated by him with great favor. He did not allow himself to be spoiled by such treatment, however, but continued to work wholeheartedly to perfect his skill as a Nō actor. In 1400 he wrote the *Kadensho*, one of the first and most important works on the theory and practice of the Nō drama, and two years later he wrote continuations to the work entitled the *Shingi* and *Ōgi*, which trace the development of the Nō and define its principles.

His father died when Zeami was twenty-one, but by that time he had already learned from him the essentials of the art of Nō and he set about working to bring the new dramatic form to perfection, borrowing elements from Kiami, a master of *dengaku*, a type of music and dance presentation that derived originally from harvest festivals, and from Dōami, a master of *sarugaku*, another type of dramatic presentation that predated the Nō. He reached the peak of his career as an actor with the Kitayama Tenran Nō performance held in 1408, when he was forty-five. Yoshimitsu died suddenly in the same year, however, and his successor to the shogunate, Ashikaga Yoshimochi, lavished favor on the *dengaku* master Zōami; as a result Zeami found himself shunned and ignored. He did not allow this to deter him from his art, however, and during the following twenty years wrote such works as the *Onkyoku kowadashi kuden* (1419), the *Shikadō* (1420), the *Kakyō*, and numerous others, and continued the task of shaping and developing the early Nō, incorporating into it the best elements of the various popular arts of the time and raising it to the level of full-fledged drama.

In 1422, at the age of fifty-nine, he turned over the post of *tayū* in the Kanze theater to his son and heir Motomasa and entered the priesthood. Two years later he was appointed chief musician to the shogun, but in 1429 the office of shogun passed to Ashikaga Yoshinori, who favored Zeami's nephew On'ami Motoshige, and Zeami and his sons suffered a sharp reversal of fortune. Zeami's second son entered the priesthood; his eldest son Motomasa, whom he had hoped would surpass his father and grandfather as an artist, died while on a journey; and he himself, though seventy-one at the time, was exiled to the island of Sado. What became of him after that is not certain, though it is said that he was eventually pardoned and allowed to return to the capital. Some scholars place his death in 1443, others in 1445.

Not only was Zeami, according to all reports, a master performer of the Nō, but he was also a playwright of unparalleled genius and productivity. He wrote over 150 plays, and approximately half of the works in the present repertory are believed to be from his hand, including nearly all of the recognized masterpieces. He was also highly skilled at other types of writing, and his critical works on the Nō hold a place of particular importance. These statements on the theory and practice of the Nō, which comprise over twenty works that were originally handed down in secret and were known only to the members of the Kanze family, reveal that he placed prime emphasis upon the quality called *hana*, by which he meant the outward wonder, beauty, and interest of the dramatic art; next to it he extolled most highly a quality called *yūgen*, the inner mystery and beauty hidden behind the outward form. As he writes, "One must perform in such a way as to bring out this mysterious beauty. When one has mastered *yūgen*, he may be said to have reached the highest level, that of perfect artistic enlightenment."

Among the more important of Zeami's plays are *Takasago, Yumi Yawata, Oimatsu, Tadanori, Izutsu, Higaki, Saigyō-zakura, Kinuta*, and *Aridōshi*. His other works include the *Kadensho* and *Kakyō* mentioned above, as well as the *Besshi kuden, Shikadōsho, Nōsakusho, Seshi rokujū igo sarugaku dangi, Museki isshi, Kintōshū*, and others.

玉津嶋

いろゝゝの玉へきゝ育むい　さゝなみや

かもつゞれか　つてもゝしゝ

いづゝ濱瑞藤に

祇ひおれてもゝ

筆に

ふ

Early Modern Period

Agatamon Sansaijo

The Three Women Disciples of the Agatamon School: Yuya Shizuko; Udono Yonoko; Shindō Tsukubako; poets and disciples of Kamo no Mabuchi.

Yuya Shizuko (1733–1752)

She was born at Kyōbashi in Edo, the daughter of a family known by the shop name Iseya, and was said to have been very beautiful. At the age of fourteen she entered service as an attendant to the wife of a daimyo, but returned to her own home three years later. Accompanying her mother on a visit to the hot springs at Ikaho in Kōzuke, she wrote an account of the journey that was said to have won the intense admiration of all those who read it. On her untimely death at the age of nineteen, her teacher, Kamo no Mabuchi, and fellow disciples of the Agatamon school of poetry were deeply grieved, and Mabuchi wrote poems in *chōka* and *tanka* form giving expression to his sorrow. Her poems are collected in a work entitled *Chirinokori* and, although Mabuchi stressed the study of the *Man'yōshū*, they employ a style that is closer to that of the *Kokinshū* or *Shin kokinshū*.

Udono Yonoko (1729–1788)

She served the lord of the domain of Kii and was known as Segawa. Her older brother was a disciple of Hattori Nankaku, and under him she studied the writing of Chinese poetry as well. She wrote a travel diary entitled *Kisojiki*, and her poems are collected under the title *Sahogawa*; other works of hers are preserved in a work entitled *Ryōgetsu isō*. Some of her poems are in Heian style, others in the style of the *Man'yōshū*.

Shindō Tsukubako (dates uncertain)

She was the adopted daughter of Shindō Seikan and married Toki Yorifusa, an official in the service of the shogunate. She is also known by the name Shigeiko. Her poems are considered to be superior to those of Udono Yonoko.

ARAI HAKUSEKI (1657–1725)

Scholar and statesman of the middle Edo period. His father was a samurai in the service of the Tsuchiya family of the province of Kazusa but later lost his position, and as a result Hakuseki grew up in circumstances of considerable poverty. At the age of twenty-five he entered the service of Tairō Hotta Masatoshi and two years later became a disciple of Kinoshita Jun'an, a teacher of the Chu Hsi school of Neo-Confucianism. He later left the service of the Hotta family and made a living as a lecturer in the Asakusa district of Edo, but on the recommendation of his teacher Jun'an, he was appointed lecturer on Confucianism to Tokugawa Ienobu, the lord of Kai. In 1709, when Hakuseki was fifty-two, Ienobu succeeded to the position of shogun, and Hakuseki became his adviser on matters of government policy. He was given the court rank of Junior Fifth Rank Lower Grade, and was appointed governor of the province of Chikugo, honors all but unprecedented for a man of scholarly background in the Edo period. When Ienobu and his successor died and Tokugawa Yoshimune became shogun in 1716, however, Hakuseki found his advice no longer wanted and he retired from government service, devoting his remaining years to writing and research.

Hakuseki's scholarly interests were very broad, covering the fields of history, geography, linguistics, and the study of the classics, and he was also renowned as a writer of Chinese verse, at one time being regarded as the finest poet in Chinese of the Edo period. He holds a place of importance in the history of Japanese literature as well, his works such as the *Hankampu*, an historical gazetteer of the feudal domains, and his famous autobiography, the *Oritaku-shibanoki*, being marked by a charm that is distinctively his own. His contribution to the study of Japanese language and literature is exemplified in the *Tōga*, a study of the etymology of Japanese words in twenty chapters; the *Dōbun tsūko*, a study of Chinese and Japanese writing systems; and the *Tōompu*, a study of *kana* spellings, all pioneering works of prime importance in their respective fields of investigation. In addition he wrote works on geography such as the *Sairan igen* and *Seiyō kibun*, which were of particular value at the time because of the information they contained on Europe and the world outside East Asia. His historical works include the *Koshitsū* in four chapters and a collection of essays on political history entitled *Dokushi yoron*. Other historical essays, along with his poems in Chinese, are found in the *Hakuseki ibun*, while the *Hakuseki sensei shinsho* and *Hakuseki-ran* contain miscellaneous writings.

ARAKIDA HISAOI (1746–1804)

Scholar of Japanese studies in the middle Edo period. He was the fourth son of Watarai Masanobu, a Shinto priest of the Outer Shrine of Ise. In 1765 at the age of nineteen he journeyed to Edo and became a disciple of Kamo no Mabuchi, the famous scholar of *kokugaku* (Japanese studies), receiving instruction from him for a period of approximately three years. Around the age of twenty-seven he was adopted by Arakida Hisayo, taking the name Hisaoi, and was appointed *gon-no-negi* in the Inner Shrine of Ise. He seems to have been a man of poetic temperament, candid in manner and indifferent to worldly concerns. Although the school of his teacher, Kamo no Mabuchi, tended on the whole to be literary and scholarly in direction, Arakida's work shows more of a philosophical bent and is pronounced in its opposition to the theories of Motoori Norinaga, his fellow student under Kamo no Mabuchi and also a native of Ise. Of particular note among Arakida's works is his study of the songs in the *Nihon Shoki*, in which he examines the diction of the songs with immense thoroughness and care. His commentaries on the *Man'yōshū* are marked by highly original linguistic interpretations and attempt to get at the underlying spirit of the songs. In his own discussions of poetic theory as well, he places great emphasis upon the tone and feeling of the poem and warns against the kind of approach that is too constricted by logic. His poems have a loftiness of style that is reminiscent of the *Man'yōshū*, and his prose pieces also are marked by grace and distinctions.

His principal works are the *Man'yōkō tsuki ochiba*, *Nihongi uta-no-ge*, *Shoku nihongi uta-no-ge*, *Kojiki uta-no-ge*, and *Itsuki-no-sono shū*, the last a collection of poems.

ARAKIDA REIJO (1732–1806)

Fiction writer of the middle Edo period. She was the daughter of Arakida Taketō, a religious official attached to the Inner Shrine of the Great Shrine at Ise; her personal name was Takako. At the age of sixteen she became a disciple of the teacher of *renga* Nishiyama Shōrin of Osaka, and later a disciple of Hananomoto Satomura Shōteki, devoting all her energies to the study of *renga*. At the age of twenty-three she became the wife of Keiji Iemasa, who fortunately seems to have been very sympathetic toward her literary interests and ambitions. When she was thirty-six she undertook the task of producing a collated edition of the famous Heian period romance known as the *Utsubo monogatari*, and this inspired her to turn to fiction writing. She seems to have followed this pursuit from around the age of thirty-eight to fifty, producing historical works such as the *Ike no mokuzu*, *Tsuki no yukue*, and *Kasa no yadori* (now believed lost), as well as other full-length novels such as the *Kiri no ha* and *Yama no i*, and collections of short tales such as the *Hiori* and *Ayashi no yogatari*. In addition, she has left behind a travel diary, the *Hatsuuma no nikki*, and collections of her prose and verse entitled respectively *Reijo bunshū* and *Reijo kushū*, her writings in all running to over four hundred volumes.

Nearly all her works of fiction deal with the world of the Heian aristocracy and are in the nature of imitations of the romances of that period, but she was so thoroughly versed in the literature of the past and commanded such felicity of style that she was able to avoid the artificialities and inaccuracies that customarily mar such works. In addition, unlike the great women writers of the Heian period, who were encouraged in their literary endeavors, she lived in an age that, because of its Confucian orientation, looked upon women as quite unsuited for such pursuits. The fact that, in the face of such bias, she still succeeded in distinguishing herself as a writer of fiction and of poetry in the *renga*, *waka*, *haiku*, and *kanshi* forms, as well as displaying outstanding talent as a calligrapher and painter, qualifies her to receive a high degree of admiration, both for the variety and volume of her work and the strength of her spirit.

Bonchō (d. 1714)

Haiku poet of the early Edo period. His surname appears to have been Miyagi, though some scholars suggest that it was Nozawa, Koshino, or Miyabe. There is no agreement as to what his childhood name or common name were, but up until around 1690 he employed the artistic name Kasei, thereafter called himself Bonchō, and in his late years also used the name Akei. He was born in the city of Kanazawa in Kaga Province. He went to Kyoto, where he made a living as a physician, and at some uncertain date took up the writing of *haiku*. His works are included in the *Itsuo mukashi*, a *haiku* anthology compiled by Kikaku in 1688, and the following year two of his poems were included in another anthology, the *Arano* compiled by

Yamamoto Kakei. He first became acquainted with Bashō around 1690, when the latter was living in the Genjū-an in Ōmi, and joined with Kyorai, one of Bashō's major disciples, in compiling the *Saru mino*, a highly influential anthology of *haiku* by Bashō and his followers. The anthology, which was published in 1691, contains forty-one *haiku* by Bonchō, more than by any other poet represented in the anthology, and he is also a participant in all of the linked verse included in the anthology. It was around this time that he began to use the name Bonchō. After the publication of *Saru mino*, however, Bonshō departed from Bashō's style in his work. Later he became involved in some affair and was imprisoned for a time, bringing about a hiatus in his artistic output. He seems to have been writing during the period from 1701 to 1703, but after that very few works by him are to be found. It would appear, therefore, that after being pardoned and released from jail, he lived in retirement somewhere in the Osaka area and died at a fairly advanced age.

In the poems included in the *Saru mino* he outshines his fellow poets as a master of the objective style, but later, as he began to turn his back on Bashō's style, his works become excessively intellectual and appear almost to have been composed by a different person. As a *haiku* poet, he is hence remarkable both for the rapidity with which he advanced to artistic maturity and the equal rapidity with which he declined in stature.

CHIKAMATSU HANJI (1725–1783)

Jōruri dramatist of the middle Edo period. His father, Hozumi Ikan (a Confucian scholar), was a close friend of the celebrated playwright Chikamatsu Monzaemon; as a result of this connection, Hanji went to study with Takeda Izumo and wrote *jōruri* for the Takemoto-za theater, taking the surname Chikamatsu. He was acclaimed as a born *jōruri* playwright. The prologue to *En-no gyōja omine-zakura* (1751), his first work, was followed by more than fifty plays, but it was only following his attainment of the position of chief playwright to the Takemoto-za in 1763 that he produced his finest work, a series of splendidly conceived plays that brought new life to the declining world of *jōruri*. He was equally at home in the field of the *jidaimono* (historical) play (for example, *Honchō nijūshi kō*, *Sekitori senryō nobori*, *Imoseyama onna teikin*), and the *sewamono* (contemporary domestic drama) (*Shimpan Utazaimon*, *Igagoe dōchū sugoroku*). His plays are varied in their conception, complex with an emphasis on dramatic inventiveness, and rely greatly on staging techniques; they are still performed today.

CHIKAMATSU MONZAEMON (1653–1724)

Playwright of the early Edo period. His original name was Sugimori Nobumori and he was the son of a samurai of the fief of Echizen, who, when Chikamatsu was about fourteen or fifteen, left the service of his lord and moved his family to Kyoto.

Chikamatsu grew up in a literary atmosphere, joining with the other members of his family in composing poems in *haiku* form. Sometime after the family moved to Kyoto, he entered the service of a court noble named Ichijō Zenkakuekan, utilizing the opportunity to deepen his knowledge of classical literature and acquaint himself with court customs and etiquette. Around the age of nineteen he left the service of the nobility and, determining to enter the artistic world, began writing puppet plays for Uji Kadayū, who was later called Kaga-no-jō, and other chanters of the puppet theater. Because of the lowly position accorded to playwrights of the puppet theater (*jōruri*), however, the plays of this period are unsigned, and it is therefore impossible to determine which ones were written by Chikamatsu. In 1683, however, he wrote a play entitled *Yotsugi Soga* to which he affixed his name, and from this time on he began to be known as a dramatist. He also wrote plays for the kabuki actor Sakata Tōjūrō, rapidly increasing his reputation in the theatrical world.

In 1695 he became a regular writer for the Miyako-za, a theater in Kyoto headed by Sakata Tōjūrō, working in close cooperation with the actor and writing dramas for him that are marked by a realism previously unknown in that genre; he also helped to establish the *sewamono* (drama on contemporary themes) as a part of the kabuki repertory. From this collaboration came such outstanding works as *Keisei Hotoke no hara* (1699) and *Keisei Mibu dainembutsu* (1702).

Meanwhile, shortly after the chanter Takemoto Gidayū opened a new puppet theater in Osaka called the Takemoto-za, Chikamatsu began writing *jōruri* dramas for him, in 1685 producing a play entitled *Shusse Kagekiyo*, which was to become of epochal importance in the development of the *jōruri* drama. In it Chikamatsu broke away from the legendary themes and stereotyped language that had characterized the early *jōruri* dramas and introduced a new note of realism and individuality. He continued to develop these tendencies in subsequent works, evolving what was to become recognized as a wholly new type of *jōruri* drama.

In 1701 the kabuki actor Tōjūrō retired from the stage, and two years later Chikamatsu wrote a play for Takemoto Gidayū entitled *Sonezaki shinjū*, which deals with the contemporary world of the Osaka townsmen and was the first *sewamono* to be written for the puppet theater. It proved to be a success of quite unexpected proportions, and this fact, along with the retirement of Tōjūrō, probably contributed largely to Chikamatsu's decision to devote himself entirely to the puppet theater. In 1706 he became a staff playwright for the Takemoto Theater, and until his death wrote almost exclusively for the puppet drama. During this period he wrote both *sewamono* and *jidaimono*, or history plays. The former category includes fifteen works dealing with love suicides, among them such masterpieces as *Meido no hikyaku* (1711) and *Shinjū Ten-no-amijima*, as well as works such as *Horikawa nami no tsuzumi* (1707) and *Onnagoroshi abura jigoku* (1721) that treat the themes of adultery or vengeance for a wife who has been wronged. In these works of his late years, Chikamatsu's powers of psychological and emotional delineation reached their highest level of development.

In his history plays he departed, as noted earlier, from the stereotypes that had characterized previous *jōruri* works in this genre and sought to give individuality to his characters and embodiment to the ideals of the warrior spirit. Among the audiences of the time, these history plays exceeded in popularity the *sewamono*, the domestic dramas. After the extraordinary success of *Kokusenya kassen* (*The Battles of Coxinga*) in 1715, Chikamatsu, heeding the advice of Takeda Izumo, the head of the Takemoto Theater at that time, turned out a number of works in this genre that made use of a larger stage and were distinguished by various novel and spectacular effects, among them *Heike nyogo no shima* (1719) and *Shinshū Kawanakajima kassen* (1721). In addition, he tried combining the *jidaimono* and *sewamono* genres to produce a domestic drama set in the past, as in his *Keisei hangonkō*.

In matters of plot conception and performance techniques, Chikamatsu's works served as models for later playwrights of the kabuki and *jōruri* theaters. But his works also stand out for their beauty of language, excelling in this respect those of all other *jōruri* playwrights and, particularly in his late years, attaining a level of maturity in both form and content that has never been surpassed. Concerning the art of dramatic writing, he put forth a new theory, declaring that "art does not lie in the mere recording of reality just as it exists; rather it depends upon the recognition of the realm of unreality, and finds its place in the narrow borderline that lies between them." Through his own art as a dramatist, he was able to take over the old *jōruri* form, which had previously been regarded as of no literary value, and raise it to a level where it came to hold a place of real importance in the history of Japanese literature. As a result, his works appeal even today and continue to be performed in the kabuki, puppet, and other types of theater.

Ejima Kiseki (1667?–1736)

Writer of *ukiyo-zōshi* or works of popular fiction of the middle Edo period. His personal name was Shigetomo and he was also known as Ichirōzaemon. Little information concerning the details of his life is preserved.

His family for some generations had been the proprietors of a shop in Kyoto that sold rice-cakes and had acquired a very considerable fortune, so that Kiseki was born into wealth. He spent his youth in dissipation, however, and eventually succeeded in reducing himself to bankruptcy. It was at this point, it would appear, that he turned to the life of a writer, drawing upon the experiences of his colorful youth to produce books of gossip and critical comment concerning actors of the time or works of popular fiction.

His first work was written sometime around the period from 1688 to 1696; though the title is unknown, it was a *jōruri* (puppet drama) composed for the chanter Takemoto Gidayū. At this time Jishō, the proprietor of a Kyoto bookstore known as the Hachimonjiya, decided to bring out some books of critical comment concerning popular actors of the day and engaged Kiseki to do the writing. The first, entitled *Yakusha kuchijamisen*, appeared in 1699, when Kiseki was thirty-two, with Jishō identified as both author and publisher. The work attracted wide attention, and thereafter the Hachimonjiya brought out a new sequel each year, for a long time enjoying a monopoly in the field of such works.

Jishō next decided to bring out a series of *ukiyo-zōshi*, works of popular fiction. Kiseki accordingly in 1701 wrote *Keisei irojamisen*, followed later by similar works such as *Fūryū kyokujamisen*, *Keisei denju zōshi*, and *Keisei kintanki*, all published under the name of Jishō of the Hachimonjiya. From around 1712, however, disharmony began to develop between Jishō and Kiseki, and they parted company. Therefore Kiseki set his son up as the proprietor of a new bookstore called the Ejimaya, from which he published works of fiction and critical comment on actors in his own name. During this period of disruption in relations between Kiseki and the Hachimonjiya, he also published works from other publishers such as Kikuya Yasubei, Tanimura Seibei, and Hishiya Magobei, but in 1718 a reconciliation took place between Kiseki and Jishō, and from then on until his death in 1736, Kiseki published works signed jointly by himself and Jishō.

Kiseki is a typical representative of the popular writer of the Edo period. For a Kyoto *chōnin* (townsman) of the time he seems to have possessed considerable culture and taste. During the thirty or more years he was active as a writer, he devoted the earlier part mainly to the production of collections of short tales or anecdotes dealing with the lives of the townsmen or the women of the licenced quarters. He is particularly noted as the creator of a genre known as *katagimono*, "character-books," which are deft and humorous sketches of various types of fathers, sons, and daughters of the time, as in his *Seken musuko katagi*, *Seken musume katagi*, and *Seken oyaji katagi*. He was also, as in the *Keisei irojamisen* and other works mentioned above, the first writer to produce books whose titles begin with the word *keisei*, a literary term for a higher-class prostitute, a practice that was much followed in later times. In his later years he spent most of his time writing longer works, some apparently based upon actual incidents of the time, others adaptations of kabuki and puppet dramas but with various original touches added by the author.

The influence of Saikaku is very much in evidence in Kiseki's works; yet he was no mere imitator of Saikaku, working instead to create a world of his own. After his death, a great many similar writers of popular fiction appeared upon the literary scene in Kyoto and Osaka, but none ever succeeded in equalling Kiseki in talent. His works exercised a strong influence upon such Edo period fiction writers as Bakin, Kyōden, Ikku, and Tanehiko, and even upon the Meiji period novelist and critic Aeba Kōson.

In addition to the titles mentioned above, Kiseki's works also include the *Wakan yūjo katagi*, *Kokusenya Minchō taiheiki*, *Kiseki okimiyage*, and others.

Enomoto Kikaku (1661–1707)

Haiku poet of the early Edo period. He was the eldest son of an Edo physician named Takemoto Tōjun. He went by his mother's surname, Enomoto, but later also used the surname Takarai. His boyhood name was Yasohachi, and he employed such literary names as Hōshinsai, Rasha, Shōsen, Shinshi, Raichūshi, and Kyōjidō. He became a disciple of the famous *haiku* poet Bashō around the age of thirteen or fourteen, and at the same time studied medicine, painting, Confucianism, and Chinese poetry. Along with Hattori Ransetsu, he was one of the earliest of Bashō's disciples. In 1680, when he was nineteen, he was permitted to take part in a *haiku*-composing assembly along with his master, the results of which were edited and published the following year by Bashō under the title *Jiin*. He soon began to distinguish himself, and in 1683 edited the *haiku* collection entitled *Minashiguri*, which in later times was hailed by Taniguchi Buson and others as the first step in Bashō's revolutionary development of the *haiku* form. Thus Kikaku in time established a position as one of the most important of Basho's followers.

Around the age of twenty-four, he lived for a time in the Fukagawa Kiba area of Edo along with Hattori Ransetsu and others, spending his days in idleness, apparently in an effort to recover from illness, and he also made trips to Hakone and Kamakura, writing a series of travel accounts known by the title *Shinsanka*. Later he also made trips to the Kyoto, Osaka, Mimeguri, Yamato, and Kii regions. On the occasion of Bashō's death in 1694 he wrote a work entitled *Bashō-ō shūenki*, and also compiled a collection of memorial verse entitled *Kare obana*. But Kikaku was by birth a member of the Edo townsman class, brilliant and talented and in temperament inclined to be rather bold and ostentatious, and he could not always bring himself into harmony with the retiring, otherworldly style of Bashō's poetry. Even while Bashō was alive, he showed a tendency to seek for novel effects and to concentrate upon technical dexterity, and after Bashō's death he abandoned the style that had become associated with his master and established a *haiku* style of his own. With this new style, which was marked by a striving for novelty and wit, he founded the school known as the Edoza, but in the process lost all trace of the spirit that had informed the best of Bashō's *haiku*.

Perhaps because of his boldness of temperament, Kikaku's best *haiku* are marked by a breadth and spirit unmatched in most other poets. His less successful works, however, are often marred by inordinate attention to technique and obscurity of language and are wholly lacking in a feeling of naturalness. Nevertheless, his works tend to be brighter and bolder in tone than those of Bashō, and though they lack depth, they often possess a beauty of melody close to that of Bashō's work.

Kikaku died at the age of forty-six, but was fortunate in having such distinguished disciples as Hayano Hajin, Matsuki Tantan, Fukagawa Kojū, and Kuwaoka Teisa, and they in turn had numerous talented followers, so that Kikaku's style in time came to exercise considerable influence in Kyoto, Edo, and Osaka. The line established by Hayano Hajin in time produced Taniguchi Buson, who is generally regarded as second only to Bashō among *haiku* poets, and Kikaku's artistic descendants continue to be active in *haiku* circles today. Kikaku's *haiku* are preserved in the *Inaka kuawase*, *Minashiguri*, and *Hanatsumi*, and his prose works in the *Shinsanka*.

Fujiwara Seika (1561–1619)

Scholar of Chinese studies in the Momoyama and early Edo periods. He was a thirteenth generation descendant of the famous poet Fujiwara no Teika and was born in the village of Hosokawa, where his father held a feudal domain, in the province of Harima. (His father later lost his domain when he was defeated by Bessho Nagaharu.) Seika at first became a monk of the Zen sect, later making his way to Kyoto to study, and in time gained considerable fame. In 1591 he was invited by Kampaku Toyotomi Hideyoshi to participate in a contest in the writing of poetry in Chinese with monks from the Gozan (five great Zen) temples of the capital, and he was also patronized by Tokugawa Ieyasu. He determined to make a trip to Ming China in search of a teacher, but when he had journeyed as far as the province of Satsuma, he acquired a copy of Chu Hsi's version of the *Ta hsüeh*, known as the *Ta hsüeh chang-chü*, and other important works of the Chu Hsi school of Neo-Confucianism. Abandoning his plans for a journey to China, he returned to Kyoto, left the Buddhist clergy, and devoted himself to the study of Confucianism and the propagation of the doctrines of the Chu Hsi school. He gained even greater fame when he was invited to lecture to Tokugawa Ieyasu on the Chinese Classics and works of history. Invitations to enter their service came to him from numerous feudal lords, but he declined them all, remaining a private teacher to the end of his life. He had a large number of disciples, including such outstanding scholars as Hayashi Razan and Matsunaga Sekigo, and was later revered as the founder of the Chu Hsi school of Neo-Confucianism in Japan. That the Chu Hsi school flourished in the Edo period and was later adopted as the official doctrine of the state by the Tokugawa shoguns was in fact due to his pioneering efforts. He was also a distinguished writer of Japanese poetry and a scholar of the *Nihon Shoki*, *Man'yōshū*, and other important texts of ancient Japanese literature, serving as a pioneer in this field of study as well and winning for himself a place of importance in the histories both of Japanese literature and of Japanese philosophy.

His works include the *Bunshō tattokuroku*, *Bunshō tattokuroku kōryō*, *Seika bunshū*, and *Fujiwara Seika shū*.

Gion Nankai (1677?–1751)

Poet and scholar of Chinese in the middle Edo period. His family were hereditary physicians to the lords of the domain of Kii. He studied under the Neo-Confucian scholar Kinoshita Jun'an and displayed great talent in the writing of verse and prose in Chinese, being highly praised by Arai Hakuseki for his ability as a poet. In 1697 he was appointed Confucian scholar to the lord of Kii, with a stipend of two hundred *koku*, but he was later implicated in a criminal affair and was deprived of his post and stipend, being forced to live a life of great poverty in the village of Nagahara in the Ito district of Kii. In 1710 he was pardoned, and six years later was restored to his post as Confucian scholar. Because of the part he played in the reception of the Korean envoy, his stipend was restored to the earlier amount, and he once more took charge of educational matters for the domain. In addition to his literary activities, he studied the works of the Ming and Ch'ing literati painters and became one of the most important figures in the early development of the *nanga* school of painting in Japan. It is said that the famous painter Ike no Taiga was one of his students. Along with Arai Hakuseki and Yanada Zeigan, he was recognized as one of the three great writers of Chinese poetry of the period. His works include the *Nankai bunshū, Shigaku hōgen, Nankai shihō, Shōun sango*, and others.

HACHIMONJIYA JISHŌ (1666–1745)

Author and publisher of the type of popular novelette known as *ukiyo-zōshi*. Hachimonjiya was his *yagō* ("shop" or "trade" name) and Jishō his pen name. He was the second proprietor of Hachimonji-ya, a firm publishing *jōruri* texts in Kyoto. An extremely able businessman, he had the idea, on taking over the family business, of publishing the texts of the kabuki plays that were then enjoying a great vogue. As a result, the Hachimonjiya, which had hitherto published only *jōruri* texts, expanded greatly. Following this, he conceived the idea of publishing *yakusha hyōbanki* (booklets providing critical comments on the kabuki actors of the day) and took on Ejima Kiseki to write them, publishing them under his own name. The first was *Yakusha kuchi-jamisen*, published in the third month of 1699, and its sequels, published regularly each year, enjoyed lasting popularity. Next, he planned publication of *ukiyo-zōshi*, a type of novelette aimed at the general public. The first, *Keisei irojamisen*, came out in the eighth month of 1701, to be followed by *Fūryū kuruwajamisen, Keisei kintanki*, and others, all published under Jishō's own name; they soon became the most popular form of reading matter in the Osaka-Kyoto area.

Eventually, Kiseki, the author, grew dissatisfied at the increasing fame enjoyed by Jishō; the two quarreled in 1713, and Kiseki left to set up an independent publishing firm called Ejima-ya. The two men kept up a stubborn crossfire in the *yakusha-hyōbanki* published by their respective houses, but finally were reconciled in 1718. Kiseki went back to Hachimonji-ya, and for nearly thirty years until Kiseki's death in 1736, *ukiyo-zōshi* and *yakusha-hyōbanki* bearing the names of both men appeared in large numbers.

Following Kiseki's death, Jishō put out *ukiyo-zōshi* jointly with Kiseki's son Kishō, but his name disappears from the publishing world following publication of *Jishō tanoshimi nikki*, probably because he had died in 1745. The publications generally known as *Hachimonjiya bon* ("Hachimonjiya books") are *ukiyo-zōshi* published by Hachimonjiya in Jishō's time; all of them are thoroughly commercial literature aimed at the popular taste. They invariably bear Jishō's own name, but it is said that they were, in fact, the work of Kiseki or other authors. Yet, though he may not have been the actual author, the *ukiyo-zōshi* that he planned and published carried on and further developed a form of the novel that had begun with Saikaku and that was to have an influence on later Edo period writers such as Takizawa Bakin, Santō Kyōden, Ryūtei Tanehiko, and Shikitei Samba, as well as Meiji writers such as Aeba Kōson and Tsubouchi Shōyō.

Other works bearing Jishō's name apart from those already mentioned include *Yahaku naisho kagami, Kankatsu Heike monogatari, Keisei denju tenarai kamiko, Hyakushō seisuiki, Akindo setaigusuri, Fūryū yasa Heike, Yoshitsune fūryū kagami, Keisei yagundan,* and *Yakusha kin-geshō*.

HATTORI NANKAKU (1683–1759)

Scholar of the Chinese classics, writer of Chinese verse, and literati painter of the middle Edo period. He also used the names Shisen, Fukyokan, Shusetsu, and Kan'ō. He was born in Kyoto, but following the death of his father, when he was thirteen, his family moved to Edo, where at the age of fifteen he went into the service of Yanagisawa Yoshiyasu, lord of the Kōfu clan and *rōjū* to the Tokugawa shogunate. In middle life he became a pupil of Ogyū Sorai and took up the study of Chinese literature and the Confucian Classics. He admired the work of Tu Fu most of all, and considered the works of the High T'ang, the period in which Tu Fu lived, as the only true poetry. He played a large part in bringing about the popularity in Japan of the anthology of T'ang poetry known as *Tōshisen*, himself producing a commentary on it entitled *Tōshisen genkai*. His master, Sorai, included among his pupils many talented "literary Confucians," and Nankaku, together with Dazai Shundai, was numbered among the most outstanding of them all, it being generally considered that Nankaku excelled in literature, while Shundai excelled in the study of the Confucian Classics. Nankaku himself considered his own verse to have attained a nobility and refinement that recalled that of Tu Fu. In later years he gave up his official post and opened his own academy; his literary reputation grew, and he was frequently invited to lecture to local lords. Of a gentle and kind disposition, he was loved and respected in the world of art. Among those who came under his influence was the *haiku* poet Buson.

His works include *Nankaku bunshū* (40 vols.), *Nankaku zekku shū*, *Tōshisen genkai*, *Daitō seigo* (5 vols.), *Tōshisen kokuji kai* (7 vols.).

HATTORI RANSETSU (1654–1707)

Haiku poet of the early Edo period. He is counted among the "Ten Philosophers," or ten major disciples of Bashō. His family name was Hattori, and his common name Hikobei, which he later changed to Magonojō; he went by such other names as Rantei Harusuke, Setchūan, Kanryōdō, and Kōrakuan. He was born in the island of Awaji and raised in Edo. At first he served under a military family but resigned his post and became a *rōnin*, interesting himself in painting and *haiku*. It is not certain when he became a disciple of Bashō, though it was said to have been some time before 1680, when he was twenty-six. He is mentioned by the name Rantei Harusuke in the preface to the collection of *haiku* compiled by Kikaku in 1680 entitled *Inaka no kuawase*, and his first *haiku*, also written under the same name, appear in the anonymously compiled collection *Tōsei kontei dokugin nijū kasen* of the same year. From around the following year he began to use the name Ransetsu. In 1687, when he was thirty-three, he published his first collection of poems, entitled *Wakamizu*, and thereafter devoted more and more time to *haiku*. Bashō had singled out Kikaku and Ransetsu by name among his outstanding disciples, and the latter was regarded as comprising, along with Kikaku, one of the pillars of Bashō's school in Edo. On the occasion of Basho's death, Ransetsu wept bitterly at the grave, and on the first anniversary of Basho's death, brought out a volume of commemorative verse entitled *Wakana shū*.

He seems to have moved about Edo any number of times, but in 1703 built a house in Hamachō, which he named the Setchū-an, and lived there until his death in 1707. His first wife was a *yuna*, or prostitute from the public baths, and when she died, he took another prostitute as a second wife, which suggests that he was a man of unconventional ways. He seldom left Edo to go on journeys, and the travel diaries he kept of such journeys as he did take are on the whole rather brief. The collection of his *haiku*, the *Gempōshū*, is also rather brief, containing only 424 poems. But it is clear that he was an unusually gifted writer, and the warmth and sincerity of his personality is clearly reflected in his poetry. His works are marked by depth and, particularly in his later years, an increasingly contemplative tone, and at times convey a sense of religious enlightenment. The school that he founded played an important role in carrying on Bashō's style in the world of Edo *haiku* and produced such eminent disciples as Sakurai Rito and Ōba Ryōwa. Under Sakurai Rito's disciple Ōshima Ryōta the Ransetsu school reached its highest point of popularity. The following *haiku* are representative of Ransetsu's best work:

> "Yellow chrysanthemum,"
> "white chrysanthemum"—there should be
> no names but these!

> One blossom of plum,
> and with each blossom
> a blossomworth of warmth.

Ransetsu's works include the *Sono fukuro*, *Aru toki-shū*, *Sono hamayū* (in conjunction with Ishiuchi Chōsō), and the *Gempōshū* mentioned above.

Hayashi Razan (1583–1657)

A Confucian and student of Chinese learning of the Momoyama and early Edo periods. He also used the religious name Dōshun. Born the son of a wealthy merchant in Kyoto, he showed a strong character and a great interest in study from an early age; at the age of thirteen he went to live and study at the Kennin-ji, a Zen temple, where he was hailed as a child prodigy and urged to become a monk, a step he refused to take. At that time there were few in Japan who studied the Neo-Confucianism of Chu Hsi, but Razan was deeply impressed on reading an annotated collection of Chu Hsi's writings, and at the age of seventeen he gathered together a number of pupils and gave lectures on the new interpretation of the Four Books. The conservative court scholars objected to his new approach, but Tokugawa Ieyasu ruled that it was not necessary to insist either on the old or the new interpretation and rejected their complaints. Razan went to study with Fujiwara Seika, known at the time as a student of Chu Hsi's writings, and soon became his most outstanding pupil. He went into the service of Ieyasu, who made great use of Razan's talent. Razan eventually came to dominate the whole academic world, from which position he further promoted the study of Chu Hsi. At the command of Ieyasu, he became a monk and assumed the religious name of Dōshun. He played a large part in Ieyasu's measures to establish the authority of the Tokugawa shogunate and he might be said to have had a hand in almost all aspects of its organization and legal code. Even after Ieyasu's death he served as political advisor to the shoguns Hidetada, Iemitsu, and Ietsuna in turn; where official shogunate ceremony was concerned, as well as in foreign affairs, he almost invariably had a say. He founded the Shōheikō, a school devoted chiefly to the study of Neo-Confucianism, which in 1790 became an official organ, thereby laying the foundations of what was to be the "official learning" of the shogunate. Successive generations of his descendants served the shogunate as Confucian scholars, the Rinke (Hayashi family) school doing much to promote the tradition of Chinese studies in Japan. Razan, in short, was responsible for the flourishing state of Chinese studies and writing in Chinese during the Edo period, and was the founder of Chu Hsi studies in Japan as an independent branch of learning.

He wrote a very large number of books. Besides studies of the Chinese Classics such as *Daigaku shō, Daigaku kai,* and *Rongo kai,* he was also well versed in Japanese literature, and produced works such as *Genji monogatari-shoshō nengetsu kō, Nozuchi* (a commentary on *Tsurezuregusa*), *Nijūichi-dai-waka-shū nengetsu kō,* and *Utai shō.* A collection of verse and prose in Chinese in 150 chapters, *Razan shibun shū,* survives.

HIRAGA GENNAI (1728–1779)

Naturalist, dramatist, and fiction writer of the middle Edo period. His original name was Hiraga Kunitomo, and he went by such literary names as Fūraisanjin, Tenjikurōnin, and Fukuuchikigai. He was the son of an *ashigaru,* or minor official, in the domain of Takamatsu in Shikoku and showed great intelligence and ability from an early age. At first he served as a *chabōzu* (tea attendant), but later he was appointed an *ashigaru* and assigned to the herb garden of the Takamatsu fief. After five years in this post he resigned and, ostensibly for reasons of regaining his health, set off on a series of journeys, visiting and studying in Edo, the Kyoto-Osaka area, and Nagasaki. In Osaka he studied botany and other fields of natural science, while in Nagasaki he took an interest in herbal medicine and the making of utensils and also took up the study of Confucianism and, under a Dutch merchant, the study of Dutch. He returned to Edo once more, where he studied rhetoric, Chinese literature, and Japanese studies, the last under the famous scholar Kamo no Mabuchi, and finally became a disciple of Tamura Motoo, an authority on the production of various commodities, organizing a production society of his own.

While pursuing these studies, he made a number of discoveries in the field of herbal medicine and made scientific improvements in the cultivation of ginseng and the refining of sugar. His abilities were recognized by the lord of his native fief of Takamatsu, who assigned him a stipend, but in 1761 at the age of thirty-three he became a *rōnin*, a masterless samurai, and continued to pursue his various interests. In the field of natural science he discovered asbestos, experimented in ways of producing electricity, and made other contributions. At the same time, having devoted considerable time to the study of drama, principally on his own, and being thoroughly versed in Japanese literature, he tried his hand at writing works of fiction in the genre known as *sharebon* and dramas for the *jōruri* (puppet theater), producing works of importance in the cultural history of the Edo period.

His first literary work, written in the *sharebon* genre in 1763 and entitled *Nenashigusa*, represents the earliest example of a full-length satirical novel, dealing in a lively and vivid style with various aspects of the contemporary world and interspersed with passages of allegory and didactic comment. It had about it an air of freshness and novelty that proved greatly attractive to the readers of the time and enjoyed a remarkable sale at the time of its publication, and its form, approach, and biting style were imitated in many works of the period that followed. In the same year he published a second work, didactic in tone and colorful in content, entitled *Fūryūshi Dōkenden*, which traces the life and adventures of a single individual. It, too, was often imitated in later periods, becoming the prototype for the *denkimono* or *henrekimono*, which concentrate upon a single fictional character. His best known *jōruri* drama is that entitled *Shinrei yaguchi no watashi*.

Being a man of scientific temperament, his approach to his work was clearheaded and marked by a materialistic philosophy, and his attitude was sharply critical, qualities that did not always endear him to the men of his time. His scientific discoveries were at times dismissed as the work of a charlatan, and in fact he seems by nature to have been somewhat too impatient for success and less than careful in choosing the means by which to achieve it. In his later years he became increasingly disappointed in his lot in life, sinking into a mood of frustration and melancholia, until finally in a fit of anger he killed a man. He was put in prison and died there at the age of fifty-one. His dramatic works may be seen as attempts to give vent to the bitterness and melancholy that he felt over his failure to win recognition. Among the intellectual class of the An'ei (1772–81) and Temmei (1781–89) eras, his works were welcomed for their independent and progressive outlook and for the way in which, indiscriminate though it might be at times, he attacked the ignorance of the masses and the illogicalities of the society of his time.

Works of fiction: *Nenashigusa; Fūryūshi Dōkenden; Hōhiron; Ki ni mochi no naru ben.*

Jōruri dramas: *Shinrei yaguchi no watashi; Genshi ōzōshi; Chūshin iroha jitsuroku.*

Other works: *Hiraga Gennai zenshū*, 2 chapters; *Hiraga Gennai shū*; *Fūrai sanjin shū*.

HIRANO KUNIOMI (1827–1864)

Poet of the late Edo period. He was the second son of Hirano Kichizō, a samurai of the domain of Fukuoka. He was well versed in literature and the military arts and was a devoted scholar of Japanese studies; he adopted the literary names Tsukinoya and Hakusha. At one time he became the adopted son of Koganemaru Tanekazu, marrying his daughter and fathering two sons and a daughter, but later he left the Koganemaru family and resumed his original surname. From his early years he was an enthusiastic exponent of the *sonnō-jōi* movement, which sought to drive the foreigners out of Japan and restore power to the emperor. In 1858 he left the domain of Fukuoka and went to Kyoto, where he became friendly with Saigō Takamori, another leader of the movement. He was almost arrested by officials of the shogunate but, in company with the priest Gesshō, managed to flee to Kyushu. After Gesshō's death in 1862, he assisted Shimazu Hisamitsu in an attempt to seize power in Kyoto but was arrested and put into prison. He was pardoned the following year and went again to Kyoto, being appointed to a post in the Gakushū-in, a school for members of the court nobility, but in the tenth month of the same year he took part in an attempted coup at Ikuno in the domain of Tajima. The attempt failed, and he was once more arrested and confined in the Rokujō prison in Kyoto. While in prison he is said to have given lectures on the Japanese historical work *Jinnō shōtōki*; he was executed the following year at the age of thirty-six.

He was dark complexioned, with a pockmarked face, high cheekbones, and white hair, and was said to have looked more like a man of sixty. He was a man of great composure and strength of will and seems to have awed the persons who came into contact with him.

Two collections of his poems exist, the *Hirano Kuniomi kashū* and *Reigo shōkō*, the latter containing poems written when he was in prison and was obliged to write with a twist of paper in place of a brush. His poems are distinguished less for technical skill or refinement than for the intensity and passionate sincerity with which he gives expression to the ideals of the restoration movement.

> Beside these thoughts
> that burn
> in my breast,
> how thin the smoke rising
> from the cone of Sakurajima!

Hori Bakusui (1718–1783)

Haiku poet of the middle Edo period. His family name was Hori. He went by the common name of Ikedaya Chōzaemon, and employed such other names as Shirakuan and Choan. He was the son of a warehouse operator in the city of Kanazawa in Kaga. He turned his back on the family business, however, and went to Nagasaki, where he studied mathematics and foreign languages. He took an interest in *haiku* from an early age, studying under Wada Kiin of the Ise school, and took particular pains to master the styles of Shikō of the Mino school and Bakurin of the Ise school, in time becoming an exclusive follower of Bakurin, or Nakagawa Otsuyū, as he was also known. Around the age of thirty-one, Bakusui went to Edo to visit various exponents of the Ise school there, and also visited Bakurin's son Bakurō in Ise. Later he made frequent trips to Kyoto, where he associated with the famous *haiku* poet Taniguchi Buson and was otherwise active in literary affairs. By around the age of forty-five, he seems to have established a reputation as a *haiku* poet in the region of present-day Niigata Prefecture.

In time he came to feel that the Mino and Ise styles, which he had studied, were vulgar betrayals of the spirit of Bashō's work, and he set about inquiring into other styles, determined to bring about a revolution in the writing of *haiku*. His conclusion was that the works collected in the *Minashiguri* represented the highest achievement of Bashō and his associates, and he accordingly became a vigorous advocate of the so-called *Minashiguri* style. Around the age of fifty-five, while residing in Osaka, he wrote a critical work entitled *Shōmon ichiya kuju* in which he expounded his views on style, and in 1777 he published an anthology of *haiku* entitled *Shin minashiguri*, which was intended to give concrete examples of the principles he advocated. Thus Bakusui devoted his late years to an enthusiastic and unquestioning espousal of the style employed by Bashō in the 1680s. His own poetry, however, seems to have suffered from his excessive adulation of the *Minashiguri* style, and the works written before he became its advocate are generally superior. He was a man of great learning and wide literary interests and was undoubtedly the finest *haiku* critic of his time; the views that he expounded contributed greatly to the "Back to Bashō" movement that arose in the Temmei era (1781–89), around the time of his death. Some idea of his poetry may perhaps be gained from the following two examples:

> The stream flowing white
> among the rocks,
> plumes of pampas grass.

> Stillness—
> and again and again
> lotus seeds popping.[1]

In addition to the *Shōmon ichiya kuju,* he also wrote a work entitled *Jōkyō shōfū kukai.*

Hosokawa Yūsai (1534–1610)

Poet and classical scholar of the late Muromachi and Momoyama periods. He was born in Kyoto, the second son of Mibuchi Harukazu, but was adopted by Hosokawa Mototsune, an official of the Ashikaga shogunate; in his later years he became lord of the domain of Nagaoka and changed his surname to Nagaoka. His personal name was Fujitaka, and he is also referred to as Hosokawa Hyōbutayū, his official title; late in life he shaved his head and became a member of the Buddhist clergy, adopting the religious name Yūsai. He began his career by joining his father in the service of the twelfth Ashikaga shogun Yoshiharu, and later served the thirteenth shogun Yoshiteru, the fifteenth shogun Yoshiaki, and the military leaders Oda Nobunaga and Toyotomi Hideyoshi, and he also held high office under their successor Tokugawa Ieyasu. He was an outstanding military leader but was also highly versed in the peaceful arts as well. One of the most cultured men of his time, he succeeded in making his way without mishap through the perilous and rapidly changing world of the late Muromachi and Momoyama periods.

He studied the writing of Japanese poetry under Sanjōnishi Sane-e and Saneyo, becoming a follower of and authority upon the orthodox line of the Nijō school of poetics and commanding great respect in artistic circles of the time. In 1572 he was initiated by his teacher Sane-e in the *Kokin-denju,* a body

---

1. As the lotus pod ripens in the autumn, the seeds one by one shoot out of the holes in the pod.

of interpretations of certain words and phrases in the *Kokinshū* that was handed down in secret to a few persons who were deemed worthy of the honor. In 1600, the year of the great battle of Sekigahara, Yūsai was defending the castle of Tanabe in Tango when he was beseiged by the forces of Ishida Mitsunari. Because Yūsai was the sole living possessor of the secrets of the *Kokin-denju*, the emperor dispatched envoys to persuade the Ishida forces to withdraw and spare Yūsai's life, an incident that became famous in the history of the time.

Yūsai's views on poetry are recorded in works compiled by his disciples such as the *Yūsaiō kikigaki* and *Niteiki*; in general he seems to have been content to pass along the traditional theories handed down from the founders of the Nijō school. His collected poems, known as the *Shūmyōshū*, were compiled after his death by his disciple Asukai Masaaki. The work contains some eight hundred poems, written in the staid and lucid style typical of the Nijō school and outstanding principally for their elegance of tone. As a master of the techniques, theories, and lore characteristic of Japanese poetry of the medieval period, he served as a cultural bridge between that era and the early modern period that was just dawning. He had numerous disciples, including Nakanoin Mickikatsu, Karasumaru Mitsuhiro, Sanjōnishi Saneeda, Shimazu Yoshihisa, Matsunaga Teitoku, and Kinoshita Chōshōshi, and passed on the secrets of the *Kokin-denju* to Prince Katsura-no-miya Tomohito, the younger brother of Emperor Goyōzei. He was also highly skilled in witty improvisation and composed a number of poems in the humorous *kyōka* genre. The following is an example of his serious work:

> In the world,
> past or present,
> these never change:
> words that flower
> from the seeds of the heart.

In addition to the works mentioned above, his writings are found in the *Hosokawa Yūsai kikigaki zenshū*, *Eika taigaishō*, and *Kyūshūmichi no ki*.

Ihara Saikaku (1642–1692)

Poet and fiction writer of the early Edo period. His name was Hirayama Tōgo; Saikaku is a literary name he adopted later in life. He was the son of a merchant family of Osaka, though little is known about his background or early life. Itō Baiu (1684–1745) in his *Kemmon dansō* writes that Saikaku "was a wealthy merchant, but at the age of thirty-four [thirty-three by Western reckoning] he lost his wife, and his only daughter went blind and later died a premature death. After the death of his wife, he turned over the family business to his chief clerk and lived a life of freedom, frequenting the pleasure quarters and the theater and having many opportunities to observe the gaudy life of the time. At times he would go off on trips to the various provinces, sometimes remaining away from home for half a year or more."

He began writing poetry in *haiku* form around the age of fourteen or fifteen, at first following the style of Matsunaga Teitoku; his earliest known verse was written at the age of twenty-four, when he used the literary name Kakuei. Around 1673, however, he joined the Danrin school of *haiku*, becoming one of the most distinguished disciples of Nishiyama Sōin, the head of the school, and taking an active part in the creation of a new style of *haiku* known as *Oranda-ryū*.

In 1677 he instituted the *yakazu*, or poetry marathon, a display of literary skill and stamina in which a poet tried to see how many linked *haiku* verses he could produce in a given period of time, composing a total of sixteen hundred linked *haiku* in a period of twenty-four hours. In 1680 he set a new record of four thousand verses, becoming the undisputed champion in the field. His successes in the *yakazu*, of which he was very proud, indicate the startling speed with which his mind worked and the wealth of his power of association; his verses follow one another like so many flashes of light, each capturing a single vivid impression.

In 1682 his master, Nishiyama Sōin, died, and Saikaku for the first time turned to the genre of prose fiction known as *ukiyo-zōshi*, producing a work entitled *Kōshoku ichidai otoko* (*The Life of a Man Who Lived for Love*). In 1684 he held his third *yakazu*, producing the astounding total of 23,500 verses in a period of twenty-four hours, and also wrote a second work of prose fiction entitled *Shoen ōkagami*, also known as *Kōshoku nidai otoko*. This was followed in 1685 by *Saikaku shokokubanashi*; in 1686 by *Kōshoku gonin onna* (*Five Women Who Loved Love*), and *Kōshoku ichidai onna* (*The Life of an Amorous Woman*); and in 1687 by *Nanshoku ōkagami* (*The Great Mirror of Manly Love*), a collection of tales dealing with male homosexuality. All these works deal for the most part with the lives of the *chōnin*, the townsmen, and depict their search for hedonistic pleasure. The year 1687, however, marks a turning point in Saikaku's fiction writing; in the works that followed, he abandoned the subject of sexual adventure to take up instead the themes of the warrior spirit and the economic life of the townsmen. His *Budō denraiki* (*Record of Traditions of the Warrior's Way*), written in 1687, and *Buke giri monogatari* (*Tales of the Knightly Code of Honor*), written in 1688, for example, deal with the former theme, while the *Nippon eitaigura* (*Eternal Storehouse of Japan*), written in 1688, treats the latter theme, being a collection of stories designed to illustrate the various ways in which men can make and lose money. It was around this time that he adopted for a while the literary name Saihō.

In 1692 appeared the *Seken munazanyō* and *Naniwamiyage,* the last works that were to be published during his lifetime. The *Seken munazanyō* (*Reckonings That Carry Men through the World*), along with the *Nihon eitaigura* and *Saikaku oridome,* a work published posthumously by Saikaku's disciple Hōjō Dansui in 1694, are regarded as the masterpieces of Saikaku's *chōnin* works, giving expression to the ideals of the merchant class and depicting both the pleasures and hardships of the townsmen living in a world where money was all powerful. Saikaku's background and talent as a *haiku* poet are reflected in the style and construction of these works of prose fiction. They are for the most part made up of collections of brief anecdotes and tales, the style tends to be highly rhythmical and poetic in tone, and all are marked by a vividness of impression and realistic presentation of the human scene.

Ishikawa Masamochi (1753–1830)

Scholar of the Japanese classics and *kyōka* poet of the late Edo period. As a writer of *kyōka* (humorous verse) he was also known as Yadoya no Meshimori (Servant at the Inn)—a reference to the fact that he ran an inn at Kodemma-chō in Edo—and he also used the pen name Rokujuen. Son of the great *ukiyo-e* artist Ishikawa Toyonobu, he himself studied painting with his father during his youth. The only formal education he had was a grounding in the Japanese classics given by Tsumura Sōan; for the rest, he is said to have been self-educated, reading widely in the Japanese and Chinese classics, so that he came to be known as the most scholarly of the *kyōka* poets. His talent was rich and varied: his intimate knowledge of the classics produced such works as *Gagen shūran* and *Genchū yoteki* as well as works of the imagination in pseudo-archaic style such as *Hokuri jūniji, Azuma namari,* and *Miyako no teburi,* while he also wrote popular novelettes in the *kibyōshi* and *yomihon* styles.

He studied *kyōka* at first with Tsuburino Hikari, but later became a pupil of Yomo no Akara (Ōta Nampo); he soon made a name for himself and formed his own school, being ranked alongside Shikatsube Magao and Baba Kinkochi as one of the leading *kyōka* poets. From *Azuma-buri kyōka bunko* on, Masamochi had many volumes of *kyōka* published by the well-known publisher Tsutajū, but in 1791 he was expelled from Edo under suspicion of running without license a *kuji-yado* (an inn in Kyoto or Edo during the Edo period for persons who came up from the provinces for law suits). For many years he was out of the limelight, but made a comeback around 1808 and attacked the *haikai-uta*, a type of humorous verse advocated by Shikatsube Magao, insisting that the true *kyōka* should contain a greater element of satire, and setting himself up as leader of the orthodox school of *kyōka*. He had followers all over the country, said to have numbered several thousand.

His works number several dozen, including collections such as *Azuma-buri kyōka bunko* and works such as *Hida no Takumi monogatari* and *Ōmi Akata monogatari*. The following is an example of his *kyōka*

> When it comes to poets,
> the clumsier, the better.
> What would we do
> if heaven and earth
> really started to move![1]

Itō Jinsai (1627–1705)

Confucian scholar of the early Edo period. Also known by the studio name Kogidō, he was the son of a Kyoto merchant. His interest in Confucianism was first aroused at the age of ten by a reading of the *Ta hsüeh* (*Great Learning*), one of the classical texts of Confucianism, particularly the passage dealing with the problem of how to "order the state and bring peace to the world." At eighteen he is said to have reread the work entitled *Yen-p'ing wen-ta* by the Sung Confucian scholar Li T'ung so many times that he wore out the paper it was printed on. As this anecdote indicates, he at first accepted the type of Confucianism that had been systematized by the Sung scholar Chu Hsi, known as the Chu Hsi school of Neo-Confucianism. From around the age of thirty-six or thirty-seven, however, he began to have doubts about the validity of the Sung interpretations, believing that they were too much influenced by borrowings from Buddhism and Taoism and did not represent the original thought of Confucius and Mencius, the founders of the Confucian school in ancient times; he also rejected the *Ta hsüeh* as a source for the study of the original Confucian doctrine. Placing great emphasis upon proper moral conduct and trusting to his own interpretation

---

1. A humorous reference to Ki no Tsurayuki's preface to the *Kokinshū*, a classic statement on Japanese poetics, which declares that "great poetry can move heaven and earth."

of Confucianism, he wrote two works on the *Mencius* and *Chung yung* respectively, entitled *Ron Mō kogi* and *Chūyō hakki*, and opened a school at Horikawa in Kyoto, where he gave instruction in Confucianism as he interpreted it. The school was known as the Kogidō, or "Hall for the Study of Ancient Meanings," and the doctrines that Jinsai taught, called the Jinsai or Horikawa school, represent a part of the general intellectual movement of the time known as the *kogakuha* (school of ancient learning), which sought to turn back to the texts of ancient China and Japan and discover their original meaning. Jinsai had over three thousand students drawn from all parts of Japan, and it is said that only the provinces of Hida, Sado, and Iki were without representatives among his disciples. His teachings were faithfully carried on by his son Itō Tōgai, who was also a prolific writer of scholarly works.

In addition to the two works mentioned above, Jinsai wrote the *Dōjimon* and *Go Mō jigi*, and his miscellaneous writings and poems in Chinese are collected under the title *Kogaku sensei shibunshū*.

Jippensha Ikku (1765–1831)

Fiction writer of the late Edo period. He was born in Fuchū in the province of Suruga, the son of a *sennin-dōshin*, or lower grade samurai official. He was sent on official business to Osaka but there resigned his position and tried his hand at writing for the puppet drama, in conjunction with another writer turning out a play entitled *Konoshita Kagehazama kassen*. Later he went to Edo, where he wrote works of popular fiction of the type known as *kibyōshi*, or "yellow cover books," and gradually gained a reputation among Edo readers. Thereafter he produced about twenty such books a year. In 1802 he wrote his best known work, a *kokkeibon* (humorous tale) entitled *Tōkaidōchū hizakurige* in twenty chapters, which deals with the amusing adventures of two happy-go-lucky travelers on the great Tōkai Highway between Edo and Osaka. It won wide acclaim for its author and was so popular that for the next twenty years Ikku continued to turn out sequels to the tale.

Ikku was also skilled at the writing of humorous verses in the *kyōka* and *senryū* forms and was an accomplished artist and calligrapher, producing the illustrations and hand-written text for many of his own books, including the *Hizakurige*. Though he was thoroughly conversant with the ways of the world, and his works abound in earthy humor, there are numerous anecdotes that suggest that he himself was a man of circumspect and fastidious temperament. The novelist Takizawa Bakin called him "the most admirable of the present-day writers," and added that he was the first author who succeeded in making a living entirely by his writings. His *Hizakurige* has become a classic of its kind, and entitles him to be regarded, along with Shikitei Samba, as one of the most outstanding writers of humorous fiction in the Edo period.

KADA NO ARIMARO (1706–1751)

Student of the Japanese classics (*kokugakusha*) during the middle Edo period. The nephew and adopted son of Kada no Azumamaro, he concentrated on the poetics and the study of ancient legal and ritual matters that formed only two aspects of his adopted father's many-faceted interests. He went to Edo in his youth, where he followed his adoptive father in serving the shogunate and also worked in the service of Tayasu Munetake, a student of the Japanese classics and second son of the eighth Tokugawa shogun, Yoshimune, but publication of his *Daishōe bemmō* invoked official displeasure. He later wrote, at the request of Munetake, a work on poetics entitled *Kokka hachiron*, but his respect for technical polish of the kind found in the *Shinkokinshū* disagreed with the views of Munetake, a champion of the more direct, unsophisticated style of the *Man'yōshū*, and in the end he resigned from the service of the Tayasu family, to die shortly afterwards.

As a man, he was marked by the greatest intellectual penetration and a sturdy uprightness of character. As a result, he argued unhesitantly and stubbornly over academic points even with his master Tayasu Munetake, never allowing other considerations to deflect him from the course of reason.

His studies of ancient rituals include *Daijōe gushaku* and *Daijōe bemmō*, the most outstanding study of the *daijōsai*, the first "harvest ritual" performed by the emperor following his accession to the throne. He also wrote various works such as *Hagura kō*, *Ryō samben*, and *Honchō dosei ryakukō*, dealing with the *ritsuryō* code, the legal code of ancient times, and related matters. His writing on poetics includes the *Kokka hachiron*, in which he attacks the old school of poetics, and champions the approach to verse shown in the *Shin kokinshū*. His theory is that although verse was originally intended to be sung, it had in practice ceased to be sung in later ages, and that it was better accordingly to concentrate on highly polished, purely verbal display. He relegates the importance of verse as "song" to second place, elevating in its stead verbal *waza*, or technique.

KADA NO AZUMAMARO (1669–1736)

Student of the Japanese classics (*kokugakusha*) and poet of the middle Edo period. He also used the surname Hagura and he was commonly called Itsuki. He was born the son of a Shinto priest, his family having for many generations been in the service of the Fushimi Inari Shrine in Kyoto. Thus from early childhood he studied the traditions of Shinto and poetics handed down in his family, and this served as the foundation on which he developed his own brand of scholarship.

At the age of twenty-eight he became a teacher of poetry and went to serve in the court Bureau of Poetry. He found favor with Prince Myōhōin, son of Emperor Reigen. However, at the age of thirty he retired from the Bureau of Poetry and went to Edo where, after a period of free study, he went into the service of the shogunate, acting as advisor, inspecting and revising old documents and records submitted by the various provinces and books stored in the shogunate's official library, and publishing various works of his own on his researches in the classics. During the last years of his life, he had his adopted son Arimaro take over his duties and went back to his home, where he devoted his time to the study of the Japanese classics and the education of his pupils.

The most outstanding of his achievements are his studies of the *Man'yōshū* and the *Nihon Shoki*, though his studies of ancient rituals and laws were also important for their influence on the development of Japanese classical studies. In both cases his role is chiefly that of commentator; he offers many highly original opinions in this field, though he has a regrettable tendency to make arbitrary emendations of the original text. He played an extremely important role in laying down a definitive model for the school of learning known as *kokugaku*, using his critical or annotative accounts of the classics as a means of elucidating the significance of the ancient learning and the old morale in the light of the studies.

In the field of Shinto studies, where his works include *Nihon Shoki jindai shō*, *Jindai no maki tōki*, and *Kojiki tōki*, he tends towards a theology of intellectualized morality. His works on poetics, which include *Manyō hekian shō*, *Manyō dōji mon*, and *Ise monogatari dōji mon*, focus chiefly on the *Man'yōshū*, and show a tendency towards an intuitive approach, though admittedly one backed up by illustrations. Apart from these, he produced studies of ancient rituals and laws such as *Ruijū sandaikyaku kō* and *Ryōgi no ge tōki*. In addition, as a poet in his own right, he published a collection of his own verse in two volumes, *Shunyōshū*. The preface to this collection explains that there are no poems on the conventional theme of love since in such works "it was impossible to achieve the true purpose of poetry—to tell the truth." There are poems descriptive of nature, but their approach is rather intellectual, nature always being linked up with human affairs in some way. His championship of *kokugaku* led him to plan the foundation of a school for that learning, and a petition on the subject entitled *Sō gakkō kei* (1728) is believed to have been written by him. He was a man of spirit and enthusiasm yet considerate in dealing with others; his pupils included the celebrated Kamo no Mabuchi as well as Kada no Arimaro and many other noted scholars who provided the driving force behind the *kokugaku* movement of the Edo period. A stroke at the age of sixty-one disabled him and he died leaving many planned works unfinished.

> Where even the sound
> of the raging storm does not reach,
> there above the clouds,
> how serenely
> the moon must shine!

Kada no Tamiko (1722–1786)

Poet and critic of the middle Edo period. She was the younger sister of Kada no Arimaro, a Kyoto poet and scholar of Japanese studies. At an early age she accompanied her brother to Edo. She later married, but was shortly after widowed and returned to her brother's home, remaining a widow the rest of her life. She studied poetic theory and the writing of poetry under her brother (and perhaps under her uncle Kada no Azumamaro as well). For a time she served as lady-in-waiting to a daughter of the Kii branch of the Tokugawa family, but retired at the age of forty-eight and lived the remainder of her life within the grounds of the Kinryū-ji temple in the Asakusa area of Edo. Her literary talents gained recognition, and she was invited to give instruction in poetry to the wives and daughters of the lords of Tosa, Himeji, and other feudal domains. She was a woman of cheerful disposition and great intellectual acumen and conducted herself with an air of authority.

Being born into a religious family—the Kada were hereditary Shinto priests of the Fushimi Inari Shrine in Kyoto—she was very devout and lived a life of impeccable propriety. She left only one scholarly work, a collated text of the *Kokinshū*, and she was not particularly distinguished as a poet, but her intelligence, wide learning, and authoritative manner reflected credit upon the Kada school of poetry and helped to contribute to its rapid rise to fame. She also deserves recognition for the contribution she made toward the education of the daughters of the feudal nobility. Her poems were collected and edited by her disciple Hishida Nuiko and were published in 1795 with a preface by Tachibana Chikage under the title *Sugi no shizue*. Her poems are graceful and employ a style somewhere between that of the *Kokinshū* and of the *Shin kokinshū*.

KAGAMI SHIKŌ (1665–1731)

Haiku poet of the early and middle Edo period. His family name was Kagami, and he employed such other names as Tōkabō, Seikabō, Shishian, Renjibō, and Hakukyō. He was born in the province of Mino, the second son of a family named Murase. At an early age he was turned over to a temple for training as a monk, but later left the temple and became an adopted member of a family named Kagami. In 1691, when he was twenty-six, he met Bashō in Ōmi and became a disciple of the latter, journeying to Edo. The following year he wrote a critical work on *haiku* entitled *Kuzu no matsubara* in which he discussed Bashō's style, and through his considerable talent and resources soon came to be numbered among the "Ten Philosophers," or ten major disciples of Bashō. In 1694 he moved to Yamada in the province of Ise, and in the ninth month of the same year accompanied Bashō on what was to be the latter's final journey.

While Bashō remained alive, Shikō continued to write *haiku* in the pure and lofty style advocated by his master. But after Bashō's death, motivated apparently by a desire for greater fame and recognition, he began moving in the direction of a simpler and more popular style, creating what was to become known, after his birthplace, as the Mino school of *haiku*. He traveled about from region to region working to spread a knowledge of Bashō's work, but at the same time he used the opportunity to publicize his own views and to strengthen his position in the *haiku* world. In 1711, anxious to learn what opinion the world held of him, he fabricated an account of his final days and put out the report that he had died. In the meantime he went into hiding in his native village and, pretending to be one of his own disciples, continued to publish works under the name Renjibō. In spite of such eccentric ways, he was a man of great creativity and organizing ability, and was the foremost *haiku* theorist among the disciples of Bashō, producing such critical works as *Haikai jūron* and *Jūron ibenshō*, and setting forth a view distinctively his own. He also invented a new type of poetry known as *washi*, which employs the Japanese syllabary but imitates the forms of Chinese poetry, and in other ways showed an inventive spirit. His *haiku*, with their rather popular and undemanding style, and his critical writings, which purported to represent the views of his teacher, Bashō, were welcomed among persons of limited education in the provinces, and his influence soon extended over the entire country. Because of the intrinsic limitations of his personality, however, and the fact that he deliberately espoused a flat and folksy style, his *haiku* are rather shallow in tone and lacking in suggestiveness. The following are two examples of his work:

> Sparrows chirping
> in the refectory,
> autumn showers at evening.

> At the sound of someone
> scolding the cows,
> a snipe flies off in the twilight.

Kaga no Chiyo (1703–1775)

Haiku poet of the middle Edo period. She was born in the province of Kaga, the daughter of a picture mounter. From an early age she showed an interest in the arts and seems to have begun writing *haiku* from around the age of fifteen or sixteen, though she does not appear to have studied under any particular teacher. In 1721 when the distinguished *haiku* poets Shikō and Rosen at different times passed through the region of Kaga, they both met Chiyo and were greatly impressed with her talent, praising her and working to publicize her writings. As might be expected, her works show considerable influence from the Mino school, the group headed by Shikō. In time her reputation spread throughout the country, and in 1725 the *haiku* poet Uchū of Komatsu made a special effort to insure recognition for her work by mentioning her in his writings. It is said that she married, but lost her husband and infant son and returned to her original home, though there is no written evidence to support this assertion. The poem that reads:

> When I get up,
> when I go to bed,
> how big and empty the mosquito net!

which supposedly refers to these sad events, has been proved to be the work of an entirely different writer, and some scholars maintain that Chiyo never married at all. As her fame spread abroad, many *haiku* poets visited her in the course of their wanderings, though her closest associations seem to have been with the members of the Mino school. Later she shaved her head and became a nun, devoting herself entirely to artistic pursuits, and in 1755 changed her name to Soen. Her reputation continued to grow, and in 1763 a selection of her poems compiled by Kikaku appeared under the title *Chiyo-ni kushū*; a further selection entitled *Matsu no koe* appeared in 1771. There appears to have been a strong tendency to idolize her and treat her as a writer of almost superhuman genius, and various works and anecdotes that originally had no connection with her have come to be associated with her name. Something of the shallow, mundane quality typical of the Mino school permeates her work, and many of her poems are characterized by mere verbal cleverness. However, although she fails to attain the highest levels of artistic expression, her works have a typically feminine delicacy of observation and feeling, and her skillful use of personification in her descriptions of nature is particularly noteworthy. Her most famous poem, which makes use of this device, is that which reads:

> By morning glories
> I have had my well-bucket captured—
> and I borrow my water![1]

Kagawa Kageki (1768–1843)

Poet and writer on poetics of the late Edo period; founder of the Keien school. His extraordinary talent as a child rapidly attracted attention, and at the age of nineteen he left his home in Tottori for Kyoto with the intention of making his way as a poet. He became a pupil of Kagawa Kagemoto, then a leading figure in aristocratic poetic circles, and was also taught by Ozawa Roan. In time his talents was recognized, and he was adopted by the Kagawa family. He subsequently split with the family for personal reasons, but he continued to use the family name and to devote his life to poetry, becoming the leading figure in the world of poetry in the Kyoto-Osaka area.

His theories on the writing of poetry center round his theory of *shirabe*, the natural, rhythmical flow of the verse; writing verse, he said, was an instinctive action for man, innocent of any intellectual motivation. Any attempt to write it as a means to some spiritual goal or for the sake of instructing society opens the doors to theory and insincerity. To do so is not the true attitude of the true poet. Verse, rather, should concern itself with setting

---

1. Translated by Harold G. Henderson, *An Introduction to Haiku*, New York: Doubleday, 1958, p. 83.

down sincere feelings just as they stand, with the aim of satisfying man's instincts, and such sincere feelings are what constitute *shirabe*. Large numbers of poets were attracted by the new type of verse he propounded, and his school came virtually to dominate poetry circles in the Osaka and Kyoto area. This school came to be known as the Keien school. The number of poets who started life as his pupils rivaled the number produced by the scholars Kamo no Mabuchi and Motoori Norinaga. His views clashed with those of Mabuchi in particular; where Mabuchi stressed the idea of spiritural return to the classics and held that poetry should go out of its way to use archaic words, Kageki insisted that the poet should use everyday language; the important thing was that the wording should be sufficiently familiar for a mere hearing of the poem to convey emotion immediately.

The popularity of the Keien style flourished unabated following Kageki's death, and the school lingered on as the "old school" even following the appearance of a new modern school of poets after the Meiji Restoration of 1868.

> In Ōi River waters
> that flow on without return
> their forms appear
> this year once more—
> blooms of the mountain cherry.

Kᴀᴊɪᴋᴏ, Yᴜʀɪ, Gʏᴏᴋᴜʀᴀɴ

Poets of the mid Edo period. Kajiko was the proprietress of a tea house situated on the south side of the entrance to the Gion Shrine in Kyoto. When the Edo poet Ameishi visited Kyoto in 1706 and became acquainted with her works, he decided they would make an interesting souvenir of the capital and, compiling a selection of some hundred or so poems and adding pictures by the Kyoto artist Yuzen, who was at that time very popular, published them in a three-chapter work entitled *Kaji no ha* in the following year. She does not appear to have studied with any particular teacher, but her works were nevertheless of such quality as to win wide acclaim. Being the mistress of a shop that catered to all types of customers, she seems to have been constantly troubled by the importuning of would-be lovers, and many of her poems are replies to romantic overtures, full of wit and charm. Her adopted daughter was known as Gion Yuriko, also a poet and author of a collection of verses entitled *Sayurishū*. Yuriko's daughter Machi became the wife of the celebrated painter Ike no Taiga and adopted the artistic name Gyokuran.

She was skilled in painting as well as poetry; her poems are preserved in a collection entitled *Shirofuyō*. The works of these three women collectively are known as the *Gion sanjo kashū* ("Collected Works of the Three Women Poets of Gion"). The following poem is by Kajiko:

> How peaceful,
> this spring morning
> in the land of Japan—
> even the heart of the river,
> even the posture of the breeze.

Kamijima (Uejima) Onitsura (1661–1738)

Haiku poet of the early and middle Edo period. His given name was Munechika, his common name Yosobee, and he also employed such other names as Kinkaō, Rarari, Inukoji, and Satoe. He was born in the town of Itami in the province of Settsu, on the border between present-day Hyōgo and Osaka prefectures. The writing of *haiku* was very popular in Itami at this time, and both Matsue Shigeyori of the Teitoku school and Nishiyama Sōin of the Danrin school worked to promote their respective styles there. In addition, Sōtan, a disciple of Matsue Shigeyori, had founded a *haiku* center of instruction known as the Yaunken and had attracted many students.

Onitsura at the age of twelve became a student of Matsue Shigeyori and participated in the *haiku* gatherings of the group. In time he also became friendly with Sōin and transferred to the Danrin school. At the age of sixteen he produced his first collection of *haiku*. Sometime around 1680 he began to feel dissatisfied with the teachings of the Danrin school and set about on his own to investigate and discover the true nature of *haiku* poetry. As a result of these researches, he announced in the spring of 1685, when he was twenty-four, that "Outside of truth there is no *haiku*," and set about to compose "true *haiku*" in accordance with this new ideal. The following year he went to Edo, but later settled down in Osaka. At some later date he also served the lords of the fiefs of Miike in Chikugo, Kōriyama in Yamato, and Ōno in Echizen respectively, but also lived at intervals in Kyoto and Osaka. At the age of seventy-two he shaved his head and entered the Buddhist clergy and died a few years later at Osaka in 1738. He was said to have been very devoted to his parents and would not journey away from home while they were alive.

Onitsura's ideal of *makoto* ("truthfulness") in *haiku* is an attempt to apply to that poetic form the principle earlier formulated for traditional *waka* style

Japanese poetry in the words *shinshu shijū*, "heart first, words second." The emphasis in either case is upon the absolute emotional sincerity and truthfulness of the poem as a requisite that takes precedence over any verbal cleverness or skill. Onitsura's theory has much in common with the ideas that Bashō was advocating at the time, both men emphasizing the need for artistic truth in *haiku*. But Onitsura divorced his concept of "truthfulness" from any ethical considerations and did not elaborate it in aesthetic terms, holding that the expression of pure and simple naturalness was sufficient to constitute *haiku*. He thus ignored the role played by rhetorical devices and skill of expression in enhancing the effectiveness of the statement, and in this respect fell far short of Bashō in artistic stature.

Onitsura appears to have been a man of very frank and open-minded disposition. He cared very little for fame or material profit, was content to live in straightened circumstances, and made no attempt to found a *haiku* school of his own. But although he could not match the profundity of Bashō, his works, because of their naturalness and grace, held a place of considerable importance in the *haiku* world of the Genroku era (1688–1703), and his theory of "truthfulness" represents a major contribution to the development of the aesthetics of Japanese literature. The following two poems are representative of his work:

> Dawn—and on
> the tips of the barley leaves,
> spring frost.

> No place to throw
> the old bath water—
> voices of insects.

Onitsura's important works include the *Inukoji, Hitorigoto,* and *Haikai nanaguruma.*

KAMO NO MABUCHI (1697–1769)

Scholar of the Japanese classics and poet of the middle Edo period. He also used the literary name Agatai. Born the son of a Shinto priest in Hamamatsu in the province of Tōtōmi, he was brought up at first as the adopted son of his elder sister's husband. However, when the sister gave birth to a child, he was adopted into the family of a cousin, whose daughter he married, but his wife died, and he went back to his own family. Subsequently, he married into a family called Umeya and had a son. He studied Chinese poetry and Chinese learning with Watanabe Mōan, a pupil of Dazai Shundai. He had also, since an early age, been friendly with Sugiura Kuniakira and Mori Terumasa, pupils of Kada no Azumamaro; through them he got to know Azumamaro himself and studied with him. At the age of thirty-six he left his wife and child behind and went to Kyoto, where he studied the classics and ancient Japanese and acquired a taste for the ancient Japanese way of life. On the death of his teacher Azumamaro, when Mabuchi himself was thirty-nine, he returned home, but the following year went to Edo, where he devoted himself to scholarship together with Arimaro, Azumamaro's adopted heir, and others of like mind. At the age of forty-nine, he succeeded Arimaro as tutor in *kokugaku* (classical Japanese studies) to Tayasu Mune-take, the second son of Tokugawa Yoshimune. Thereafter, thanks to a stable livelihood and ample facilities for study, his ideas matured steadily, and from the age of sixty-three, when he retired, until his death at the age of seventy-two, he wrote a large number of books and instructed a large number of outstanding pupils—men such as Motoori Norinaga, Arakida Hisaoi, Murata Harumi, and Katō Chikage.

The underlying idea behind his studies was to foster a correct understanding of and to restore the "spirit of the past." His work ranged over Shinto, poetics, linguistics, and court manners and etiquette. His ostensible aim was to elucidate the "way of old," especially as embodied in the *Kojiki*, but his achievement in practice lay rather in his studies of ancient poetry and the ancient language, especially as found in the *Man'yōshū*. He championed a return to the style of the *Man'yōshū* and in his own verse made much use of the vocabulary and style of that anthology; he also drew on the *Kojiki*, the *norito* (Shinto prayers) and ancient songs, calling for a return to the natural, unsophisticated, noble spirit peculiar to ancient Japan as embodied in concepts such as *makoto* (sincerity), *shirabe* (natural rhythmical flow), and *masaoburi* (manliness). These ideals he contrasted with the more "effeminate" *Kokinshū* and later anthologies, which he considered effete and overoccupied with technique. In this way he was largely responsible for the marked revival of interest in classical Japanese studies during his period.

An example of Mabuchi's verse is:

> The crickets singing,
> in my country lodge
> how bright the moonlight—
> if only someone
> would come to call!

KARAI SENRYŪ (1718–1790)

His name was Karai Hachiemon, and he was a *nanushi*, community head of Shinhoribata in the Asakusa district of Edo; Senryū is his literary name. He first became a *haiku* critic at the age of forty and promptly outstripped his fellows, so that verses that he had selected came to be known as *Senryū-ten* (approved by Senryū), and eventually simply as *senryū*. For thirty-three years, until his death at the age of seventy-two, he published selections of verse every year, and the result of his labors is embodied in *Senryū hyō Yorozu-ku-awase*, a collection of some eighty thousand verses to which he gave high marks from a total of some 2.3 million verses submitted. This collection was so voluminous, however, that Senryū's pupil Goryōken Arubeshi made a further selection of 756 outstanding verses taken from thirteen years' collections, all of these verses capable of being understood on their own without the concluding lines. The *senryū* began as a kind of game in which one person composed the last two lines (7-7) of a *tanka* and gave them to another person who had to supply the first three lines (5-7-5). The result of Arubeshi's effort is the first edition of *Haifū yanagidaru*. This work was epoch making in that it omitted the 7-7 syllable couplet usual in the *Yorozu-ku-awase*, thus in one move establishing the 5-7-5 *senryū* as a literary form in its own right. Senryū himself died the year preceding the appearance of the twenty-fourth version of *Yanagidaru*, and thereafter the judges and editors changed many times, the work continuing under the same name until the 167th edition. However, *Yanagidaru's* value is limited to the first twenty-four editions.

The most important collection apart from *Yanagidaru* is *Haifū yanagidaru shūi*, which ran to ten versions; these focus on the work of Senryū I, but also include works selected from the collections of other judges. They contain much excellent work and are distinguished by being divided up into sections, arranged chronologically, in the manner of the *Kokinshū*.

The *senryū* has a humor and irony that makes it a typical art of the common people; it excels in searching out the innermost workings of human feelings and even today conveys a sense of the emotions of the man in the street.

> Son of an official—
> just remember
> to grab, grab, grab!

> Mothers!
> how precious they are to us—
> and so easy to fool.

He showed me the way,
pointing with the radish
he'd just pulled up.

KAWATAKE MOKUAMI (1816–1893)

Kabuki dramatist of the late Edo and Meiji periods. Unwilling to take up the
family business of pawnbroking, he became a pupil of the playwright
Tsuruya Namboku and at the age of nineteen went to work for the Ichimura-
za theater in Edo. At the age of twenty-seven he took the name of Kawatake
Shinshichi II. From then until the time when he reached the age of forty-one
was a kind of apprenticeship during which, as a playwright, he undertook
work of every nature. What might be called his second period lasted from the
age of forty-two to the age of fifty and established his position as a playwright; it was also his most energetic period, during which, in collaboration
with the actor Ichikawa Kodanji, he produced a large number of *sewa* plays
(contemporary domestic dramas) and *shiranami* plays (centering round the
activities of thieves), such as *Bunya goroshi*, *Izayoiseishin*, *Sannin Kichiza
kuruwa no hatsukai*, etc., portraying from every angle the emotional outlook
of the common people of the city of Edo.

His third period, from the age of fifty-one to the age of sixty-five, saw him
at the peak of his powers and produced his most characteristic work. His
style underwent a great development, and the new plays he produced were
conceived on a much grander scale. They include works such as *Youchi Soga*,
Ōshio Heihachirō, and *Ten'ichibō*. Besides these works based more or less on
historical episodes, he also produced *zangiri-mono* (lit. "short-haired plays,"
an allusion to the compulsory cutting-off of the topknots worn by most
Japanese men prior to the Meiji Restoration of 1868), contemporary dramas
that incorporated the new manners and speech of the Meiji period. In addition, he wrote—mostly at the instigation of the celebrated actor Danjūrō—
historical plays produced so far as possible in a manner faithful to the facts
and striving after greater psychological truth. At the age of sixty-five he
determined to retire and wrote a play entitled *Shimachidori tsuki no shiranami*,
which he announced would sum up his life's work. At this point he changed
his name from Kawatake Shinshichi II to Furukawa Mokuami.

His fourth period, extending from the age of sixty-six to the age of
seventy-seven, saw the opening of the new Kabuki-za theater in Tokyo. He
undertook the staging of kabuki or puppet plays by Chikamatsu and produced
for Danjūrō dance-dramas such as *Suō otoshi* and *Kagami-jishi*, while for

Kikugorō V he wrote *Sakanaya Sōgorō, Fudeya Kobei, Tsuchigumo,* and *Ibaragi.*

In all Mokuami left some 360 works that bring together all the varied elements of the drama of Edo. They are brilliant and inventive in themselves, but he is also noteworthy for giving kabuki a new, richly poetic expressiveness and musical quality and for his role as a kind of bridge between the old age and the new.

Keichū (1640–1701)

Priest and scholar of Japanese studies of the early Edo period. He came from a family named Shimokawa, his grandfather Motonobu having been a highly placed retainer of the Katō family, the lords of the domain of Kumamoto in Kyushu. With the downfall of the Katō family, however, the members of the Shimokawa family became scattered, and Keichū was born in Amagasaki, near the city of Osaka. A precocious child, he suffered from a serious illness at the age of six. Praying fervently for recovery, which in time came about, he determined to become a monk and devote his life to religion.

At the age of ten he accordingly entered the Myōhō-ji, a temple situated in the Imazato district of Osaka, and became a disciple of the head priest Kaijō. Two years later, he entered the monastery on Mt. Kōya and pursued his Buddhist studies under Kaiken, and by the age of twenty-three he had attained the high ecclesiastical rank of Ajari. In time he became head priest of the Mandara-in in the Ikutama section of Osaka and there became acquainted with Shimokōbe Chōryū, who was to be his lifelong friend. Around the age of twenty-six, however, he embarked on a life of wandering, staying for a time at Mt. Murō, visiting Mt. Kōya to take, under Kaien, the special religious vows known as Bosatsukai, and living as a guest of the Tsujimori family in the village of Kui in Izumi, south of Osaka. Some five years later he moved to the residence of Fuseya Jūemon Shigekata, a wealthy man of Manchō in Osaka and began making a study of his host's collection of works on Japanese and Chinese literature. At the same time he continued his association with Shimokōbe Chōryū, becoming increasingly interested in poetics and laying the foundation for his later studies of Japanese literature. In order to provide for the care of his mother, he took a position as head priest of the Myōhō-ji around the age of thirty-nine, remaining there for the following ten years or more and, with the encouragement of Chōryū, produced his great study of the *Man'yōshū* entitled *Man'yō daishōki.*

In 1690, after his mother's death, he retired to a small temple named Enjuan in the Kōzu area of Osaka, living there for the remainder of his life and devoting himself to scholarship. His works include the *Waji shōranshō*, a study of the history of *kana* spellings; a commentary on the songs included in the *Kojiki* and *Nihon Shoki* entitled *Kōganshō*; and other commentaries on Japanese poetry and literature such as the *Yozaishō*, *Seigo okudan*, *Hyakunin isshu kaiganshō*, *Genchū shūi*, and numerous others. In his late years, at the request of his disciples Ikan, Jakuchū, and others, he gave lectures on the *Man'yōshū*, and composed poems in *waka* form to commemorate the conclusion of the lectures. A devout and learned follower of the Shingon sect of Buddhism, he at the same time made an important contribution to the study of Japanese poetry and the classics of Japanese literature. Beginning with a pure and disinterested desire to discover the truth, he pursued his studies by the inductive method, being careful to provide corroborative evidence to support his findings, and through his pioneering efforts laid the foundation for the study of the Japanese classics in the Edo period. With the *Man'yōshū* as his focus of interest, he explored textual and linguistic problems and produced annotations and critical comments on the text. His most significant works are the *Man'yō daishōki* and *Waji shōranshō*, but the critical comments on the *Genji monogatari* contained in his *Genchū shūi*, particularly his emphasis upon the role of emotionalism in the *Genji*, are worthy of note, adumbrating as they do the theory of *mono no aware* later expounded by Motoori Norinaga.

His disciples included Kaihoku Jakuchū, Imai Ikan, and others, and his works exerted an influence upon Kada no Azumamaro and Kamo no Mabuchi, though the scholar who honored him most highly and acknowledged the greatest debt to him was undoubtedly Motoori Norinaga.

He was also a poet of considerable importance, turning out a large volume of works that have been collected under the title *Manginshū*. He was particularly skilled in the writing of *chōka* and religious poetry, but he could also achieve an elegance of tone reminiscent of the *Shin kokinshū*.

The following is an example of his poetry:

> Buffeted and blown
> by wind and rain,
> in my village
> the scattering petals
> forlorn—an evening in spring.

Kɪ no Kaion (1663-1742)

Poet and dramatist of the early and middle Edo period. His name was originally Enami Kiemon, but he later changed his personal name to Zempachi; as a writer of *kyōka*, humorous or satirical poems in *tanka* form, he went by the literary name Taiga. His father, Enami Zenemon, was the proprietor of a confectionery shop called the Taiya in Osaka and at the same time was skilled in the writing of *haiku* poetry, being known by the literary name Teiin. Kaion's older brother Yuensai Teiryū was a *kyōka* poet, while his younger brother (or, according to some authorities, his cousin,) was well known as a *haiku* poet. In his youth Kaion entered the priesthood, but shortly after returned to lay life and established himself in Osaka as a physician. At the same time he studied Japanese literature under the noted scholar Keichū, *haiku* under Yasuhara Teishitsu, and *kyōka* under his elder brother Teiryū. Coming from such a literary family and having received considerable training in literature himself, it is not surprising that, when the opportunity presented itself, Kaion should try his hand at writing dramas for the puppet theater. He was engaged as a playwright for the Toyotake Theater, his task being to write dramas that would compete with those of Chikamatsu Monzaemon, the playwright for the Takemoto Theater. He wrote his first work, entitled *Keisei futokorogo*, in 1702, when he was thirty-nine, and thereafter devoted nearly all his time to writing dramas for the puppet theater, most of the new plays that were presented by the Toyotake Theater being from his hand. He seems to have lived a rather wild life in his youth, but in 1724 he succeeded his father as proprietor of the Taiya, thus ending his career as a playwright. He wrote some fifty plays, of which the most outstanding are *Onikage musashiabumi*, *Kamakura sandaiki*, *Shinjū futatsu haraobi*, and *Osome Hisamatsu tamoto no shiroshibori*. Many of his plays, such as *Shinjū futatsu haraobi*, deal with the same subject matter as plays by Chikamatsu, but it appears that in most cases it was Chikamatsu who borrowed material from Kaion, rather than the other way around. In construction of plot and literary skill, however, he was no match for Chikamatsu. His plays are rather staid and lacking in charm, and the language is often labored, as though the author had difficulty making his lines fit into the proper rhythmical patterns, yet by the variety of scenes presented he manages to achieve considerable dramatic interest and effect, and he deserves to be regarded as one of the best playwrights of the period. He is also important because, like Chikamatsu, he wrote both historical dramas and plays of the *sewamono*, or domestic drama, type, which dealt with contemporary events.

His other important works, in addition to those mentioned above, include the *Wankyū sue no matsuyama, Yaoya Oshichi koi no hizakura, Tomihito Shinnō Saga nishiki, Keisei mumonshō, Shinoda no mori onna uranai,* and *Keisei Kokusenya.*

KINOSHITA CHŌSHŌSHI (1569–1649)

Poet of the Momoyama and early Edo periods. His personal name was Katsutoshi and he was a nephew by marriage of the military leader Toyotomi Hideyoshi. Because of Hideyoshi's influence, he became lord of the castle of Obama in the province of Wakasa, but was deprived of his domain after the great battle of Sekigahara in 1600. From the age of thirty-one until his death some fifty years later, he withdrew from worldly affairs and lived a life of quiet seclusion at Ryōzen in the Higashiyama area of Kyoto and elsewhere. When he was a warrior he had taken an interest in Japanese poetry and studied for a period under Hosokawa Yūsai. He also exchanged views on scholarly matters with Fujiwara Seika, the exponent of Neo-Confucian philosophy, and with other learned men of the time, and after going into retirement, he devoted all his energies to matters of poetry, at the same time associating with most of the well-known painters, calligraphers, and men of letters of the day.

He attempted to revitalize and inject a note of innovation into the poetic world of the time, which had sunk into a state of lifeless conservatism, introducing fresh topics and a greater freedom of treatment, employing Chinese loan words to lend greater force and virility to his diction, and in other ways showing a spirit of experimentation and originality. He thus sought to realize the ideals of the Kyōgoku school, opposing himself to the conservative Nijō school, which adamantly adhered to the poetic canons of medieval style verse, and predictably was criticized by the latter for his unconventionality. The *Kyohakushū*, which contains his poetry and prose works, includes some eighteen hundred poems in *waka* form, many of them marked by boldness of expression and an air of freshness and novelty. In some works, in fact, these tendencies have been carried to such an extent that they have been labeled as *haikai uta* or "frivolous verse."

In addition to the *Kyohakushū* mentioned above, his works are also found in the *Chōshōshishū.* The following is an example of his poetry:

> To the echo of the
> nightingale's cry

> petals from fading cherries
> softly fall—
> twilight in spring.

KINOSHITA TAKABUMI (1779–1821)

Poet of the late Edo period. He used the *gō* (literary name) Sayasayanoya. A native of the province of Bitchū, he started composing *waka* and writing prose at the age of eleven or twelve. He was still young when he went to Kyoto and became a pupil of the poet-priest Chōgetsu, and then, on the latter's death, of Jien. However, while he was still studying with Jien he conceived an admiration for Kagawa Kageki and began going to him for instruction. Eventually, when he was nineteen, he moved to Okazaki village to the east of Kyoto, near the home of Kageki, and officially became a pupil of his, much to Jien's disappointment and annoyance. Following this move, he worked with his new master to bring about a reform of the *waka*, but it seems that his brilliance often brought him into competition with Kageki and that relations between the two were frequently strained. Nevertheless, he is known as one of the finest products of Kageki's school, his style showing a blend of the freedom bestowed by his fearless outlook and the weakness occasioned by his naivete.

For a while following his arrival in Kyoto, Takabumi worked as a copyist, but later he lived mostly by teaching *waka*. In 1819 he moved to Osaka, took the pseudonym Sayasayanoya and produced a collection of his verse entitled *Sayasaya ikō*, which remains one of the more striking collections of Edo period verse despite the undeniable influence from works such as Okura's famous *Man'yōshū* poem on the poverty of the common people. He himself wrote a work entitled *Hinkyū hyakushu* ("One Hundred Poems of Poverty"), and he was, in fact, a poor man. He studied Zen and was also adept at Chinese verse and painting.

> Wet with showers
> of early summer rain
> I came,
> to this hill-shaded path
> strewn with chestnut blossoms.

Works: *Sayasaya ikō* (posthumous), *Sayasaya sōshi*.

Kitamura Kigin (1624–1705)

A noted scholar of early Japanese literature and a *waka* and *haiku* poet of the early Edo period. His original name was Kitamura Kyūsuke and he also went by such literary names as Ryoan, Shūsuiken, Kogetsutei, and others. He was born in the village of Kitamura on the shore of Lake Biwa in the province of Ōmi. Both his father and grandfather, while making a living as physicians, took an interest in *renga*, and his grandfather, in particular, is said to have been a disciple of the *renga* teacher Satomura Shōha. Accordingly, Kigin received instruction in poetry at home from a very early age and later went to Kyoto to study under Yasuhara Teishitsu, a disciple of the famous Matsunaga Teitoku, and eventually became a disciple of Teitoku himself. At the age of twenty-three he published a collection of *haiku* entitled *Yama no i*, and soon became known as an important member of the Teitoku school. At the age of twenty-nine he is also said to have received instruction in *waka* poetry from Asukai Masaaki and Shimizudani Sanenari.

In this same year he produced his first commentary, an annotated edition of the *Yamato monogatari* entitled *Yamato monogatari-shō*. In 1661 he completed similar works on the *Tosa nikki* and *Ise monogatari* entitled *Tosa nikki-shō* and *Ise monogatari shūsuishō*, which he presented to Retired Emperor Gomizuno-o for the latter's inspection. In 1674 he produced a commentary on the *Genji monogatari* entitled *Genji monogatari kogetsushō*, which he had the honor of being allowed to present to Shogun Ietsuna. In 1689, at the age of sixty-five, he was invited by the Tokugawa shogunate to come to Edo, and spent the remainder of his life there in very comfortable circumstances.

Kigin confessed in one of his poems that:

> The unfathomable literature
> of China,
> the art of Japanese poetry—
> although I do my best
> to master both—

In the end, however, he proved to be at heart a scholar rather than a poet, and his poetic works were too pedantic and moralistic to attract real interest. But his lucid commentaries on earlier works of literature were of great benefit to readers of the time and played an important part in reviving interest in the classics of the past, while his works on the proper methods for composing *haiku* cannot be too highly praised for the benefit that they have given to followers of that art.

In addition to the commentaries mentioned above, he also wrote commentaries on the *Tsurezuregusa, Makura no sōshi,* and *Hyakunin isshu, Man'yōshū,* and other anthologies of poetry, and produced such works on *haiku* as the *Inagoshū, Haikai ryōginshū, Shoku renju, Kigin haikaishū* and *Haikai umoregi,* and collections of *waka* entitled *Kigin shika, Kigin hyakushu,* and *Iwa tsutsuji.*

Kobayashi Issa (1763–1827)

Haiku poet of the late Edo period. His given name was Nobuyuki, and his common name Yatarō. In his youth he went by such artistic names as Ikyō, Kikumyō, Adō, and Ungai, but he is best known by the *haiku* name Issa, which he employed throughout his life. He also used such studio names as Nirokuan and Haikaiji.

He was the first son of a farmer of middling circumstances of the village of Kashiwabara in the northern part of Shinano, in present-day Nagano Prefecture. He lost his mother when he was two, and when he was seven his father remarried. Two years later a younger half-brother named Senroku was born, and thereafter there was constant disharmony between him and his stepmother. His father, at a loss to deal with the situation, finally sent him to Edo in the spring of his fourteenth year to take service as an apprentice.

Little is known about his life in Edo during the following ten years, though it was apparently a period of great hardship. At some point he began to take an interest in the writing of *haiku,* and at the age of twenty-four he was enrolled as a student in the school of Nirokuan Chikua, where he studied *haiku* of the so-called Katsushika school. After the death of his teacher, Nirokuan Chikua, three years later, he succeeded him as head of the school, but in the spring of his twenty-ninth year he set off upon a walking tour of western Japan, spending the following seven years in wanderings through the areas of Kyoto, western Honshu, and the islands of Shikoku and Kyushu. During this period he devoted himself to the composition of *haiku,* and in Kyoto brought out his first collection of poems entitled *Tabi shūi.* From the age of thirty-five until the spring of his forty-ninth year he lived in various localities in Edo or wandered about the Bōsō Peninsula, living in considerable poverty and loneliness, though he at the same time became acquainted with such outstanding *haiku* writers as Seibi, Sōchō, and Ippyō and worked to perfect the distinctive type of *haiku* that came to be known as the "Issa style." When he was thirty-eight his father fell ill and Issa returned to his home in Shinano to nurse him in his last days, leaving a diary account of the period known as the *Mitori nikki* or *Chichi no shūen nikki.* His father appears to have left dying instructions that Issa was to receive a share of the property, but his stepmother and younger half-brother prevented him from receiving his inheritance, and he returned to Edo full of resentment. He made subsequent journeys to his old home, carrying on the fight with his stepmother and half-brother until, in the fifth month of his fiftieth year, the ten-year dispute was finally ended and he settled down at last in his native village as master of his own house. The following year he married for the first time, taking for his wife a village girl named Kiku, and began to live a more sedentary life, though he continued to perfect his *haiku* style and from time to time journeyed to Edo to keep abreast of new literary developments. Kiku bore him three sons and a daughter, but all of them died in infancy, and Kiku herself died when Issa was sixty. The following year he remarried, but divorced his wife after only two months. At the age of sixty-two he took a third wife named Yao. In 1827, when he was sixty-four, his house was destroyed by fire and, obliged to shelter in a storehouse that had survived the blaze, he died of a stroke in the eleventh month of the same year. His wife was pregnant at the time, and the following year bore a daughter named Yata, whose descendants survive to the present.

Issa appears to have been a man of very forceful and passionate nature, and the poverty, hardship, and repeated frustration that he was forced to endure fostered in him a highly complex and in some ways distorted personality. His *haiku*, which clearly reflect his unusual temperament, are marked by a unique tone that has come to be known as the "Issa style." Its outstanding characteristics are humor, satire, and deep compassion, and it is frequently distinguished by an underlying sense of pathos and anger. Issa did not hesitate to employ colloquial or dialect expressions in his poetry, and his highly subjective manner conveys a vivid sense of his own personality and environment. His poems dealing with the farm life of Shinano, with their sharp realism, and the candor and simplicity of the poems written in the style of children's songs are of particular note. His works did not exert a very great influence in the *haiku* world of the time but have attracted increasing attention since the Meiji period, until at present Issa has come to be ranked beside Bashō and Buson as one of the greatest *haiku* masters of the Edo period. The following are typical examples of his work:

> Come play with me,
> sparrow
> without any mother!

> Looks good enough to eat—
> snow falling

fluffy, fluffy.

In addition to the works mentioned, Issa's writings include *Shichiban nikki,
Oragaharu, Hōgen zasshū, Issa hokku-shū,* and *Issa ichidai-shū.*

Kumagai Naoyoshi (1782–1862)

Poet of the late Edo period. His personal name was Nobukata; in his youth
he used the name Yasohachi, which he later changed to Sukezaemon and also
employed the literary names Keishūtei and Chōshuntei. He was the son of a
samurai in the fief of Iwakuni in the province of Suō. From an early age he
displayed a fondness for learning and gave evidence of literary talent. He
began studies of Japanese poetry in his native fief, but at the age of fifteen
enrolled under the well-known poet Kagawa Kageki in Kyoto, sending poems
to the capital with a request for Kageki's corrections. Kageki enclosed the
following poem by way of encouragement when he returned the first batch of
corrected poems:

> Think of fall
> when crops are about to ripen—
> the real joy comes
> in watching rice grains
> as they form in mountain paddies.

At the age of eighteen Kumagai journeyed to Kyoto and for the first time
received instruction from Kageki in person, studying under him for a year
and at the same time undergoing Zen training at Shōkoku-ji, a famous Zen
temple in Kyoto. He was soon on very close terms with his teacher and
thereafter journeyed back and forth between Kyoto and Iwakuni numerous
times. The prose description that he wrote of one such journey by sea made
when he was twenty-five is famous for the beauty and flow of its style.

Kagawa Kageki had earlier been adopted into the Kagawa family of
Iwakuni, but for certain reasons had become estranged from them. A law
suit arose between him and the family, and Kumagai, because he was an
official in the fief of Iwakuni, was obliged to supervise the matter. The suit
was finally settled in favor of Kageki's family rather than of Kageki, which
placed Kumagai in a very difficult position with regard to his teacher. As a
result, in 1825 he finally left the fief of Iwakuni and went to Osaka, where he
spent the remainder of his life as a teacher of poetry.

He was a skilled poet and a warm and engaging personality and, along with Kinoshita Takabumi, was recognized as one of the two most important poets of the Keien school, as Kagawa Kageki's school was known. He held first place among the members of the school as a scholar of poetics and in 1842, when he was sixty, produced three important works during a very short period of time, including the *Kokinshū seigi jochū tsuikō*. These embodied various interpretations that Kagawa Kageki had expounded earlier, along with Kumagai's own theories. The *Ryōjin kōshō*, which contains notes and explanations on the types of songs known as *kagura* and *saibara*, is especially famous. He used to declare that "A poem has served its function once it has been put into rhythmic form (*shirabe*)," and for this reason kept no copies of his works. As a result, he left no collection of his poetry when he died, and his disciplies were obliged to assemble one from other sources.

He was looked upon with great favor by his teacher Kagawa Kageki, and throughout his life honored his teacher's principles. Kagawa Kageki had declared that "A poem is the natural melody (*shirabe*) in which sincerity finds expression," and Kumagai did his best to realize this theory in practice, producing works marked by a musical quality that is elegant and fluid, as may be seen in the following examples:

> All alone,
> pouring saké for myself,
> and boundless
> emotions of spring
> come piling in upon me.

> As the tide runs out
> it turns into
> an arm of the beach—
> what I took for
> a little offshore island.

In addition to the works mentioned above, his writings include the *Kokinshū seigi sōron hochū*, *Ura no shiogai*, and others.

Matsunaga Teitoku (1571–1653)

Haiku poet (founder of the Teitoku school of *haiku*), classical scholar, and writer of *waka* and *kyōka* during the Momoyama and early Edo periods. His childhood name was Katsuguma, and he went by the literary names Shōyōken, Chōzumaru, and Meishin *koji*. He was born in Kyoto, the son of the *renga* poet Matsunaga Nagatane. During early childhood he was educated by his father, and later by Kujō Tanemichi. He studied the classics and *waka* with Hosokawa Yūsai and *renga* with Satomura Shōha.

Teitoku lived during the period of Toyotomi Hideyoshi and the establishment of the Tokugawa shogunate. The new government's emphasis on civil administration and education encouraged the rapid rise of a culture of the common people, and Teitoku, as a student of the classics, poet, and student of poetics, contributed greatly to the education of the younger generation and helped to encourage interest in the classics. Particularly during the period beginning in 1624, when he was fifty-two, he devoted himself in earnest to the writing of *haiku* and became the central figure of the world of *haiku*; before long the vogue for this verse form spread all over the country, and almost all *haiku* poets of note appear to have come directly or indirectly under his influence, so that the period came to be referred to as the age of the Teitoku school.

As a scholar, his interest lay in educating the masses; he acted as a bridge, making the scholarship of the upper classes available to the common people, and his *haiku* style was designed to be interesting and easily understood. As a result, his verse made use of colloquial terms and Chinese loan words seldom employed in *waka* verse and tended at times to lapse into stylistic tricks or plays on works. He also laid down a set of rules for the writing of *haiku*—something that had not existed before—and expounded them in detail in his work *Gosan* (1651). Besides this, he published a large number of collections of work by himself and his pupils, noteworthy among them being *Enoko shū* (1633, Matsue Shigeyori) and *Shinzō inu tsukuba* (1643), which includes *Abura-kasu* and *Yodogawa*, both grouped with *Gosan* as Teitoku's three most important works. His pupils included Kitamura Kigin, Matsue Shigeyori, Yasuhara Teishitsu, and Yamamoto Saimu. Two of Teitoku's *haiku* are:

> Was it some anxiety
> made them wilt and lose their color,
> the apricot flowers?

(The poem is built around a pun on *anzu*, "apricot"/"anxiety.")

> Even the spring mists
> show spots—
> Year of the Tiger.

Matsuo Bashō (1644–1694)

Haiku poet of the early Edo period. He was born in Ueno in the province of Iga, the second son of Matsuo Yozaemon; as a child he was called Kinsaku, and later Jinshichirō, Tōshichirō, or Chūemon; he adopted the artistic names Tōsei and Bashō.

At around the age of nine he became a page to Yoshitada, the son of Tōdō Shinshichirō Yoshikiyo, the lord of the castle of Ueno. Yoshitada was fond of *haiku* and studied under Kitamura Kigin, a Kyoto *haiku* poet of the Teitoku school, being assigned the artistic name Sengin, and Bashō likewise became a devotee of *haiku*. In 1666, when Bashō was twenty-two, his young lord, Yoshitada, died suddenly. Bashō journeyed to the great Buddhist monastery on Mt. Kōya to deposit his lord's mortuary tablet, but thereafter left the service of the Tōdō family. The shock of his lord's death and a romantic involvement with a woman later known as Jutei have been suggested as possible reasons for his sudden departure, though the facts are uncertain.

After leaving the domain of Iga, he seems to have gone to Kyoto and studied under Kitamura Kigin, but later journeyed to Edo, where he moved from place to place, staying in the homes of various friends and acquaintances. At the same time he became friendly with Nishiyama Sōin, the founder of the Danrin school, and in time gained a reputation as a *haiku* poet under the literary name Tōsei, gathering about him a group of followers. In 1680, at the age of thirty-six, he published an anthology of poems by himself and his disciples entitled *Tōsei montei dokugin nijū kasen*, which gave the first clear indication of the distinctive style that was to become associated with his name. At the same time he took up residence in a small cottage in Fukagawa built for him by one of his disciples named Sampū and called it the Bashō-an, from the *bashō* (plantain) trees planted about it, and from these trees he took the literary name Bashō. It was in this period that he first began to compose works marked by a tone of quiet loneliness such as the famous verse:

> On a withered branch
> a crow has settled—
> autumn nightfall.[1]

and to show the influence of the Taoist thought of Lao Tzu and Chuang Tzu in his writings. He also began serious Zen study under a master named Butchō, and his Zen experiences in time came to exert a profound effect upon

---

1. Translated in Harold G. Henderson, *An Introduction to Haiku*, Doubleday & Co., 1958, p. 18.

his outlook on life and his poetry. In 1684 he set off on a journey, partly for the purpose of visiting his birthplace, thus initiating a series of wanderings that he undertook in imitation of the poet-priests Saigyō and Sōgi of earlier times. He wrote an account of the journey, which is known as the *Nozarashi kikō* or *Kasshi ginkō*. This was followed by a journey to view the full moon at the Kashima Shrine in Hitachi, described in his *Kashima kikō*; a cherry viewing expedition to Mt. Yoshino described in the *Oi no kokumi* (also called *Yoshino kikō* or *Udatsu kikō*); and a second moon viewing journey to Sara-shina recorded in the *Sarashina kikō*. In 1689 he set out on an extended journey through the northern part of the island of Honshu, and the account he wrote of this expedition, the *Oku no hosomichi*, or *The Narrow Road to the Far North*, is the longest and greatest of his works in this genre.

In 1692 he once more took up residence in the Bashō-an, which had been newly rebuilt for him and where he was visited by his nephew Tōin; the nun Jutei, an old friend and possibly his mistress in his younger days; and other friends and acquaintances. But Tōin died the following year, and the year after that, while Bashō was on a journey to western Japan, he learned of the death of the nun Jutei. He himself fell ill shortly afterward and died on the twelfth day of the tenth month of 1694 at the home of one Hanaya Nizaemon in Minami Midō in Osaka at the age of fifty. It was during this illness that he composed what has come to be regarded as his farewell verse:

> On a journey, ill,
> and over fields all withered, dreams
> go wandering still.[1]

Bashō began by writing in the style of the Teitoku school, moved to that of the Danrin school, and eventually evolved a style distinctively his own, playing a central role in the development of the theory and practice of *haiku* and for the first time succeeding in raising it to the level of a profoundly serious art form. Bashō's verses have customarily been praised for their embodiment of *sabi* (quiet contemplation), *shiori* (the state of mind capable of perceiving deep suggestiveness), and *hosomi* (delicacy of perception), qualities that derive from the artistic ideals of the *waka*, *renga*, and Nō drama of the medieval period, with their emphasis upon *yūgenbi*, mysterious beauty, but which he succeeded in translating into the language of his own time, making of the *haiku* an art form that was at once profound and popular in nature. In his *Oi no kobumi*, Bashō remarks that "Whoever would achieve artistic excellence must follow along with nature and take the four seasons to

1. *Ibid*, p. 30.

be his friends, . . . must follow along with nature and return to nature!" As this indicates, Bashō's ideal in poetry was to achieve a level of total identity with nature. Only when all private thoughts and emotions have been cast off and one has immersed himself completely in the world of nature can true art be achieved. The following are further examples of his work:

> As the sea darkens,
> the cries of the mallards
> grow faintly white.

> This road—
> no one to walk it—
> autumn evening.

> Stillness—
> and the locust's shrill
> sinking into the rock.

Miyoshi Shōraku (1696?–1772)

Puppet theater playwright of the middle Edo period. Born in the province of Iyo in Shikoku, he was originally the priest in charge of a temple in Matsuyama, Iyo, but was for some reason forced to leave the temple. He made his way to Osaka, returned to lay life, and is said to have made his living as a physician or as the proprietor of a tea house. At the end of the text of the puppet drama *Imoseyama onna teikin* there is a notation that reads, "Kōken Miyoshi Shōraku, age seventy-six," and from this it may be surmised that he died in the early years of the An'ei era (1772–81) around the age of seventy-nine. He studied the *jōruri* (puppet drama) under Takeda Izumo and was a contemporary of Hasegawa Senshi. His career as a playwright began in 1736 with a work entitled *Akamatsu enshin midori-no-jinmaku*, which he wrote in conjunction with Bunkōdō and which was produced at the Takemoto Theater, and continued to be active for the next thirty-six years, being listed as *kōken*, or stage assistant, for a play entitled *Sakura goten gojūsan eki* produced in 1771.

He is listed as the author of over fifty plays, and in addition he served twice as *tate-sakusha* (chief playwright) and was active throughout his career as a co-author or assistant to other playwrights, no doubt holding a position of considerable importance in the theater to which he was attached, although his work was not always of the kind to attract public attention. His best work seems to have been done at times when he did not have to act as leading playwright, a task that involved the planning of the overall structure of a play and the working out of various complications of plot, but he excelled in the handling of short passages of dramatic intensity and beauty. The fact that he was willing to turn over the position of chief playwright to other dramatists would appear to indicate that he was well aware of his own abilities and shortcomings. Working under the direction of other chief playwrights, however, he succeeded in turning out pieces of great distinction such as *Goshozakura Horikawa youchi*, which he wrote in conjunction with Bunkōdō; *Sugawara denju tenarai kagami*, *Yoshitsune sembonzakura*, and *Kanadehon chūshingura*, written in conjunction with Takeda Izumo, Namiki Senryū, and others; and *Honchō nijūshi kō* and *Ōmi Genji senjin yakata*, written with Chikamatsu Hanji, all classics of the puppet theater repertory.

Morikawa Kyoriku (Kyoroku) (1656–1715)

Haiku poet of the early Edo period. His name was originally Morikawa Hyakuchū. He was a retainer of the Ii family, the lords of the fief of Hikone in present-day Shiga Prefecture. He began *haiku* studies under the scholar and poet Kitamura Kigin, but later became a follower of the Danrin school. After reading the published works of Bashō and being deeply impressed by them, he determined to become a disciple of Bashō, and in the eighth month of 1692 visited Bashō and was duly accepted as a follower. Though Bashō was by this time well along in years, he recognized Kyoriku's cleverness and literary talent and treated him with great respect. Kyoriku was well versed in painting and in turn was said to have given Bashō lessons in that art. After his teacher's death, Kyoriku returned to Hikone and founded a branch of the Bashō school of *haiku* there, at the same time devoting much time to the writing of critical works on *haiku*, an undertaking at which he showed great aptitude. Though ill for the last six years of his life, he continued his literary activities up until the time of his death at the age of fifty-nine.

Kyoriku was one of the most important critics and theoreticians among Bashō's followers and was skilled at prose as well as poetry. A glance at his writings reveals that he was a man of great confidence and frankness who did not hesitate to state his opinions freely and without reservation. His *haiku*, likewise, though marked by skillful handling of the traditional themes, keen observation, and originality of expression, are most noteworthy for their accurate and direct descriptions of nature, as may be seen in the following two examples:

Cool breeze—
cloud shadows
passing over the green paddies.

On the water where
rice seedlings are growing,
scattered cherry petals float.

Kyoriku is more important as a critic and a writer of *haibun* (prose pieces in the *haiku* manner) than as a poet. His critical estimates of his fellow disciples, though at times reflecting his own prejudice and arbitrariness, are often extremely perceptive. His *haibun* are marked by wit and resourcefulness and are rich and varied in mood. He left many works, among them the *Infutagi* and *Rekidai kokkeiden*, and his *Fūzoku monzen* is particularly important as the first anthology of *haibun*.

Motoori Norinaga (1730–1801)

Scholar of Japanese studies and poet of the middle Edo period. He was born in Matsuzaka in the province of Ise, the son of a merchant family named Ozu. The family name was later changed to Motoori, and he is also known by the literary names Shun'an and Suzunoya. His father was Ozu Sadatoshi, and he was the son of a second marriage. His father died when he was ten, and his elder half-brother when he was twenty-one, leaving him the heir of the family. His mother, Katsuko, however, perceiving that he was not suited to carry on the family business, sent him to Kyoto to study medicine. For a period of six years ending in 1757 he pursued his medical studies in Kyoto; at the same time he applied himself to Chinese studies under Hori Keizan, a teacher of the Chu Hsi school of Neo-Confucianism and an expert writer of Chinese verse and prose who was also deeply versed in Japanese studies and the writing of *waka* poetry. Under his influence, Norinaga also became interested in Japanese studies and poetry, familiarizing himself with the works of the scholar of Japanese studies Keichū and concentrating in particular upon the study of the *Genji monogatari*. It was during his years in Kyoto that he wrote the work entitled *Ashiwake obune*.

Upon returning to Matsuzaka he practiced medicine and at the same time continued his studies of Japanese literature, lecturing to his disciples on the *Genji monogatari*, *Man'yōshū*, and other classics, holding poetry matches, and devoting much time to writing. In 1762 he took a wife, named Tamiko, and the following year completed his works on literary theory entitled

Shibun yōryō and *Isonokami no sasame no koto*. He also fulfilled a long-standing ambition to meet the great scholar Kamo no Mabuchi, discussing with him plans for a study of the *Kojiki* and receiving his advice. In 1792 he received an invitation to take service with the Maeda family, lord of the domain of Kaga, and shortly after a similar invitation from the Tokugawa family of the domain of Kii; since the lord of Kii was willing to let him remain at his home in Matsuzaka, he accepted service under the latter. In 1796 at the age of sixty-six he completed his *Genji monogatari tama no ogushi*, and two years later brought to completion his greatest work, the *Kojikiden*, upon which he had labored for a period of over thirty years. He died in the ninth month of 1801 at the age of seventy-one.

Norinaga's greatest contribution was in the study of the classics of Japanese literature, and he holds a position of primary importance among the scholars of Japanese studies in the Edo period. Among his commentaries, that on the *Kojiki* mentioned above, actually a combination of commentary and critical study, is of the greatest importance, and he also wrote philological commentaries on the *semmyō* (imperial proclamations) and contributed new insights into the understanding of the language of the *Genji monogatari* and *Man'yōshū*. In addition he provided modern language paraphrases for the poems of the *Kokinshū* and critical comments on the *Shin kokinshū*. His comments on poetic theory are contained in the *Isonokami no sasame no koto*, while in his *Shibun yōryō* and *Genji monogatari tama no ogushi* he dealt critically with the *monogatari* as a literary genre. In his critical works he attached particular importance to the *Genji monogatari* and the *Shin kokinshū*, expounding in connection with them his famous theory of *mono no aware*. According to his views, the quality of *mono no aware*, the "sensitivity to things," constitutes the basic characteristic of the *Genji monogatari* and in fact of all great poetry and literature. In the field of linguistics he wrote the *Kotoba no tamao*, a study of the function of particles in the Japanese language, and the *Te-ni-o-ha himokagami*, which deals simply and lucidly in diagram form with the use of particles, as well as other works, all of epoch-making importance in their field. It is important to note that Norinaga's studies were of significance not only in his own time but continue to constitute an indispensable starting point for modern studies of the classics as well. His poetry is noteworthy in that he sought through it to express the ideals of the Japanese nation, employing the cherry blossom in particular as a symbol of those ideals. As a poet, however, he does not equal his teacher, Kamo no Mabuchi, and his literary talent is seen to better advantage in his prose writings and collections of miscellaneous pieces such as the *Tamakatsuma*. His most famous poem is that which reads:

If one should ask,
what is the spirit of Japan—
Shining in the morning sun,
these blossoms of the mountain cherry!

Among the works of Norinaga not already mentioned are the *Naobi no mitama*, *Tama kushige*, *Uiyamabumi*, and others.

MUKAI KYORAI (1651–1704)

Haiku poet of the early Edo period. His given name was Kanetoki, and he went by the common names of Heijirō or Jirotayū. In addition to the artistic name Kyorai, he also used the name Rakushisha. He was one of the "Ten Philosophers," or ten major disciples of Bashō. His father, Genshō, was a Confucian scholar and physician and acted as head of the Seidō, the Confucian temple and school in Nagasaki. His younger sister Chine was also a distinguished *haiku* poet, as were other members of his family.

At the age of seven he accompanied his father to Kyoto, where he began training in the military arts. It was hoped that he would enter the service of some important feudal lord, but he adamantly declined such a career. In addition to the military arts, he also studied the science of divination and was skilled at painting. He became a disciple of Bashō around the age of thirty-five or thirty-six, and sometime around this period built a little retreat called the Rakushisha (Cottage of Falling Persimmons) in Saga in the suburbs west of Kyoto, where he lived in retirement. In 1689, as a disciple of Bashō he undertook to edit a collection of *haiku* called the *Arano*, which contains works representative of the style of Bashō and his followers. He also invited Bashō to his home in Saga and entertained him with great care. Following this, he and Bonchō, another important disciple of Bashō, under the direction of their teacher compiled the anthology entitled *Sarumino*. Noted for the tone of quietness and loneliness that pervades it, the anthology stands in the same relation to the *haiku* tradition as does the great *Kokinshū* anthology to the tradition of *waka* poetry. As a result of this undertaking and the poems by him included in the anthology, Kyorai became established as a poet of major importance.

Kyorai was extremely diligent in looking after the wants and desires of his teacher, Bashō, did his best to carry out Bashō's wishes faithfully, and took charge of the funeral arrangements on the occasion of Bashō's death. In his own late years he moved to a lodging near Higashiyama, Nanzen-ji Shōgoin, in the eastern suburbs of Kyoto, where he devoted his time to teaching *haiku* and helping to maintain the traditions of the Bashō school. The anthology *Tabine-ron*, which he finished compiling in 1699, illustrates how diligently he worked to transmit faithfully his teacher's views on poetry. He died five years later at the age of fifty-three, having devoted his life to the service of Bashō and his art.

Kyorai's style is lofty and refined and shows a solid understanding of Bashō's principles. Though he was not a genius by nature, his constant effort brought him to the highest level of attainment. Bashō himself remarked that "In solidness of content, no one can equal Kyorai," and referred to him as the "arbiter (*bugyō*) of *haiku* for the western provinces." He was the most outstanding of Bashō's disciples living in the Kansai area, rivaled only by Jōsō, and, in fact, he and Jōsō are often mentioned as the two most important disciples of Bashō in western Japan, the counterparts of Kikaku and Ransetsu in the east. His reputation has continued undiminished in later ages, and he remains today one of the major figures in the *haiku* world of early Edo times. The following poem is representative of his work:

> The waters of the lake
> have overflowed—
> early summer rains.

Kyorai's writings include the *Zō Shinshi Kikaku sho*, *Tō Kyoshi monnan ben*, *Tabine-ron*, and *Kyorai-shō*.

Murata Harumi (1746–1811)

Poet and scholar of Japanese studies of the middle Edo period. His common name was Heishirō and he used such artistic names as Kotojiri no Okina and Nishigori no Ya no Aruji. He was the son of a wealthy merchant family of the Kobune district of Edo and replaced his elder brother as successor to the family business.

At first he concentrated his attention upon the study of Chinese literature and learning, but later joined his father and elder brother in becoming a disciple of Kamo no Mabuchi, the distinguished scholar of Japanese studies. He particularly excelled at writing *waka* poetry and prose pieces in antique style, and soon became recognized as one of the most distinguished *waka* poets of the Edo school, rivaled only by Tachibana (Katō) Chikage. He lived very extravagantly, being numbered among the "Eighteen Connoisseurs" (*jūhachi daitsū*), wealthy merchants of Edo who prided themselves upon their taste and savoir faire, particularly in matters pertaining to the theater and the licensed quarters. In time he exhausted the family resources and was for a while reduced to a life of poverty, but he later received stipends from Matsudaira Sadanobu, lord of the fief of Shirakawa, and other powerful patrons. Around the age of sixty-five he built himself a small study in which he placed the *koto* handed down to him by his father, a fine instrument of the type known as an *azuma-goto*, built a small cabinet to store his books, and slept and worked in their midst, adopting the artistic name Kotojiri no Okina, The Old Man Back of the Koto.

He was a scholar of great ability and wide learning, and was particularly versed in matters pertaining to the *kana* syllabary and the phonemes of the Japanese sound system. He is also important for having discovered the earliest Chinese-Japanese dictionary, a ninth century work entitled *Shinsen jikyō*, and brought it to the attention of scholars. In addition to works in Japanese, he was a skilled writer of prose and poetry in Chinese.

His Japanese prose is noted for its elegance of style and lucidity and clarity of argument. Its excellence, as in the case of his poetry, would appear to derive from the fact that he spared no effort in rewriting and polishing his compositions. In poetry he strove for an effect of naturalness, eschewing anything that smacked of artificiality and paying particular heed to the freshness and rhythm of the work. He sought to understand why *waka* poetry had fallen upon such poor times and advocated a return to the ways of antiquity as an antidote. The "antiquity" that he advised returning to, however, was not the *Man'yōshū* and pre-*Manyōshū* poetry espoused by his teacher Kamo no Mabuchi, but included all early poetry up to the *Kokinshū*, and his own works often adopt a style as late as that of the *Shin kokinshū*. The freshness and novelty that he strove for was likewise little more revolutionary than that achieved by some of the forerunners of the school of Kagawa Kageki who were working in Kyoto at the time. He stressed the importance of the *chōka* and experimented in composing works in the form, but he did not succeed in recapturing the spirit of the great *chōka* of antiquity. The following are two examples of his *tanka*:

> As dawn breaks,
> they cry,
> and in the voices of the pheasants
> the spring mountain paddies
> gradually whiten.

> The boat tied up,
> sounds of dripping

from the rush roof fade away—
in the night, the early winter rain
has given way to snow.

His writings include the *Gojūon bengo, Kanajitaii-shō, Utagatari, Nishigori
no Ya zuihitsu,* and *Kotojiri-shū.*

Muro Kyūsō (1658–1734)

Confucian scholar of the Chu Hsi school in the early and middle Edo period.
His personal name was Naokiyo, his common name Shinsuke, his formal
name Shirei or Jogyoku, and he employed such literary names as Kyūsō,
Sōrō, and Sundai. His father, Muro Gemboku, was a physician in the fief of
Bitchū in present-day Okayama Prefecture but later moved to Edo. Kyūsō
was born in the Yanaka section of Edo. In 1672, when he was fourteen, he
lectured on the *Ta-hsüeh chang-chü,* Chu Hsi's commentary on the *Ta-hsüeh*
(*Great Learning*), in the presence of Maeda Tsunanori, the lord of the fief of
Kaga, and composed poetry in Chinese, winning recognition for his literary
talents. Shortly after, he was ordered by the fief of Kaga to proceed to
Kyoto, where he studied the Chu Hsi school of Confucianism under Kinoshita Jun'an, later becoming known as one of the ten most outstanding of
Jun'an's disciples.

Though a scholar himself, he greatly admired men who played an important role in political affairs and in particular looked upon Sugawara no
Michizane as the ideal Confucian, writing a famous "Prayer and Oath to the
God Sugawara" and pursuing his studies with a determination and refusal to
compromise reminiscent of that of Michizane himself. Around the age of
twenty-four he completed his studies and took a position under the lord of
Kaga, whose residence was in the city of Kanazawa. In 1711, however, on
the recommendation of the scholar and statesman Arai Hakuseki, he was
summoned to Edo to take a position as a Confucian scholar in the service of
the shogunate. In 1716 he was appointed *jikō,* lecturer in attendance, to the
eighth shogun Tokugawa Yoshimune and enjoyed great honor.

He remained faithful to the teachings of Chu Hsi while at the same time
displaying ability in political and economic affairs and gaining a reputation
for brilliance and breadth of learning that placed him side by side with Ogyū
Sorai and Arai Hakuseki as one of the outstanding intellectual figures of the
time. Illness, however, forced him to retire from the post of lecturer in
attendance, and he spent his remaining years writing his *Sundai zatsuwa* in

five chapters and other works. His poetry in Chinese and his prose works are marked by vigor and erudition, beauty of diction, and elegance of tone. In 1909 he was posthumously awarded the court rank of Junior Fourth Rank. In addition to the *Sundai zatsuwa*, his works include the *Rikuyu engi taii* and *Kyūsō sensei bunshū*.

Naitō Jōsō (1662–1704)

Haiku poet of the early and middle Edo period. He was one of the "Ten Philosophers," or ten major disciples of Bashō. His common name was Rin'uemon and he used such other names as Ranka and Butsugen'an. He was the eldest son of a samurai of the fief of Inuyama in Owari, in present-day Aichi Prefecture. He served the younger half-brother of Naruse, the lord of the fief, but at the age of twenty-six retired on grounds of ill health. He thereupon entered the Buddhist clergy, left Inuyama, and lived in retirement in Fukakusa on the southern outskirits of Kyoto. He appears to have first become a disciple of Bashō in 1689, and in 1691 contributed a postface written in Chinese to the collection of *haiku* by Bashō and his followers entitled *Sarumino*. He later moved to the nearby province of Ōmi, and shortly after Bashō's death in 1694, wrote a work called the *Nekorobigusa* in which he gave expression to his views on the world and life. After observing a three-year mourning period for this teacher, he retired to a small residence called the Butsugen-an at Awazu in Ōmi, where he lived a life of great simplicity. For three years beginning in 1701, he cut himself off from ordinary social intercourse and devoted his time to services for the repose of his teacher's soul. In 1704, when he was forty-two, the illness that had troubled him for the preceding three years took a turn for the worse, and he died in his hermitage.

Jōsō was both a *haiku* poet and a priest, and his character represents a combination of sternness and keen aesthetic sensibility. His *haiku* are marked by sincerity and artistic integrity and appear to have been composed in moments of strong inspiration. To the end of his life he remained faithful to the style he had learned from Bashō, and his poems in their purity of conception and tone of touching melancholy often rival those of his master. The two poems that follow are examples of his work:

> How many people
> scampering through the autumn showers—
> the bridge at Seta.

A fallen leaf
settles on the rock
at the bottom of the water.

In addition to the *Nekorobigusa*, his works include the *Jōsō hokku-shū*, *Jōsō bunshū*, and *Jōsō-shū*.

NAMIKI GOHEI (1747–1808)

Kabuki dramatist of the late Edo period. It is not known what his original name was. He was the son of a townsman of Osaka and at first ran a tobacco store, a wine shop, and various other businesses. He studied under the playwright Namiki Shōzō and in 1772, at the age of twenty-five, became a writer for the Kado no Shibai, a kabuki theater in Osaka. Until 1793 he was active mainly in the Osaka area, but after that date he wrote for the kabuki theater in Edo. From his Osaka period, when he succeeded the well-known playwright Namiki Kamesuke, date *Temmangū natane no gokū*, *Kimmon gosan no kiri*, *Keisei kogane no shachihoko*, *Kanjin kammon tekuda no hajimari*, *Godairiki koi no fūjime*, and other famous works, and after he moved to Edo he wrote many outstanding works in the *sewamono* (domestic drama) category. His plays are noted for their realism and logical, well-constructed plots, and after his move to Edo, he succeeded in injecting a new note of Osaka rationalism into the Edo kabuki drama, which until that time had been dominated by pure emotionalism, leading it in the direction of greater intellectual content. In all, he was active for a period of around forty years from the end of the Meiwa era (1764–72) to the beginning of the Bunka era (1804–18) and left more than 160 works.

The principal works of his Osaka period, in addition to those already mentioned above, are *Hanasakuragi Ako no shiogama*, *Anakashiko kuruwa-no-bunshō*, and *Shimameguri uso-no-kikigaki*, while from his Edo period date *Sumida no haru geisha katagi*, *Satokotoba awasekagami*, *Tomigaoka koi no yamabiraki*, and others.

NOMURA BŌTŌ-NI (MOTO-NI) (1806–1867)

Poet of the late Edo period. She was the third daughter of Urano Katsutsune, a samurai of the domain of Fukuoka. She married at the age of sixteen but separated shortly after; at twenty-three she became the second wife of

Nomura Sadatsura, also a samurai of the domain of Fukuoka, and raised his three children by a previous wife, managing her wifely duties with great efficiency. In 1859, when her husband died, she shaved her head and became a nun, taking the religious name Bōtō-ni. She was fond of learning and excelled in many of the arts; she studied the writing of Japanese poetry under Ōkuma Kotomichi and produced many works of distinction. She was on very close terms with Hirano Kuniomi, Takasugi Shinsaku, and other leaders of the *sonnō* movement, which called for restoration of power to the emperor, and many of them visited her home at Hirao-san. In 1864, when Takasugi Shinsaku was forced to flee from the domain of Chōshū, he took refuge in her mountain home and there laid plans for another attempt to realize his ideals, and when the priest Gesshō was on his way to the domain of Satsuma, he stayed at her home and from there paid a visit to the court official Sanjō Sanemi, at that time in confinement at Dazaifu. In these and other ways, she aided the movement that in time was to lead to the Meiji Restoration. In 1865, when the faction favorable to the Edo shogunate seized power in the domain of Fukuoka, she was tried on charges of assisting the *sonnō* movement and was banished to the island of Himejima, but the following year was rescued by Takasugi Shinsaku and his allies and fled to Shimonoseki. She later took up residence in Mitajiri but died there shortly after. Along with the Kyoto nun Ōtagaki Rengetsu-ni, she was one of the leading women poets of the movement to restore power to the emperor, and her strength of character and poetic talent led to the production of works that, while marked by a feminine delicacy of expression, at the same time are charged with great emotional power. In addition to the collection of poems entitled *Kōryōshū*, she also left two diaries, the *Himejima nikki* and *Bōshū nikki*, as well as other works.

Ogyū Sorai (1666–1728)

Confucian scholar of the early Edo period. He is also known as Ogyū Mokei or Ken'en. His father was personal physician to the fifth shogun, Tokugawa Tsunayoshi, but when Sorai was still a boy of thirteen, his father was accused of a fault and left Edo for the province of Kazusa. Sorai accompanied his father there, and though he had no teacher or friends, he studied on his own and read all the books he could lay his hands on. In 1690 his father was pardoned, and at twenty-four Sorai returned to Edo and set up a private school in front of the Zōjō-ji in Shiba, where he taught the Neo-Confucian doctrines of Chu Hsi and the Ch'eng brothers. When he was thirty, he was befriended by Yanagizawa Yoshiyasu, a powerful official under Shogun Tsunayoshi, and was given an important post in the government, even being called into the presence of the shogun himself. In 1709, with the death of Tsunayoshi and the fall from power of Yanagizawa Yoshiyasu, Sorai's political influence came to an end, and thereafter he devoted his time to the teaching of Confucianism and Chinese studies in the city of Edo.

At first Sorai defended the doctrines of the Sung scholars Chu Hsi and the Ch'eng brothers against the attacks of Itō Jinsai and others of the *kogakuha* (School of Ancient Learning), who wished to discard these later interpretations and return to the original meaning of the Confucian texts. Around the age of forty-nine, however, he had a change of heart, discarded the orthodox Neo-Confucianism of the Sung scholars, and advocated a philological approach, instituting a revolution in the field of Japanese studies of Chinese literature.

Sorai's philological approach, known as *komonji-gaku*, or the "study of ancient words," was originally inspired by the classical revival in Ming literary circles, a movement that was mainly concerned with the proper diction to be used in the writing of poetry and prose, but Sorai extended his philological interests much farther, insisting that one could not properly understand the classical texts of Confucianism and ancient Chinese philosophy if he did not devote himself to a study of the origin and historical development of the words used therein. His theories on philological study attracted wide attention at the time and in some instances gave rise to certain abuses, but at the same time they contributed greatly to the growth and improvement of Chinese studies in Japan and to the writing of prose and poetry in Chinese. Previous to his time, most of the poetry and prose in Chinese by Japanese writers had been marked by certain peculiarities of phrasing and usage deriving from Japanese linguistic habits and modes of expression, but Sorai, through his emphasis upon intensive linguistic and philological study, taught his students to write prose and poetry that was correct by Chinese standards. His passion for Chinese language and culture even led him to adopt a Chinese style name, taking the character "mono" from his clan name Mononobe and giving it its Sino-Japanese reading "butsu," thus creating the name Butsu Sorai. Others began to imitate him, and soon it became a fad to replace Japanese personal names, official titles, and even place names with Chinese sounding equivalents. In his collection of miscellaneous writings known as the *Narubeshi*, Sorai also offered some important suggestions on the origins and historical development of certain Japanese words, and his philological methods were taken over and used by later scholars in the study of ancient Japanese literature and culture.

His works include the *Kyōchū kikō, Yakumon sentei, Ken'en zuihitsu, Bendō, Bemmei, Rikuyu engi, Seidan, Rongo-chō,* and others.

Ōkuma Kotomichi (1798–1868)

Poet of the late Edo period. His surname was originally Kiyohara and he was also known by the name Seisuke and the literary name Hyōdō. He was the son of a wealthy merchant family said to have descended from Imperial Prince Toneri. Born in Fukuoka, he studied under Futagawa Sukechika, a teacher of calligraphy in Fukuoka, applying himself to the study of Japanese poetry and calligraphy; at the same time he studied on his own the *Man'yōshū* and *Kokinshū* and was also thoroughly versed in the collection of poems by the poet-priest Saigyō known as the *Sankashū*, in time becoming recognized as an authority in his own right. At the age of thirty-eight he turned over his inheritance rights to his younger brother and moved to a place in the suburbs of the city known as Imaizumi, living a life of retirement in a home called the Chihyōdō and devoting all his time to the writing of poetry.

His views are recorded in his collection of remarks on poetry entitled *Hitorigochi*, where he urges that one should write poetry appropriate to one's own time. Hoping to gain wider recognition, he journeyed to Osaka at the age of fifty-nine and remained there for some ten years, but his hopes were disappointed, and he returned to Fukuoka to live out his remaining years at his home, the Chihyōdō. The celebrated poet and supporter of the restoration movement Nomura Bōtō-ni, who was also a native of Kyushu, studied under him. A collection of his poems in three chapters entitled *Sōkeishū* was published while he was in Osaka, but it failed to attract any attention during his lifetime. It was not until 1898, when Sasaki Nobutsuna introduced the *Sōkeishū* to the reading public and pointed out its true value, that Kotomichi's poetry gained the recognition it enjoys today. His works are marked by deftness and originality and convey a sense of vivid impressionism and liveliness of tone.

Ōtagaki Rengetsu (1791–1875)

Poet of the late Edo period. Her personal name was Nobu; her parents were in the service of the Chion-in, a large temple at Higashiyama in Kyoto. She exhibited a talent for poetry at an early age and was also proficient in the military arts. A son was adopted into the family to be her husband, but because of his dissolute behavior the marriage was annulled. She married once more, but when her husband and child both died, she shaved her head and took the religious name Rengetsu. She made pottery, which she inscribed with her own poems, and supported herself on the proceeds, her pottery being known as Rengetsu-yaki. In her last years she resided in a dilapidated little temple on Higashiyama, keeping only one bowl and cooking pot for her own use and giving all the rest of her possessions to the poor, living out her last days in lonely austerity.

Her poetry, like her pottery, strikes one as being a natural expression of her personality. She lived at a time when the poetic world of Kyoto was dominated by Kagawa Kageki and his disciples, known as the Keien school, and though she does not appear to have studied under Kageki, she was no doubt influenced by the work of his school. Her style is simple and lucid, and most of her works are graceful descriptive pieces. Her poetry is less important for any technical skill or intellectual content that it may possess than for the air of purity that breathes throughout it, a reflection no doubt of the writer's own integrity and purity of heart. For this reason she holds a place of importance among the women poets of the early modern period. Her poems are found in the *Rengetsu Shikibu nijo wakashū* and the *Ama no karumo*. The following is an example of her work:

> How I envy them!
> cherries that bloom
> as they please,
> then in no time
> lightly, carelessly scatter.

Ōta Nampo (Shokusanjin) (1749–1823)

Kyōka and *kyōshi* poet and author of *sharebon* and *kokkeibon* during the middle and late Edo period. Son of a foot soldier in the service of the shogunate, he himself became a foot soldier at the age of sixteen and remained in the shogunate's service for more than fifty years thereafter. He acquired a knowledge of Chinese verse and prose at an early age and studied with Uchiyama Gatei and Matsuzaki Kankai. At the age of eighteen he was introduced to Hiraga Gennai, which inspired him to write *Neboke-sensei bunshū*. The work, which poked fun at human life and society in simple Chinese verse and prose, aroused an unexpected public response, and he became famous almost overnight as a writer of *kyōshi* (humorous verse in Chinese). He also started writing *kyōka* (humorous verse in Japanese). It was, ultimately, the breakdown in the shogunate's administrative policies and the contradictions becoming apparent within society that accounted for the popularity of this type of literature, and also of the hedonistic type of novel such as the *sharebon*. Nampo produced a large number of *kyōshi*, *kokkeibon*, and *hanashibon* and by his late twenties had come, it seemed, to dominate the world of literature.

The *kyōka* that he wrote under the name of Yomo no Akara won great favor with their characteristic wit; the number of his admirers increased steadily, and with the publication of *Manzai kyōkashū*, a collection of *kyōka* verse by contemporary poets, his popularity knew no bounds and he became the leading exponent of the "Temmei *kyōka*," as it was known from the name of the era during which the form enjoyed a special vogue. He also wrote a number of *kibyōshi*, becoming, in fact, the central figure not only in the *kyōka* world but in what is known as "Temmei culture" as a whole.

Using the pen name Shokusanjin almost exclusively from 1790 onward, he continued to write humorous verse until his death. He wrote a very large number of works that display the breadth of his tastes and the scope of his learning.

> The young fiddleneck ferns
> lift up their tight fists,
> in the spring wind
> shaking them
> right in the face of the mountain.

Ozawa Roan (1723–1801)

Poet and critic of the middle Edo period. His name was Ozawa Harunaka, and he was also known by the names Tatewaki and Kankadō. His father was a retainer of the Naruse family, lords of the castle of Inuyama in Owari. He lived in Kyoto from an early age, serving as caretaker for the Naruse family residence in the capital, and studied the writing of Japanese poetry under Reizei Tamemura. Later, however, he developed a new style of his own in which he worked to avoid the shortcomings of Kamo no Mabuchi and others of the Giko-ha, or Classical school, as well as those of the Dōjō-ha to which his teacher Reizei Tamemura belonged; his own style, known as the Tadakoto-ha, stressed the direct and honest expression of genuine feeling in language that is simple to understand.

In 1788, when he was sixty-five, the area of Okazaki in the eastern suburbs of Kyoto, in which his home was situated, was leveled by fire, and he moved to Jizōdō in Uzumasa, west of Kyoto; it was here that he wrote his first work on poetic theory, the *Chirihiji*, which was followed in rapid succession by a number of other works of similar nature. It was also at this time that, along with Ban Kōkei, Chōgetsu, and Jien, he became known as one of the Four Deva Kings of Heian; of this group of four poets, he was by far the most talented and original. He was on particularly close terms with Ban Kōkei and the well-known poet and fiction writer Ueda Akinari and was also a long-time friend of the poet Kagawa Kageki. In his later years he became very friendly with the scholars of Japanese literature Tachibana Chikage and Motoori Norinaga, and the latter remarked in praise of him that "In Kyoto the poet Roan is the one, while in Edo it's the scholar (Murata) Harumi!" Later Roan moved back to the area of Okazaki, where he died. In addition to the *Chirihiji* already mentioned, his works include the *Ashikabi, Arutoi, Furiwakegami, Shūchū waka rokujō,* and *Kokin rikugi shosetsu,* and a collection of his poems entitled *Rokujō-eisō.* The following poem on the Ōi River west of Kyoto, a spot noted for its cherry blossoms, will perhaps give some indication of his style:

> Ōi River—
> A night when
> moon and flowers grow hazy,
> only the sound of its waves
> undimmed.

Rai San'yō (1780–1832)

Scholar of Chinese studies and poet of the late Edo period. His personal name was Noboru or Shisei and he is also known by the literary name Sanjūroppō-gaishi. He was born in Osaka, but at the age of one his father, Shunsui, a scholar of the Chu Hsi school of Neo-Confucianism, became a teacher of Confucianism in the fief of Aki in present-day Hiroshima, and San'yō grew up in the Hiroshima area. He began writing verse in Chinese at the age of twelve, and his works were praised by the Edo Confucian scholar Shibano Ritsuzan. At the age of seventeen he journeyed to Edo and became a disciple of the Chu Hsi school scholar Bitō Nishū, receiving instruction in the Chinese Classics and works of Japanese history, but the following year he returned to the fief of Aki. He married at the age of nineteen but separated from his wife the following year because of an illness from which she was suffering. In 1804 he completed the first draft of a work in Chinese on Japanese history entitled *Nihon gaishi*, covering the period of the great military leaders from the time of the Taira and Minamoto families of the late Heian down to the rise of the Tokugawa family and interspersed with historical essays embodying the principles of the Chu Hsi school of philosophy. In 1809 he entered the school of Kan Sazan, a Chu Hsi school teacher of the fief of Bingo, holding a position as overseer of students, but resigned after a year in the post and later made his way to Kyoto. He remarried at the age of thirty-five. His father died the following year, and after the customary period of mourning, he made an extended trip around the island of Kyushu. Returning to Kyoto at the age of forty-three, he purchased a house at Sambongi, which he named the Suiseisō, and built a thatched cottage for himself in the garden. In 1827 he made public the finished version of the *Nihon gaishi* in twenty-two chapters, and the following year produced a set of poems in Chinese dealing with events and persons important in Japanese history, entitled *Nihon gafu*. In 1832 he completed another work in Chinese on Japanese political history, the *Nihon seiki*, and died in the ninth month of the same year.

San'yō was a distinguished historian and scholar of the Chu Hsi school of Confucianism, but was renowned as well for his outstanding works of Chinese prose and verse. He was particularly skilled in the composition of long poems dealing with contemporary events and the personages of history. In his poems in Chinese he strove for simplicity and purity of diction and liveliness of emotion and, not content merely to produce imitations of Chinese models, attempted to endow his works with a distinctively Japanese flavor, using the medium of Chinese verse to create works that were contemporary in spirit and truly meaningful to his fellow countrymen. He was a highly talented prose writer as well and was ranked with the Edo scholar Satō Issai as one of the outstanding Chinese prose stylists of the time, succeeding to the position held earlier by the "Three Professors of the Kansei Era (1789–1800)," Shibano Ritsuzan, Koga Seiri, and Bitō Nishū. In his *Nihon gaishi* San'yō labored to adapt the medium of Chinese prose to the needs of his narrative, deliberately employing certain distinctively Japanese phrases and usages. As he himself states, "Japanese colloquial phrases can be used directly to bring out the true flavor of the narrative. But one must know how to employ them with skill and discretion if his writings are to be worthy of consideration."

Works by Rai San'yō in addition to those already mentioned include *Tsūgi, San'yō shishō,* and *San'yō ikō.*

Ryōkan (1758–1831)

Poet and priest of the late Edo period. His original name was Yamamoto Eizō, Ryōkan being the religious name that he used after becoming a Buddhist monk. Born the eldest son of a village headman and Shinto priest at Izumozaki in the province of Echigo, he relinquished the right of succession to his younger brother and became a Buddhist monk at the age of seventeen, going to live in a Zen temple. At the age of twenty-one, he became a pupil of the itinerant monk Kokusen, and accompanied him as far as the province of Bitchū (present Okayama Prefecture), where he underwent a further period of monastic discipline at the Entsū-ji temple in Tamashima. From then on until the age of forty-two he spent his time—apart from a period following his mother's death, when he returned to his home—traveling about Shikoku, Kyushu, and other parts of western Japan. He then returned to his native district and served as priest at various temples until finally, at the age of forty-seven, he settled in the Gogō-an at Kugamiyama, where he lived until the age of sixty. He struck up a friendship with Abe Sadayoshi, an influential religious benefactor and lover of literature. He became acquainted with the *Man'yōshū* and verse of the celebrated Chinese Zen monk Han-shan, studied ancient calligraphy such as the *Kohōjō* and *Shūshūjō*, and began to produce noble poems in both Japanese and Chinese, as well as calligraphy. At times he would join the village children in their innocent games, at others he would go with the women of the village to gather young herbs in the country. The following well-known poems date from this period.

> Long spring days
> when the mists rise—
> hitting the little handball
> along with the children,
> I've passed one more of them.

> The breeze is fresh,
> the moonlight bright—
> come, together let's dance
> the whole night through
> in memory of my old age.

He lived in poverty yet was always content. At the age of sixty-eight, when he began to grow rather feeble, he moved to a cottage in the back garden of Kimura Gen'emon, at the foot of Kugamiyama. Here he developed an affectionate and pure master-pupil relationship with a twenty-eight-year-old nun, Teishin-ni, and continued to produce poetry of undiminished skill until his death at the age of seventy-three. His verse is contained in the collection *Hachisu no tsuyu*, edited by Teishin-ni, and he also left fine calligraphy in the *sōsho* (cursive) style and many Chinese poems of an austere simplicity.

Ryū Rikyō (1704–1758)

Literati painter and writer of the middle Edo period. His real name was Yanagizawa Kien and he was the son of the *karō* (chief retainer) of Kōriyama in the province of Yamato. He was accomplished in a great variety of arts and was renowned as a man of taste and refinement. He was particularly distinguished as a painter and was one of the leading early figures in the *nanga*, or literati, school of painting in Japan. Ike no Taiga, a later master of the school, as a youth studied under him for a period. One of his specialities was *shitōga*, painting made by applying ink with the tip of the finger, and the paintings of bamboo that he produced by this technique have been highly praised. He was a man of warm and magnanimous disposition, delighting in the company of all kinds of persons, talented and untalented alike, and it is said that his house was always overflowing with guests. He was, in fact, one of the outstanding eccentrics of the time. He left a collection of miscellaneous jottings entitled the *Umpyō zasshi* and dealing with events of everyday life, a kind of compendium of "laudable sayings and examples of exemplary conduct" that faithfully reflects the ideals of feudal society as seen from the standpoint of a member of the samurai class. But because Rikyō was a representative of the cultured society of middle Edo times and a man of broad interests, the topics dealt with are unusually varied in scope, and the style of the work is simple and lucid, making it one of the most outstanding works in the *zuihitsu* genre. He also produced other works such as the *Hishirinen* and *Hitorine*.

Ryūtei Rijō (?–1841)

Writer of *kokkeibon* of the late Edo period. A man of many skills, he played the *shamisen*, appeared at variety show theaters, and is said to have also worked as a *taikomochi* (professional male entertainer at parties). The well-known writer of popular novelettes Tamenaga Shunsui was his younger brother. As his first models he took Juppensha Ikku and Shikitei Samba. Thus his earliest *kokkeibon* were works such as *Ōyama dōchū kurige no shiriuma*, an imitation of Ikku's *Hizakurige*, or sequels to Samba's *Ukiyodoko* and *Ningen banji uso bakkari*. With the works for which Rijō was to become best known, however—*Hanagoyomi hasshōjin* (1824) and *Kokkei wagōjin* (1823) —he succeeded in creating a world of his own and acquired a skill that none of his contemporaries could emulate. Although the works give a vivid portrait of the vulgar and decadent amusements of the citizens of Edo during the late Edo period, when the long period of peace and seclusion had sapped the sterner standards of earlier days, he also gives some idea of the underlying desire of those citizens to free themselves from the fetters of a still feudal society and morality. Thus he became one of the leading writers of *kokkeibon*, a successor to Juppensha Ikku and Shikitei Samba who, like them, left a special mark on the history of the form.

Ryūtei Tanehiko (1783–1843)

Late Edo period writer of popular fiction of the type known as *gōkan* or *kusazōshi* (illustrated tales). He was descended from the Yokote family, who had earlier been retainers to the Takeda family of Kōshū. He was a samurai in the direct service of the Tokugawa shogunate, but in addition to ordinary academic pursuits and the study of the military arts, he also became proficient in painting and the composition of *haiku*, *kyōka*, and *senryū*. He was also an avid kabuki fan and was said to have been skilled at impersonating the famous kabuki actors of the day. Inspired by the example of the Edo fiction writer Santō Kyōden, he began writing *yomihon* (historical novels), his first work appearing in 1807, when he was twenty-four. In the same year he published the historical novels *Awa no Naruto* and *Yakko no Koman monogatari*, and thereafter brought out a new book almost every year. In 1811 he produced a work of the *gōkan* or *kusazōshi* type, an illustrated tale entitled *Suzuki hōchō aoto no kireaji* and, apparently realizing that this was his real forte, thereafter produced mainly works in this genre. Among these, *Nise murasaki inaka Genji*, which appeared over the years from 1829 to 1842, was particularly popular among the women of Edo, partly because of the elaborate illustrations by Utagawa Kunisada that accompanied the text, and brought its author widespread fame. He also tried his hand at writing other types of works such as the romantic tales known as *sharebon* or *ninjōbon*. It is apparent, however, that his talents were best suited for the *kusazōshi*, and he achieved no distinction in the other genres he attempted to work in. He was active as a book collector and antiquarian and left such works on the subject as *Kōsho-kuhon mokuroku* and *Yoshiwara shoseki mokuroku, utsushi,* and the collections of essays entitled *Sukikaeshi* and *Yōshabako.* In 1842, when the so-called Tempō era reforms were instituted, the *Nise murasaki inaka Genji* was ordered to be withdrawn from circulation. No official reason was ever given for the ban, but it was rumored that the contents of the novel had offended those in high places, and even that the illustrations were modeled upon the life in the women's quarters of the shogunal residence. Tanehiko is said to have taken sick and died as a result of the shock, though there is also a theory that he committed suicide.

His works are characterized by carefully planned construction and variety of incident. The plots are drawn largely from the kabuki and *jōruri* drama or earlier works of fiction and are freely adapted and elaborated. His works are also noted for their clarity of expression. Through the medium of the *kusazōshi,* he converted the type of historical fiction that had earlier been treated in the *yomihon* genre into something even more popular, dramatic, and easily accessible to the mass of readers, thus acting as the forerunner of the writers of popular fiction of the present day. It is this contribution that merits him a place of importance in the literary history of the period, representing as he does the foremost exponent of the *kusazōshi* genre. In addition to the works mentioned above, his major writings also include the *yomihon Asamagatake omokage zōshi, Ōshū shūjaku monogatari, Moji tesuri mukashi ningyō,* and *Seta no Hashi ryūjo no honji,* and the *kusazōshi Shōhon-jitate, Mukashi-mukashi kabuki monogatari, Oatsuraezome tōyama kanoko,* and *Kantan shokoku monogatari.*

Santō Kyōden (1761–1816)

Playwright, fiction writer, and *ukiyo-e* artist of the middle and late Edo period. His name was Iwase Samuru, his common given name Denzō, and he also used the names Seisai and Seisei-rōjin. He was the son of a pawnbroker of Fukagawa in Edo, and from his youth was versed in music and dancing. He became a student of the painter Kitao Shigemasa and in time began a career as an *ukiyo-e* artist and illustrator for the *kibyōshi,* popular fiction. Soon after, he tried his hand at writing *kibyōshi* himself, at the age of seventeen publishing his first work, *Kaichō riyaku no meguriai,* and two years later, in 1780, published *Musume katakiuchi kokyō no nishiki* under the pen name Santō Kyōden, which he used thereafter. He continued to write works of fiction, and in 1785, with the publication of *Edo-umare uwaki no kabayaki,* won recognition at the age of twenty-four as a major writer. At the same time he drew upon his long familiarity with the world of the licensed quarter to write a work in the *sharebon* (gossip book) form entitled *Musuko-beya*, which was published in 1785, and thereafter continued to write both *kibyōshi* and *sharebon*. His works, rich in content, characterized by keen sensitivity and detailed observation, and illustrated by the author himself, gained wide popularity, and he was also active as a writer of humorous prose and verse.

In 1790, at the age of twenty-nine he married a geisha named Kikusono with whom he had long been familiar, and she seems to have made him an excellent wife. In 1791 three of his *sharebon* were condemned by the authorities for violation of the morality laws and he was sentenced to wear handcuffs for a period of fifty days. Thereafter he wrote no more *sharebon* and took care to inject a note of didacticism into his works in *kibyōshi* form. His wife died sometime after, and he opened a shop on the Ginza selling pipes and tobacco pouches. He turned his attention to the writing of *yomihon*, works of didactic fiction, for a time competing in this genre with his former student Takizawa (Kyokutei) Bakin, though he was no match for Bakin in erudition. In the writing of *kibyōshi*, however, he was acknowledged as a master. Around the age of forty he married another geisha, this one named Tamanoi or Yuri. In his late years he devoted most of his time to the writing of carefully researched essays on the customs and manners of Japan in the Edo period, which have been recognized for their scholarly value and include such well-known works as *Kinsei kiseki-kō* and *Kottō-shū*. He had no children and apparently led a rather bleak and lonely life in his late years. He died of illness in the ninth month of 1816 at the age of fifty-five. The work entitled *Iwademono ki* by his contemporary Bakin provides considerable data concerning his life, though some of it is probably distorted because of Bakin's feelings of antagonism toward him. However that may be, it is certain that no writer of the Edo period can rival Kyōden in breadth and variety of activities. The following is a list of his major works in various genres:

kibyōshi: *Edo-umare uwaki no kabayaki, Shingaku hayazome-gusa, hitogokoro kagami utsushie.*

sharebon: *Musuko-beya, Tsūgen sōmagaki, Tsūki suigoden, Keisei-kai shijūha-chi-te.*

gōkan: *Orokugushi Kiso no adauchi, Kasamori musume nishiki no orizuri.*

yomihon: *Fukushū kidan Asaka no numa, Udonge monogatari, Sakura-hime zenden akebono no zōshi, Mukashi-gatari inazuma-byōshi, Sōchōki.*

kokkeibon: *Komon gawa, Kimyōzu.*

essays: *Kinsei kiseki-kō, Kottō-shū, Ukiyo-e ruikō.*

ehon: *Tanagui awase, Kokin kyōka-bukuro*

Shikitei Samba (1776–1822)

Fiction writer of the late Edo period. Born in the Asakusa district of Edo, he became an employee in a bookstore at an early age. Later he opened a second-hand bookstore of his own and at the same time devoted himself to writing works of fiction. His first work, entitled *Tentō ukiyo no dezukai*, appeared in 1794. This was followed by a work in the *kibyōshi*, or popular fiction, genre called *Kyan Taiheiki mukō hachimaki*, a *kusazōshi* work entitled *Kusazōshi kojitsuke nendaiki*, and others. He also carried on the traditions of the *sharebon* and *kokkeibon*, genres dealing with amorous or comical tales and anecdotes, producing works such as the *Ikazuchi Tarō gōaku monogatari*, as well as many works in the *gōkan* genre, another type of popular fiction. But his talent shows to best advantage in his *kokkeibon*, or humorous works, such as his masterpiece, the *Ukiyoburo*, and the *Ukiyodoko*, which deal with the lives of the common citizens of Edo. In other works such as the *Hayagawari mune no Karakuri*, *Shijūhachi kuse*, *Ningen banji uso bakkari*, and *Kokon hyaku baka*, he explores the ins and outs of various human idiosyncrasies and personality types, capturing through the medium of highly realistic dialogue and soliloquy the exact manner of speech and peculiarities of behavior characteristic of each different type. Through his detailed descriptions of the daily lives of the common people of the time, he succeeds in exposing the foibles of human nature, and his works abound in sarcasm and satirical humor. He ranks with Jippensha Ikku as one of the two greatest writers of humorous fiction of the time.

Shimizu Hamaomi (1776–1824)

Poet and scholar of Japanese studies of the late Edo period. His *tsūshō*, or common name, was Harunaga, and he adopted the literary name Sazanaminoya. He was the son of a physician and himself conducted a medical practice near Shinobazu Pond in Edo. He pursued Japanese studies under Murata Harumi and was a proficient writer of both poetry and prose, enjoying the patronage of Matsudaira Sadanobu, the lord of the domain of Shirakawa, and other feudal lords of the time. He was also a close friend of the scholar of Chinese studies Kariya Ekisai. He produced studies and commentaries on the classics and in addition wrote a number of works relating to Japanese language and literature. He worked to publicize the achievements of the Agata-mon, the school of Japanese studies founded by Kamo no Mabuchi, compiling and publishing a work entitled *Agata-mon ikō*, and also compiled a collection of recent *chōka* or "long poems," an ancient poetic form that had largely gone out of use but was revived in the Genroku era (1688–1704), publishing it under the title *Kin'yō suganeshū*. Through these and other scholarly works such as the *Gorin ruiyō*, he contributed to the literary world of the time, while his collection of prose writings, the *Sazanaminoya bunsō*, won him fame as a stylist. His poems were collected after his death in a work entitled *Sazanamiyoya shū*, and reveal that he was skilled in the use of the diction of ancient poetry. After the death of Murata Harumi, his disciples increased in number greatly, and include such scholars of Japanese studies as Maeda Natsukage, Okamoto Yasutaka, and others.

> Puffs of wind
> swaying the tip
> of the fishing line—
> setting sun on the face
> of a lonely autumn stream.

Shimokōbe Chōryū (1624–1686)

Poet and scholar of Japanese literature of the early Edo period. He was the son of a samurai family of Yamato named Ozaki, but was later adopted into the Shimokōbe family, to which his mother belonged. In his youth he entered the service of the Katagiri family, but later resigned and went to Edo. Failing to find the kind of employment there he desired, he went to Osaka, and then to Kyoto, serving there for several years under the Sanjōnishi family. He went once more to Edo, and finally settled down in Osaka, living a life of retirement and devoting the remainder of his years to the arts.

From the age of seventeen or eighteen he was an avid reader of the *Kokinshū*; in matters of poetic theory he was an admirer of Kinoshita Chōshōshi and he is said to have received guidance in the writing of *renga* or linked verse from Nishiyama Sōin. He was particularly fond of *waka* poetry, was well versed in poetics, wrote commentaries on collections of poetry and matters pertaining to *makura kotoba* and other types of poetic diction, and compiled anthologies of poetry. His particular speciality was the *Man'yōshū*. Many persons came to study under him, but he was a man of rather difficult temperament and did not care for the company of others. Only with the priest and scholar of Japanese studies Keichū did he maintain a deep and lasting friendship, exchanging poems with him with great frequency. Because of his knowledge of the *Man'yōshū*, he was invited by Tokugawa Mitsukuni, the

lord of the domain of Mito, to write a commentary on the text, but due to
the vagaries of his mood he made little progress at the task and meanwhile
fell ill. At his urging, Keichū undertook to carry on the project, eventually,
after Chōryū's death, producing the great work known as the *Man'yō
daishōki*.

Chōryū believed that poetry should be used to express one's reactions to
sights and sounds around him and could be written by any Japanese, old or
young, noble or humble in station. Accordingly, when he compiled an
anthology known as the *Rin'yō ruijinshū*, he included poems by commoners,
attempting to free *waka* poetry from the stultifying dominance of the Dōjō
school, with its rigid conventions and its "secret interpretations" of the
Kokinshū that were handed down from one adept to another, and to infuse it
with a spirit of innovation and vitality. This was also the reason that he
concentrated his attentions upon the *Man'yōshū*, a text regarded with contempt by the members of the Dōjō school, and in his collection of comments
and glosses on the text entitled *Man'yōshū kanken* offered many new theories
on its interpretation. Keichū was the successor to Chōryū's efforts in this
field, building upon the foundation that Chōryū had laid, and through him
Chōryū's scholarship came to exercise an important influence upon later
students of Japanese studies and early Japanese literature.

His other works include the *Man'yōshūshō*, *Man'yō koji narabini kotoba*,
Makurakotoba shokumyōshō, *Tosa nikkishō*, and a collection of his poems known
as *Bankawakashū*.

TACHIBANA AKEMI (1812–1868)

Poet of the late Edo period. His family name was Ide, and as a child he went
by the given name Gosaburō; he was born in Fukui in the province of
Echizen to a branch of the Shōgen, a family prominent in the eighth century
and descended from Minister of the Left Tachibana no Moroe. He lost
his mother at the age of one and his father at the age of fourteen. Determining to enter the priesthood, he became a disciple of Myōdō, the head
priest of a Nichiren sect temple known as the Myōtai-ji, receiving instruction
in Buddhist doctrine, Chinese, and the writing of poetry in Chinese and Japanese. Later he journeyed to Kyoto and studied under Kodama Saburō, one of
the leading disciples of Rai San'yō, but soon after returned to his home in
Echizen. At the age of thirty-four he decided to devote himself to Japanese
studies, becoming a student of Tanaka Ōhide, a disciple of Motoori Norinaga. He later turned over his family inheritance to his younger brother,

moved to a house in Jōsei that he named the Waraya, and gave all his time to literary pursuits. Matsudaira Yoshinaga, the lord of the domain of Fukui, greatly admired Akemi's learning and character, bestowed upon him the literary name Shinobunoya, and frequently urged him to take service in the castle and give lectures on the classics of Japanese literature, but Akemi firmly declined the invitation. Matsudaira Yoshiaki, Yoshinaga's successor as lord of the fief, struck by Akemi's devotion to literature and his determination to maintain his independence and integrity even though it meant living a life of poverty, saw to it that Akemi received a certain amount of rice each year from the granaries of the fief.

He was a supporter of the *sonnō* movement, which sought to restore power to the emperor, and when he learned that some of the samurai of the domain were in doubt as to whether to support the movement or ally themselves with the forces loyal to the shogunate, he was deeply distressed and composed a poem, which reads:

> For what purpose
> do you wear a sword?
> So that you may carry out
> the commands of the emperor!

He looked forward to the day when the system of imperial government would be restored, and was accordingly overjoyed when in 1867 the shogunate officially returned the power of government to the court. Unfortunately, he died some ten days before the era name was changed to Meiji and the ceremonies marking the beginning of the Meiji Restoration took place.

Akemi was a man of broad learning, thoroughly conversant with Japanese and Chinese literature, but his lifelong passion was poetry in the *waka* form. In philosophical approach he reserved his highest admiration for Motoori Norinaga and attempted to perpetuate his doctrines, but in poetry he favored the *Man'yōshū* style advocated by Kamo no Mabuchi and his followers. To this, however, he added elements of the freer style propounded by Ozawa Roan and Kagawa Kageki, writing poems about the events of everyday life and helping to initiate a new era in the history of Japanese poetry. Particularly famous is the series of poems beginning with the line *Tanoshimi wa*, "It is a pleasure when. . . .", in which he describes the simple joys of eating and drinking with his family and friends, writing poetry, and pursuing his scholarly studies.

He left behind two collections of poetry, the *Shinobunoya kashū* and *Warayaeisō*, and a collection of miscellaneous writings entitled *Iroritan*.

Tachibana Chikage (1735–1808)

Poet and scholar of Japanese studies of the middle Edo period. His family name was Katō, and he is hence commonly known as Katō Chikage, though the Katō family had originally borne the surname Tachibana. His common name was Matazaemon, and he also went by the literary names Hagisono, Ukerasono, and the *kyōka* name Tachibana no Yachimata.

He was the son of Tachibana Enao, a poet and scholar of Japanese studies who held office as a *yoriki*, a lesser official in the service of the Edo *machibugyō-sho*, the office in charge of the administration of Edo. From an early age he studied under his father, and at the age of nine became a student of the famous poet and *kokugakusha*, or scholar of Japanese studies, Kamo no Mabuchi. His extreme diligence and innate intelligence in time led him to be counted among the twelve foremost disciples of the Agatamon, as Kamo no Mabuchi's school was known. He and Murata Harumi, another disciple of the Agatamon, came to be recognized as the two most important figures in the so-called Edo school of poetry.

At the age of fifteen he entered the service of the Edo *machibugyō-sho*, and at twenty-nine succeeded to his father's office, becoming a *gimmikata yoriki*, an official in charge of investigating persons suspected of crimes. Later he became a *sobayōnin*, or attendant, in the service of the high shogunate official Tanuma Okitsugu, but when Okitsugu fell from power and the so-called Kansei era reforms began (1787–93), he retired from office in 1788 at the age of fifty-three. Following his retirement, he devoted all his efforts to poetry and scholarship, and in 1800 completed his most important scholarly work, a commentary on the *Man'yōshū* entitled *Man'yōshū ryakuge*. But he excelled more as a poet than as a scholar, and his collection of literary works completed in 1802 and entitled *Ukeragahana* is considered a masterpiece.

He took over and carried on the modern style that had been one of the styles of his master Kamo no Mabuchi, producing many works marked by a refined delicacy and grace appropriate to a citizen of a great city such as Edo; he especially excelled in descriptive pieces.

In his late years he became acquainted with Lord Tominokōji Sadanao, a member of the court nobility, and was invited to submit poems to Myōhōin-no-miya, a prince of the imperial family. Thus, from powerful statesmen and members of the aristocracy down to the women of the licensed quarters, all sought his advice and instruction in matters pertaining to poetry. He was also a distinguished painter and calligrapher, formulating a distinctive style of *kana* writing known as the Chikage school, which enjoyed great popularity at the time, and works of pottery and textiles with reproductions of his paintings on them, known respectively as *Chikage yaki* and *Chikage donsu,* were also popular.

In addition to these many talents, he developed a taste for *kyōka*, humorous verse, establishing friendly relations with such noted poets of that genre as Tegara Okamochi and Shokusanjin, and took an interest in the *kibyōshi* and similar types of humorous and satirical popular literature of the time. Among his disciples were Kimura Sadayoshi and Hitotsuyanagi Chifuru.

Following are two examples of his poetry:

> Sumida River—
> the raftsmen coming down it
> wear straw raincoats,
> and I know that
> a misty morning rain must be falling.

> Today too
> will be another quiet day—
> shining through the dawn mist,
> the light
> of the morning star.

Takebe Ayatari (1719–1774)

Haiku and *waka* poet, author of *yomihon*, student of *kokugaku*, and artist during the middle Edo period. As a *haiku* poet he used the pseudonyms Kasso, Toin, and Ryōtai, as a painter the pseudonym Kan'yōsai, and also went by other names, such as Katauta no Michimori. He was born into the Kitamura family, his father being chief minister of the Tsugaru clan, while his great-grandfather was Yamaga Sokō, the celebrated military theorist and Confucian scholar. He was given a typical samurai education, but fled from home at the age of nineteen on account of an illicit love affair with his elder brother's wife and embarked on a life of wandering.

He went first to Kyoto, where he became a Buddhist monk for a while, but subsequently returned to lay life and took up the study of *haiku*, studying first with Shida Yaha in Osaka and subsequently with a succession of poets of the Ise school. In 1747 he went to Edo, where, under the pseudonym Ryōtai, he adapted the plain style of the Ise school of *haiku* (so called because it first arose in Ise) to the more sophisticated taste of the large city and eventually became head of a school of his own. Besides the *haiku*, he was also an aspiring painter. He was a pioneer of the *nanga*, or literati, style of painting and under the pseudonym Kan'yōsai gained recognition along with such other famous *nanga* artists as Ike no Taiga and Yosa Buson. In 1762 he developed an interest in *kokugaku*, the study of the Japanese classics, which was flourishing at the time, and became a pupil of Kamo no Mabuchi in order to pursue the subject. By nature ambitious, with a taste for novelty and self-advertisement, he conceived the idea of launching a new *haiku* style in competition with the prevalent Shōmon school of Bashō and his followers; as a result, he came to denounce the *haiku* itself as a debased form, advocating in its stead an old verse form known as *katauta*, consisting of nineteen syllables in three lines of five, seven, and seven respectively. He campaigned vigorously for this ancient form in which he himself wrote a great deal of verse. Apart from a few followers that it won in the provinces of Shinano and Kōzuke, however, the *katauta* was greeted mostly with scorn, so he turned this time to prose and painting.

His work as a painter is seen at its best in such works as the album *Kan'yōsai gafu* (1760), while his popular novelettes gave way to novels in the pseudo-archaic style following his conversion to *kokugaku*. His works in this vein, the *yomihon Nishiyama monogatari* and *Honchō suikoden*, can hardly be said to have great literary value, any more than can his travel books and belles lettres, but they were precursors of the *yomihon* that later became so important in the popular literature of Edo and as such are important in the history of literature. Although he tried his hand at various art forms, his innate excess of ambition prevented him, despite undoubted talent, from great accomplishment in any of them.

Takeda Izumo (1691–1756)

Puppet drama playwright of the middle Edo period. The name Izumo is an abbreviation for Izumo-no-jō, a name used by a group of men who originally broke off from Takeda Ōmi of the Takeda Puppet Theater of Dōtonbori in Osaka. At some point, one of the holders of the name Takeda Izumo succeeded the great *jōruri* chanter Takemoto Gidayū as head of the Takemoto Puppet Theater and began calling himself Takeda Izumo I. The man to be dealt with here is his son, Takeda Izumo II, popularly referred to by the respectful title Oyakata Izumo and a writer of high repute. He, in turn, was succeeded by his son Koizumo, who was also a playwright, but who died three years before his father.

Takeda Izumo II bore the personal name Kiyosada and adopted the literary name Senzenken. From an early age he applied himself to the study of the theater, receiving guidance from Chikamatsu Monzaemon and others, and sometime early in the Kyōho era (1716–36) was allowed by his father to take over the professional name Takeda Izumo. In 1724 he wrote his first play entitled *Shokatsu Kōmei teigundan*, and thereafter until the time of his death continued to act as both playwright and proprietor of the Takemoto Theater, displaying great skill in both capacities and admirably reviving the fortunes of the business.

If the four plays listed under the name *Takemoto-geki* are included, his complete works total about forty plays; of these, ten were written entirely by him, while the remainder were written in collaboration with such other playwrights as Hasegawa Senshi, Bunkōdō, Miyoshi Shōraku, Namiki Senryū, and Yoshida Kanshi. His independent works were written fairly early in his career and include the *Daidairi Ōtomo no Manatori* (1725), *Sanshōdayū gonin musume* (1727), and *Ashiya Dōman ōuchi kagami* (1734), which, although they have undergone a certain amount of revision, still retain the qualities characteristic of his work. Later, in collaboration with Namiki Senryū and Miyoshi Shōraku, he wrote such outstanding works as *Sugawara denju tenarai kagami* and *Yoshitsune senbonzakura* in 1747, *Kanadehon chūshingura* in 1748, and *Futatsuchōchō kuruwa nikki* in 1749, being responsible for the selection and handling of the material and the staging of the completed works.

There are several characteristics that mark his work, among them the fact that in the plots of his plays the dictates of *ninjō* (human feeling) are customarily sacrificed to the demands of *giri* (duty), leading to scenes of great pathos and beauty; in addition, his works are distinguished by their scenes of spectacular visual impact and by the perfect coordination achieved between the chanted text and musical accompaniment and the lively movements of the puppets. The fact that his most famous works have been adopted into the repertory of the kabuki theater and are presented today in very nearly their original form is an indication of his great skill as a playwright and master of the dramatic arts. Most of his works, it may be noted, are historical pieces dealing with the heroes of the past. He had many disciples, including Tamenaga Tarobei, Nihodō, Takeda Shōzō, Takeda Izumi, Takeda Heishichi, and others.

Takizawa (Kyokutei) Bakin (1767–1848)

Writer of the forms of popular fiction known as *yomihon* and *kusazōshi* during the late Edo period. His surname was Takizawa; his father was in the service of the Matsudaira family, a man of a proud, fierce character who was skilled at the martial arts. From him, Bakin received a samurai style training and a strong, unyielding disposition. His father, however, died when Bakin was eight, and he embarked on a shifting, unsettled life. He went into the service of two or three different *hatamoto* (retainers of the shogun), but none of these engagements lasted for long; he tried his hand at various other callings, including medicine, Confucianism, and calligraphy, but failed in every case.

In 1790, at the age of twenty-three, he became a pupil of the popular storywriter Santō Kyōden. His first work was *Hatsukaamari shijūryō tsukaihatashite nibu kyōgen*. At the age of twenty-six he married into the family of a wooden clog (*geta*) merchant and went into the *geta* trade, adopting his wife's surname, but two years later took a dislike to this in turn and reverted to his original surname of Takizawa. He now became a teacher of reading and writing, but gave this up too at the age of thirty-nine. His writing activities were stepped up following the publication of his *Takao senjimon* and *Chinsetsu yumihari-zuki*, large-scale works, acquiring an unrivalled reputation as a writer of *yomihon*. His son Sōhaku, who had studied medicine, died before him, and he was obliged to shoulder sole responsibility for keeping the Takizawa family alive. He lost the sight of his right eye through overwork at the age of sixty-seven, and his writing activities did not go as well as he could have wished. At the age of seventy he held a sale of his paintings and calligraphy, from which he made a profit of two hundred *ryō*, using the money to buy a house at Yotsuya, Edo. Following his removal there, he finally lost his sight entirely but managed with the aid of his daughter-in-law to complete his celebrated work *Nansō Satomi hakkenden* before his death at the age of eighty-one.

Bakin's literary life extended over sixty years and ranged over many genres—*kibyōshi*, *gōkan*, and *yomihon* especially, but also *haiku*, *sharebon*, *kokkeibon*, belle-lettres, and *gikobun* (works in a mock archaic style), but outstanding is the series of long works such as *Hakkenden*, which takes its framework from a Chinese novel and required twenty-eight years to complete, and others such as *Asahina Juntōki* that are set in the period of civil wars (ca. fifteenth—sixteenth centuries) and take historical heroes as their central characters. The feudal outlook is marked in all of them, and they are strongly influenced by Confucian morality and by ideas of karma. Their style is brilliant and their structure well organized, and they show the historical-romance type of *yomihon* at its highest point.

Tamenaga Shunsui (1790–1843)

Fiction writer of the late Edo period. His orginal name was Sasaki Sadataka, and he was also known by the *tsūshō*, or common name, Echizenya Chōjirō; he seems to have been the son of an Edo townsman family. At first he operated a bookstore called the Seirindō, which did most of its business by lending out books. Later, hoping to exploit the knowledge that he had gained from his spare-time reading, he became a professional storyteller, appearing at various small theaters in Edo, but failed to attract a following. He then became a student of the well-known fiction writer Shikitei Samba, producing works under a variety of literary names, but once more success eluded him. Finally, adopting the literary name Nansenshō Somabito II, he wrote in conjunction with another author a work entitled *Akegarasu nochi no masayume*, which, published in 1821, won unexpected popularity. Thereafter, using the same name, he produced a series of works such as the *Tamagawa nikki* (1827) in the fiction genre known as *ninjōbon*, becoming known as one of the most outstanding writers in that genre.

Having established his reputation as an author, he in 1829 abandoned the name Somabito and began turning out works of the *ninjōbon* type under the name Tamenaga Shunsui, and in 1832 published a work entitled *Shunshoku umegoyomi*, which was greeted with wild acclaim. (It has been suggested that many of the works attributed to him during the period when he was using the name Somabito were actually written by men who were studying under him; the *Shunshoku umegoyomi* and subsequent works, however, appear to be from his own hand.) In 1837 he published the *Eitai dango* and *Harutsugedori* and began referring to himself grandiloquently as the "father of all Edo *ninjōbon* writers." In the years following he turned out over ten more works in the *ninjōbon* genre, which were avidly read by the young men and women of Edo, mainly, it would seem, because of their amorous content. In 1842, however, the high shogunate official Mizuno Tadakuni began a vigorous campaign to reform ethical standards; Shunsui was accused of writing works that were injurious to public morality, his books were banned, and he was condemned to punishment. He died the following year, a bitter and despondent man.

Shunsui was the virtual creator of the *ninjōbon* genre, which describes in rich and elegant language the daily lives of the citizens of Edo and the romantic intrigues of its young men and women, opening the way for later writers of this type of fiction. In a broader sense, he also helped to lay the foundation for the creation of the modern Japanese novel, which in time was to grow out of the *ninjōbon* and other genres of Edo period popular fiction.

His works of importance other than those mentioned above include the *Nezame no kurigoto*, written under the name Somabito, the *Shunshoku megumi no hana*, *Shunshoku umemibune*, *Agemaki musubi yukari no fusaito*, and others.

TODA MOSUI (1629–1706)

Poet and scholar of Japanese studies of the early Edo period. He was born in Sumpu Castle, the son of Watanabe Kemmotsu Tadashi, a samurai in the service of the Edo shogunate. His name was Yasumitsu. When he was three, his father went into retirement in the province of Shimotsuke, and Mosui accordingly spent his childhood there; later he was adopted by his uncle in Edo, took the surname Toda, and entered the service of a lord of the Honda family. When reforms were carried out in the administration of the Honda domain, however, he became a *rōnin* (masterless samurai), and lived a life of retirement as Mt. Kinryū in the Asakusa region of Edo. From around 1692 he began to produce works in considerable number, but hung a sign reading "House of the Hermit Mosui" over his gate and otherwise behaved in such a way as to gain a reputation throughout Edo for his eccentricity.

He was skilled in the military arts, learned in matters pertaining to both Japanese and Chinese culture, and in general a man of copious talent, but he seems never to have found an opportunity to advance in the world, and much of the tone of vehemence that characterizes his writings on poetry is no doubt a reflection of his feelings of frustration and anger at his lot in life.

His achievements covered a number of fields, but he is perhaps most outstanding as a critic of poetry. In 1665, at the age of thirty-six, he wrote a work entitled *Bunji* in which he launched an attack on the poetic theories handed down from the medieval period. This was followed by the *Hyakunin isshu zōdan*, *Higagotoshirabe*, and other works in which he criticized the poetics of the courtier families, particularly those who derived their literary theory from the Nijō school of poetry and from the time of Hosokawa Yūsai had handed down the so-called *Kokin-denju*, the secret interpretations of the *Kokinshū*. Mosui declared that the *Kokin-denju* was worthless and in 1698. at the age of sixty-nine, brought out a work entitled *Nashimotoshū* in which he propounded his ideas for a revolution in poetic theory and practice.

No collection of Mosui's own poems has been preserved, but scattered examples of his poetry are found in some of his works such as the *Murasaki no hitomoto* and the anthologies that he compiled entitled *Kakurega hyakushu*, *Tori no ato*, and others. Such poems of his as exist, rather than being the kind of violent revolutionary departures from tradition that he calls for in his critical works, are wholly devoted to a simple and unaffected celebration of the pleasures of a life of retirement. The following is an example of his work:

> While the lights
> that cross the sky
> go their way unchanged,
> what month, what day
> did I grow old?

He also wrote a work entitled the *Ise monogatari zōdan* in which he introduced the concept of *mono no aware* or "sensitivity to things," a phrase that was later taken up and made famous by the great scholar of Japanese literature Motoori Norinaga. It was, however, as a leader in the attack on the traditions of court poetry that he won fame. He holds a place of importance in the history of Japanese literature because of these attacks and because he assisted in the development of the *kogaku* (ancient learning) movement, which sought, through commentaries and studies, to reawake interest in the classics of early Japanese literature.

In addition to the works mentioned above, Mosui also wrote the *Man'yōshū kuden daiji* and *Gotōdaiki*. His writings have been collected under the title *Toda Mosui zenshū*.

Tokugawa Mitsukuni (1628–1700)

Scholar of the Japanese classics (*kokugakusha*) and poet of the early Edo period. He was the third son of Yorifusa, son of Tokugawa Ieyasu. During his early life, he played a distinguished role as head of the Mito clan, one of the three main branches of the Tokugawa family. Following his retirement, when he was known as Nishiyama-kō (Lord of Nishiyama) or Mito Kōmon, he also achieved great stature for his devotion to literature and to the study and the encouragement of learning. In 1657, he established the Shōkōkan, a center for research, dispatching scholars to gather old books from various parts of the country, as well as having copies made of rare documents in the possession of various families. In 1665 he invited to his center a Chinese scholar who remained loyal to the defunct Ming dynasty and who had taken refuge in Japan, Chu Shun-shui, and studied with him. He himself devoted much energy to the completion of the *Dai Nihon shi*, an enormous work in 379 chapters written in Chinese and aimed at tracing the history of the imperial family and making clear the nature of the relationship between the emperor and his people. Another work, the *Fusō shūyō shū*, was seen by the emperor himself. He also devoted much energy to the study of the *Man'yōshū* and engaged Shimokōbe Chōryū and Keichū to make studies of the work. Keichū produced two versions of a commentary on the *Man'yōshū* entitled *Man'yō daishōki*, on the basis of which Mitsukuni compiled a *Shaku Man'yōshū*.

Mitsukuni's works include *Jōzan eisō, Seizan kō zuihitsu, Sankō Gempei seisuiki, Sankō Taiheiki, Sankō Hōgen monogatari,* and *Sankō Heiji monogatari.*

Tsuruya Namboku IV (1755–1829)

Kabuki dramatist of the late Edo period. The first three men of the same name were all kabuki actors, but the fourth became as a playwright the most respected figure in the kabuki world of his day. In 1775 he became a pupil of Sakurada Jisuke I, and soon started writing kabuki plays himself, but his apprenticeship, as it were, was long; he was already forty-seven when he became a *nimaime* ("second rank") dramatist and fifty when he became chief dramatist of the Kawarazaki Theater.

Neverthelesss, even in his younger days he showed originality, and his *Tenjiku Tokubei ikoku-banashi*, which he wrote for the summer season in 1804, captured Edo audiences with the unprecedented dramatic inventiveness of its stagecraft. This was the work that made his name, and from then until his death at the age of seventy-four he turned out a succession of outstanding works. He made a speciality of plays on supernatural or ghostly themes, but he also wrote works with a more human appeal, based on the lives of the lower classes, and is noteworthy in the history of the theater for having established the *kizewamono* (domestic drama on purely contemporary themes) as an independent genre. He wrote between 150 and 200 works, of which the most famous include *Tōkaidō Yotsuya kaidan* and *Osome Hisamatsu ukina no yomiuri.*

Ueda Akinari (1734–1809)

Fiction writer of the middle Edo period. His personal name was Tōsaku, and he also went by the literary names Wayakutarō, Senshikijin, Muchō, and Uzurai. He was born in the Sonezaki section of Osaka; his mother was said to have been a geisha or the daughter of a brothel-keeper; the identity of his father is unknown. At the age of three he was adopted by a family of paper and oil merchants named Ueda. Though well cared for, he seems to have been very sickly, and the fingers of both hands were so crippled by smallpox as to be all but useless. His illnesses and the circumstances surrounding his birth seem to have cast a shadow over his personality and contributed no doubt to the tone of discontent, sarcasm, and bitterness toward the world that marks the literary works he later produced. His animosity toward the world was not, however, motivated solely by feelings of injustice and self-pity; rather it seems to have been based upon a strong sense of idealism and personal integrity that would not let him go along with the foibles of the time but impelled him to speak out in opposition and outrage.

At the age of twenty-six he married, but in the years previous to his marriage he lived the life of a *tsūjin*, or man of the world, studying the writing of *haiku* under Takai Kikei, becoming an avid devotee of the theater and dramatic literature, and frequenting the world of the pleasure quarters. Sometime after the age of thirty-six he published, under the literary name Wayakutarō, two works in the *ukiyo-zōshi* genre entitled *Shodō kikimimi sekenzaru* and *Seken tekake katagi*. Both are short pieces; the former, in particular, reveals a satirical attitude toward the world of the time and abounds in epigrammatical observations. Following this, he came under the guidance of Tsuga Teishō, Takebe Ayatari, and other writers in the *yomihon* (historical fiction) genre, and subsequently under that of Katō Umaki, a scholar of Japanese studies, and for the first time began the serious study of literature. At the age of thirty-four he completed what was to be his greatest work, the *Ugetsu monogatari*, a collection of demonic and macabre tales written in a classical style colored by romantic overtones. Among such collections of ghost and wonder stories, it holds a place of unparalleled excellence and exerted a powerful influence upon writers of historical fiction in the period following his time. At the age of thirty-seven he lost his home in a fire nad thereafter turned to the study of medicine. He began practice as a physician in Osaka at the age of forty-one, gained a reputation for his ability, and was able to build himself a new house. He also took an interest in the school of Japanese studies founded by Kamo no Mabuchi, producing works on the *Man'yoshū, Kokinshū, Ise monogatari*, and other texts that hold a place of importance in the study of ancient Japanese literature. His studies of phonology led him into a controversy with Motoori Norinaga, one of the outstanding scholars in that field at the time, and he also displayed his versatility of talent in areas pertaining to Japanese history, the tea ceremony, and the writing of *haiku*.

At the age of fifty-four he abandoned his medical practice and moved to the suburbs, and two years later he lost the sight in his left eye. Some years later, his wife died and he became totally blind. In addition, he does not seem to have gotten along well with his adopted daughter, but in spite of these buffetings of fortune and the pitiful condition to which he had been reduced, he continued his studies, producing a critical work on the *Man'yōshū* entitled *Kinsha*, a collection of poems and prose pieces entitled *Tsuzurabumi*, a work of historical fiction called *Harusame monogatari*, and a collection of miscellaneous writings entitled *Tandai shōshinroku*. He died at the age of seventy-five. His other important writings include the *Kakizome kigenkai* in the *ukiyo-zōshi* genre; the *Yasumigoto* on Japanese studies; a collection of miscellaneous pieces called *Kuse monogatari;* collections of *waka* and *haiku,* and others. There is also a collection of his poems compiled by Asano Sampei entitled *Ueda Akinari kashū.*

Yokoi Yayū (1702–1783)

Haiku poet of the middle Edo period. His given name was Tokitsura, his common name Magouemon, and he employed such artistic names as Eigensai, Ryōkakō, Shiinri, Keramaro, Rain, Bosui, Chiutei, and Hanzōan. He served as an important minister in the fief of Owari, a post that his forebears had held before him, but at the age of fifty-two resigned his position and took up residence in a house called the Chiutei at Maetsu in Nagoya, where he lived in retirement and engaged in various pastimes. He died at the advanced age of eighty-one. His father and grandfather had both been *haiku* poets, the former employing the artistic name Issui, the latter the name Yasō, and he thus came by his interest in *haiku* quite naturally. He had no fixed teacher of *haiku,* but from time to time consulted with Hajaku and Hajō, disciples of Shikō of the Mino school of *haiku,* on artistic matters. By birth and training he was proficient in the military arts, and he also displayed great talent in the Heike *biwa,* Nō drama, painting, calligraphy, and Japanese and Chinese poetry, but he particularly excelled in the composition of *haiku* and *haiku*-style prose.

The *Uzura-goromo,* a polished and witty work in one chapter combining prose and *haiku,* is the composition by which he is chiefly remembered. Though from a highly distinguished family, he never boasted of his background, but appears to have been a man of simple and unassuming character. In *haiku* he favored the plain and rather low-class style advocated by Shikō of the Mino school and showed little sympathy for the more refined and elegant style of Gyōtai, another Nagoya poet, and his followers. Yayū's works deal mainly with the occurrences of everyday life and often display a touch of wit or humor. In spite of their cleverness, however, they are almost uniformly bland in tone and lack the intensity of feeling needed for truly great poetry. His prose works as well, though put together with extreme skill and well modulated in tone, lack a feeling of complete naturalness. It is the lightness and deftness of touch that constitute the chief assets of his work and that appealed in particular to the tastes of his time, winning him a degree of acclaim that has not been sustained in succeeding ages. The following are representative examples of his work:

> Short night,
> but I have
> dreamed a long dream.

> The lark
> I missed seeing
> because I stopped to sneeze.

In addition to the *Uzura-goromo*, his works include the *Kokawago* and *Rayōshū*.

Yosa (Taniguchi) Buson (1716–1783)

Painter and *haiku* poet of the middle Edo period. He went by both the surnames Yosa and Taniguchi. As a poet he employed such artistic names as Saichō, Keisō, Shikoan, and Yahantei, and as a painter the names Chōkō, Shain, and Shunsei.

He was born in the village of Kema in Higashinari District of the province of Settsu in present-day Osaka Prefecture, but nothing is known of what kind of family he came from, what his father and mother's surnames were, or what surname he himself went by as a child. It is known, however, that his father owned property in the village, that he himself grew up in the village, and that he showed a fondness for painting from the time he was a child. When he was in his early twenties, he for some reason turned his back on his inheritance and wandered about until he reached Edo.

In Edo he at first studied *haiku* under Uchida Senzan, but later enrolled under Hayano Hajin, a disciple of Kikaku and Ransetsu, who in turn had been disciples of Bashō. At this time he used the artistic name Saichō, which he later changed to Yahantei. His teacher Hajin died when he was twenty-six, and he thereafter went to live in the town of Yūki north of Edo, the home of a fellow disciple named Isaoka Gantō. There he lived in rustic surroundings and spent his time wandering about the countryside gathering ideas for paintings and poems. He also took an extended walking trip to the far northern area of Honshu, which helped to deepen his appreciation of natural beauty. After this journey, he stayed for awhile in Utsunomiya. At this time, when he was around twenty-seven, he first began to use the name Buson.

Around the age of thirty-five, he suddenly set off on a journey west, spending several years in Kyoto and three years in Yosa, a village in Tango Province north of Kyoto, which was said to have been his mother's home. After working to perfect his talents as a painter, he returned to Kyoto and thereafter went by the surname Yosa. His skill in painting improved rapidly and he was soon ranked with Ike no Taiga as one of the outstanding founders of the *nanga*, or literati, school of painting. Eventually he moved to a house at Shijō Karasumaru, gathering a group of disciples around him and devoting more and more attention to *haiku*. In time he formed a *haiku* association called the Sankasha made up of Tan Taigi, Kuroyanagi Shōha, and various of Hayano Hajin's former disciples. He went to Sanuki in Shikoku for a time on business connected with painting, and after his return to Kyoto, held meetings of his *haiku* association several times a month. In 1768 his poetry attained a degree of refinement it had not displayed before and continued to mature with accelerating rapidity until he reached the height of his poetic powers and established a firm position as a great teacher, a worthy successor to his own teacher, Hayano Hajin. Just as Bashō's greatest works were produced during the last ten years of his life, so Buson's last years from 1772 until his death in 1783 represent the culmination of his career both as a *haiku* poet and teacher and as a painter. He died at the end of the twelfth month of the third year of Temmei (1783) at the age of sixty-six, surrounded by his family and disciples.

While Buson was still living in Edo, he perceived the need to bring about a reform in *haiku* writing, advocating as his ideal the motto "Return to Bashō!" This represented the general direction of reform efforts in the *haiku* world as a whole, but Buson actually succeeded in his late years in recapturing the spirit of Bashō's poetry.

Nevertheless, the *haiku* of Bashō and Buson differ very markedly in their essential nature. Bashō in his best work was able to confront the natural scene directly and to respond to it with such depth and sensitivity that he actually became merged in spirit with the scene itself. Buson, on the other hand, stressed the necessity for the *haiku* poet to study the works and artistic ideals of the great men of the past, to seek at all times a unity of artistic mood, and to work in an atmosphere of intense aesthetic devotion. His ideal in both painting and poetry was to rise above the level of the common and vulgar, and to achieve that aim he sought to improve his taste and understanding through constant reading and also worked to develop a highly refined aesthetic sensitivity. His aesthetic sense clearly owes much to the ideals of classical poetry, and both his paintings and *haiku* achieve a kind of romantic lyricism that is based upon delicate sensitivity. His works therefore do not necessarily reflect his own personality and daily life, for he looked upon art and life as belonging to wholly different dimensions, with art taking firm precedence over life. His works represent a beauty that is carefully and thoroughly planned. Drawing upon his knowledge of classical Japanese and Chinese literature, he succeeded in imbuing his *haiku* with a kind of classical feeling, fusing fantasy and legend with reality, or treating reality in such a way that it is beautified and fantasized into something wholly aesthetic in nature. Finally, as might be expected from a painter, many of his poems reflect the painter's objective eye. In addition to *haiku*, he also wrote poems in free form, such as the *Shumpū batei-kyoku*. The following are representative of his *haiku*:

> Fragrance of plum blossoms
> rising, ascending—
> ring around the moon.

> Early summer rains—
> beside the big river,
> two houses.

> Toward Toba Hall[1]
> five or six riders hasten—
> an autumn storm.

He was the author or editor of such works as the *Tamamoshū*, *Yahanraku*, *Shin-hanatsumi*, and *Momosue*.

YOSHIDA SHŌIN (1830–1859)

Thinker of the late Edo period. He was born in Hagi, the second son of Sugi Yurinosuke Tsunemichi, a samurai of the domain of Chōshū. He was adopted by his uncle Yoshida Taisuke, a teacher of the Yamaga school of military science to the Mōri family, lords of the domain of Chōshū. He also received

1. Toba Hall was the residence of Emperor Toba, who ruled in the early twelfth century during a period of great civil unrest.

education from another uncle, Tamaki Bunnoshin, and at the age of nine lectured on military science at the Meirinkan, the school maintained by the fief, and manifested other evidences of extraordinary talent. Around the age of fifteen he came under the influence of Yamada Matasuke, a teacher of the Naganuma school of military science, for the first time becoming aware of the situation in the world outside Japan and learning something of Western battle formations. His abilities were recognized by the lord of his domain, who allowed him to leave Chōshū and travel to other provinces for the purpose of study. At Nagasaki and Edo he broadened his information and gained new knowledge of the world, but when it was learned that he did not intend to return to Chōshū, he was accused of attempting to escape from his domain and was brought back to Hagi and placed in confinement.

Around this time he began to be seriously concerned for the future of Japan and to immerse himself in the study of Japanese history. Being pardoned and allowed to journey to Edo once more, he became a disciple of Sakuma Zōzan. It was at this time that Perry appeared with his squadron of ships at Uraga and began pressing for the opening of the country, and Japan was in a state of excitement and turmoil. Shōin turned to writing and became a strong advocate of the group who opposed the making of any concessions to foreign demands. In the third month of 1854, when Perry returned to Japan, Shōin, hoping to journey to Europe and America, attempted to stow away on one of Perry's ships, but he was apprehended, chastised by the shogunate, and put into prison. He was later sent back to Hagi and confined in the Noyama Prison there. He was twenty-four at the time. Released after three years, he opened a private school in Hagi known as the Shōka Sonjuku, where he gave instruction to a large number of disciples, at the same time vigorously supporting the *sonnō-jōi* movement, which sought to drive out the foreigners and restore power to the emperor.

In the Ansei era (1854–59), when strong repressive measures were taken by the shogunate against the supporters of the *sonnō-jōi* movement, Shōin was one of those marked for surveillance because of his extreme views and he was once more imprisoned and eventually executed at the Temma-chō Prison in Edo; he was twenty-nine at the time of his death. Among his disciples were such men as Takasugi Shinsaku, Kusaka Genzui, Itō Hirobumi, Kido Kōin, and others, men who later played an important role in the overthrow of the Edo shogunate and the early years of the Meiji Restoration. Though his life was a short one and his career as a teacher at the Shōka Sonjuku lasted only a year, his superior learning and pure and impassioned spirit of patriotism seems to have exerted a profound influence upon the young men under his instruction. Along with the stormy events of his life, his poems in *waka* form gained wide fame among the people of the time, particularly the verse that he composed to accompany a letter to his parents informing them of his imminent execution, the first of the following two.

> Greater even than
> my love for them,
> my parents' love—
> How will they bear
> the news today?

> Though my body
> rot on the plain
> of Musashi
> I would leave behind a soul
> worthy of Japan.

In 1889 he was posthumously awarded the court rank of Senior Fourth Rank.

水晶の珠數藤の

梅の花に雪の

、るいみじ、

兒の笞

康成

Modern Period

AKUTAGAWA RYŪNOSUKE (1892–1927)

Fiction writer. He was born in Tokyo. Shortly after his birth, his mother went insane, a tragedy that was to haunt him all his life. While a student in Tokyo Imperial University, he joined with Kume Masao, Kikuchi Kan, and other fellow students in publishing the third and fourth continuations of the magazine *Shinshichō*. In one issue he published a short story entitled *Hana*, which won extravagant praise from his teacher, the novelist Natsume Sōseki, and launched him on his career as a writer. In 1916 his first collection of short stories, *Rashōmon*, established him as a figure of unique importance among the younger generation of writers. This was followed by a number of other stories such as *Imogayu* and *Hankechi*. Over half of these stories of his early years have a historical setting, borrowing the events and figures of the past to deal with themes and problems that deeply concerned the writer himself. They include stories set in the Heian period, the period of the Christian missionaries in the sixteenth century, and the Edo period, stories which deal with the modernization and Westernization that took place in the Meiji era, and adaptations of old Chinese stories, displaying a great variety of themes and drawing upon material from the literatures of both East and West. They vary in style as well, depending upon the type of theme being treated, some employing a novelistic style, others a style reminiscent of the traditional tale or some other style, and the diction varies also, displaying a mastery of technique unmatched in the literature of the time. Through these works, he established himself as the leader of the intellectual school of writers of the period.

From 1924 on he began to write stories with a modern setting that are detached in manner though narrated in the first person. But his health was poor and he was troubled by various personal problems, which reduced his creativity and introduced a note of pervading gloom into his work. Stories such as *Tenkibo, Genkaku sambō,* and *Shinkirō* illustrate the morbid sensitivity and somber outlook that are characteristic of his work at this time. Finally, in 1927, at the age of thirty-five, he ended his life by drinking poison in his home. His death took place at a time when the proletarian and popular literary movements were coming to the fore to challenge the values and methods of the writers of the intellectual school. Akutagawa's death aroused wide comment, for it seemed to many to symbolize the crisis and unease faced by the intellectuals of the time. After his death, a number of works such as *Seihō no hito, Haguruma,* and *Aru ahō no isshō* were published posthumously.

Ariga Nagao (1860–1921)

A jurist, he graduated from the philosophy course of Tokyo Imperial University and was a professor of Tokyo and Waseda universities. A contemporary of Tsubouchi Shōyō, he is said to have been the model for one of the characters in Shōyō's novel *Tōsei shosei katagi.* In a work entitled *Seimon tetsugaku-ron,* which comprises the second volume of the *Bungaku sōsho,* he attempted to present a systematized version of the cultural sciences of the Orient in such a way as to integrate philosophy, history, and literature. He acted as an assistant to his teacher at Tokyo University, Ernest Fenollosa, and produced a two-volume translation of Fenollosa's study of Oriental art entitled *Tōa bijutsu shikō.* He also published a work entitled *Bungaku-ron* about the same time that Tsubouchi Shōyō produced his famous *Shōsetsu shinzui,* propounding a theory of literature that stressed the harmonious blending of the various elements that go to make up a literary work.

Arishima Takeo (1878–1923)

Novelist and critic. Born in Koishikawa, Tokyo, son of a Finance Ministry official who had originally been a samurai of the Satsuma fief, he was the oldest of seven, the Western-style painter Arishima Ikuma and the novelist Satomi Ton both being younger brothers. He was given a traditional Confucian-style education at home, but at the same time learned English from an American and received his primary school education at a mission school. On leaving the Gakushūin Middle School he entered the Sapporo Agricultural

College (present Hokkaidō University) in the hope of bringing about a reform of agriculture. On graduating, he went to study in America, as a result of which he became critical of Christianity. He also for the first time came under the influence of modern thinkers such as Emerson, Whitman, and Ibsen and adopted the ideal of the "free man."

In 1908 he went to Sapporo to take a post as lecturer at his old college but in 1914 returned to Tokyo on account of his wife's illness. In 1910, when Mushanokōji Saneatsu and other literary figures founded the coterie magazine *Shirakaba*, he became a member and his own literary activities began. He first attracted attention in literary circles with his novel *Aru onna no glimpse* (later to be revised and published under the title *Aru onna*). Not long after this he lost both his wife and father within a short space of time, which prompted him to turn to full-time literary activity; he published in rapid succession a number of carefully written works that earned him considerable popularity. In the period from 1918 to 1921, he published a large number of works, among them *Cain no Matsuei, Umareizuru nayami, Oshiminaku ai wa ubau*, and won a following among young intellectuals with his erudition and his dignified humanism. His work has rich ideological overtones—a love of man learned from the Bible, a deep understanding of humanity learned from Tolstoi, and an anarchistic socialism learned from Kropotkin. His works portray, with a deep compassion and fellow-feeling, the sorrows and tragedies of the daily lives of lower-class working people in a manner found almost no place in other writers of the *Shirakaba* school, most of whom came from the upper classes. They also portray women as objects of social oppression. These ideas of his were to come into conflict with the realities of life in society following World War I, when class antagonism first came into prominence; gradually the kind of self-negation found in *Sengen hitotsu* became more pronounced, and he suffered an increasing failure of creativity and sense of futility and despair. As a way out, he gave up his own property, making his farm in Hokkaido available to tenants, but these attempts to find some solution to the questions tormenting him failed to translate themselves into any new ideological drive, and he ended by committing suicide with his mistress, Hatano Akiko, at his villa in Karuizawa. The works of his last years include the drama *Domomata no shi* and the short stories *Shunkyō* and *Oyako*. He experienced more deeply and at an earlier date than any other novelist the problems that tormented the social conscience of the intellectual during the decade following World War I.

Awano Seiho (b. 1899)

Haiku poet. Born in Nara Prefecture, he began by studying with Takahama Kyoshi in the 1910s, then in the late 1920s formed a group of poets including, besides himself, Mizuhara Shūōshi, Yamaguchi Seishi, and Takano Sujū— The Four—who contributed to *Hototogisu* magazine and thanks to whom the magazine enjoyed its golden age. The deafness that had afflicted him since boyhood cast a constant shadow of loneliness over his verse, also imparting to it, according to some, a mood of lament and humor that reflects the feelings of the common people. He is at present advisor to the Association of Haiku Poets and, along with Yamaguchi Sesshi and Takano Sujū, one of the most venerable figures in the *haiku* world in the Kansai area. *Katsuragi*, which he founded and became editor of in 1929, continues today. Collections of his verse include *Manryō, Kunibara, Haru no tobi,* and *Kōyō no ga.*

> Only the drip drip
> of early summer rain—
> the Floating Hall.[1]

Doi (Tsuchii) Bansui (1871–1952)

Scholar of English literature and poet in the modern style. His surname was originally pronounced Tsuchii, but in 1932 he changed the reading to Doi. Born in Sendai, he entered the English literature course of Tokyo Imperial University in 1894. He made the acquaintance of such other modern style poets as Shioi Ukō and Ōmachi Keigetsu and formed an association for the study of modern poetry. In 1896 he joined Togawa Shūkotsu and others in becoming a member of the editorial board of the literary magazine *Teikoku Bungaku* and published *Koryū* and a number of other poems in it in rapid succession. In 1898 he published such works as *Banyū to shijin, Hoshi to hana,* and *Boshō,* and soon came to be ranked beside Shimazaki Tōson as one of the most prominent writers of modern style verse. The following year saw the publication of his first collection of verse, *Tenchi ujō.* In 1900 he returned to his native city of Sendai to become a teacher in the Second High School there. The publication of a collection of songs entitled *Chūgaku shōka,* which contained his famous *Kōjō no tsuki* ("Moon over the Ruined Castle") set to music by Taki Rentarō, and of his second collection of verse, *Gyōshō,*

---

1. A small Buddhist hall built out over the water on the west shore of Lake Biwa.

helped to spread his fame throughout the country. In 1901 he embarked upon a four-year visit to Europe and on his return published a number of translations of Western verse. In 1950 he became the first writer of modern style verse to receive a Cultural Medal.

Bansui wrote a number of long poems on themes drawn from history and legend, which are cast in a grandiose style that employs a large number of Chinese phrases. His poetry enjoyed particular popularity among students and young people, and for a time all school songs and other songs for the young seem to be cast in the Bansui style. At a period when most poetry in modern style dealt with romantic love, he succeeded in creating a unique style and tone of his own, one marked by grandeur and manliness tinged with a note of melancholy. It was these qualities that won such wide popularity for his works and insure them a place of special importance in the history of modern style verse.

ENCHI FUMIKO (b. 1905)

Novelist. She was born in Tokyo, the second daughter of the scholar of Japanese linguistics Ueda Kazutoshi. From an early age she was well acquainted with the classics of Japanese literature and also took an interest in the works of the aesthetic school of the late Edo period and the kabuki and *shingeki* forms of drama. She published a number of dramas and in 1928 saw her work entitled *Banshun sōya* performed by the Tsukiji Little Theater. In 1930 she married Enchi Yoshimatsu and very shortly after turned to the writing of fiction, publishing her works in such literary magazines as *Nichireki* and *Jimmin Bunko*. *Sambun ren'ai*, published in 1936, was her first major novel, but in the years immediately preceding and during the Pacific war she produced no works of significance. In 1946, the year following the end of the war, she underwent surgery for cancer of the womb, spending a considerable time in the hospital. In 1951 she published serially in a magazine a work entitled *Kōmyō Kōgō no e*, and from this time on her literary output increased rapidly. Her work *Himojii tsukihi* won the 1953 prize for a work by a woman author and was followed by such works as *Yō*, *Futaomote*, and *Namamiko monogatari*, the last also the recipient of a prize for the work of a woman author. She is unique among women writers of the present time for the great variety of subjects with which she has chosen to deal. She is particularly noted for her treatments of the themes of human vindictiveness, feminine subtlety and charm, and the ugliness of old age. Her full-length novel *Onnazaka* was awarded the Noma Literature Prize.

Fujioka Sakutarō (1870–1910)

Scholar of Japanese literature. He was born in Kanazawa. In 1894 he graduated from the Japanese literature course of Tokyo Imperial University and in 1897 became a teacher at the Third High School in Kyoto. In 1900 he moved to the position of assistant professor of Tokyo University. A man of keen intelligence and great artistic understanding, he made brilliant and original contributions to the study of Japanese literature and painting. His works include *Kokubungaku-shi kōwa*, *Shōun-kō shōden*, *Kinsei kaiga-shi* and *Nihon fūzoku-shi*, the last written in conjunction with Hiraide Kenjirō. Of particular importance is his study of the literature of the Heian period entitled *Kokubungaku zenshi Heianchō-hen*. Though strongly influenced by the views on literary history of the French critic Hippolyte Taine, the work is remarkable for the scale of its construction and the critical acumen displayed and stands as one of the finest Meiji period works on Japanese literature. Fujioka employed what was as that time a new approach, adopting a scientific attitude and basing his studies upon a critical examination of a wide variety of sources. His works on the history of art likewise are unique for their originality of insight. As a result, his scholarly writings retain their importance even today and continue to be read by students in the field. Among the works of his that were published posthumously are *Kokugaku-shi*, *Nihon hyōron-shi*, *Kokubungaku to fūzoku*, *Kamakura Muromachi jidai bungaku-shi*, and *Kindai shōsetsu-shi*.

Funahashi Seiichi (1904–1976)

Novelist and playwright. Sickly as a child, he spent a great deal of time reading and also became very fond of the theater, developing a love for it, which, along with his passion for sumo wrestling, has remained with him throughout his life. In 1926 he entered the Japanese literature course of Tokyo Imperial University and became a contributor to the magazine *Shumon*. He made the acquaintance of Abe Tomoji and Iketani Shinsaburō, who, like him, were destined to become important writers. He formed a new theater group called Kokoro-za, which staged a production of his, *Koshitsu-sha*, starring Kawarazaki Chōjūrō. The group disbanded in 1928, but shortly after he formed another theater group called Kōmori-za, which played an active role in the movement to create a new literature. In 1935 he published a novel entitled *Daibingu*, which caused considerable stir in the literary world because of its call to activism. The left-wing movement in Japan had by this time lost much of its force, and there was a strong tendency to question the kind of activism among the members of the intelligentsia such as was evident in French literary circles in the thirties. It was in this atmosphere that Funahashi's proclamation in favor of activism aroused controversy. With the publication of *Bokuseki* in 1938 he gradually began to develop a style of his own and entered upon his most prolific period. During the war he remained aloof from events of the time, instead working to complete his important novel *Shikkaiya Yasukichi*.

After the war, his works, which had always been marked by an air of emotionalism in their descriptive passages, tended to focus more and more on the world of sexual desire, creating a distinctive kind of romanticism that became inseparably linked with his name. His most important book-length works of the early postwar period include *Susono, Yuki fujin ezu, Hana no sugao,* and *Hana no shōgai. Geisha Konatsu,* which appeared in 1952, proved so popular that he followed it with a number of other works dealing with the same character and known collectively as "Konatsu stories." His novel *Aru onna no enkei* won the Mainichi Prize for literature.

He has also written plays and scripts for the kabuki, Shimpa, Tōhō Modern Theater, and other groups, establishing an important place in the dramatic world. In addition to these activities, he has participated in efforts to reform the Japanese language and played an active part in various writers' associations. He is a member of the Japan Art Academy.

F UTABATEI SHIMEI (1864–1909)

Novelist and translator. He was born in Ichigaya in the Edo residence of the lord of the Owari clan; his father was a samurai of the clan who in later life became a minor official of the Finance Ministry. He hoped to become a soldier, and applied several times for admission to the Army Officers' School, but was rejected because of poor eyesight. In 1880 he entered the Department of Russian in what was then the Foreign Languages School, hoping to become a diplomat; in 1886 he met Tsubouchi Shōyō and struck up a close friendship with him, and around the same time attempted translations of Gogol, Turgenev, and other Russian writers. In the same year he published *Shōsetsu sōron* ("The Theory of the Novel"), and the following year, at the age of twenty-three, won instant fame with the publication of the first part of his novel *Ukigumo*. The second part appeared the following year, as did *Aibiki* and *Meguriai,* both translations from Turgenev. In 1888 he began publication of the third part of *Ukigumo* but broke off halfway and left it unfinished. Nevertheless, the influence of the novel on modern Japanese literature is undeniably great both in its structure, which is that of a modern realistic novel, and its painstaking psychological descriptions, as well as in its pioneering of the compromise between the literary and colloquial styles that was to become the basic style of modern Japanese literature. Following *Ukigumo*, he wrote no more fiction until after the turn of the century. He tried various occupations, even going abroad at one stage, but nothing, it seems, satisfied him. In 1904 he joined a newspaper, the Osaka *Asahi Shimbun* and worked as its representative in Tokyo, at the same time, with works such as *Sono Omokage* and *Heibon*, making his return for the first time in almost twenty years to the world of fiction. In 1908 he went to Leningrad as the newspaper's correspondent there, but in less than a year his tuberculosis took a turn for the worse. He was aboard ship in the Bay of Bengal, on his way home to Japan, when he died.

As his aspirations first to become a soldier then a diplomat show, he did not necessarily feel literature to be his vocation, yet the mark he left on literary history is great. *Ukigumo* was the precursor of the modern novel in Japan, while his translations from the Russian had a strong impact on the literary world. These translations were a major source of inspiration and artistic education to later writers, especially those of the naturalist school, while the fine colloquial style that he developed for the purpose did much to free Japanese literature from the fetters of the old styles. Thus the formative role that he played in modern Japanese literature is truly great.

HAGA YAICHI (1867–1927)

Scholar of Japanese literature. He was born in Fukui Prefecture. His father was Haga Masaki, a Shinto priest and disciple of the late Edo period poet and scholar of Japanese literature Tachibana Akemi. He thus grew up in an atmosphere of devotion to such studies and determined to follow in his father's footsteps. In 1898 he became an assistant professor of Tokyo Imperial University. From 1899 to 1902 he studied in Germany, acquainting himself with German methods of philological study, which he found to be very similar to those employed by scholars of Japanese literature in the Edo period. Likewise similar in the case of both Germany and Japan was the tendency to treat literary history as the history of the national spirit of the respective poeples involved. After his return to Japan he became a professor of Tokyo University and took on responsibility for the courses on Japanese literature. With breadth of vision and an attitude of tolerance, he assumed leadership in the field of Japanese literature studies, becoming its virtual founder in the modern period. His works include *Kokubungaku dokuhon* (1890), which he wrote in conjunction with Tachibana Senzaburō, *Kokubungaku-shi jūkō* (1899), *Kokubungaku-shi gairon* (1900), *Kokuminsei jūron* (1907), *Setsugetsuka* (1909), *Nihonjin* (1911), and *Fude no mani mani* (1915). His *Kōshō Konjaku monogatari-shū* in three volumes (1913–1920) served an important purpose by identifying the sources from which the *Konjaku monogatari* drew its material. His lectures were published posthumously, comprising such works as *Nihon bunkengaku*, *Nihon bumpō-ron*, *Rekishi monogatari*, *Kokugo to kokuminsei*, and *Nihon kambungaku-shi*. He was, as stated above, the virtual founder of Japanese literature studies in the modern period, working to promote the philological method of study and to establish a historical view of Japanese literature, while at the same time playing an important role in the development of Japanese language education.

HAGIWARA SAKUTARŌ (1886–1942)

Poet. He was born in Maebashi in Gumma Prefecture and from the time he was a student in Maebashi Middle School took an interest in literature. He contributed poems to the magazine *Bunko*, and was associated as a "friend" with the Shinshisha (New Poetry Society). In 1908 he entered the German literature course of the Sixth High School but withdrew because of illness. Around 1911 he began to contribute to Kitahara Hakushū's magazine *Zamboa* and became acquainted with Kitahara. At the same time, having read and admired immensely some poems by Murō Saisei, he wrote a letter to the author, thus initiating what was to become a close lifelong friendship. In 1916 he joined with Saisei in founding a magazine entitled *Kanjō*, which departed from the abstract and intellectual tone pervading the world of modern poetry at the time and introduced a wholly new style. The following year his first collection of poems, *Tsuki ni hoeru* (*Howling at the Moon*), was published, containing works marked by a free and masterful handling of colloquial language and an air of morbid fantasy. They differed completely from the works of Takamura Kōtarō and the other idealist poets and helped set the style for much of the poetry of the Taishō era. In 1923 he published *Ao neko*, which further consolidated his position as a poet of importance. In 1933 he founded a magazine of his own called *Seiri*, and the following year published *Hyōtō*. He also became a contributor to the poetry magazine *Shiki* and in time its most important writer. In 1938 he published a critical work entitled *Nihon e no kaiki*.

Hagiwara is a highly distinctive poet, one of the finest in modern Japanese literature and the first, it is generally agreed, to write completely successful works in free verse form and employing the colloquial language. His works convey the psychological landscape of an injured human being and a sense of fin de siècle decadence, creating a strange world of morbid sensibility and bizarre fantasy. At the same time the inner rhythms of the language in which they are cast exploit to the fullest degree the musicality and beauty of modern colloquial Japanese. In his late years he showed an increasing interest in traditional Japan.

Hasegawa Nyozekan (1875–1969)

Critic. He was born in the Fukagawa area of Tokyo. In his youth he attended a private school headed by Tsubouchi Shōyō and later, after completing Tokyo English Language School, entered the law course of Chūō University. In 1902, after graduating, he became a reporter for the newspaper called *Nihon*. In 1906, when Miyake Setsurei withdrew from the newspaper, Nyozekan joined the group of persons who resigned along with him and the following year he became a reporter for the newspaper headed by Miyake Setsurei called *Nihon oyobi Nihonjin*. In 1908 he transferred to a position on the Osaka *Asahi Shimbun*. After a visit to England, he embarked upon a highly active literary career, attracting attention as a writer of works for the intelligentsia. In 1918 he aroused the ire of the Terauchi cabinet because of his writings on democracy and was forced to resign his position with the newspaper. Thereafter he made his living solely as a writer. The following year he joined with Ōyama Ikuo and Kawakami Hajime in founding a magazine called *Warera* (the name was later changed to *Hihan*) and served as its chief editor. His thought during this period of his life is reflected in such works as his *Gendai kokka hihan* and *Gendai shakai hihan*. In 1932 he participated in the founding of the Yuibutsuron Kenkyū-kai (Society for the Study of Materialism) and in 1939 he joined with Miki Kiyoshi and others in forming the Kokumin Gakujutsu Kyōkai (National Science Association), writing a number of vigorous essays dealing with various aspects of Japanese culture as viewed from the standpoint of liberalism. After the war he was elected a member of the House of Councilors and was selected to become a member of the Japan Art Academy. In 1948 he received a Cultural Medal. He was the author of many books such as *Nihon fashizumu hihan*, *Nihon-teki seikaku*, and *Aru kokoro no jijoden*.

During the long years of his intellectual development he held fast to the principles of liberalism. For a time he embraced radical democracy, leveling strong criticisms against the Japanese state and moving close to the position of the Marxists, but in time he made it clear that his stance was based upon rationalism. He always took actual experience as his point of departure and examined all phenomena in the light of a broad critique of civilization as a whole, factors that help to explain the unusual longevity his thought has enjoyed. His literary endeavors were not confined to social and intellectual criticism, but extended to fields of creative literature such as the drama, novel, and essay forms.

Higuchi Ichiyō (1872–1896)

Novelist and poet. Her father was a low-ranking civil servant with the Tokyo Urban Prefectural government. She acquired a taste for novels while still at primary school and was also given instruction in writing verse. In 1886, she entered the Hagi-no-ya Academy run by the *waka* poet Nakajima Utako. Before long, however, both her elder brother and her father died, and the family was left totally without support. She therefore conceived the idea of making a living by writing, and eventually sought the advice of Nakarai Tōsui. This led her to study the novels of the Edo period and her own times, and also to study the techniques of the kind of novel, resembling the popular novelettes of the Edo period, that Tōsui himself wrote. These studies resulted in her first work, *Yamizakura*. In early 1892 rumors concerning her relationship with Tōsui led her to give up studying with him. In the summer of 1893, she moved to Ryūsenji in Shitaya, where she started a shop selling sundries and confectionery, which proved a failure. Nevertheless, her life in Ryūsenji was to provide her with a major source of poetic inspiration, and she began to devote herself to creative activity. She won fame with *Yuku kumo*, published in the magazine *Taiyō* in 1895. With *Ōtsugomori*, published at the end of 1894, her work began to develop its own original world; in *Nigorie* (1895) she demonstrated a superb feel for reality, while *Jūsanya* (1895) shows her writing at its most lyrical. Her most famous work, *Takekurabe* (1896), was highly praised by Mori Ōgai among others, and she became not only the leading woman writer of the day but one of the major figures of the Japanese literary world as a whole. She followed up with *Ware kara* and *Ura-Murasaki*, but her health deteriorated rapidly, and she died at the early age of twenty-four. Her diary, of which she left several dozen volumes, has a value scarcely inferior to that of her other works.

Her works, which are based on her own experiences, present a realistic portrait of the pathetic world of a young woman to whom fate was not kind. Her style, with its blend of the classical and the colloquial, extremely serious approach to the task of creative writing, and the pervasive truth and sense of pathos of her work combine to create an atmosphere that is deeply moving. She appeared and vanished like a comet—she had only four years of creative activity—yet she enjoys a special place in the history of Meiji literature as a writer whose work shows a degree of perfection that borders on genius.

Hirabayashi Taiko (b. 1905)

Novelist. She was born in Nagano Prefecture. While still in the upper grades of elementary school she became an avid reader of Russian literature and the works of the socialist critic Sakai Toshihiko. Determined to become a writer and an active member of the socialist movement, she went to Tokyo, where she supported herself by working at various jobs such as waitress and telephone switchboard operator. She became acquainted with members of the anarchist group and for a time wandered about Korea and Manchuria, living with one or another of the male members of the group. She also came to know the writers Hayashi Fumiko and Tsuboi Shigeharu and his wife Sakae In 1927 a story of hers entitled *Azakeru* was selected for publication in the Osaka *Asahi Shimbun,* and the same year she joined the proletarian literature movement that centered around the magazine *Bungei Sensen.* She married Kobori Jinji, a leader of the movement, and with the publication of her story entitled *Seryōshitsu ni te* she became recognized as an important new writer of proletarian literature. In 1937 she and her husband were arrested for their involvement in the Front Populaire incident, and the years that followed saw her engaged in a desperate battle with poverty and sickness, from which she did not emerge until 1943. After the war she was among those chosen for the First Women Writers' Award. Her postwar works such as *Kōyū onna* (1946) and *Hitori yuku* show her to be less interested in the class struggle than in the basic human will to live and the passionate battle for survival that it so often entails. Many of these works, which have a special flavor of their own, are semipopular in nature. Her lengthy autobiography, entitled *Sabaku no hana* and published in 1957, attracted considerable attention because of the frankness with which she wrote of the experiences of her early years.

Hori Tatsuo (1904–1953)

Novelist. Born in Kōjimachi, Tokyo, he began study with Murō Saisei and Akutagawa Ryūnosuke while he was still at the First High School. He entered the Department of Japanese Literature of Tokyo University, where he, Nakano Shigeharu, and others joined in founding the literary coterie magazine *Roba*. He was fond of French writers such as Cocteau, Appolinaire, and Radiguet and published a large number of translations. Subsequently most of the members of the *Roba* association were absorbed into left-wing movements, but he continued to devote himself to literature, until in 1930 the publication of *Seikazoku* bore concrete witness to the keenness of his sensibility and his interest in exploring the latest techniques of the novel. In October of the same year he suffered a severe haemorrhage of the lungs and thereafter was obliged to continue his literary activities as a semi-invalid in high-altitude resorts such as Karuizawa and Fujimi. Around the same period he began to read Proust and published in instalments a novel entitled *Utsukushii mura*, which differed somewhat from the light, Radiguet-like style he had employed hitherto.

His interest in Rilke also deepened, a fact that was to have a profound influence on the essential nature of his work. The death of his fiancée led him to brood on the theme of love and death, which resulted in the work in several parts entitled *Kaze tachinu*. He also acquired a great interest in the Japanese classics and the literature of the Nara and Heian eras, an interest that inspired *Kagerō no nikki* and *Hototogisu*. He undertook to write a full-length novel that would synthesize the themes of love-and-death and the mother-and-daughter relationship, and the outcome was *Naoko*. He died in Shinano, where he had gone to convalesce.

Hori's poetic temperament found admirable expression in the lyrical prose of his works. One may trace two mainstreams to his development: his gradual progress to maturity as a novelist who grafted elements of the French literary tradition onto the modern Japanese novel, and the progress towards spiritual maturity that took him back, via the media of Rilke and Origuchi Shinobu, to the Heian era and, ultimately, to the *Man'yōshū*. The outstanding feature of his work is constant preoccupation with the themes of death, life, and love—themes that he progressively deepened and developed. The style that he established, with its development of a consistent theme via a treatment blending the intellectual and the lyrical, and the gently lyrical atmosphere created by his characteristic prose, occupies a unique position in the literature of the Shōwa era.

Igarashi Chikara (1874–1947)

Scholar of Japanese literature. He was born in Yamagata Prefecture and graduated from the literature course of Waseda University. A member of the literary and scholarly group headed by Tsubouchi Shōyō, he received his literary doctorate in 1925 for his work entitled *Kokka no taisei oyobi hattatsu.* He is known for his studies of Heian literature and of the war tales, as well as for studies of rhetoric such as the *Bunshō kōwa* and others. There is a collection of essays dedicated to him entitled *Igarashi Chikara hakase kinen ronshū.* The wealth of knowledge displayed in his numerous writings indicates the scope and depth of his understanding of cultural history.

Iida Dakotsu (1885–1962)

Haiku poet. He was the eldest son of a landlord of Yamanashi Prefecture. Since *haiku* of the traditional type were popular in the Yatsushiro region of Yamanashi, he was well acquainted with *haiku* poetry from his youth. He studied in the Faculty of Letters of Waseda University and tried his hand at writing novels and poems in the "new style," but found his interest drawn increasingly to *haiku.* In time he was selected to become a member of the group known as the Haikai Sanshin, being the youngest writer of the group. The Haikai Sanshin, which centered about the poet Takahama Kyoshi, was dedicated to preserving the traditions of *haiku* poetry, opposing the innovations of Kawahigashi Hekigodō and others that were attracting much attention in poetic circles at the time. In 1908 Takahama Kyoshi announced that he was retiring from literary life, and for this and other reasons, Dakotsu returned to his home in Yamanashi the following year. When the literary magazine *Hototogisu,* formerly edited by Kyoshi, began once more to devote itself to *haiku* poetry, however, he became active again, editing the magazine *Ummo* and, along with such men as Murakami Kijō and Watanabe Suiha, carrying on the traditions of the *Hototogisu* line and establishing a place of eminence for himself in the world of *haiku.* In the early years of the Taishō era, he produced a number of works in a romantic vein, such as the following:

> By the brazier
> the beautiful nails
> of one dying of a fatal disease.

His poems, which deal with both human affairs and the world of nature, succeed through their elevation of tone and freedom from distortion in achieving a kind of harmony between the classical and modern styles of *haiku* and will probably in the future continue to be recognized as among the best works of the Taishō and Shōwa eras. There are two collections of his *haiku*, the *Sanroshū* and *Kodamashū*, as well as numerous critical essays and miscellaneous writings such as the *Haiku bungei no rakuen*, *Gendai haiku no hihan to kanshō*, and others.

IKETANI SHINZABURŌ (1900–1933)

Novelist and dramatist. In 1922 he obtained leave of absence from Tokyo Imperial University and went to study in the Department of Law of Berlin University, but spent much of his time pursuing his interest in drama, music, and the dance. A short novel entitled *Bōkyō*, which he based on his life at this stage, won a competition organized by the *Jiji Shimpō* newspaper, and from then on he devoted himself to writing. Along with Murayama Tomoyoshi, Funabashi Seiichi, Kawarazaki Chōjūrō and others, he organized a theatrical company called Kokoro-za, which staged a work by him entitled *Sangatsu sanjūninichi*. From then on, he was an enthusiastic champion of the new drama movement, but the Kokoro-za itself soon split up on account of ideological differences among its members. In 1930 he joined Kon Hidemi and others in forming another troupe, the Kōmori-za, in protest against the left-wing tendencies of the new drama movement, but fell ill the following year and died at the early age of thirty-three. His light, urbane style won him attention as an exponent of the "Neo-Sensationalism." He died, however, before he could go beyond a superficial modernism in his work.

IKUTA CHŌKŌ (1882–1936)

Critic, novelist, playwright, and translator. He joined with Morita Sōhei while still a student in the First High School in putting out a circulating magazine and also contributed to the magazine *Myōjō*. While a student in college he attracted notice by a long critical piece dealing with the novelist Oguri Fūyō that he published in *Geien*. Having completed the aesthetics division of the philosophy course of Tokyo Imperial University, he became an English language instructor in Seibi Women's School. He formed a literary association called the Keishū Bungakkai, or Women's Literary Group, lecturing on philosophy and literature. Among his listeners were such important women literary figures as Hiratsuka Raichō and Yamakawa Kikue, who in time formed an association of their own known as the Seitō, or Blue-stockings. Ikuta became increasingly interested in Nietzsche, producing a translation of the *Zarathustra*. Thereafter, Neitzsche's thought became the foundation for his critical remarks on literature and civilization, and he devoted much of the remainder of his life to the complete translation of Nietzsche's writings. He also translated D'Annunzio's novel *The Victory of Death* and wrote a work entitled *Tettei jindō shugi*, playing a provocative and highly active role as a free thinker in the field of social criticism. He worked very hard at a translation of *Das Kapital*, but was prevented by difficulties from completing it. In addition to Neitzsche, he also developed a strong interest in William Morris and Edward Carpenter, and in a work entitled *Burujiyoa wa kōfuku de aru ka* went so far as to advocate a return to the traditional culture of the Orient with its emphasis upon the primacy of agriculture. In *Tōyōjin no jidai kitaru* and *Chō-kindaiha sengen* he attacked the "Neo-Sensationalist" school that had come to play an important part in the literary world of the time and criticized the elegant sensitivity displayed in the psychological novel and the preoccupation with the details of daily life. In his late years he devoted himself to writing religious works such as *Shakuson* and a collection of essays on religion entitled *Shūkyō shijō*. He also produced translations of various works such as the *Odyssey* and the *Divine Comedy*. His *Saikin no shōsetsuka* published in 1912 is a discussion of the novelists of his time and illustrates his own unique standards of judgment.

Ishibashi Ningetsu (1865–1926)

Critic and novelist. He was born in Fukuoka Prefecture and graduated from the German law course of Tokyo Imperial University. He won recognition as a critic for his *Imo to Sekagami wo yomu*, dealing with the works of Tsubo-uchi Shōyō, and *Ukigumo no hōben*, dealing with the novel *Ukigumo* by Futabatei Shimei. After 1888 he wrote for the magazine *Kokumin no Tomo* and was the most active critic until Mori Ōgai appeared upon the scene. He based his critical approach mainly upon Aristotle's *Poetics* and Lessing's *Laocöon*, adopting an idealistic and romantic approach and conducting his investigations in a thorough and methodical manner. He engaged in critical debate with Mori Ōgai and played an important role in elevating the status of the literary critic in Japan. The essential nature of his criticism is best revealed in his *Shijin to gairaibutsu*, *Shiika no seishin oyobi yojō*, and *Genjitsu-ron*. In addition, he did much to gain recognition for the works of Kōda Rohan, a writer who at that time was not very highly regarded, and succeeded in raising him to a position equal to that of Ozaki Kōyō. His own novels include *Sute-obune*, *Yae*, and *Tsujiurauri*. After retiring from the literary world, he lived a very active and varied life, serving as a lawyer, judge, and a member of his prefectural assembly. He is the father of the well-known critic Yamamoto Kenkichi.

ISHIDA HAKYŌ (1913–1969)

Haiku poet. Born in Matsuyama, he was only in fourth grade at Matsuyama Middle School when he contributed his first verse to the *haiku* column of a newspaper. He joined a *haiku* association of the Shibugaki school, but soon got to know Ikazaki Kokyō of the *Hototogisu* school and started to study the realistic style as a result. *Katsushika*, a collection of verse by Mizuhara Shūōshi, awakened him to a new world of *haiku* and he began to contribute verse to the coterie magazine *Ashibi*. In 1933, at the age of twenty, he joined the association that published *Ashibi* and became one of its editors. In 1935 he published his first collection of *haiku*, *Ishida Hakyō kushū*, at the age of twenty-two, thereby attracting much attention as a promising young poet. In 1937 he founded and became editor of *Tsuru*. As the new *haiku* movement gathered strength, he became known, along with Nakamura Kusatao and Katō Shūson, as one of the "incomprehensible" or "human exploration" group, and he occupied a secure if unspectacular place in the *haiku* world. In 1942 he severed his connection with *Ashibi* and the following year started working for the National Writers Patriotic Association (Nihon Bungaku Hōkoku-kai). He was drafted into the army and sent overseas but was sent back to Japan on account of sickness in 1945 and remained there until the end of the war. He founded the magazine *Gendai Haiku* and wrote a large number of verses dealing with the postwar desolation. His sickness recurred, and the collection *Shakumyō* is an account of four years of struggle against it. In 1954 he was awarded the Yomiuri Newspaper Prize for literature. He did important work as *haiku* judge for the *Asahi Shimbun* and as secretary of the Association of Haiku Poets.

ISHIKAWA TAKUBOKU (1886–1912)

Poet. Born in Iwate Prefecture, he grew up in the village of Shibutami, where his father served as head of a local Buddhist temple. He entered primary school there and was soon recognized as a child of great promise. At the age of twelve he entered Morioka Middle School and, deeply impressed by the *Tōzai namboku*, a collection of poems by Yosano Hiroshi, he determined to devote himself to literature. In time he became acquainted with the members of the Shinshisha, a poetry association in Tokyo headed by Yosano and, hoping to pursue these connections, in 1902, at the age of sixteen, left school and went to Tokyo. His plans did not work out as he had hoped, however, and illness and lack of funds forced him to return to Iwate in an effort to recover his health. During his recuperation, he devoted himself to writing poetry, producing a number of long poems in the so-called new style, which appeared in *Myōjō*, the magazine put out by the Shinshisha, and in 1905 were collected and published under the title *Akogare*. He later took a position as a substitute teacher in the primary school in Shibutami, but continued as before to suffer from lack of sufficient funds. Making a second trip to Tokyo in connection with the publication of another volume of verse, he became acquainted with the naturalist movement, which at that time was attracting attention in literary circles, and was inspired to turn his hand to the writing of fiction, turning out such works as *Omokage, Kumo wa tensai de aru*, and others.

In search of a change of scene, he went to Hokkaido in 1907, but after moving about from one job to another as a newspaper reporter, he returned to Tokyo the following year. There he went about from magazine to magazine, seeking without success to interest someone in his writings and suffering many disappointments. At the same time, he began turning out works in *tanka* form, using this brief traditional form to give vivid expression to the experiences of his daily life and infusing it with a vitality and freshness it had not known for a long time. These poems were eventually collected and published in 1910 under the title *Ichiaku no suna*, or *A Handful of Sand*. Sometime earlier, he had become associated with a magazine called *Subaru*, publishing his *Sokuseki* and other works in it, only to be met by such severe critical comment that his hopes of becoming recognized as a writer were considerably dampened. Shortly after, in 1909, he was hired as a proofreader for the *Asahi Shimbun*, and for the first time was able to gain a measure of financial security. In the same year he published his essay *Kuu beki shi*, or *Poems to Eat*, in which he described his own experiences and ideals as a poet and set forth what he believed should be the guiding principles for a new type of poetry in the *tanka* form. Toward the end of the year, he began to take an interest in the socialist movement. He was greatly shocked by the arrest in 1910 of Kōtoku Shūsui and other socialists on charge of lèse-majesté, and thereafter devoted himself to the study of socialism, writing an essay on the subject entitled *Jidai heisoku no genjō*. Continually beset by financial difficulties and ill health, he died in 1912 at the age of twenty-six.

His poetic style exercised a strong influence upon the development of *tanka* in the modern language and upon the *tanka* of the school of proletarian literature. In addition, Takuboku Societies have sprung up in many parts of the country, devoted to the study of his works and the carrying on of his literary ideals.

ISHIKAWA TATSUZŌ (b. 1905)

Novelist. Born in Akita Prefecture. On leaving the Department of English Literature of Waseda University before graduation, he combined working for a magazine publisher with study of the novel. In 1935 he won the first Akutagawa Prize with his short story *Sōbō*, thereby establishing himself as an up-and-coming writer. Even in his "apprentice" days he did not, as often happens in Japan, attach himself to any older author who would give him guidance in his creative activities; his works, rather, developed on the basis of individual research into his materials and on social observation. He published a series of full-length novels including *Ikite iru heitai, Tenraku no shishū*, and *Kekkon no seitai;* his activities continued after the war, especially in the field of the newspaper serial. The long list includes such works as *Nozomi naki ni arazu, Seishoku kakumei, Yonjūhassai no teikō,* and *Aku no tanoshisa,* while *Kaze ni soyogu ashi* and *Ningen no kabe* are major, representative works that well illustrate his preoccupation with social questions. In the intervals of such works, he also wrote short and medium-length works of "pure literature," works such as *Kamisaka Shirō no hanzai* and *Jiyū shijin,* while *Shosai no yūutsu, Fuan no rinri* and other critical essays give evidence of the practical, positive interest that he took in politics and society. He has few rivals in the range of his subject matter, and his whole work is pervaded by a typical writer's sensitivity to the trend of the times and a characteristic sense of justice that has the courage to take the middle road in the face of the radical and is firmly rooted in a belief in progress by gradual stages.

IsHIKURE CHIMATA (1869–1942)

Poet. Born in Ehime Prefecture, he entered the Chikuhaku-kai, a poetry association headed by Sasaki Nobutsuna, in 1893 at the age of twenty-three. He helped to found the magazine *Kokoro no Hana,* which represented the association, and acted as one of its chief editors during the following forty years, when the magazine was at the height of its influence. In 1888 he also helped to found the Teikoku Suinan Kyūsai-kai (Imperial Sea Disaster Relief Association), serving as one of its directors for the following fifty years or more. He published several collections of poetry such as *Shionari, Kamome,* and *Umi.* As the titles of these collections—*Tide Roar, Seagull,* and *The Sea*—suggest, many of his poems, among them his finest works, deal with themes related to the sea.

> On broad leaves
> of sea tangle he rides
> rocking, dipping,
> drifting from side to side—
> the seagull.

Ishizaka Yōjirō (b. 1900)

Novelist. Born in Hirosaki city, Aomori Prefecture, he returned to his birthplace on graduating from the Department of Japanese Literature of Keiō University in 1925 and for thirteen years thereafter made his living as a teacher, at the same time pursuing his literary activities. His position as an author was first established by *Wakai hito,* which was serialized for three years in the magazine *Mita Bungaku,* beginning in 1933. His next work, *Mugi shinazu,* published in 1936, provoked a violent controversy for its criticism of the left-wing movement, then on the verge of annihilation. During the war he served in the South Pacific with the Japanese army as member of a press squad, and following the war won great popularity among young readers with his newspaper serials *Aoi sammyaku* and *Yama no kanata ni.* At the same time, in *Ishizaka-sensei gyōjō ki* he created a comedy of modern manners that opened up a new genre in the modern novel. A consistent feature of his work is its faith in goodwill and progress and its portrayal of characters who try to live honestly, humbly, decently, and healthily; his works achieve popularity without vulgarity, their man-in-the-street morality and the plebeian humanism that pervades them making them highly valued as works for family reading.

Itō Hitoshi (1905–1969)

Novelist and critic. Born in Hokkaido, he published a collection of verse at his own expense at the age of twenty-one. He entered the Tokyo Commercial

College in 1928 but before long decided to become a writer. He soon attracted the attention of Kawabata Yasunari, and with *Seibutsusai*, a collection of
stories, he established himself as a promising young writer. He also undertook translations of Joyce's *Ulysses* and Lawrence's *Lady Chatterley's Lover*.
He advocated a "new psychological realism" and was also active as a critic,
doing valuable pioneering work in the literature of the early Shōwa period
as a leader of the Shingeijutsu-ha, combining both theory and original creation. During the war he published a series of stories centering round a figure
known as Tokunō Gorō and examining the question of the intellectual's
place in society, which include *Tokunō Gorō no seikatsu to iken* and *Tokunō
monogatari*.

   In 1950, he published *Narumi Senkichi*, in which he gave free rein to humor
and satire in portraying the intellectual's efforts to cope with the confusion
and decadence of the postwar years. He considered ways of using Joycean
methods to produce Western style logic-oriented novels. At the same time,
he systematized the original literary theories that he had been working out
for half a lifetime into a *Method in the Novel*. Publication of the unexpurgated
translation of *Lady Chatterley* involved him in a celebrated court case. The
case dragged on for more than seven years, but during his long struggle as
defendant he stated his views with an unwavering conviction that bore
witness to his intellectual integrity. His experience during the case inspired
several works, of which *Saiban* is a "documentary novel" based on the event.
In the following years he published a large number of novels and critical
works, among them *Nihon bundan shi, Hi no tori, Hanran, Shōsetsu no nin-
shiki*, and *Kyūdōsha to ninshikisha*. At the same time he was active in literary
circles as vice-president of the Japan P.E.N. Club, assistant director of the
Museum of Modern Japanese Literature, and so on. Along with Abe Tomoji
he played a valuable role in establishing modern, logical thought as an
ingredient of the Japanese novel.

Itō Sachio (1864–1913)

Poet and novelist. Born in Chiba Prefecture, he entered Meiji Legal School
(later Meiji University) in Tokyo at the age of seventeen but withdrew
midway because of eye trouble. At twenty-five he started a milk business, an
undertaking that he pursued until his late years. From the age of thirty-
three he began attending the monthly poetry gatherings of Kirinoya Keishi.
In 1900 he first met the outstanding poet and critic Masaoka Shiki and in
time became one of Shiki's most diligent and admiring disciples, playing an

important role in furthering the work of the Negishi Tanka Society, which had been founded by Shiki a few years earlier. After Shiki's death, he became editor of the *tanka* magazine *Ashibi*. When this ceased publication and was replaced as the official organ of the Negishi Society by the magazine known as *Araragi*, he lent his full support to the latter. He produced poems and critical essays, lectured on the *Man'yōshū*, and had numerous disciples. He also wrote works in the kind of realistic prose style that Shiki had advocated, producing *Nogiku no haka* and other novels. His poetic style is somewhat more subjective and emotional than that of Shiki, and the works of his late years in particular, straightforward in tone and steeped in quietism, are unlike anything to be found in Shiki's work.

Kambara Ariake (1876–1952)

Poet. Born in Tokyo, he first became acquainted with *shintaishi*, modern style poetry, in 1886 through the work entitled *Shintai shika* by Takeuchi Takashi. Later he was influenced by a volume of Western verse translations put out by Shinseisha under the title *Omokage* and also attended lectures on Byron by Takahashi Gorō. In 1897 his novel *Daijihi* won first prize in a contest sponsored by the *Yomiuri Shimbun*, and he became acquainted with the judge for the contest, the novelist Ozaki Kōyō. At the same time he familiarized himself with the works of the British Romantic poets such as Keats and Shelley and became deeply interested in the poet and painter Dante Gabriel Rossetti, pouring over Iwamura Tōru's voluminous studies of Rossetti. These various influences are evident both in the form and content of the works in his second collection of poems entitled *Dokugen aika*. Through the works in this volume, he succeeded in bringing Japanese poetry in the modern style to full maturity. He also became acquainted with the poetry of Verlaine and, through the studies of Arthur Symons, with the modern French Symbolist movement, and was deeply impressed by the translations of European poetry by Ueda Bin. He began producing works of his own that employed Symbolist techniques, publishing them in a collection entitled *Shunchōshū*. Both in theme and technique, these poems had about them a freshness and novelty previously unknown in the Japanese literary world and they established his reputation as the outstanding symbolist poet of the Meiji era. His symbolist style reached its highest point of development in his fourth collection of verse, published in 1908 and entitled *Yūmeishū*, which won him a place beside Susukida Kyūkin as one of the two leading figures of modern style poetry. His works are remarkable for their maturity of aesthetic consciousness and subtle expression of modern psychology and exerted a strong influence upon Kitahara Hakushū and other younger poets of the time. In 1908 he retired from the world of poetry, devoting his remaining years to revision of his early works, translation, and critical writing. In addition to his collections of poems, he produced such prose works as *Nozarashi no yume* and *Hiunshō*.

KANEKO KUN'EN (1876–1951)

Poet. He was born in the Kanda district of Tokyo. In 1893 he became a member of the Asakasha, a poetry association headed by Ochiai Naobumi, and helped to bring about a revitalization of poetry in the *waka* form. In 1898 he became acquainted with Satō Giryō and accepted a position as poetry editor for *Shinsei*, a magazine put out by Satō. In 1901 he published a collection of poems in graceful lyric style entitled *Kataware tsuki* and the following year he joined with Onoe Saishū in publishing *Jokeishi* ("Scenic Poems"). Their aim in this collection was to combat the influence of the *Myōjō* school, which placed great emphasis upon the theme of romantic love, and to restore the natural landscape to its rightful place among the major themes of Japanese poetry. In 1903 Kun'en formed an association known as the Shiragiku-kai (White Chrysanthemum Society), which fostered such poets as Hirai Kanson and Toki Aika (Toki Zemmaro). In 1904, when the magazine *Shinchō* began publication, he became editor of its poetry column and also assisted in the general editorial work of the magazine. In the following year he formed the Tanka Kenkyū-kai (Tanka Study Association), working to train the younger generation of poets. In 1948 he became a member of the Japan Art Academy. In his poetry, he carried on the graceful style created by Ochiai Naobumi, writing most often on the beauties of nature and striving for clarity and simplicity of tone, but he also wrote experimental works in which he abandoned the traditional syllabic pattern of *tanka* verse for freer forms of versification.

KATŌ SHŪSON (b. 1905)

Haiku poet. He was born in Yamanashi Prefecture, where his father held an official post. After completing Kanazawa Middle School, he became an elementary and middle school instructor. He began writing *haiku* at the age of twenty-five, studying under Mizuhara Shūōshi. He submitted poems to the magazine *Ashibi* and quickly gained recognition as an avant-garde writer. In 1937 he entered the Japanese literature course of Tokyo Bunri University, graduating in 1940. He founded and edited the magazine *Kanrai*, and in 1942 severed his connections with *Ashibi*. His poetry became marked by a human warmth and earthiness, turning increasingly to the concerns of daily life and concentrating upon the expression of man's wants and needs. As a result, he and Nakamura Kusatao came to be known from around 1939 on as the Ningen Tankyū-ha, or Human Quest School. His poetry was distinguished in particular by its strongly plebeian tone. During the war years he was active as a teacher, playing a large part in training the younger generation of *haiku* poets who became active after the war. He also produced important studies of the poetry of Matsuo Bashō. His collections of *haiku* include *Kanrai*, *Taifūgan*, and *Hodaka*, and he has also published a collection of essays entitled *Oki*. The following is an example of his work:

> In the heart of the fire
> I saw
> a peony crumble.

Kawabata Bōsha (1900–1941)

Haiku poet. He was born in the Nihonbashi section of Tokyo, the younger brother of the painter Kawabata Ryūshi. His ambition at first was to become a Western style painter, and he studied for that purpose under Kishida Ryūsei. At the same time he began writing *haiku* at an early age, publishing his works in *Myō no Hana*, *Dojō*, *Ummo*, and other magazines. He devoted himself intensively to both painting and poetry, but in the early twenties was hospitalized by illness and remained bedridden for the rest of his life, studying under Takahama Kyoshi and continuing to write *haiku*. He won recognition throughout the *haiku* world as one of the outstanding new poets associated with the magazine *Hototogisu*. He regularly contributed not only *haiku* but essays and critical pieces to the monthly issues of *Hototogisu* and published in such other magazines as Hoshino Tatsuko's *Tamamo* and Takahama Toshio's *Haikai*. Takahama Kyoshi in his introduction to Bōsha's second collection of poems, *Kegon*, called Bōsha the "top man in the mysteries of nature poetry," by which he meant that Bōsha's works do not simply present an objective recording of the natural world, but convey a deeper sense of religious introspection and quest for truth.

KAWABATA YASUNARI (1899–1972)

Novelist. He was born in Osaka and lost his parents and most of his close relatives at an early age, an experience that inflicted upon him a sense of loneliness and isolation that was to remain with him throughout his life. The griefs of these early years prepared the way for the deep air of melancholy that characterizes his mature works. The remarkable diary he wrote at the age of fifteen, in which he records his ministrations to his dying grandfather, reveals a keenness of perception and realism hardly conceivable for a youth of that age. In 1920 he entered the Japanese literature course of Tokyo Imperial University and the following year helped to publish the sixth continuation of *Shinshichō*. Around this time he became acquainted with Kikuchi Kan and, when the latter founded the magazine *Bungei Shunjū* in 1923, he became a member of the staff; in the years that followed he enjoyed the patronage of the older writer. In 1921, through the introduction of Kikuchi Kan, he also became acquainted with Yokomitsu Riichi. With his graduation from Tokyo University in 1924 he joined Kataoka Teppei, Yokomitsu Riichi and others in founding the magazine *Bungei Jidai*, which became the organ for the group known in time as the Neo-Sensationalists. The movement, with Kawabata and Yokomitsu as its most prominent exponents, opposed the realism that had been in vogue up to this time and sought to approach life from a wholly new and different standpoint, creating works that were highly innovative in style. In 1925 Kawabata published his first important work, *Izu no odoriko*, followed in 1929 by *Asakusa kurenai-dan*, which appeared serially in the *Asahi Shimbun*, and from this time he, along with Yokomitsu Riichi, came to be recognized as one of the most promising and important writers of the period. *Kinjū* and *Yukiguni* are regarded as particularly noteworthy among his works of the prewar years. In the postwar period he produced such outstanding works as *Sembazuru*, *Yama no oto*, *Mizuumi*, and *Koto*. In 1948 he became president of the Japan P.E.N. Club, and in 1958 vice-president of the International P.E.N. Club. In 1960 he received an award for his literary activities from the French government, and in 1968 he was awarded the Nobel Prize in literature. Many of his works have been translated and are well known and appreciated abroad.

From the time he became associated with the Neo-Sensationalist movement, Kawabata has been recognized for his unique lyricism. His unique contribution is a highly poetic style and delicate sensitivity combined with a kind of cold detached view of humanity. He exercised a profound influence upon many younger writers, such as Mishima Yukio and Sawano Hisao.

Kawada Jun (1882–1966)

Poet. Born in Shitaya in Tokyo. His father, Kawada Takeshi, was a Doctor of Literature and tutor to the crown prince. He became a pupil of Sasaki Nobutsuna at the age of fourteen, while he was still at the Jōhoku Middle School. In 1902 he entered the Department of English Literature of Tokyo Imperial University, where he attended the lectures of Koizumi Yakumo (Lafcadio Hearn) and Natsume Sōseki, but switched to the Department of Law in 1904. In the same year he joined Osanai Kaoru and Takebayashi Musōan in founding the literary magazine *Shichinin*. Besides flinging himself into the surging new literary movements of the day, he was an ardent lover and produced a succession of love poems that gave him an outstanding place in the magazine *Kokoro no Hana* edited by Sasaki Nobutsuna. On graduating from Tokyo University in 1907, he became a businessman and devoted himself to office work until in 1918 a collection of verse, *Gigeiten*, marked his return to the world of poetry. He followed it in 1921 with *Kagerō*, in 1922 with *Sankaikyō*, and with still further collections in the following years. During the period of *Gigeiten* and *Kagerō* his style showed to a considerable degree the aesthetic, romantic tendencies that prevailed in the world of poetry at the time, but gradually he developed a more solid, rough-and-ready style of his own, which enabled him in time to single out and give accurate expression to the essentials of nature. He also published a succession of studies of the *Shin kokinshū* that acted as a healthy check to the tendency of the poetic world to become occupied exclusively with the *Man'yōshū*. In business life, he became an executive director of his company, but resigned following the February 26 attempted coup d'état and devoted himself to literature. His collection of verse *Washi* (1940) and his collection of *kabun* (prose and poems) *Kokusho seiseki ka* (1941) won him the first Japan Art Academy Award, and he was also given the Asahi Cultural Award for his studies of three wartime poetry anthologies. In his collection *Kanrinshū*, published following Japan's defeat, he ponders on the correct course for a poet in the postwar years. His scholarly works include, besides his studies of Saigyō, *Yoshino-chō no hika* and *Sengoku jidai wakashū*.

Kawahigashi Hekigotō (1873–1937)

Haiku poet. He was born in the city of Matsuyama in Ehime Prefecture. He studied the writing of *haiku* poetry under Masaoka Shiki and, along with his friend Takahama Kyoshi, became recognized as one of the most promising young poets of the time. After gaining notice as one of the group working under Shiki to infuse new vitality into *haiku* poetry, he was appointed in 1896 as editor of the *haiku* section for the magazine *Shinsei*. The following year, when Shiki and his associates founded the *haiku* magazine *Hototogisu*, he contributed to its activities as well. In 1899 he published his first works, *Haiku hyōshaku* and *Shoku haiku hyōshaku*, and in 1902, after the death of Shiki, he became *haiku* editor for the magazine *Nihon*. In the *Onsen hyakku*, a collection of his poems, he carried on a controversy with Takahama Kyoshi, opposing what he regarded as the defects of the conservative faction and calling for a more progressive and contemporary approach to *haiku* poetry. Around 1906 he founded an association called the Haizammai-kukai, which in time came to dominate the world of *haiku* poetry and produced such writers as Ōsuga Otsuji and Ogiwara Seisensui. Seeking for new styles and areas of expression, Hekigotō and the others of his group created what came to be known as "New Trend" *haiku*. In 1907 Hekigotō set out on his first nationwide tour of Japan and in 1909–11 he made a second such tour, working to promote interest in his new type of *haiku*; he also published a prose account of his trips entitled *Sanzenri*. Borrowing elements from naturalism, which was then at the height of its influence in the literary world, he urged people to give expression to their individual personalities and to employ the *haiku* form to describe their everyday lives. The movement that he led in time split into several factions, while he himself in 1915 founded a magazine called *Kaikō* and eventually abandoned the seasonal references and 5–7–5 syllabic form of traditional *haiku* in favor of a freer form of versification.

In his late years his works became increasingly difficult to understand and showed signs of failing poetic powers and, abandoned by his disciples, he was left in a position of isolation. In 1933 he announced his retirement from the world of *haiku* poetry and for the remainder of his years devoted himself almost entirely to the study of the works of Buson. Whatever the final critical estimate of his poetry may be, it is certain that he earned a place of importance in the history of *haiku* poetry by his pioneering efforts in leading it along the difficult path toward greater modernity. His works, in addition to those mentioned above, include *Hekigotō kushū, Kayatsurigusa,* and others.

KAWAI SUIMEI (1874–1965)

Poet. He was the son of a merchant family of Sakai. From around the age of twelve he became interested in poetry in free verse or modern style form as well as such traditional forms as *haiku, tanka,* and *imayō*. He published modern style poems in *Bunko* and for a while served as editor of the poetry column for that magazine. In 1900 he moved to Tokyo, where he became a regular writer for *Bunko* and associated with Yosano Tekkan and other leading literary figures. His first collection of poems, entitled *Mugenkyū*, was published in 1901 and was distinguished by its tone of tranquil lyricism. His second collection, *Tōei*, came out in 1905, and attracted considerable attention. In 1907 he resigned from the staff of *Bunko*, ending an association of thirteen years during which he helped to bring to light a number of promising young poets such as Yokose Yau, Kitahara Hakushū, Shimagi Akahiko, and Kawaji Ryūkō, and himself gained recognition as the leading poet of the *Bunko* group. *Kiri*, published in 1910, showed a distinct change in style, moving in the direction of colloquial diction and greater freedom of form. In 1930 he founded a women's magazine called *Josei Jidai*, which continued publication until 1944. In 1937 he was made a member of the Japan Art Academy.

Suimei devoted his entire life, which spanned the Meiji, Taishō, and Shōwa eras, to the art of poetry, producing important works of his own and acting as a teacher and guide to many younger poets. His poems are marked by an invariable feeling of sympathy for the subject treated and an air of profundity and eloquence.

KAWAJI RYŪKŌ (1888–1959)

Poet. Born in Mita, Tokyo, he attended the Kyoto School of Fine and Decorative Arts and the Japanese Painting Department of the Tokyo College of Fine Art. In 1907 he startled the world of poetry by publishing *Hakidame* in the magazine *Shijin*, the first free-form poem in the colloquial language to be created consciously as a work of art. Besides collections of his own verse such as *Michibata no hana*, *Kanata no sora* (1914), *Shōri* (1918), *Yogen* and *Ayumu hito* (1922), he also published *Verlaine shishō*, a collection of translations, and a volume of criticism *Sakushi no shin-kenkyū*. He was active as a central figure in the group known as Shiwa-kai (The Versifiers), and in 1918 launched the Shokōshisha, a poetry society, through which he worked to encourage younger poets. A trip abroad in the late 1920s was followed in the next decades by publication of a large number of collections of verse and works on poetics; in 1957 he was awarded the Japan Art Academy Award for his *Nami*. He worked constantly to develop rules for the new verse by following up all its possibilities, giving predominance to intellectual organization and employing the kind of witty techniques seen in his serialized work

Sūgaku ("Mathematics"). He also did useful work in introducing the work of the futurists and surrealists.

KIKUCHI KAN (1888–1948)

Novelist and playwright. He was born in the city of Takamatsu in Kagawa Prefecture and grew up in poverty. He was extremely fond of reading, and is said to have read nearly all the books in the Takamatsu Public Library. In 1913 he entered Kyoto Imperial University and while a student published such plays and stories as *Okujō no kyōjin, Chichi kaeru,* and *Minage kyūjogyō* in the third and fourth continuations of the magazine *Shinshichō* edited by Akutagawa Ryūnosuke, but he failed to gain recognition as a writer. After graduation, he worked for a time as a reporter for the *Jiji Shimpō* and the Osaka *Mainichi Shimbun.* Beginning in 1918 he published in *Chūō Kōron* a succession of stories such as *Mumei sakka no nikki, Tadanao-kyō gyōjōki, Aoki no shukkyō,* and *Onshū no kanata ni,* which, with their freshness of style, established him as a writer of unshakable reputation. He also wrote such highly individualistic works as *Tōjūrō no koi, Kami no gotoku yowashi,* and *Gimin Jimbei.* He developed the so-called thematic novel, which deals with a clearly defined subject and employs incisive novelistic techniques and a straightforward manner of expression. Through his numerous plays, he helped to introduce a keynote of realism into the drama of the time and in the middle years of the Taishō era was active in the movement to create a new type of drama. With the beginning of the Shōwa era in 1926 he devoted his time mainly to the writing of works of popular fiction, such as *Shinju fujin,* busily turning out new books to satisfy the demand of his wide readership, and through his impressive accomplishments came to be looked on as the doyen of Japanese letters. He founded the Writers' Association and in numerous other ways worked to benefit literature. In 1923 he established the magazine *Bungei Shunjū* and through various means returned the profits from it to the men of the literary world, establishing the Akutagawa Prize, the Naoki Prize, and the Kikuchi Kan Prize. He was a liberal and thoroughgoing humanist, and through his words and actions during the war showed himself to be a man of simple patriotism as well.

KIMATA OSAMU (b. 1906)

Poet. He graduated from Tokyo Higher Normal School and became a professor of Shōwa Women's College and later Jissen Women's College. In his youth he contributed poems in modern style to the magazine *Akai Tori* and became acquainted with the well-known poet Kitahara Hakushū. Later he helped to found the magazine *Tama*, which Hakushū headed, and as one of Hakushū's most energetic followers took part in the movement to establish what was termed the "modern *yūgen* style." His first collection of *tanka* poems, *Koshi*, was published in 1942, the following being representative of the type of works it contains:

> Fields of Iwase—
> watching
> flocks of white herons
> cross the deep snow.

After Hakushū's death in 1942 he took over the task of editing *Tama* and also worked to put Hakushū's unpublished papers into order. The collection of poems entitled *Tōreki*, published after the war, shows Kimata departing from the symbolism and impressionism of Hakushū's work in favor of a soberly realistic style, but one with rich undercurrents of lyricism. In 1953 he founded the magazine *Keisei*, acting as its chief editor. In addition to his work as a poet, he has contributed greatly to the study of modern *tanka*, his works on the subject including *Hakushū kenkyū*, *Shōwa tanka-shi*, *Kindai tanka no kanshō to hihan*, *Kindai tanka no shiteki tembō*, and *Taishō tanka-shi*.

KIMURA MASAKOTO (1827–1913)

Scholar of Japanese literature. He was born in the city of Narita, in what was later to become Chiba Prefecture. After studying Japanese and Chinese literature, he became a disciple of Okamoto Yasutaka, devoting himself to the study of Chinese and Japanese script and phonology. He became assistant director of the Wagaku Kōdansho, a school for the study of Japanese literature supported by the Edo shogunate, and after the Meiji Restoration held a succession of posts in the Ministry of Education, Ministry of Justice, and other branches of government. He also taught in the Faculty of Letters of Tokyo Imperial University and in Tokyo Higher Normal School. He retired from public office in 1893, and in 1902 was appointed a member of a committee set up by the Ministry of Education for the study of the Japanese language. Early in his career he became interested in studies of the *Man'yōshū* and, distressed by the rapidity with which so many modern scholars resorted to textual emendation in their efforts to interpret the *Man'yoshū*, he examined numerous versions of the work and conducted a careful and exhaustive study and evaluation of the text, endeavoring wherever possible to arrive at satisfactory interpretations that did not involve textual emendation. In many instances he offered original and creative suggestions based upon his wide knowledge of ancient Chinese and Japanese literature and phonology. His principal works are the *Man'yōshū shomoku teiyō*, *Man'yōshū jion benshō*, and *Man'yōshū mifugushi*, and he also left a collection of poems and prose writings entitled *Tsukinomi kashū*.

Kinoshita Rigen (1886–1925)

Poet. Born in Okayama Prefecture, he studied at the Gakushūin and later graduated from the Japanese literature course of Tokyo Imperial University. At the age of twelve he became a member of the Chikuhaku-kai, a literary association headed by Sasaki Nobutsuna, and continued his membership into his late years. He joined with Shiga Naoya, Mushanokōji Saneatsu, and others in founding the magazine *Shirakaba*; though most of the men associated with *Shirakaba* and the group it represented were novelists, Senge Motomaro used the medium of modern style verse and Rigen that of traditional style verse to give expression to the literary ideals of the group. In his early works, Rigen employed a sensual style influenced by Kitahara Hakushū, but in time his poetry came to reflect the humanism characteristic of the *Shirakaba* group, displaying a forceful realism and sympathy for his fellow beings, as in the poem:

> Under his load
> of drooping sheaves
> the farmer walks unsteadily
> step by step.

In his collection of poems entitled *Ichiro*, he achieved a purity and transparency of style all his own; the works in this collection deal mainly with the contemplation of nature and are marked by the abundant use of colloquial expressions and frequent departures from the traditional *tanka* syllabic pattern. These characteristics are illustrated in the following poem:

> The shrikes
> call noisily,
> and beside the road
> red *manjushage* lilies glow—
> this village is a good one.

Though long afflicted by tuberculosis and confined to his bed in his latter years, he continued to write poetry up to the time of his death at the age of thirty-nine.

KITAHARA HAKUSHŪ (1885–1942)

Poet. He was born in Fukuoka Prefecture in Kyushu, the son of a prominent family of merchants dealing in marine products in the Yanagawa region of Kyushu. Around the age of seventeen he began contributing poems in *tanka* and other forms to the magazine *Bunko*, and his unusual poetic talent was soon recognized by Kawai Suimei. In 1906 he became a member of the Shinshisha, a poetry association headed by Yosano Hiroshi and began publishing poems in *Myōjō*, the organ of the association, distinguishing himself as one of the most promising figures of the rising generation. In 1907 he visited the Amakusa Islands in Kyushu and became fascinated with the accounts of the Christian missionaries who were active in that area in the sixteenth century, an interest that found expression in his remarkable poem *Jashūmon hikyoku*, "Secret Song of the Heretics." Toward the end of the same year he left the Shinshisha and set out on a course of his own, producing a number of innovative works marked by a colorful and sensuous symbolism. At the same time he founded the Pan-no-kai, challenging the naturalism that dominated the literary world of the time and espousing the principles of aestheticism and art for art's sake. In 1909, when Mori Ōgai founded the literary magazine *Subaru*, he became one of its contributors. Around the same time he published *Jashūmon*, a collection of poems rich in exotic feeling and fin de siècle decadance, which established him as a figure of major importance in the history of modern poetry in Japan. In 1911 he published a collection of short lyric pieces entitled *Omoide*, which was highly praised by the critic and translator Ueda Bin. In 1918 he became editor in charge of children's songs for the *Akai Tori*, a publication headed by Suzuki Miekichi, and began writing children's songs himself, displaying a striking talent in this new field of endeavor. Eventually he produced over 870 lyrics of this type, a number of which were set to music by Yamada Kōsaku and became popular throughout the nation. In 1937 illness reduced him to a state of near blindness, but he continued as before to devote his energies to poetry. He also founded a magazine entitled *Tama* devoted to poetry in *tanka* form, which was highly regarded in literary circles of the time. In 1941 he became a member of the Japan Art Academy.

Hakushū was a poet whose talent matured early, establishing him almost from the time of his literary debut as a figure of prime importance. His works, which overflow with color and bouyant rhythm, are dominated by emotion and sensuality. A man of unparalleled breadth of talent, he produced poetry of outstanding excellence in both the *tanka* and modern styles, as well as children's songs, folk songs, and songs in the traditional genre known as *kouta*. He published some two hundred volumes in his lifetime, of particular importance being the collection of poems entitled *Jashūmon*, mentioned above, and *Kiri no hana, Shirahae, Kurohi, Hakushū dōyōshū*, and *Hakushū kouta-shū*.

Kobayashi Hideo (b. 1902)

Critic. Born in Tokyo, he graduated from the Department of French Literature of Tokyo Imperial University in 1928 and shortly afterwards made his literary debut when a piece entitled *Samazama naru ishō* won a prize in a contest organized by the magazine *Kaizō*. In 1930 he published *Ashiru to kame no ko* in the magazine *Bungei Shunjū* and thereafter published every month in the same magazine an article on contemporary literature written in an original style, gradually establishing himself in the front rank of prewar literary critics. He mercilessly attacked the "I-novel"—a kind of relic of naturalism that persisted in contemporary Japanese literature—while at the same time violently attacking the intellectualism—the "deception through ideas"—of the proletarian literature movement of the late 1920s and 1930s. In a sense, he represented the beginnings of modern literary criticism in Japan. In 1933, he joined with Hayashi Fusao and others in founding the magazine *Bungakkai*, in which he serialized his "Life of Dostoevsky." His "On the 'I-Novel' " aroused much controversy, and he counducted a celebrated argument with Masamune Hakuchō on the subject of "Ideas and Real Life" (*Shisō to jisseikatsu*). During the war he led a solitary life in which he developed his love of ancient art and the classics and published a series of essays, such as *Taima* and *Mujō to yū koto*.

Following the war, he took up the subject of Rimbaud and Dostoevsky again, and at the same time summed up his own view of aesthetics in *Watakushi no jinseikan*. His *Letters of Gogh* won the Yomiuri Literary Award, and at the end of 1952 he embarked on a tour of Europe, the fruits of which were embodied in *Kindai kaiga*, for which he won the Noma Literary Award. In recent years he has outlined his views on Bergson's philosophy in *Kansō* and on the Japanese thinkers of Edo period Japan in works such as *Motoori Norinaga* and *Sorai*. He brought literary criticism in Japan to the point where it could stand on its own as a literary form with its own independent function and value, and his achievement and influence have been of great importance.

KŌDA ROHAN (1867–1947)

Novelist, dramatist, essayist, and historian. Born in Kanda, Tokyo, he attended a private academy, where he was set to study the *Classic of Filial Piety* at an early age, and also frequented libraries, reading avidly among Chinese works, Buddhistic works, and miscellaneous works of the Edo period. He was deeply impressed by Tsubouchi Shōyō's *Essence of the Novel*, with its rejection of old literature, but also developed a taste for the work of Saikaku. In 1889 he published *Tsuyu dandan*, a romantic tale set in America. He followed it with *Fūryū-butsu*, a poetic portrayal of ideal love written in a lofty style; this work established his reputation on a level comparable to that of Yamada Bimyō and Ozaki Kōyō. In 1891–92 he published *Gojū no tō*, generally rated as his finest work, and in 1893–95 wrote the massive *Fūryū mijinzō*. In 1896 he revived the literary magazine *Shin Shōsetsu* and as its editor provided new authors with a forum for their work. In 1903 he began publication of his lengthy *Sora utsu nami*, but it was destined to remain unfinished. In 1911 he was awarded a doctorate of literature. During the 1910s he turned increasingly to historical biography, essays, and historical research; the period produced such outstanding works as *Ummei, Doryokuron*, and *Senshinroku*. In 1937 he was given the first Award of Cultural Merit and became a member of the Japan Art Academy. His work also includes travel writing, plays, and works on *haiku* poetry; *Hyōshaku Bashō shichibu shū*—a commentary on seven collections of verse by Bashō and his disciples—is particularly outstanding, with literary value in its own right.

Rohan ranks alongside Ozaki Kōyō as one of the two masters of Meiji literature, his work being characterized by its fanciful, idealistic elements in contrast to the realistic portrayal of human emotions and manners favored by Kōyō. His works, with their fierce awareness of the self and their masculine vigor, are vivid expressions of the pure Japanese spirit and have won a lasting place in the history of Japanese literature.

KOIZUMI YAKUMO (1850–1904)

Writer of fiction, essays, and travel accounts. His original name was Lafcadio Hearn. He was born in Greece of an English father and a Greek mother and was educated in England and France. As a result of an accident during his school days in England, he lost the sight in his left eye. Around the age of twenty he went to America, where he became a newspaper reporter. At the age of twenty-seven he settled in New Orleans, where he worked his way up from reporter to chief editor of the literary section of the paper that employed him. During his approximately ten-year stay in New Orleans, he turned more and more to literary activities, producing translations and original works and writing literary criticism. He came to Japan in 1890 as a correspondent for *Harper's Monthly* and soon after took a position teaching English at the Matsue Middle School and married Koizumi Setsuko, the daughter of an old Matsue family. From 1891 to 1894 he taught English at the Kumamoto Fifth High School and later worked as a reporter for the *Kobe Chronicle*, and during this time became a naturalized citizen of Japan, taking the name Koizumi Yakumo. From 1896 to 1903 he was a teacher of English at Tokyo Imperial University and later served in the same capacity at Waseda University.

Yakumo was a man of strong emotions and acute sensibility and also possessed a rich power of imagination. He devoted much time and energy to the study of Japanese life and was particularly attracted to Buddhism. His *Japan: An Attempt at Interpretation*, published in 1904, is a collection of his studies on Japan. It was preceded by a number of lesser works, which, as his familiarity with Japan deepened, were marked by an increasingly Oriental flavor and richness and cast in an English style at once simple and suggestive. Among these works the most widely read is probably the collection of weird tales entitled *Kwaidan*, which he based upon legends and early Japanese collections of stories such as the *Kokon chomonshū*. His writings have been collected in a work entitled *Koizumi Yakumo zenshū*.

Konakamura Kiyonori (1821–1895)

Scholar of Japanese literature. He was born in Edo and studied under teachers trained in the tradition of Motoori Norinaga. He was particularly well versed in the *ritsuryō*, the elaborate rules drawn up in ancient times to define the nature and duties of the bureaucratic state, and at the time of the Meiji Restoration he was often called into consultation on matters pertaining to institutional reform in the government. He also helped to set up courses in the reading of Japanese classics at Tokyo Imperial University and, as a professor of the same university, lectured on Japanese literature. His works include *Kabu ongaku ryakushi* and *Ryō-no-gige kōgi*, and he took part in the compilation of the encyclopedia known as the *Koji ruien*. Living the earlier part of his life in the Edo period and trained in the old traditions of Japanese studies handed down from such scholars as Motoori Norinaga, he played an important role in carrying on those traditions during the early part of the Meiji period, when there was a strong reaction against the past, and worked to lay the foundations for modern style studies of Japanese literature. Living in an age of transition, his importance lies in the continuity that he provided between the methods of the past and those that were to take shape in the future.

Kondō Yoshimi (b. 1913)

Poet. A graduate of Tokyo Industrial University, he is an architect by profession. In 1933 he met Nakamura Kenkichi and became a member of the *Araragi* poetry society; with Nakamura's death the following year he began to study under Tsuchiya Bummei. His first collections of verse, *Sōshunka* and *Hokori fuku machi*, were published in 1948. In 1951 he founded the poetry magazine *Mirai*. His works, intellectual in approach and marked by a keen sensitivity to the confusions of the postwar era, have succeeded in capturing in novel fashion the anxieties of the period, and he continues to the present to be one of the most productive and important *tanka* poets to appear since the war. "The new poetry," he has stated, "must be founded upon realism in the true sense of the word," and he has accordingly been active in defining the standards for such realism in the world of *tanka* poetry. His collections of poetry include *Shizuka naru ishi*, *Rekishi*, and *Fuyu no ginga*, as well as the two mentioned earlier, and he has also published two critical works on poetry, *Atarashiki tanka no kitei* and *Gendai tanka*. At present he is active as editor of *tanka* for the *Asahi Shimbun*.

Kubota Utsubo (1877–1967)

Poet and scholar of Japanese literature. He was born in Nagano Prefecture. Leaving Matsumoto Middle School, he entered Tokyo Semmon Gakkō (present Waseda University) but left before long. There followed an unsettled period during which he lost both his parents and worked as a replacement teacher in primary school. Later he returned to Waseda and graduated in 1904. Under the influence of Uemura Masahisa he became a Christian.

After working for newspapers and magazines, he became a professor in the Department of Literature of Waseda University and remained in that position until his retirement in 1947.

He first became interested in writing poetry in 1899 when he was twenty-two; he joined the Shinshisha (New Poetry Association) a literary group organized by Yosano Hiroshi and others, and had his work published in the magazine *Myōjō*. Eventually he left the Shinshisha and, along with Yoshie Kogan, Nakazawa Rinsen and others, launched a new magazine entitled *Yamabiko*, devoting himself to verse and novels. In the late 1920s, as his studies of classical Japanese literature progressed, he increased his poetic activity and played the leading role in the founding of the literary magazines *Kokumin Bungaku* and *Tsuki no Ki*. The principal collections of his verse number nineteen. To mention only the most important of them, *Mahiruno* (1905) reveals a kind of graceful clarity and realistic tendency that is essentially different from the style of the *Myōjō* school. *Nigoreru kawa* (1915) shows a greater sobriety and plainness, and the general approach increasingly resembles that of the *Man'yōshū*. *Tsuchi o nagamete* (1918) is largely inspired by the death of the poet's wife, while *Kagamiba* (1926) is characterized by maturity and objectivity.

Kubota also produced many works in his capacity as classical scholar, including annotated editions of the *Ise monogatari* and the *Shin kokinshū*.

Kunikida Doppo (1871–1908)

Poet and novelist. As a boy his father's work obliged him to move about frequently from one part of the country to another, including Iwakuni, Hiroshima, and Yamaguchi, and works such as *Hatsukoi, E no kanashimi*, and *Yama no chikara* embody his reminiscences of this period. In 1887 he went to Tokyo, where he entered Waseda University. Reading Carlyle, he developed an interest in Christianity and received baptism. In 1894 he joined the staff the *Kokumin Shimbun* newspaper. With the outbreak of the Sino-Japanese War, he accompanied the Japanese army as a reporter, and the article entitled *Aitei tsūshin* that he sent back won him a reputation for the freshness of its style. In the autumn of 1895 he married Sasaki Nobuko and went alone to Hokkaido to find some place where they could live together; this provided him with the material for his later *Sorachi-gawa no kishibe* (1902), together with *Musashino* (1901), one of the finest examples of Doppo's works dealing primarily with nature. His marriage failed, however, after a mere six months, and he fell into deep gloom. In 1902 he went to live in

Kamakura and in a burst of creative activity completed *Shōnen no hiai*, *Tomioka sensei*, *Kamakura fujin*, and *Shuchū nikki* in rapid succession. He also produced short stories such as *Gen oji*, *Gyūniku to bareisho*, and *Ummei ronja*, and embarked on a full-length novel, *Bōfū*, but illness obliged him to give it up uncompleted. In his late years, he dabbled in a number of commercial publishing ventures, all of which failed. He also developed a deep affection for the world of the poor, and in works such as *Kyūshi* and *Take no kido* portrayed their lives with objective detachment. In the midst of the rapid cultural upheaval of the Meiji period, Doppo, through his passion and intelligence, managed to bring reality to the romantic trend of the early years and was one of the few writers who tried to view the individual's life in terms of society as a whole. If *Gen oji* is typical of the romantic works of his early period, works such as *Take no kido* and *Kyūshi* can be seen as forerunners of naturalist literature.

MAEDA YŪGURE (1883–1951)

Tanka poet. He was born in Kanagawa Prefecture. After a childhood spent largely in sickness and wandering, he went to Tokyo in 1904 and became a disciple of the poet Onoe Saishū, joining with Onoe's other students Wakayama Bokusui and Miki Rofū in the association known as the Ōbakosha. His dry intellectual approach and artless manner contrasted markedly with the sentimentalism of Wakayama Bokusui. In 1906 he formed an association of his own known as the Hakujitsusha and published a magazine entitled *Higuruma* in which he sharply attacked the romanticism of the *Myōjō* school of poetry in vogue at the time. In 1910 his first collection of poems, entitled *Shūkaku*, appeared and, along with the collection entitled *Betsuri* by Wakayama Bokusui, attracted attention as an important work in the naturalist manner. He founded a magazine called *Shiika* and was on close terms with such other important poets as Yamamura Bochō, Hagiwara Sakutarō and Murō Saisei. He and Wakayama Bokusui were at this time at the height of their popularity.

The poems in *Shūkaku* and *In'ei* employ a naturalist manner often marked by a strong feeling of nihilism and ennui, and many of them depart from the traditional syllable pattern for *tanka*. The following is typical of the work of this period:

> On the lumber
> piled in the loading area
> beside the canal

> a man sits
> staring at the sky.

In later collections such as *Ikiru hi ni* and *Shinrin*, however, his work took on a brighter tone suggestive of the impressionist school. The best known work of this period is probably the following:

> The sunflower,
> body bathed
> in oil of gold,
> swaying, towering—
> beside it, the sun seems so small!

From 1929 on he began to write *tanka* that employed the colloquial language and did not observe the traditional syllable pattern, at the same time emphasizing the importance of rhythm and a sense of density in *tanka* and working actively to promote his views. Eventually, however, he returned to the traditional *tanka* form.

Masaoka Shiki (1867–1902)

Waka and *haiku* poet. He was born in Matsuyama in the province of Iyo (present Ehime Prefecture). He started writing prose and verse at a very early age, left Matsuyama Middle School in 1883 and went to Tokyo. The following year he entered the University Preparatory College (later the First High School). In 1889 he suffered a haemorrhage of the lungs; around this time he adopted the literary name Shiki. In 1890 he entered the Department of Literature of Tokyo Imperial University. Around the same time he traveled in various parts of the country and wrote a considerable amount of travel literature. In 1892, he moved to Kami-Negishi in Shitaya; here for the first time he devoted himself completely to *haiku* and set about compiling works such as *Haiku bunrui* and *Haisho nempyō*, a chronological bibliography of works related to *haiku*. He also published *Dassai shooku haiwa* serially in the newspaper *Nippon*, in which he criticized the intellectualized, stereotyped approach to *haiku* and advocated a new naturalism in which the subject of the poem would be described honestly and realistically. He left the university in 1893 and soon after published *Bashō zatsudan*, in which he criticized the idolized concept of the poet Bashō.

In 1895, he went to China as a war correspondent to cover the Sino-Japanese War and was on his way home in May of the same year when he had a severe haemorrhaging of the lungs. He soon recovered, however, and went back to Matsuyama, where his presence stimulated great activity in *haiku* circles. In 1896 the fashion for writing the new type of *haiku* that he advocated gradually spread, and his name acquired increasing importance in literary circles. His health in the meantime declined steadily, and he developed tuberculosis of the spine, which left him largely bedridden. In 1897, he founded the *haiku* magazine *Hototogisu*. In 1899 he published a critical work on *haiku* entitled *Haijin Buson*. The following year *Shin haiku*, a collection of verse by the *Hototogisu* group, was published. In the same year, he published *Utayomi ni atauru sho*, which created a stir in poetry circles by proposing reforms in the writing of *waka*. He also proposed, with his theory of "a narrative," a new kind of prose style based on description. He produced large numbers of *tanka* and writings on poetics, which led to the formation of the Negishi *Tanka* Association. In 1901 and 1902 he published such pieces as *Bokujū itteki*, *Byōshō rokushaku*, and *Gyōga manroku*, continuing vigorous activity up until his death in September, 1902.

Shiki insisted that the *haiku* held just as important a place in Japanese literature as other verse forms, and he advocated a new, more realistic style as a way of rescuing it from the moribund state in which it found itself in the early years of the Meiji era. He helped to clarify the literary achievements of Bashō, Buson, and other earlier *haiku* poets and established a new style of *haiku*. He also joined in the movement to reform the *tanka* and helped its rebirth as a modern verse form by advocating a realism similar to that he stressed in the *haiku*. He also created a new prose style based on realism, his championship of realism in various fields of literature having a great effect on the literary world of his day.

Half his short life was taken up with the struggle against disease, and as his illness progressed it became impossible for him even to turn over in bed. Yet despite his suffering, his extraordinarily clear intelligence continued to manifest itself in his literary activities. This, and the large number of first-rate proteges such as Takahama Kyoshi, Kawahigashi Hekigotō, and Itō Sachio, whose development he watched over, make him one of the most important contributors to the development of modern Japanese literature.

Mishima Yukio (1925–1970)

Novelist and playwright. He was born in Tokyo. After completing the Gakushūin, he entered Tokyo Imperial University. In 1944 he published his first story, *Hana-zakari no mori*, and in 1946, with the publication of *Tabako*, made his debut in the literary world. His early short stories, which show a strong influence of fin de siècle hedonism, soon attracted wide attention. For a time he worked as an official in the Ministry of Finance, but soon resigned to devote himself to creative activities. In 1949 his first full-length novel, *Kamen no kokuhaku*, appeared, followed by *Ai no kawaki*, establishing his reputation as a writer of major importance, and thereafter he began to enjoy great popularity. These works were followed by *Kinjiki* and *Shiosai*, the latter an idyllic tale of youthful love and innocence that won particular acclaim. His works are characterized by a style that combines a refined aesthetic sensibility with a keen critical spirit and a harmony and balance of elements that seeks to recreate the classical beauty of the past in present-day language. These qualities are evident in such ambitious works as *Kinkaku-ji*, *Kyōko no ie*, and *Utage no ato*. The first of these won the Yomiuri Prize for literature, while the last involved him in a law suit with the politician who served as the model for its protagonist on grounds of invasion of privacy.

At the same time he was stirring up controversy in the literary world because of these events, he was also becoming active in dramatic circles, establishing himself as one of the most brilliant playwrights of the postwar period with such works as *Rokumeikan*, *Bara to kaizoku*, and *Tōka no kiku*. His dramas, marked by sound construction, probing psychological analysis, and creativity of ideas, as well as brilliance of language, have succeeded in exploiting the potentialities of the postwar theater in Japan to create a superb world of their own. He himself became a member of the Bungaku-za theater group, playing an important role in its leadership, though he later withdrew from the group as a result of a controversy over his play *Yorokobi no koto*. Thereafter he appeared in various movies and was given special permission to become associated with the Self-Defense Force, attracting wide comment through these and other unconventional actions and pronouncements. Eventually he organized a militaristic group of his own called the Tate no Kai (Shield Society). In November of 1970 he and his group forced their way into the Self-Defense Force army post at Ichigaya in Tokyo, where Mishima, after reading a proclamation and attempting to incite the troops to action, committed ritual *harakiri* in the commanding officer's room. This unprecedented act startled and amazed the world at the time.

Mishima's works have been translated into many languages and are widely read and admired abroad. His *Kindai nōgaku-shū*, modern Nō plays, have been performed in Stockholm and New York, winning wide critical acclaim, and his name has been mentioned as a candidate for the Nobel Prize in literature. Because he was a figure of international prominence, his sudden and unusual death became the subject of widespread comment. Just before his death, he completed work on a massive tetralogy entitled *Hōgyō no umi* (*The Sea of Fertility*).

Mitomi Kyūyō (1889–1917)

Poet. He was born in Nagasaki Prefecture. While a student in the English literature course of Waseda University, he joined with Hitomi Tōmei, Imai Hakuyō and others in forming the Jiyūshisha, an association to promote free-verse poetry. The association published a monthly magazine entitled *Shizen to Inshō*, which introduced the works of French symbolist poets such as Mallarmé, Verlaine, and Rimbaud. After graduating from Waseda, he remained deeply under the influence of modern French poetry and devoted himself to detailed studies of the works of various poets and to the writing of a prose-poem entitled *Seikatsuhyō*. The poem, which shows the influence of French poetry, is marked by delicate feeling and sensitivity, cheerful in tone but with a touch of melancholy. It is especially noteworthy for its freshness of poetic feeling. In August of 1917 the poet was drowned while swimming with his friend Imai Hakuyō at Inubōzaki, thus ending his life at the young age of twenty-eight.

Miyake Setsurei (1860–1945)

Thinker and critic. He was born in Kanazawa, the son of a physician in the service of the Maeda clan. He studied Confucianism in his youth and in 1876 entered the Faculty of Letters of the Kaisei Gakkō (later renamed Tokyo Imperial University), concentrating upon the study of philosophy. During his student days he took special interest in Spencer and Carlyle and began to lay the groundwork for his own philosophy. In 1883 he published *Nihon minzoku no tokushoku*. He was made the equivalent of an assistant professor in the editorial office of Tokyo University, devoting himself to the study of Japanese Buddhism, and later transferred to a post in the editorial division of the Ministry of Education, where he assisted the British scholar Basil Hall Chamberlain in his studies of Japanese language and literature. In 1887 he resigned his post and thereafter remained in private life. The following year he joined with Sugiura Shigetaka and others in forming an association known as the Seikyōsha, publishing a magazine entiled *Nihonjin* and writing articles advocating nationalism and the preservation of traditional Japanese values. In the pages of *Nihonjin* he repeatedly attacked the members of the Satsuma and Chōshū groups for the arbitrary way in which they dominated the government, and as a result the magazine was forced to suspend publication.

As may be seen in his work entitled *Shinzenbi Nihonjin* published in 1894, the type of nationalism that he advanced, though stressing the uniqueness of the Japanese people, placed greater emphasis upon the individual than upon the people as a whole. In 1892 he married Tanabe Tatsuko (Kaho), a writer of traditional Japanese poetry, and in 1901 he was awarded a doctorate. After the Russo-Japanese War, he published a work entitled *Uchū* serially in the magazine *Nihon oyobi Nihonjin*, a reissue of the earlier *Nihonjin* under a new title. In works such as his *Tōzai bijutsu no kankei* and *Gakujutsujō no tōyō seiyō*, he discussed the definition of such concepts as *shin*, (truth), *zen* (goodness), and *bi* (beauty), while in his *Jinrui seikatsu no jōtai* he adopted an evolutionary standpoint in discussing problems relating to the life and thought of present-day mankind. Through the magazine *Nihon oyobi Nihonjin* he played an important part in encouraging the arts, particularly the writing of *haiku* and poetry in Chinese, and the magazine served as the stronghold of the new movement in *haiku* writing that centered about Kawahigashi Hekigotō. He also contributed to the literary world by introducing previously unpublished writings of the *haiku* poet Masaoka Shiki. He exercised a major influence upon the development of the thought and culture of post-Meiji times and counted among his followers such eminent men as the historian Naitō Konan and the critic Hasegawa Nyozekan.

MIYAMOTO YURIKO (1899–1951)

Novelist. She was born in the Koishikawa section of Tokyo. For a time she attended Japan Women's College. She made her literary debut with a short story entitled *Mazushiki hitobito no mure*, which appeared in *Chūō Kōron* magazine. In 1919, while studying in America, she married, but was divorced in 1924. *Nobuko*, a novel dealing with the events in this period of her life and one of her most important works, was completed in 1926. In 1930, after returning from a three-year tour of western Europe and the Soviet Union, she immediately became a member of the Japan Proletarian Writers' League and of the Japan Communist Party and began to take a very active part in the proletarian movement in literature, working energetically to introduce Soviet culture and literature. In 1932 she married Miyamoto Kenji, a fellow writer in the proletarian movement, and two months later was arrested and held in custody for a time because of her political beliefs. Around this time her husband embarked upon underground activities, and the couple were obliged to live separately until the end of the war, a period of thirteen years. In the years following her initial arrest, she was frequently arrested and held in custody and was forbidden to continue her writing career, suffering a number of severe economic and spiritual blows, among them the news of her husband's arrest. As a result of the repeated interrogations she was forced to undergo, her health had deteriorated badly by the time the war came to an end. After the war she formed the Shin-Nihon Bungaku-kai (New Japanese Literature Association) and entered upon her period of greatest activity. In addition to publishing works of fiction and criticism such as *Utagoe yo okore*, *Banshū heiya*, *Fūchisō*, and *Futatsu no niwa*, she was very active as a lecturer and political organizer. She died suddenly in 1951, shortly after finishing her novel *Dōhyō*. Her life in the troubled society of Japan in the first half of the present century was distinguished by a powerful determination to confront the facts of reality and to fight on behalf of the workers, the poor, and disadvantaged women. Her works reveal the course of her development from a humanist to a champion of socialism.

Miyazaki Koshoshi (1864–1922)

Novelist, critic, and poet. He was born in Fukuoka Prefecture. He graduated from Waseda University and became a convert to Christianity. He joined the staff of the newspaper *Kokumin Shimbun* and in it and the magazine *Kokumin no Tomo* published poems, works of fiction, and critical essays over the following thirty years. He was particularly noted in the field of modern style poetry and, before the appearance of Shimazaki Tōson, was probably the most outstanding lyric poet writing in the modern style form in the 1890s. His novels such as *Kisei* and *Kūya*, though lacking in realism, give expression to the Christian view of nature and have a pastoral charm and simple lyricism that lend them freshness of feeling. His collections of poems, such as *Koshoshi shishū* and *Jojōshi*, demonstrate that he was one of the most important pioneers in the writing of romantic lyrics in the modern style. He also wrote a critical biography entitled *Wordsworth*. In his later years he became a member of the clergy and devoted his time to teaching in a divinity school and to preaching activities.

Miyazaki Sammai (1859–1919)

Novelist. He was born in the Shitaya section of Edo. In 1880 he joined the staff of the newspaper *Tokyo Nichinichi Shimbun* and, after working for other newspapers in turn, became a reporter for the Tokyo *Asahi Shimbun* in 1890. Around 1888 he began writing fiction, producing such works as *Saga no amamonogatari*, *Katsura-hime*, *Ban Dan'emon*, and *Nio no ukisu*, all historical novels that are carefully researched and serious in tone. He also became involved in the movement to reform the theater and worked to bring out a reprint of an early edition of Ueda Akinari's *Ugetsu monogatari*. For a time he was ranked beside Kōda Rohan and Murakami Namiroku as one of the most important writers of historical fiction, but he was unable to free himself from the adverse influence of the *kusazōshi*, the works of popular fiction of the late Edo period, and his writings are lacking in creativity, both factors that probably contributed to his eventual decision to quit the field of literature.

Mizuhara Shūōshi (b. 1892)

Haiku poet. He was born in Tokyo, the eldest son of a doctor who headed a maternity hospital. After graduating from the medical department of Tokyo Imperial University, he took over his father's practice. He began writing *haiku* as a member of the Shibugaki school headed by Matsune Tōyōjō, but later became a student of Takahama Kyoshi, joining Yamaguchi Seishi, Takano Sujū, and the other poets who in the late Taishō and early Shōwa eras centered their activities around the magazine *Hototogisu* when it was at the height of its influence.

Shūōshi had a passionate fondness for nature and attempted in his poetry to create a sense of beauty out of elements drawn from the natural world, aiming for an approach that might be called subjective realism. But this conflicted with the objective realism advocated by Takahama Kyoshi, and in 1917 Shūōshi therefore left the *Hototogisu* group and became head of the magazine called *Ashibi*. He worked to introduce a richer note of human sentiment into *haiku*, and in doing so acted as the forerunner of what in time was to become a new movement in the *haiku* world. He also advocated the composition of poem sequences and experimented in the composition of a number of such sequences himself, though eventually he abandoned these efforts, having concluded that sequences tended to weaken the impact of the individual poem. From this time on, he devoted himself solely to the celebration of the beauties of nature. After the war, he gave up his medical practice and concentrated all his attention upon poetry, achieving a kind of artistic rejuvenation and displaying increasing richness and purity in his work. He has published over ten collections of poems including *Katsushika*, *Shinju*, and *Shūen*. In 1963 he received a Japan Art Academy prize, and in 1966 he became a member of the Art Academy.

MORI ŌGAI (1862–1922)

Novelist. He was born in Shimane Prefecture, where his family had for many generations served as official physicians to the Tsuwano clan. In 1881, at the age of nineteen, he graduated from the Department of Medicine of Tokyo Imperial University and entered the army. In 1884 he went to study in Germany. Returning to Japan in 1888, he became a teacher at the Army College. The following year he began vigorous literary activity, publishing a collection of translated verse entitled *Omokage* in the magazine *Kokumin no Tomo* and also founding the magazine *Shigarami Sōshi*. In 1890 he published his first novel, *Maihime*, which was soon followed by *Utakata no ki* and *Fumizukai*. These established him almost overnight at the center of the literary world as an early leader of the romantic movement in Japan. In the following years he devoted himself with intense energy to translation and criticism. In 1896, he founded the magazine *Mezamashi Gusa*, successor to *Shigarami Sōshi*, and embarked on an almost belligerently active life as a critic, his views depending largely on the aesthetics of Hartmann.

The verbal battles in which he engaged over a broad field of ideas—his emphasis upon the autonomous nature of literature, his controversy with Ishibashi Ningetsu concerning *Maihime*, and his controversy with Tsubouchi Shōyō concerning the "lack of ideals," as well as the argument concerning the improvement of the drama—were backed up by a rich knowledge and cultural background and had an important influence on the world of writers. He was responsible for a celebrated translation of Andersen's *Improvisator* (1891–1901), and countless other translations including *John Gabriel Borkman* (1909) and *Faust* (1913). In order to help bring about a reform of the theater he also published plays such as *Tamakushige futatsu Urashima* (1902) and *Nichiren Shōnin tsuji seppō* (1904). In the late Meiji period he once more turned his attention to fiction, which he had neglected since *Fumizukai*, and began writing pieces for *Mita Bungaku, Subaru* and other magazines. Various well-known works such as *Vita Sexualis*, *Mōzō*, and *Gan* were produced around this time. In the early Taishō period (1912–25), he produced the historical novels *Okitsu Yagoemon no ishō* and *Abe ichizoku*, as well as *Takase-bune, Kanzan Jittoku,* and the historical biographies *Shibue Chūsai* and *Izawa Ranken.* During the Meiji period he had served as an army doctor in both the Sino-Japanese and Russo-Japanese wars, holding a number of important posts and finally reaching the highest post available to an army doctor. He was active in medical research and published a number of papers on medical subjects. He held doctorates of both literature and medicine and occupied a number of important posts in various cultural fields, such as director and curator of the Imperial Household Museum and Library, head of the Imperial Art Academy, and chairman of the Provisional Commission on the Japanese Language, applying his vast knowledge and energy to achievements in many different fields.

Ōgai stands with Natsume Sōseki as one of the two giants of modern Japanese literature: like Sōseki, he adopted an antinaturalist approach and based his literary activities on a broad and deep background in which a sound knowledge of Western literature played a large part. He acted constantly as a pioneer, indicating the path that he felt should be taken not only by Japanese literature but by Japanese culture as a whole, and his practical achievements, whether in the fields of translation, criticism, or creative writing, are astonishing in both their quantity and their quality. In the extent of his influence he was perhaps unequalled by any other figure in modern Japanese literature.

Murai Gensai (1863–1927)

Fiction writer. He was born in Aichi Prefecture. In 1874 he entered the Russian language course of Tokyo Gaigo Gakkō but was forced by sickness and lack of funds to discontinue his studies. In 1885 he made a trip to America, and after his return became a member of the staff of the newspaper *Hōchi Shimbun,* by 1895 advancing to the position of managing editor. The stories *Shōsetsuka* and *Koneko,* which were published in the paper, soon gained him recognition as a writer, and the work entitled *Hinodejima* was greeted with such interest that it eventually ran to a total of twelve hundred installments. In addition he wrote such widely read works as *Shokudōraku, Kinugasajō,* and *Sakura no gosho,* gaining a reputation as an outstanding writer of popular fiction. In 1906 he became editorial adviser to a women's magazine called *Fujin Sekai,* to which he contributed articles on such practical subjects as cooking and home medicine, an innovation for the women's magazines of the time.

Murakami Kijō (1865–1938)

Haiku poet. His father was a samurai of the fief of Tottori, and he was born at the official clan residence in Edo but grew up in Takasaki. Because of an ear ailment he gave up all hope of an official career and instead made a living as a public letter-writer. In 1899 he requested criticism from the poet Masaoka Shiki and as a result became a contributor of *haiku* and descriptive pieces to *Hototogisu*, the poetry magazine that Shiki edited. In 1913 he was chosen to be a member of the staff of *Hototogisu* and also acted as *haiku* editor for such other magazines as *Yamabato*, *Honryū*, and *Wakatake*, gradually gaining a place of importance in the *haiku* world. The *haiku* poet and critic Ōsuga Otsuji designated Kijō's works as "the poetry of circumstance" and went so far as to compare them with those of the great Edo period poet Issa. Because Kijō was already in his fifties when his poetry began to gain recognition in the early years of the Taishō era, many of his best-known works deal with loneliness, old age, and death and are imbued with a tone of deep melancholy, as may be seen in the following examples:

> The winter wasp,
> with no place to die,
> goes on walking.

> How sad—
> the face of the hawk
> grown terribly old.

His collections of poems include *Kijō kushū* and *Teihon Kijō kushū*.

Murakami Namiroku (1865–1944)

Novelist. He was born in the city of Sakai south of Osaka. His father died when he was two, and he was raised by his mother in conditions of great poverty. He went to Tokyo in 1881 with dreams of becoming a politician or a businessman and thereafter moved about from place to place, living a life marked by constant vicissitude. In 1890 he joined the staff of a newspaper called the *Hōchi Shimbun* and wrote a novel titled *Mikazuki*, which was well received. This was followed by other works such as *Yakko no Koman*, *Tōsei go'nin otoko*, and *Hakken nagaya*, which established him as a major writer of popular fiction. Though he remained a favorite with readers over a period of many years, he himself seems never to have been satisfied with his life as a writer. His works are devoid of any descriptions of background or natural surrounding, but concentrate entirely upon the actions and words of the characters. His characterizations are stereotyped and his outlook on life anything but original, but his conversational passages have an appeal of their own. Though he never transcended the limitations of the old style fiction of the late Edo and early Meiji period, he holds a place of importance in the development of popular fiction in modern times.

MUSHANOKŌJI SANEATSU (b. 1885)

Novelist and playwright. He was the eighth son of Viscount Mushanokōji Saneyo. In the same year that he finished Gakushūin Middle School, he for the first time read the Bible and the works of Tolstoy and became an avid admirer of the latter. In 1903 he entered the sociology course of Tokyo Imperial University but left school before graduating, devoting all his efforts to literature instead. In time he gradually began to divest himself of the influence of Tolstoy's thought and in 1910 joined with Shiga Naoya, Arishima Takeo, and others in founding a magazine called *Shirakaba*. The group associated with the magazine, known as the *Shirakaba* school, advocated a literature characterized by humanism. Mushanokōji's literary career, which extends over half a century, can, according to Kamei Katsui-chirō, be divided into the following five periods.

The period from the founding of *Shirakaba* in 1910 until the establishment of Atarashiki Mura (New Village) in 1918 comprises the first period. Under the influence of Tolstoy, Mushanokōji espoused egocentricity and published such works as *Omedetaki hito* and *Seken shirazu*. As may be seen in his full-length work *Kare ga sanjū no toki*, however, his egocentricity was becoming modified in the direction of humanism. From this period date such plays as *Sono imōto* and *Aru seinen no yume*.

During the second period, his devotion to humanism became more intense, and he attempted to put his ideas into practice through the founding of his so-called New Village. For this purpose he left his home in Abiko in 1918 and moved to a remote village in Hyūga in the southeastern part of Kyushu, where he organized a cooperative community. This period from the founding of the New Village until the Kantō earthquake in 1923 was one of the most active in the author's life and saw the writing of one after another of his most celebrated works such as the novels *Kōfukusha*, *Yūjō*, and *Aru otoko*, as well as plays.

The third period saw the further growth of the New Village experiment, but Mushanokōji's thinking becaming increasingly communistic in tone, and as a result his ideals and activities were often subjected to severe ridicule and abuse. During this period he produced many biographical novels and began to paint.

The fourth period was marked by the writing of an account of the author's trip to Europe, novels dealing with romantic love, and works on fine arts. Among the many full-length novels dating from this period are *Ai to shi* and *Kōfuku na kazoku*.

During the fifth, or postwar, period he was barred from holding public office, but he staged a comeback in the literary world with his long novel *Shinri sensei*, and also gained recognition as a painter. Because of the construction of a dam in the area, he moved the site of his agricultural community from Kyushu to Saitama Prefecture; by this time his New Village experiment was beginning to be looked upon with greater sympathy and understanding.

Mushanokōji in his writing and thought has attempted to combat the tendencies toward excessive objectivity and suppression of the ego that mark naturalism, encouraging each individual to give full expression to his ego. A characteristic of his thought is the belief that, when the individual ego is allowed full rein, the result will be harmony among all men. His literary works are conceived on a grand scale and are marked by a sunniness and sense of humor that are uniquely his own. But, as demonstrated in *Aiyoku*, his is the sunniness and optimism of a man who at the same time is fully sensitive to the troubles and darker aspects of the times. For all their simpleness and directness of expression, one feels that his works are constantly grappling with the fundamental problems of human existence, and it is this quality that gives their author a place of unique importance among Japanese thinkers and writers. In 1955 Mushanokōji was awarded a Cultural Medal.

NAGAI KAFŪ (1879–1959)

Novelist. He was born in Tokyo, the son of a prominent family of the intelligentsia. After finishing middle school, he entered the foreign language school that was attached to Tokyo Higher Normal School, but soon began to devote all his attention to literature. At the age of nineteen he showed a short story entitled *Sudare no tsuki* to the writer Hirotsu Ryūrō and was accepted as a student. Around this time he also studied Japanese dancing and the type of traditional ballad singing called *kiyomoto* and frequented the variety theaters and the rooms backstage where the kabuki playwrights did their work. In 1903, when he was twenty-four, his father, hoping to equip him for a career in business, sent him to America for a period of study, but he did not like life abroad and in 1907, contrary to his father's wishes, he journeyed to France and the following year returned to Japan. The collection of stories entitled *Amerika monogatari*, which was published shortly after his return, as well as *Reishō, Furansu monogatari*, and the numerous others works that followed it, in no time established Kafū as a major writer. In 1910 he became a professor of Keio University and editor of the university's literary magazine *Mita Bungaku*, through which he promoted what came to be known as the Mita school of literature. In 1916, however, he resigned his teaching and editorial positions and founded a magazine of his own called *Bummei*, which was followed shortly by another called *Kagetsu*. In 1920 he built a Western style house, which he called the Henkikan ("Eccentricity House"), living there in a manner appropriate to the appellation. Thereafter he began to write about the world of the geisha and the licensed prostitute, spending much of his time in the environments that he described. Such outstanding works as *Udekurabe, Okame-zasa, Tsuyu no atosaki*, and *Bokutō kidan* were published at this time. During the war he wrote *Odoriko, Fuchin*, and other stories that were published after the end of the war. In the postwar years he produced *Katsushika miyage* and other works. He lived a very solitary life in these late years, evincing a great interest in the downtown area of Tokyo, particularly the amusement center in Asakusa, and nearly every day was to be found walking about the neighborhood. In 1952 he received a Cultural Medal.

He began his career as an advocate of Zola style realism, but after his return from abroad, while the naturalist movement was at the height of its popularity among other writers, he proceeded to turn out works marked by a subjective hedonism. He voiced sharp criticism of the way of life in Japan in his own day, while at the same time expressing a deep sense of nostalgia for the traditional culture of the Edo period and the vanished world it represented. He went his own way as an artist, rising above the various fashions and movements that swayed the general run of writers and in the end achieved the status of a truly great literary figure. In addition to his works of fiction he left a fine diary entitled *Danchōtei nichijō*, some ten plays, and a volume of translations of foreign poetry entitled *Sangoshū* that exercised a strong influence upon the poetry world of the time.

Nagatsuka Takashi (1879–1915)

Poet and novelist. He was born in Ibaragi Prefecture, the eldest son of a local landlord. He attended Mito Middle School but left before completing the course. Having read Masaoka Shiki's "Letter to *Waka* Poets," he was filled with deep respect and at the age of twenty visited Shiki in Tokyo and asked to receive instruction from him. After Shiki's death in 1902, he was a member of the group associated with the *waka* magazine *Ashibi*. His poems deal mainly with rural scenes and are marked by delicacy of sentiment and expression. Though he was a landlord, he farmed his own land and studied ways to improve the raising of bamboo and the making of charcoal and compost heaps and had a wide and firsthand knowledge of the life of the farmer. At the same time, he was very fond of walking trips and composed many of his finest poems while on the road. In 1905 he published a collection of poems entitled *Kiryo zatsuei*, which gave clear proof of his abilities. Though a number of his poems, such as *Nōmu no uta* and *Norikuradake wo omou*, were recognized for their excellence, he temporarily abandoned poetry and in 1908 plunged with great enthusiasm into the writing of sketches and works of fiction. The result of these labors was the famous novel *Tsuchi*, which was published in 1910. The following year, when he was stricken with tuberculosis of the larynx, he returned to the writing of poetry, producing the collection entitled *Byōchū zatsuei* and in 1914–15 he published a collection of 231 poems entitled *Hari no gotoku*, which are marked by delicacy of tone and introspective sentiment. Throughout his works he attempted to achieve the note of realism that his teacher, Masaoka Shiki, had advocated as the ideal in poetry.

Nagayo Yoshirō (1888–1961)

Novelist, playwright, and critic. His father, Nagayo Sensai, studied medicine in the private school in Osaka headed by Ogata Kōan and was one of the leaders in the medical field in the Meiji era. The surroundings in which, as the eighth and youngest child of such a prominent family, he grew up, and his acquaintance with the highly individual members of the group associated with the literary magazine *Shirakaba*, played a large role in his intellectual and spiritual development. After graduating from Gakushūin, he entered Tokyo Imperial University, but withdrew before receiving his college degree. In 1914 he published two largely autobiographical stories, *Mōmoku no kawa* and *Karera no ummei*, in *Shirakaba*. The play *Kō U to Ryū Hō* established his reputation as a playwright. In addition, as a champion of the humanitarian principles espoused by the *Shirakaba* group he wrote numerous critical essays and reflective pieces. The most important works of fiction of his middle years are *Seidō no Kirisuto* and *Takezawa sensei to iu hito*. In the middle thirties he made frequent trips to Manchuria and China, which resulted in such works as *Man-Shi kono-goro*, *Daitei Kōki*, and *Yūko no ryokōki*. He continued to be active in his late years, bringing to completion a dynamic description of his intellectual development entitled *Waga kokoro no henreki*. A man of great energy and a fighter for justice, he devoted his life to the support of liberalism. His personality has a powerful and distinctive appeal, and his literary works have won high critical acclaim.

Naitō Meisetsu (1847–1926)

Haiku poet. He was born in Shikoku, the eldest son of a samurai of the fief of Matsuyama in present-day Ehime Prefecture. He studied Chinese in the fief school and later attended the Shōheikō, the official school of the Tokugawa shogunate in Edo, but with the Meiji Restoration and the end of the feudal system, he returned to Shikoku and became an official in the government of Ehime Prefecture. From 1881 to 1891 he served as an official in the Ministry of Education in Tokyo and later headed the dormitory set up for students from the former fief of Matsuyama, holding that post until 1901. In 1892 he began taking instruction in the writing of *haiku* from Masaoka Shiki, who was a student in the dormitory at that time, and thus at the age of forty-five began a career as a *haiku* poet. Though Shiki was some twenty years younger than Meisetsu, the two men seem to have established a very warm and lasting relationship. Meisetsu had a vast knowledge of Japanese and Chinese studies and a frank and open manner. He was highly respected as the eldest member of the group of poets surrounding Shiki and assisted in training the younger men of the group. His style is simple and graceful and has a somewhat classical tone to it. In addition to his poems and remarks on poetry, which are preserved in the *Meisetsu haikushū* and *Meisetsu haiwa*, he produced various commentaries and exegetical works.

Nakae Chōmin (1847–1901)

Thinker, critic, and scholar of French studies. He was born in Kōchi in the fief of Tosa in Shikoku. In 1865 he was sent to Nagasaki as an official student from the fief and three years later, with the assistance of Gotō Shōjirō, he was able to go to Edo and take up the study of French. In 1871 Ōkubo Toshimichi arranged for him to go to France to continue his studies. After devoting himself to literature, philosophy, and history, he returned to Japan in 1874 and opened a private school of French studies called the Futsugaku-juku. The following year he was appointed head of the Tokyo School of Foreign Languages, but he soon resigned. He also served as a member of the Genrō-in (Senate) but resigned and thereafter did not hold any official posts. In 1881 he founded a newspaper called the *Tōyō Jiyū Shimbun* with Saionji Kimmochi as head and himself as chief editor, but pressure from the government forced it to suspend publication after the thirty-fourth issue. From his own school, the Futsugaku-juku, he issued a semimonthly entitled *Seiri Sōdan*, in which he published serially a translation of Rousseau's *Social Contract*, later printed separately under the title *Minyaku yakukai*. He eloquently expounded French political concepts of liberty and equality and attacked the Japanese government of the time for its failure to come closer to them.

His ideas and activities exercised considerable influence upon the society of the period, and Chōmin himself came to be referred to as "the Oriental Rousseau." In 1887 he published a French-Japanese dictionary entitled *Futsuwa jirin*. He was elected a member of the Lower House of the Diet in the first election, held in 1890, and was a member of the Jiyūtō (Liberal Party). He also served as manager of the *Jiyū Shimbun* when it was refounded, of the *Rikken Jiyū Shimbun* and *Minken Shimbun*, and other organizations. Told that, because of cancer of the throat he had only a year and one-half to live, he published a collection of essays entitled *Ichinen yūhan* ("Year and a Half"), and a philosophical work entitled *Shoku ichinen yūhan*. One of the outstanding intellectual leaders of the early Meiji period, his varied activities as an advocate of liberalism and popular rights exercised a powerful influence upon the thinking of the time. He produced a translation of E. Veron's *Esthétique* (1878), the first volume of which appeared in 1883 and the second the following year. Among his disciples was Kōtoku Shūsui.

Nakamura Kusatao (b. 1901)

Haiku poet. Following graduation from the Department of Japanese Literature of Tokyo Imperial University, he taught at Seikei Gakuen, joined the Tokyo University *Haiku* Association and received advice from Mizuhara Shūōshi. In 1933 he was made a member of the *Hototogisu haiku* association, and his verse began to appear in the magazine of the same name. Around 1939 he began to be grouped with Ishida Hakyō and Katō Shūson because of the difficulty of his verse; he also became known for the exploration of human nature in his poetry. Kusatao caused a stir in *haiku* circles and acquired a considerable following, though there were also cries of heresy within the *Hototogisu* association. He remained constantly critical of the new *haiku* movement, but, at the same time, was dissatisfied with the dilettantism of the *Hototogisu* group. In 1944 he finally left the group and in 1946 founded a magazine called *Banryoku*, acting as its editor. He inherited the realism of Masaoka Shiki, deepening it to include the faithful depiction of every aspect of human nature, thereby endowing it with a new, typically modern awareness of the self. He published several collections of his verse, including *Chōshi, Hi no shima,* and *Ginga izen,* while his collections of criticism include *Buson shū,* and *Renga, Haikai, Haiku, Senryū.* He has also published many other works; his consistently progressive outlook has won him constant attention in *haiku* circles, in which he plays a leading role.

NAKAZAWA RINSEN (1878–1920)

An electrical engineer, he graduated from the Engineering Department of Tokyo Imperial University and managed the Nakazawa Electrical Company. He was also active as a critic, though less of literature than of human civilization in general, and showed a special fondness for philosophy and literature characterized by passion. His first collection of writings, entitled *Binkashū,* contains critical essays, translations, and reflections marked by sentimentalism. In time he came to concentrate upon the study of Russian literature, in a critical work entitled *Shizen shugi hanron* discussing the naturalist movement in France, Germany, and Russia. He also wrote on Tolstoy, James, and Bergson, and published a collection of essays on Romain Rolland and Eucken entitled *Hakai to kensetsu* and another collection on civilization entitled *Furuki bummei yori atarashiki bummei e.* He advocated nationalism and statism as a transitional step from individualism to internationalism. He also interested himself in matters pertaining to management and labor, producing such works as *Seigi to jiyū* and *Denshi-setsu kara mita sekai.* In addition he left two unpublished works, *Shinshakai no kiso* and *Arashi no mae.*

Natsume Sōseki (1867–1916)

Novelist. He was born in Tokyo. His early interest was in Chinese literature and *haiku* poetry, but he later took up the study of English literature and, after finishing the First High School, entered the English literature course of Tokyo Imperial University in 1890. In 1895, after graduation, he became a teacher of the Matsuyama Middle School in Shikoku and the following year moved to Kyushu to take a teaching position in the Fifth High School in Kumamoto. In 1900 he was sent by the government to England to continue his studies, where he remained until 1903. During his years abroad he developed a serious nervous disorder that continued to trouble him in the years after his return to Japan. He became a lecturer in both the First High School and Tokyo Imperial University, lecturing on literature and literary criticism. His lectures, later published in book form, demonstrate that he was an excellent scholar.

In 1905 he published his first work of fiction, *Wagahai wa neko de aru* (*I Am a Cat*), in the magazine *Hototogisu*, followed by such short stories as *Rondon-tō* and *Maboroshi no tate* and the novels *Botchan, Kusamakura,* and *Nihyaku tōka,* which established him as a creative writer of major importance. He also began to gather about him such promising young followers as Morita Sōhei, Omiya Toyotaka, Suzuki Miekichi, and Terada Torahiko. In 1907 he resigned his teaching positions and joined the staff of the *Asahi Shimbun,* determined to devote all his time to creative writing. Thereafter his works all appeared first in serialized form in the *Asahi.* In such works as *Kōfu, Sanshirō,* and *Sore kara,* the rather light satirical note and concern with manners that had characterized his early writings gave way to a deepening tone of seriousness and increasing attention to the problem of egoism. Though he advocated what he called "self-centeredness," he at the same time expressed repeated horror at the ugliness of excessive egoism, thus placing himself in clear opposition to the writers of the naturalist school, with their adulation of the self. It is not surprising, therefore, that the literary column of the *Asahi,* which Sōseki edited, came to be regarded as the stronghold of opposition to the naturalist movement.

In 1909 he made a trip to Korea and Manchuria, but the stomach trouble from which he had long suffered became greatly aggravated and the following year, while staying at the hot spring resort of Shuzenji, he vomited a large quantity of blood from a hemorrhaging ulcer and for a time was in extremely critical condition. Around this time he startled the world by rejecting an honorary PhD degree that the Ministry of Education wished to confer upon him. Resuming his literary work, he produced *Mon, Higan-sugi made,* and *Kōjin,* but during the writing of the last was troubled by a recurrence of his nervous disorder and by his stomach condition. In spite of this, he was able to complete two more novels, *Kokoro* and *Michigusa.* Around this time Akutagawa Ryūnosuke, Kume Masao, Matsuoka Yuzuru, and other young writers associated with the magazine *Shinshichō* began to study under him. He started work on a major novel entitled *Meian,* but in November of 1916 his stomach condition suddenly worsened and he died in the following month, leaving his last work uncompleted.

Sōseki began his writing career with a rather generous and detached attitude toward life, but this in time gave way to an attitude of greater seriousness that sought to come to grips squarely with the problems of man and society. His works evince a profound scepticism concerning the civilization of his time and concern themselves with the fate of the intellectual class, probing tenaciously into the problems of egoism and lack of human trust that characterize its members. After his near encounter with death at Shuzenji, his outlook on life became graver and more profound, resulting in novels marked by a new seriousness. In this late years he attempted to achieve a view of life that transcended egoism, as summed up in the motto *sokuten kyoshi,* "abandoning self and following Heaven." His works display a powerful moral concern such as cannot be found in the writings of the naturalists, and they have exerted a profound influence upon later literature. In addition, many important writers emerged from the group that studied under his direction.

Niwa Fumio (b. 1904)

Novelist. He was born in Mie Prefecture, the eldest son of a Buddhist priest. While a student in the Japanese literature course of Waseda University, he became acquainted with the novelist Ozaki Kazuo and determined to become a writer himself. With his graduation in 1929, however, he was obliged to return home and take up duties as a priest in the family temple. But the religious life was not to his liking, and he continued his efforts to become a writer. A work entitled *Hogaraka naru saisho,* which was published in the literary magazine *Shinseitō-ha,* won praise from the writers Nagai Tatsuo and Kawabata Yasunari, and with this as encouragement he went on to publish *Ayu* in the magazine *Bungei Shunjū* in 1932. Convinced of his chances for success, he left his home and his duties as a priest and went to Tokyo, where he published a number of works in rapid succession. The abandoned ways of the women of modern times is a dominant theme in his works, and he often drew upon an actual incident in his own life, describing how his mother left her husband and ran away from home when he was still a small child. During the war he produced works in a patriotic vein such as *Kaisen* and *Suien*, but with the end of the war he was able to return once more to themes that were more congenial to his nature, depicting characters who are blinded by passion and achieving a new level of artistic excellence. His most famous works are *Iyagarase no nenrei*, *Hachūrui*, *Nichinichi no haishin*, and *Kao*, which show him as in the main a genre novelist who is remarkable for the range of subjects he has dealt with. In 1965 he became a member of the Japan Art Academy and the following year he was elected president of the Japan Writers' Association. He publishes a literary magazine called *Bungakusha*.

Nogami Yaeko (b. 1885)

Novelist. She was born in Ōita Prefecture in Kyushu and at the age of fifteen entered the Meiji Women's School in Tokyo. She made the acquaintance of a student of the First High School named Nogami Toyoichirō, and through him was able to meet the novelist Natsume Sōseki and experience something of the atomosphere of literary endeavor surrounding him and his group. Upon graduation from Meiji Women's School she married Nogami Toyoichirō. She began to write fiction, and at the urging of Natsume Sōseki published a work entitled *Enishi* in the magazine *Hototogisu*, thus embarking upon a literary career.

Her early works are short stories in a realistic vein, but gradually she worked her way toward an English type intellectualism based upon moral attitudes, and eventually undertook in her works to deal with large-scale social themes. The works entitled *Kaishin-maru* and *Sumiko*, the latter dealing with the family of a man who is struggling to overcome the handicap of a physical disability, date from this period. In the early years of the Shōwa era, which began in 1926, she produced *Machiko*, a full-length novel describing in a dispassionate manner the efforts of the members of the younger generation to carry out some kind of social reform in a period of upheaval. She next embarked upon the writing of what in time was to become a six-part work entitled *Meiro*, but after publication of the first two parts, *Kuroi gyōretsu* and *Meiro*, the rising tide of ultranationalism in Japan obliged her to discontinue her work. She set off upon a tour of Europe and America, where she was caught by the outbreak of the Second World War.

After the war, she resumed work on *Meiro*, completing publication of the six-part work in 1956, twenty years after the first part was published. The novel examines the lives of the conscientious young people of the late thirties and early forties, and at the same time exhaustively describes the structure and various levels of the society of the period. Since then, though less prolific than in her earlier years, she has produced such outstanding works as *Hideyoshi to Rikyū* and *Kijo Sambō ki*. There is a certain excessive intellectualism and poverty of warmth and feeling in her work, and yet its spiritual freshness and underlying humanism have assured her a position as one of the most widely and perennially read of all modern Japanese women authors. In 1971 she was awarded a Cultural Medal.

Oᴄʜɪᴀɪ Nᴀᴏʙᴜᴍɪ (1861–1903)

Poet and scholar of Japanese literature. He was the son of an important official of the domain of the Date family, but later was adopted by Ochiai Naoaki. He pursued Chinese studies at the Nishō Gakusha in Tokyo under the historian Naitō Chisō and others and in 1882 entered the Japanese classics course of Tokyo Imperial University. In 1888 he published a long poem entitled *Kōjo Shiragiku no uta* in the *Tōyō Gakkai Zasshi*. Appearing at a time when the poetic world of Japan was in a state of great confusion, this poem, with its air of freshness and innovation, attracted wide attention and exercised a considerable influence upon the poets of the time. In 1889 Naobumi was appointed chief lecturer of the Japanese Language Institute, and he also taught at the First High School and Waseda University. He was at the same time associated with the novelist Mori Ōgai in the publication of the literary magazine *Shigarami Sōshi*. In collaboration with Hagino Yoshiyuki and others he edited and published the *Nihon bungaku zensho* and compiled an anthology of poetry entitled *Shinsen katen*, which provided fresh inspiration as a guide to the writing of poetry. In 1893 he formed a literary association known as the Asakasha, whose aim was to reform and infuse new life into *tanka* poetry, attracting about him such promising figures as Ōmachi Keigetsu, Shioi Ukō, Yosano Hiroshi, and Onoe Saishū. Though each of these men moved in his own particular direction, all worked under the leadership of Naobumi to create a new style of classical Japanese poetry. The Asakasha remained in existence for only two or three years, yet it is of great historical significance because of the literary talent that it served to engender. Naobumi also compiled such reference works as the *Nihon daibunten* in 1897 and *Kotoba no izumi*, published a collection of poems entitled *Kono hana*, and was active in many other fields of endeavor. Of particular note is the fact that he worked to develop a new style of classical Japanese diction to be used in the writing of poetry.

Okamoto Kidō (1872–1939)

Dramatist and novelist. He was born in Tokyo and finished Tokyo Prefectural First Middle School. In his youth he studies Chinese poetry under the direction of his father and took lessons in English from his uncle and an English student attached to the British legation. His language studies served a useful purpose in his selection of material as a creative writer, for they allowed him to read European works of fiction in the original. In 1890 he became a reporter for the *Tokyo Nichinichi Shimbun* and thereafter wrote dramatic criticism for it and other newspapers. In 1908 he wrote a work entitled *Ishin Zengo* for the kabuki group headed by Ichikawa Sadanji II and produced a number of dramas for the same group. His historical dramas such as *Shuzenji monogatari*, *Muromachi gosho*, *Sasaki Takatsuna*, *Toribeyama shinjū*, and *Banchō sarayashiki* are among the most outstanding of modern kabuki pieces and are still performed frequently today.

In his later years he came to dislike labored themes and artificial plots and instead produced many dramas marked by simplicity and homeyness and based upon incidents in the daily lives of the people, such as *Gonza to Sukejū* or *Sōma no Kinsan*. His dramatic writing is characterized by great skill and technical dexterity and succeeds in creating a world marked by romanticism and a sensibility that is distinctively Japanese. In 1937 he became a member of the Art Academy, the first dramatist to be so honored.

The world of Edo depicted in Kidō's works is distinguished by its remarkable degree of historical accuracy, indicating that he had a profound and detailed knowledge of the old city and its ways of life. In addition to plays, he also wrote works of popular fiction such as *Hanshichi torimonochō* and *Miura rōjin mukashibanashi*. His works of fiction run to over 100 stories and his dramatic works to 196 pieces, making him one of the most prolific as well as one of the most widely read writers of the time. Among his disciples were such figures as Nakano Minoru and Hōjō Hideji, who continue to be active in the literary world today.

Ōmachi Keigetsu (1869–1925)

Critic and poet. Born in Kōchi in Shikoku, he came to Tokyo in 1880 after the death of his father. Having completed the First High School, he entered the Japanese literature course of Tokyo Imperial University, graduating in 1896. He became a member of the editorial board of the literary magazine *Teikoku Bungaku*, publishing highly ornate prose pieces and works of modern poetry in its pages. He also joined with his former classmates at Tokyo University, Shioi Ukō and Takeshima Hagoromo, in writing a work entitled *Bibun imbun hana momiji*, which brought him considerable literary fame. For a time he taught at Hagawa Middle School in Izumo, but later became a member of the publishing company Hakubunkan and succeeded Takayama Chogyū as a literary critic for the magazine *Taiyō*, at the same time publishing critical pieces in other magazines such as *Bungei Kurabu* and *Chūgaku Sekai*. From 1909 to 1918 he was editor of a magazine called *Gakusei*, devoting all his attention to the moral and intellectual training of young people, but in his late years he developed a passion for travel, publishing pieces descriptive of his journeys in the magazine *Chūō Kōron*. He was particularly fond of the hotspring resort named Tsuta on the shore of Lake Towada, making it his official place of residence and dying there in 1925. Believing firmly that "style is the individual," he wrote in an elegant and flowing manner that reflected his own frankness and openness of disposition. As he grew older, he became increasingly unconventional in his ways, and his writings similarly take on a light and witty tone. His essays, and in particular his travel pieces, have a flavor not to be found in the work of any other writer. His complete works in twelve volumes have been published under the title *Ōmachi Keigetsu zenshū*.

Onoe Saishū (1876–1957)

Tanka poet, calligrapher, and scholar of Japanese literature. He was graduated in 1901 from the Japanese literature course of Tokyo Imperial University and the following year in conjunction with Kaneko Kun'en published a collection of verse entitled *Jokeishi*, the purpose of which was to oppose the romantic tendencies of the *Myōjō* school of poetry. Following this, he acted as editor for the poetry columns of the *Shinsei*, *Bunko*, *Chūō Kōron*, and other publications, and in 1905 formed a literary association known as the Ōbakosha, which produced such poets as Maeda Yūgure and Wakayama Bokusui. He taught at the Tokyo Women's Higher Normal School, Gakushūin, and Waseda University, and served as a member of the Nihon Shodōkai, Taitō Shoin, and other organizations, contributing to the promotion of Japanese poetry and calligraphy. In 1923 he received a PhD for his study of the Heian *kana* syllabary entitled *Heianchō sōgana no kenkyū*. In his later years he devoted all his time to the study of the Chinese novel.

He published a number of collections of poems including *Ginrei*, *Seiya*, *Eijitsu*, *Shirokimichi*, and *Sora no iro*, which are marked by elegance of tone and reflect his temperate and intellectual personality. Among his other works, the most famous is his translation of the poetry of Heine.

ORIGUCHI SHINOBU (1887–1953)

Scholar of folklore and Japanese classical literature and poet. He employed the pen name Shakuchōkū. He was born in Osaka and, upon completion of his lower education, entered Kokugakuin University in Tokyo in 1905. In 1909, while still a student, he made the acquaintance of such notable poets as Itō Sachio and Tsuchiya Bummei of the Negishi poetry society. After graduating from the Japanese literature course of Kokugakuin, he returned to Osaka and took a position as a middle school teacher. In 1911, when the eminent folklorist Yanagida Kunio founded the journal called *Kyōdo Kenkyū*, Origuchi submitted an article entitled *Sangō kōdan*. In this way he became acquainted with Yanagida and began folklore studies under him, acknowledging him as his lifelong teacher and making frequent contributions to the field. In 1914 he went to Tokyo and in 1917 became a member of the group of poets associated with the magazine entitled *Araragi*, publishing poems and critical pieces in its pages. Later, however, he became associated with another literary magazine entitled *Nikkō*, which advocated ideals in poetry that were in marked contrast to those of *Araragi*. Origuchi's poetry possesses a romantic tone that could not be encompassed within the strict realism demanded by the *Araragi* group, and his works, while dealing with the everday events of human life, are marked by a freshness of feeling and approach. It was these characteristics, as well as the originality of observation and interpretation that he developed in the course of his travels as a folklorist, that caused his poetry to develop along different lines from that of the *Araragi* group. In 1925 he published his first collection of poems entitled *Umi yama no aida*, which was followed later by the collections entitled *Haru no kotobure* and *Tōyama hiko*.

In addition to his activities as a poet, Origuchi taught at Kokugakuin and Keiō universities and produced a number of works on Japanese literature and folklore, including a modern language version of the *Man'yōshū*. His free-verse poems, which combine traditional poetic diction with a distinctly modern sensitivity, are preserved in a collection entitled *Kodai kan'aishū*; he also wrote a novel, *Shisha no sho*, and was active in other fields of literary endeavor.

Ōta Mizuho (1876–1955)

Tanka poet and scholar of Japanese literature. He was born in Nagano Prefecture; while still a student in Nagano Normal School he began contributing poems to the literary magazine *Bungakkai*. He became acquainted with Shimazaki Tōson and Kubota Utsubo, poets from the city of Komoro in Nagano, and in 1900 formed the association known as the *Kono hana kai* with the latter. His first collection of poems, *Tsuyu kusa*, was published in 1902, and in 1905 he published a collection entitled *Sanjō kojō*, written in collaboration with Shimagi Akahiko. In 1909 he married the poetess Shiga Mitsuko. He contributed to *Sōsaku*, and in 1911 took the lead in founding a new magazine called *Chōon*. In the following years he published critical essays and studies in this magazine, at the same time working to develop his own poetic style; he also produced a number of studies of the Japanese classics and classical poetic theory. In 1948 he became a member of the Japan Art Academy.

During the Meiji era he wrote works in a romantic manner, which combined the lofty tone of the *Man'yōshū* with the elegance of the *Kokinshū* and *Shin kokinshū* style. From the end of the Taishō and the beginning of the Shōwa eras, he turned to poetry with more of a *haiku* flavor and eventually developed his own distinctive style, a modernized version of the symbolistic verse of the medieval period.

His collections of poems include *Unchō*, *Fuyuna*, *Sagi*, *Raden*, and *Ryūō*, and he wrote works on poetic criticism such as *Tanka ritsugen*, *Waka haikai no shomondai*, *Kachō yoron*, and *Fūga hishō*, as well as numerous scholarly works.

Ōyama Tokujirō (1889–1963)

Tanka poet and scholar of Japanese literature. He was born in Kanazawa, Ishikawa Prefecture. At the age of fourteen he lost his right leg and was obliged to use a crutch for the rest of his life. At the age of twenty he went to Tokyo, where he worked for a number of literary magazines including

Wakayama Bokushui's *Sōsaku*, Maeda Yūgure's *Shika*, and Kubota Utsubo's *Kokumin Bungaku*. He had a wide acquaintance among novelists and poets; he was also a skilled painter and calligrapher and a noted classical scholar, devoting himself to the study of the *Man'yōshū* and producing studies of Ōtomo no Yakamochi and Saigyō. His first collection of verse, *Sasurai*, was published in 1912 when he was twenty-three; it was followed by eleven more volumes, including, notably, *Akaru tae*, *Manjushage*, and *Heimeicho*. His tenth collection, *Tofu no sugagomo* was given the award of the Japan Art Academy. His style is on the whole plain but illuminated with flashes of his highly personal character and depends less on realistic description than on evocation of atmosphere, creating a characteristic art that is deeply imbued with the Oriental tradition. Doubtless the influence of the classics, and of Saigyō in particular, is partly responsible. His poetic criticism is noted for its frankness and incisiveness.

OZAKI KŌYŌ (1868–1903)

Novelist. Born in Shiba, Tokyo. His father was a well-known carver in ivory. He attracted attention even in early childhood with his intelligence and quick wit. In 1883 he began studying at Tōdai Yobimon (later incorporated in Tokyo University). He began his literary activities around this time, founding an association known as the Bun'yūkai, "Friends of Literature." In 1885 he joined with Yamada Bimyō, Ishibashi Shian, and others in founding the association known as Ken'yūsha and established the circulating magazine *Garakuta Bunko*, based on contributions from members of the association. This is said to have been the first of the many coterie magazines that played such a large part in the history of modern Japanese literature. Ken'yūsha was joined in time by men such as Kawakami Bizan, Iwaya Sazanami, and Hirotsu Ryūro, and gradually its influence began to make itself more strongly felt. In 1885 he transferred to the Literature Department of Tokyo Imperial University, and *Garakuta Bunko* issued its first number printed by movable type. He himself contributed *Fūryū Kyōningyō*, written in a blend of the literary and colloquial styles devised by himself, which gradually won him a literary reputation. The period around the late 1880s and 1890s saw a cooling-off of the enthusiasm for Westernization and the first stirrings of nationalism; the neo-classical novels of the Ken'yūsha, matching the temper of the times as they did, were eagerly welcomed. *Ni'nin bikuni iro zange*, published in the same year, was the first work to bring him real fame, and his place in the literary world was established overnight. He joined the *Yomiuri Shimbun* at the same time, taking charge of the literary section, and over a period of twelve or so years thereafter published in its pages a series of works, each of which served to increase his fame still further. Some of his principal novels such as *Kyara-makura*, *Sannin-zuma*, and *Tajō takon*, as well as a large number of short stories, appeared first in the *yomiuri*. Around the time when he started work on his celebrated novel *Konjiki yasha*, his health began to deteriorate; in 1901 he suffered from a violent gastrointestinal disorder, and the following year was obliged to resign from the newspaper. In 1903, he died of stomach cancer at the early age of thirty-six.

At the time of the inception of *Garakuta Bunko*, Kōyō's approach resembled that of the writers of popular novelettes during the Edo period, but in time he developed a taste for Saikaku and began to study the realistic manner. The brilliant style that he thus developed, a compound of both classical and more popular elements, and the interest of his stories, with their abundance of incident, won his works an overwhelming popularity at the time, though there were those who criticized the flatness of his realism, a certain vulgarity of sensibility and moral outlook, and the commonplace quality of his observations. Despite such shortcomings, the influence he exerted on the world of literature—his untiring efforts to polish his style; his creation of the *de aru* style (Futabatei Shimei used *da* and Yamada Bimyō *desu*) that was to link the colloquial and literary styles and serve as the basis for much later literary style; the leading role that he played throughout in the Ken'yūsha group; and his role as teacher to younger writers such as Izumi Kyōka, Oguri Fūyō, and Tokuda Shūsei—earned him a lasting place in the literature of the Meiji period.

SAGANOYA OMURO (1863–1947)

Novelist and poet. He was born in Edo and grew up in the troubled times that accompanied the fall of the shogunate and the restoration of imperial rule, suffering considerable hardship. After graduating from the Russian language course of Tokyo Gaigo Gakkō, he made the acquaintance of the novelist Futabatei Shimei and became a disciple of the writer and critic Tsubouchi Shōyō. He worked for a time for the newspapers Tokyo *Asahi Shimbun* and *Kokumin Shimbun*, but resigned and thereafter made a living as a writer. His early works *Shusendo no hara* and *Hitoyogiri* are lightweight romances written very much under the influence of late Edo period fiction, but in time his works became more idealistic and deeply felt in tone, and during his finest period he was ranked beside such masters as Yamada Bimyō and Ozaki Kōyō. He was a Christian and was much influenced by Russian literature. His works include *Ajiki nashi, Kusare tamago, Hatsukoi,* and *Nozue no kiku,* of which the last two are regarded as his masterpieces. His poems, written in modern style and comprising nine chapters entitled *Itsumatekusa,* are pure in concept, but from the first showed a strong tendency to moralize, and as time went on they became increasingly didactic and allegorical in nature and lacking in romanticism. Eventually he abandoned literature, his career as a writer coming to an end in 1910.

Saisho Atsuko (1825–1900)

Poet. Born in Kyoto, at the age of nineteen she became the second wife of Saisho Atsuyuki, a samurai of the domain of Satsuma in Kyushu. After the death of her husband eight years later, she became an attendant to the heir of the lord of Satsuma, Shimazu Nariakira, but the child died at an early age. In 1875, at the recommendation of the poet Takasaki Masakaze, she became a member of the Imperial Household Department in Tokyo, serving as an instructor in traditional style poetry to the empress and empress dowager. She studied poetry under Chigusa Arikoto and Hatta Tomonori, followers of the Keien school, and during the early and middle parts of the Meiji period ranked beside Takasaki Masakaze as one of the most important poets of the school associated with the Imperial Household Ministry. Many of her poems deal with womanly virtues or the life of the court and are marked by a tone of refinement and modesty, as seen in her poem:

> In the quiet
> dawn moonlight
> I open the window—
> and see the dew
> gathered on bush clover leaves.

She also tried writing works on nontraditional themes, a practice that was becoming popular at the time, as in the following poem entitled *Clocks,* which comments on the uncertainty of human life:

> Even the hands
> of the devices that measure time
> sometimes linger, sometimes rush ahead—
> how much more so
> in the world of men!

Her poems are collected in the *Mitama no shitakusa* and *Mitama no shitakusa shūi*.

Saitō Mokichi (1882–1953)

Poet. He was the son of a farm family of Yamagata Prefecture. He went to Tokyo in 1896 and, after attending Kaisei Middle School there, entered the First High School and later the medical course of Tokyo Imperial University. In his high school days he was deeply impressed by a collection of poems by Masaoka Shiki published posthumously and entitled *Take no sato uta* and determined to become a poet himself. The following year, when he entered Tokyo University, he began to study poetry under Itō Sachio, contributing poems to *Ashibi*, a *tanka* magazine of which Itō was editor. In 1916 he was adopted into his wife's family and assumed the surname Saitō. He went to Europe in 1921 for a period of study, and after his return four years later until 1948 he acted as director of the Aoyama Mental Hospital, an institution established earlier by his wife's family.

When the magazine *Araragi* was founded, he joined Itō Sachio in becoming one of its contributors, and after Itō's death he and Shimagi Akahiko became the leaders of the group that centered about the magazine. He advocated the writing of poetry that is based upon close observation of the real world, and himself wrote poems of this type that are highly modern in subject and feeling, which soon distinguished him as the leading writer of Japanese traditional style verse. His first collection of poems, published in 1913 and entitled *Shakkō*, contains works marked by passionate lyricism and a feeling of fresh and intense vitality. The skill with which the writer has succeeded in harmonizing modern-day sensibility with the demands of the traditional *tanka* form distinguishes him as one of the finest writers of modern *tanka* poetry and amply explains why he exercised such a wide influence in the literary world of the time. In his later poetry, the lyrical element takes on a quieter tone and, as seen in his *Aratama*, there is a deepening objectivity. In 1940 he completed his great five-volume study of the *Man'yōshū* poet Kakinomoto no Hitomaro, for which he was awarded the Imperial Academy prize. In 1951 he received the Order of Culture.

Sasakawa Rimpū (1870–1949)

Critic, art historian, and *haiku* poet. He was born in the Kanda district of

Tokyo and graduated from the Japanese history course of Tokyo Imperial University. He acted as editor of the magazine *Teikoku Bungaku* and was a contemporary of such men as Takayama Chogyū and Anezaki Chōfū. His works of literary and art criticism include the *Shina shōsetsu gikyoku shōshi* and *Nihon kaiga-shi*, and in 1924 he was awarded the doctorate for his study entitled *Higashiyama jidai no bijutsu*. He began writing *haiku* during his student days and joined with Ōno Shachiku, Sassa Seisetsu, and others to form the Tsukuba-kai, an association to encourage the writing of *haiku*. His other writings include a historical study entitled *Namboku seitō-ron* and a serial novel *Nichiren Shōnin*. He also joined with Izumi Kyōka and others to form the Bungei Kakushin-kai, an association that opposed literary naturalism, and organized the Masumi-kai to preserve the type of late Edo period *jōruri* singing known as *katō-bushi*. He was well known as a collector of editions of popular fiction of the Edo period.

SASAKI NOBUTSUNA (1872–1963)

Poet and poetry critic. He was the eldest son of the scholar of Japanese studies Sasaki Hirotsuna. He went to Tokyo at the age of nine and began studying the writing of traditional style verse under Takasaki Masakaze. At the age of twelve he entered the library division of the Japanese classics course of Tokyo Imperial University and after his graduation at sixteen devoted himself to the writing and study of *waka*. From 1890 on he cooperated with his father in compiling a two-volume work entitled *Nihon kagaku zensho*. After the Sino-Japanese War, when changes and innovations were taking place in the Japanese poetry world, he joined with Ochiai Naobumi, Yosano Tekkan, and Masaoka Shiki in endeavoring to promote the new styles. He headed the association known as the Chikuhaku-kai, published a magazine called *Kokoro no Hana*, and attracted a large number of disciples. In 1903 he published a collection of his poems, the *Omoigusa*, and at the age of thirty-two became a lecturer at Tokyo University, giving lectures on the *Man'yōshū* and on the history of Japanese poetic theory and *waka* poetry. At this time he devoted all his attention to such studies, and in the years between 1897 and 1915 published such scholarly works as the *Shoku Nihon kagaku-shi* in 12 volumes, the *Kagaku ronsō*, *Nihon kagaku-shi*, and *Waka-shi no kenkyū*. In recognition of the latter two works he was awarded a prize by the Japan Academy. Following this, he determined to compile a collated edition of the *Man'yōshū* and, with the cooperation of such scholars as Hashimoto Shinkichi, Takeda Yūkichi, and Hisamatsu Sen'ichi, he carried out the compilation and publication of the *Kōhon Man'yōshū* in 25 volumes. In 1920 he was made a member of the Japan Academy, and in 1923 received a Cultural Medal and was made a member of the Japan Art Academy.

His accomplishments fall into two categories, the scholarly and the artistic. As a scholar he was important first for his studies of the *Man'yōshū*, second for his researches in the history of Japanese poetic theory and *waka* poetry, and third for his efforts in arranging for reproductions of old manuscripts of the *Man'yōshū* and other classics. He investigated every aspect of the *Man'yōshū* and laid the foundation upon which all later studies of the work have been based, as well as cooperating with other scholars in the preparation of English, German, and Chinese translations of the anthology. In addition, his *Nihon kagaku-shi*, which is based upon the lectures he delivered at Tokyo University, contains systematic discussions of all the anthologies and works on poetic theory dating from the middle and early modern periods of Japanese history.

His own poems are marked by freshness, grace, and deep feeling, reflecting his conviction that poetry should be "the flowering of the heart" and "the religion of beauty." He had many disciples, encouraging each to develop his own distinctive style; among the more famous are such men and women as Kinoshita Rigen, Kawada Jun, Ishikure Chimata, and Kujō Takeko.

SASSA SEISETSU (1872–1917)

Scholar of Japanese literature and *haiku* poet. He was born in Kyoto. In 1896 he graduated from the Japanese literature course of Tokyo Imperial University. During his student years he wrote his first work on the history of *haiku* entitled *Rempai shōshi*, which was published serially in the periodical *Teikoku Bungaku*. He also wrote works of fiction such as *Shimbun-uri* and *Isōrō nikki*. After serving as a teacher in the Second High School in Sendai and the Yamaguchi High School, he moved to Tokyo in 1901, founded the magazine *Bungeikai*, and became very active as a critic. In 1906 he became a lecturer at the Tokyo Higher Normal School and also taught at Tokyo and Waseda universities. He was a man of extremely varied activities. In 1894 he joined with Sasagawa Rimpū and others in forming an association called the Tsukuba-kai to encourage *haiku* writing and in particular to oppose the school of *haiku* writers known as the Nihon-ha. From this association emerged such *haiku* scholars as Ōno Shachiku and Nunami Keion. Seisetsu, in addition to producing various studies of *haiku*, also published commentaries and studies on works of Edo period literature, devoting particular attention to research on the types of songs known as *kouta* and *jōruri*. His most important works are probably his *Zokkyoku hyōshaku* and *Kinsei kokubungaku-shi*, and he also produced pioneer studies on the subject of rhetoric such as his *Shūjihō kōwa*. In all, he made a very great contribution both as a teacher and a scholar. His most important *haiku* were written in his college days and are characterized by the unusually large number of works that deal with daily human activities.

SATOMI TON (b. 1888)

Novelist. His eldest brother was the novelist Arishima Takeo and his second eldest brother the writer and Western style painter Arishima Ikuma. While a student at the Gakushūin he became acquainted with Shiga Naoya, who was to exercise a profound influence upon him for much of his life. In 1909 he entered the English literature course of Tokyo Imperial University but, determined to become a writer, he withdrew shortly after. The following year he became associated with the newly-founded magazine *Shirakaba*, publishing his first work entitled *Otomisan*. In 1911 he wrote *Irumagawa* for the magazine *Zamboa* and in 1913 published *Kimi to watakushi to* in *Shirakaba*, but thereafter he dissociated himself from *Shirakaba*, which at the time was becoming increasingly humanistic in tone. In 1915 he published *Osoi hatsukoi* in the *Chūō Kōron* magazine, and the following year wrote *Zenshin akushin*. From around this time until the Kantō earthquake in 1923 was his most productive period.

His works take up the theme of unrestrained affirmation of the self in all its uniqueness of temperament. In 1917 he wrote *Kōfukujin*, which further developed this theme of self-affirmation. His thought has something in common with that of Mushanokōji Saneatsu, who likewise stresses the importance of the life and self of the individual. But Satomi's concept of self, unlike that of Mushanokōji, emphasizes the need for free expression of the emotions and is based upon the ideals of self-realization and sincerity. In addition to his short stories, he has written a number of full-length novels, such as *Kirihata, Tajō busshin*, and *Anjō-ke no kyōdai*. *Tajō busshin*, perhaps his most outstanding work, is particularly important for its embodiment of the concept of *magokoro* (sincerity). *Gokuraku tombo*, published in 1961, is the most noteworthy of his postwar writings.

Senke Motomaro (1888–1948)

Poet. He was born in Tokyo, the son of a baron who held various distinguished posts such as metropolitan governor and minister of justice. He began to write *haiku* and *tanka* around the age of sixteen or seventeen and also showed an interest in the novel and the theater. In 1913 he founded the coterie magazine *Terracotta*. The extreme praise he accorded Mushanokōji Saneatsu's *Seken shirazu* brought him into contact with the *Shirakaba* movement in which Mushanokōji figured so prominently. He himself wrote large quantities of verse under the strong influence of the *"Shirakaba* spirit,"* with its philanthropy, respect for the individual, and general good will, and of the literary outlook of Mushanokōji Saneatsu, for whom he had particular respect. He also worshiped Gogh, Beethoven, Dostoevsky, and Whitman, and gave expression to their type of humanistic sentiments in plain, readily understandable verse. His first collection, *Jibun wa mita,* appeared in 1918. His work, product of a great sincerity of feeling, conveys a suggestion of an essentially innocent soul and breathes a relaxed manner and an incomparable healthiness of outlook. His many other collections include *Niji, Mugi, Enten,* and *Natsukusa.*

Shiga Mitsuko (b. 1885)

Poet. She was born in Nagano Prefecture and graduated from the Nagano Normal School and Tokyo Women's Higher Normal School. During her years at normal school she became familiar with *Myōjō,* the organ of the New Poetry Society, and in 1903 she became acquainted with the poet Ōta Mizuho, joined the society known as the Kono-hana-kai, which he founded with Kubota Utsubo and others, and in 1909 became his wife. In 1916, when Ōta organized the Chōon-kai, she became a member, and after Ōta's death she and her adopted son Ōta Seikyū acted as the leaders of the group. As the most eminent of the elder women poets, she was chosen to serve from 1957 to 1966 as a judge in the imperial poetry contest held at the beginning of each year. Her collections of verse include *Fuji no mi, Asazuki,* and *Asaginu,* and show a gradual progression from a style marked by grace and pure lyricism to one of simplicity and realism. She has published a collection of essays entitled *Waka sakusha no tame ni,* and in conjunction with her husband produced such works as *Shin kokinshū meika hyōshaku, Dentō to gendai waka, Kamakura zakki,* and *Yuku kokoro kaeru kokoro.* The following is one of her best-known poems:

Even my black hair
softly scented;
on an evening when
cherries bloom,
coming home from the bath.

Shiga Naoya (1883–1971)

Novelist. He attended the elementary, middle, and high school of the Gakushūin. For some seven years, beginning in 1900, he received instruction from the Christian leader Uchimura Kanzō, by whom he was greatly influenced. In 1906 he entered the English literature course of Tokyo Imperial University, and around this time, determined to become a writer, produced his first stories, *Aru asa, Abashiri made, Hayao no imōto, Araginu,* and others. In 1908 he withdrew from college and two years later joined with Arishima Takeo, Mushanokōji Saneatsu, and others in founding the literary magazine *Shirakaba,* embarking on a career as a writer. But his father opposed his ambitions in this direction, and further discord developed between them over the question of his marriage. The period from 1910 on saw the production of his first important works, *Kamisori, Ōtsu Junkichi, Seibee to hyōtan,* and others. In 1912, at the age of twenty-nine, he left home, living successively in Onomichi, Matsue, Kyoto, and other cities, but in 1917 the differences between him and his father were finally resolved. In the same year he published *Kinosaki nite, Akanishi Kakita,* and other stories, as well as the novel *Wakai.* Around thirty-five at the time, he was gradually outgrowing his youthful rebelliousness and, while continuing to assert an attitude of positive egoism, was developing a more moderate view of life and moving in the direction of the psychological novel, as may be seen in his work *Kōjinbutsu no fūfu.* In 1922 the first half of what was to be his finest work, *Anya kōro,* was published. From this period on his literary output declined. He retained a position of importance in the literary world, but with the beginning of the Shōwa era in 1926 attention focused upon the new proletarian writers who were coming to the fore. In 1932-33 he published *Manreki akae, Taifū,* and other stories, and in 1937 brought out the second part of *Anya kōro,* thus completing his only full-length novel, the writing of which had occupied him from the ages of twenty-nine to fifty-four.

In the postwar period he took almost no part in literary activities, but continued to be respected as an elderly writer of established reputation. It is generally conceded that he brought the short story form to a level of perfection it had never known before in Japanese literature, and his skill in expression and thoroughly realistic style for a time completely dominated the literary scene and exerted a powerful influence upon other writers of the period. In 1949 he was awarded a Cultural Medal.

SHIMAGI AKAHIKO (1876–1926)

Poet. His first published work was a volume entitled *Sanjō kōjō*, which he wrote in conjunction with Ōta Mizuho, a friend and fellow student at the Nagano Normal School; Ōta contributed poems in *tanka* form to the volume, while Akahiko contributed works in the *shintaishi* or "new style verse" form. Akahiko taught for a time at a primary school in Nagano and held other positions such as school principal. During this period, he became an admirer of the poetic style associated with the Negishi Tanka Society, organized in 1889 by Masaoka Shiki, and eventually became a student under Itō Sachio, one of Shiki's most important disciples. In 1914 Akahiko went to Tokyo and devoted all his time to poetry, succeeding Nagatsuka Takashi as editor of the magazine *Araragi*, the organ for the poets of the Negishi group. He thus came to be regarded as one of the principal members of the *Araragi* school, as the group was known. Though his literary interests were very wide, he concentrated upon the *tanka* form. Like Saitō Mokichi, he emphasized realism in *tanka*, stressing the need for total mental concentration when writing poetry and the types of training required to achieve such concentration, often setting forth his opinions in highly moralistic terms. In his collection of poems entitled *Bareisho no hana* he employed a very simple and almost artless style, but his *Kiribi* and *Hio* showed a broadening of scope and experimentation with a variety of styles. In his *Taikyoshū* he concentrated entirely upon achieving greater depth in his works. A final collection of poems entitled *Shiinshū* was published posthumously.

SHIMAMURA HŌGETSU (1871–1918)

Critic, aesthetician, and leader of the *shingeki* drama movement. He lost both parents at an early age and faced considerable difficulty in acquiring an education, but he was assisted by a district attorney named Shimamura Bunkō and eventually was able to enter Waseda University (known at that time as Tokyo Semmon Daigaku). His scholastic record was outstanding, and he seems to have profitted particularly from the instruction that he received in literature from Tsubouchi Shōyō and in philosophy and aesthetics from Ōnishi Sōzan. His graduation thesis, entitled *Shimbi-teki ishiki no seishitsu wo ronzu*, was published in the journal *Waseda Bungaku*. Following his graduation he published a number of outstanding works of criticism and became known as a meticulous and thorough scholar and critic. Among these was a work on rhetoric, *Shinbijigaku*, which was of epochal importance in its field at that time.

In 1902 he went to Europe for further study, attending Oxford and Berlin University and pursuing such subjects as aesthetics, psychology, and the history of art. At the same time he became an avid theater-goer and acquired the foundation in understanding and appreciation of drama that was to serve him later in his role as leader of the Shingeki. He returned to Japan in 1905 and became a lecturer at Waseda, at the same time resuming his activities as a critic of the arts. He revived publication of the journal *Waseda Bungaku*, and in the first issue of the new series published a lengthy essay entitled *Torawaretaru bungei*, in which he urged that the arts be freed from their bondage to intellectualism and returned to the realm of emotion. He worked vigorously to promote the movement toward naturalism in Japan, his most important statements on the subject being his *Bungeijō no shizenshugi* and *Shizenshugi no kachi*, both published in 1908. As a result of his efforts, naturalism became the dominant trend of the time, and a new realism was introduced into the arts in Japan. At the same time his writings entitle him to be regarded as the first truly modern critic of the arts in Japan. In addition, he played an important role in encouraging the new dramatic movement known as Shingeki, laboring to lend freshness and vigor to the movement and to improve the quality of the works being presented, as well as to transform it into a truly popular theater rather than one appealing only to a small group of intellectuals. For all these varied accomplishments he deserves to be regarded as one of the major figures in the cultural history of the period.

Shioi Ukō (1869–1913)

Poet and scholar of Japanese literature. He was born in Hyōgo Prefecture and graduated from the Japanese literature course of Tokyo Imperial University. He taught at Japan Women's University and Nara Women's Higher Normal School, where he was respected by his students for his earnestness and sincerity. During his student days at Tokyo University, he became a member of the Asakasha, a poetry society headed by Ochiai

Naobumi, and in 1894 published a translation of Scott's *The Lady of the Lake* done into the five-and-seven-syllable rhythms of classical Japanese literature, a translation that won wide recognition for its grace and brilliance. In the journal *Teikoku Bungaku* he published such original poems as *Miyama no bijin* and *Iso no fuetake*, which, cast in a pure and elegant style and marked by a mastery of classical diction, established his reputation as the leading writer of poetry in the archaic manner. His works are contained in the *Hana momiji*, a collection that he authored in conjunction with Ōmachi Keigetsu and Takeshima Hagoromo, and in other collections such as *Kono hana* and *Ankō soei*. He produced scholarly works on Japanese literature, such as the *Shin kokinwakashū hyōshaku* and *Kagawa Kageki*, and also wrote poetry in *waka* form, as well as biographies of famous women, historical anecdotes, and miscellaneous essays. After his death a collection of his works edited by Takeshima Matajirō and Ōmachi Keigetsu was published under the title *Ukō zenshū*.

Shimazaki Tōson (1872–1943)

Poet and novelist. He was born into an old family that had run a *honjin* (officially recognized inn for exalted personages), acted as wholesale merchants, and served as *shōya* (village heads responsible to the local lord) at Magome on the old Kiso Highway. In his youth he studied works such as the *Classic of Filial Piety* and the *Analects* with his father, Masaki, who was a student of *kokugaku*. Going to Tokyo in 1881, he soon came into contant with Christianity and Western literature and ideas, by which he was greatly impressed. At the same time, he became acquainted with the Japanese classics and began to evolve literary ideas of his own. Following graduation from Meiji Gakuin in 1891, he contributed a translation to a magazine, *Jogaku Zasshi*, which brought him into contact with Kitamura Tōkoku. In 1893 he had a hand in the founding of the magazine *Bungakkai*, chief champion of the romantic movement in Japanese literature of the day, but received a profound shock from the suicide of his associate Tōkoku the following year.

Around 1896 he made marked improvements in the verse he was composing and published his first collection, entitled *Wakana shū*. It was followed by other collections, *Hitoha-bune*, *Natsukusa*, and *Rakubai shū*. With these collections, all published within somewhat less than five years, Tōson firmly established the "new form" verse (*shintaishi*) in the literary world and was to have an epoch-making influence on poetry in modern Japan. Through his verse he gave Japanese poets for the first time a means other than the classical verse forms of conveying their emotions as Japanese. In time, Tōson came under the influence of the naturalism of French, Russian, and German literature and gradually began to turn from poetry to prose. He wrote a series of short stories entitled *Chikumakahan no monogatari*, and shortly afterwards began writing *Hakai*, in which he embodied his own inner conflicts personalized in the character of a schoolteacher from the "outcast" *burakumin* class; he completed the work in 1906. This work, the first true naturalist novel in Japanese literature, at once gave him a place in the front rank of Japanese letters. Next he wrote *Haru* and *Ie*, which have something of the nature of autobiographical novels. The latter, the model for which was provided by the family into which his younger sister married, is a realistic depiction of the gradual decline of an old feudalistic family and became one of the representative works of naturalist literature in Japan. In 1913 he went to France and was still there when the First World War broke out. In 1919 he published *Shinsei*, in which he boldly confessed sexual relationship with his young niece in an attempt to achieve a kind of rebirth in middle age. During the same period he also published collections of children's stories such as *Furusato* and *Osana monogatari*. In 1929 he began publication of *Yoake mae*, in which his father's life provided the framework for a vast historical novel portraying the coming into being of modern Japan. The next seven years were devoted to the completion of this work, which was to become one of the monumental works of modern Japanese literature. He died in 1943, leaving half-finished another full-length novel. *Tōhō no kon*.

Susukida Kyūkin (1877–1945)

Poet and essayist. Born in Okayama Prefecture; went to Tokyo in 1894, where he worked as assistant teacher at a school of Chinese studies, at the same time continuing his own education by frequenting the Ueno Library and avidly reading Japanese, Chinese, and Western works alike. A collection of thirteen pieces entitled *Hanamitsu ni shite kakurete miegatashi* in the monthly *Shincho Gekkan* in 1897 won praise from Shimamura Hōgetsu and others, but his health was poor and life continued to be a struggle for him. In 1899 his *Botekishū* won favorable notice. It was followed by a second collection, *Yuku haru*, and by the time his well-known collection *Kōson juka ni tachita* appeared, he ranked with Kambara Ariake as leader of the world of poetry, since Shimazaki Tōson had by this time ceased writing. Of a weak constitution, he led the life of a semi-invalid, in which his friendship with

Tsunashima Ryōsen played a large part. The isolated, introverted frame of mind in which his days were passed is reflected in many of the poems of his collection *Nijūgo-gen*. With his collection *Hakuyōkyū*, which contains his finest work, he turned his attention to symbolist poetry. Deservedly famous are two particular pieces, *Aa Yamato ni shi aramashikaba*, which deals with nature and history in the Yamato district, and *Bōkyō no uta*, which deals with the four seasons in Kyoto. The lengthy lyrical poem entitled *Katsuragi no kami* (1906) marked the peak of his poetic activity; from then on he showed a rapid decline in vigor and poetic inspiration.

In 1912 he joined the Osaka *Mainichi Shimbun* newspaper. His regular column, *Chabanashi*, won a wide readership, and from then on he worked principally as an essayist. He displayed considerable ability as a newspaperman and rose to be chief of the Arts and Literature section, but the progress of Parkinson's disease forced him to retire in 1923. Thereafter he continued to dictate essays of a serenely subjective nature until his death in autumn of the year in which World War II ended. He was known as a man of wisdom, discretion, and integrity. The severity with which he treated himself was matched by great tolerance and kindness in dealing with others, and his poetic style, always maintaining a certain propriety, was firmly rooted in his personality. As a poet, he began by following the romanticism typified by Shimazaki Tōson, but eventually developed into a Kōtō-ha poet midway between that school and the symbolism of Kambara Ariake, sharing with Ariake the distinction of having developed the *bungo teikeishi*, a type of poetry employing classical Japanese and fixed rhythmical patterns but unrestricted in length. As an essayist, too, his wide learning and his skill with words earned him a special place in Taishō and Shōwa literature.

TAKAHAMA KYOSHI (1874–1959)

Haiku poet and novelist. He was born in Matsuyama in Ehime Prefecture in Shikoku. During his days in Iyo Middle School, he was a fellow student of Kawahigashi Hekigotō, who was also destined to become famous as a writer of *haiku*. In 1891 he made the acquaintance of the well-known *haiku* poet Masaoka Shiki and began to write *haiku* himself. In 1892 he entered the Third High School in Kyoto. His ambition at this time was to become a novelist, but at the urging of Shiki he continued to write a considerable number of *haiku*, and when the movement to reform the writing of *haiku* that Shiki launched in 1892 began to gain momentum, Kyoshi and Hekigotō, along with Shiki himself, came to prominence.

In 1895 Kyoshi moved to Tokyo. The following year he began experimenting intensely in the writing of *haiku* that do not conform to the traditional 5-7-5 syllable pattern, gaining attention for works of the kind that Shiki described as "objective descriptions of human affairs," or "momentary *haiku*," of which the following are examples:

> The angry waves bite the rocks;
> am I too a god
> this misty night?

> On the hat
> stolen from the scarecrow
> fierce rain beats down.

In 1898 he took over the editorship of the monthly literary magazine *Hototogisu*, which Shiki had founded the previous year, and the magazine remained the center of Kyoshi's literary activities during the years that followed, playing a vital role in the development of *haiku* during the late Meiji, Taishō, and Shōwa eras. In addition, the work entitled *Asakusadera no kusagusa*, which he published serially in the magazine, constituted the first of what he called *shaseibun*, "sketch pieces," an attempt to employ in literature the technique used by the Western style painter in sketching.

Around 1907 a new movement came to the fore in the *haiku* world and for a while swept all other styles from the scene, but at this time Kyoshi was engrossed almost entirely in the writing of "sketch pieces" or works of fiction. It was only in the early years of the Taishō era, which began in 1912, that he returned to the writing of *haiku*, working through the magazine *Hototogisu* to combat the new movement headed by Kawahigashi Hekigotō and others and seeking to redirect the writing of *haiku* into channels he felt to be more appropriate to it. The outcome of these efforts was the work entitled *Susumu beki haiku no michi* ("The Proper Direction for Haiku"), which Kyoshi published in 1918. At this time Kyoshi was working to develop the talents of such young writers as Murakami Kijō and Iida Dakotsu, and under his guidance *Hototogisu* came to be a major influence in the *haiku* world. In the latter years of the Taishō era, the style advocated by Kyoshi and others of the *Hototogisu* group continued to gain ever wider acceptance, and the magazine reached its peak of prominence, now numbering among its followers such poets as Mizuhara Shūōshi, Yamaguchi Seishi, and Kawabata Bōsha. However, with the beginning of the Shōwa era in 1926, a new movement arose among *haiku* writers that was sharply critical of the *Hototogisu* style, though it was largely led by writers such as Mizuhara Shūōshi, who had previously been associated with the *Hototogisu* group.

Thus, although this new style came in time to dominate the scene, it was in a sense an outgrowth of the *Hototogisu* movement. In the end, it was Kyoshi's tolerant leadership that provided the most important moving force for the high degree of artistic excellence attained by the *haiku* writing of the Taishō and Shōwa eras.

Kyoshi followed Shiki in advocating objective realism in the writing of *haiku*, and early in the Shōwa era propounded his theory of *kachō fūeiron* or "poeticizing on nature," in which he stressed the need for the poet to contemplate nature exactly as it is. His *haiku* are contained in the *Kyoshi kushū* and *Ku nikki*, while his works of fiction include *Haikaishi* and *Fūryū sempō*.

Takami Jun (1907–1965)

Novelist. He was born in Fukui Prefecture but almost immediately moved to Tokyo with his mother and grandmother, where he attended the First Middle School and First High School before entering the English Literature Department of Tokyo University in 1927. The period around the time of his graduation from university in 1930 saw the rise of such avant-garde movements as the Neo-Sensationalists and proletarian literature, as well as the suicide of novelist Akutagawa Ryūnosuke; the turbulent literary activity stimulated his own literary aspirations and led him—sensitive child of his age that he was—to toy with dadaism, Marxism, anarchism, and other such literary trends. He became a member of the Japan League of Proletarian Authors and at the same time assisted in the campaigns of the Japan Metal Workers Union, for which he was arrested in 1933. His subsequent political apostasy and the breakdown of his family life left scars, but he in time recovered and launched the coterie magazine *Higoyomi*, which was later joined by Tamiya Torahiko and Enchi Fumiko. In 1935 he began serialization of *Kokyū wasureubeki* in the same magazine and thereby won recognition as a promising young writer. From 1939 to 1940 he serialized *Ika naru hoshi no shita ni*, a full-length novel that records with poetic insight the joys and tribulations of the ordinary people in wartime society. During World War II he went to the front in Burma and central China as a member of the press corps. After the war, he developed an interest in poetry; he began to contribute to the poetry magazine *Nihon Miraiha* and in 1947 published a collection of his verse entitled *Jumokuha*. In 1958 he was appointed Director of the Japan P.E.N. Club, in which capacity he visited the Soviet Union. In the period 1959–63 he completed the first part of *Gekiryū*, and in 1960–63

Iya na kanji. In 1962 he joined with Itō Hitoshi, Odagiri Susumu, and others in preparing the foundation of a Nihon Kindai Bungaku-kan (Museum of Modern Japanese Literature). He died of cancer of the esophagus the day after work was started on the building. The poems that he wrote on his sickbed have a profound sincerity that is deeply moving and were awarded the Noma Literary Prize, published under the title *Shi no fuchi yori.*

Faced with the spiritual turmoil affecting the literary world following the collapse of the left-wing literary movement, he wrote a piece entitled *Byōsha no ushiro ni nete irarenai* ("Don't Take Refuge Behind Description"), in which he proposed a new methodology, and himself evolved a characteristic discursive narrative style. His novels give memorable human portraits in this characteristic style.

TAKASAKI MASAKAZE (1836–1912)

A samurai of the fief of Satsuma in Kyushu, he played an active role in the Meiji Restoration. In 1868 he served as a staff officer under the commander of the imperial forces and was later appointed a lesser counselor and sent on an inspection tour of Europe and America. He studied the writing of traditional Japanese verse under Hatta Tomonori, a follower of the Keien-ha, the leading school of poetry in the late Edo period. In 1876 he was appointed a member of the *outadokoro*, the Bureau of Poetry in the Imperial Household Ministry, which had been revived by the Emperor Meiji, and in 1886 he was made chief of the bureau. In 1887 he was created a baron and in 1895 was appointed a councilor of the *sūmitsuin*, or Privy Council. He was the leader of the movement to revive the Keien school of poetry in Meiji times and served as instructor in poetry to the Emperor Meiji. He carried on the orthodox traditions of the Keien school, and his style is marked by the grace and refinement typical of the *Kokinshū*, which the Keien school took as its ideal. Through his position as head of the Imperial Bureau of Poetry, he played an important part in training poets of the younger generation. The following is typical of his work:

> Only the peak of Fuji
> left in the sky—
> over the long road to Azuma,
> where cocks crow,
> drift banks of mist.

His works include the *Utagatari*, *Shinkō hikki*, and *Tazugane shū*.

TAKAYAMA CHOGYŪ (1871–1902)

Critic and thinker. He was born in Yamagata Prefecture. From the time he was a middle school student he won praise for his literary ability and while still a student in high school he founded a magazine called *Bungeikai Zasshi* and published several articles in it. In 1893 he entered the philosophy course of Tokyo Imperial University. The following year, his novel *Takiguchi nyūdō* won the prize in a competition sponsored by the *Yomiuri Shimbun* newspaper, and he gained recognition as a writer. In 1895 he became literary critic for the magazine *Taiyō*. Upon his graduation from Tokyo University he took a position as a teacher in the Second High School, but in 1897 returned to his former job as literary critic for *Taiyō*. Around this time he joined Inoue Tetsujirō and others in advocating nationalism, setting forth his arguments with great vigor and eloquence. He attacked both Christianity and Buddhism on the basis of their foreign origin, engaged in debate with the critic Tsubouchi Shōyō on questions relating to historical drama and painting, and was active in other ways on the intellectual scene. In 1901 ill health forced him to abandon plans for studying abroad. Around this time his earlier nationalism began to give way to individualism, and in a series of writings, such as *Biteki seikatsu wo ronzu*, he espoused romanticism and a satisfaction with the native instincts of the individual, at the same time exerting considerable influence over the romantic movement that was coming to prominence at the time. In his last years he embraced the philosophy of Nietzsche, moving from individualism to the worship of genius, and expressed particular veneration for the Japanese Buddhist leader Nichiren. He was a man of highly emotional temper, and the frequent shifts in his philosophical position inevitably led to certain contradictions and illogicalities in his thinking. But the passionate and unequivocal nature of his pronouncements and his sensitivity to the trend of the times, along with his sonorous prose style, captured the hearts of his readers, and as a result his writings exercised a profound influence upon the literature and thinking of the period. The sudden popularity enjoyed by the romantic movement at this time owed much to his efforts. His scholarly works include *Sekai bummei-shi, Ronrigaku,* and *Kinsei bigaku.*

TAKESHIMA HAGOROMO (1872–1967)

Poet. He was born in Tokyo and graduated from the Japanese literature course of Tokyo Imperial University. He held a teaching position at Tokyo

University of Music and later at Japan Women's University. He was known along with Shioi Ukō and Ōmachi Keigetsu as a member of the Akamon-ha, or Tokyo University school of poetry, and was also famous as a prose stylist. He cooperated with the other two poets mentioned above in producing a collection of verse entitled *Hana momiji*. He wrote such works as *Shinsen eikahō* and *Kokka hyōshaku* and the collections of verse and prose entitled *Bibun imbun, Geishō bigin,* and *Kamo no Mabuchi,* and he also wrote the lyrics for the song *Tennen no bi*. He was a member of the Bureau of Poetry in the Imperial Household Ministry. In style his works do not venture beyond the traditional.

Tanaka Ōdō (1867–1932)

Philosopher and critic. He went to America in 1889 and studied at the University of Chicago, where he was profoundly influenced by John Dewey. While embracing pragmatism, however, he combined it with a strong emphasis upon symbolism to form a unique philosophy of his own. After his return to Japan, he devoted most of his time to the propagation of this new philosophy. The basis of the philosophy is a critical spirit deriving from a combination of functionalism and symbolism, and he employed it to attack the naturalism that was so popular in the late years of the Meiji period. He wrote many works, including *Shosai yori gaitō ni, Tetsujin shugi, Waga hitetsugaku, Kaizō no kokoromi, Tettei kojin shugi,* and *Shōchō shugi no bunka e*. In his late years he withdrew from literary circles and became a professor of Waseda and Rikkyō universities. A four-volume work entitled *Tanaka Ōdō senshū* presents a selection of his writings.

Tanizaki Jun'ichirō (1886–1965)

Novelist. He was the son of a merchant family of the Nihonbashi section of Tokyo. Because of his father's failure in business, it appeared for a time that he would not even be able to attend middle school, but he was evidently a child of unusual talent, and funds were eventually scraped together to allow him to finish both middle and high school. In 1908 he entered the Japanese literature course of Tokyo Imperial University, but had to withdraw in 1910 because of inability to keep up with tuition payments. He joined with Osanai Kaoru and others in initiating the second continuation of *Shinshichō*, publishing in it a short story entitled *Shisei*, and published another story,

Shōnen, in *Subaru*, thus making a brilliant debut as a writer. These initial works were followed by *Atsumono*, *Otsuya-goroshi*, *Itansha no kanashimi*, and other works that helped to consolidate his position as an important writer. These early works, written in a dazzling and sensuous style, deal with themes marked by eroticism, decadence, and a fascination with the grotesque, and celebrate the power and attraction of evil in a manner that led their author to be dubbed a diabolist. This aestheticism and preoccupation with morbid sensuality found its most impressive expression in his novel *Chijin no ai*. After the Kantō earthquake in 1923, Tanizaki left Tokyo and moved to the Kobe-Osaka-Kyoto area. The novels *Manji* and *Tade kuu mushi*, written early in the Shōwa era, show an increasing appreciation for the beauties of Japan and the traditional Japanese way of life, a tendency continued in the works that followed, *Mōmoku monogatari*, *Yoshino kuzu*, *Ashikari*, and *Shunkinshō*. After the war, *Sasame yuki*, a lengthy novel that he had been working on during the war, appeared, revealing Tanizaki's full artistic maturity, to be followed by *Shōshō Shigemoto no haha*, *Kagi*, *Fūten rōjin nikki*, and other works. His late years showed no diminution in his creative powers, and he is, in fact, almost unrivaled in the great length of his artistic career, which spanned the Meiji, Taishō, and Shōwa eras. His style underwent various changes during this long period of productivity, but throughout he remained essentially a romanticist, a teller of tales, an artist whose basic aim was to transform life through the power of art. Through his brilliant and unconventional works he was able to break away from the arid realism that dominated Japanese fiction at the time of his appearance on the literary scene, and went on to become the most important exponent of aestheticism in recent years and a figure of unmatched stature and influence. In addition to novels, he wrote a number of plays and produced a modern language version of *The Tale of Genji*.

Tayama Katai (1871–1930)

Novelist. He was born in Gumma Prefecture. His father was killed in the campaign to put down the Satsuma rebellion in 1877, and as a result he grew up in poverty and received very little formal education. Outside of some instruction in Chinese studies and the writing of Japanese poetry, he was largely self-taught, and devoted much time to the study of modern European literature, particularly the works of the naturalist writers. In 1891, at the age of twenty, he published his first work, a short story entitled *Uribatake*. In 1895 he became acquainted with such leading writers as Shimazaki Tōson and Kunikida Doppo and by the early 1900s had gained recognition as a writer of highly romantic and sentimental novels dealing with love. In 1902, however, he published *Jūemon no saigo*, a work written in quite a different style that showed the influence of Western naturalism and attracted considerable attention. In 1906 he became the chief editor of the magazine *Bunshō Sekai*. The following year he published *Futon*, a work of crucial importance both in his own career and in the Japanese literary world in general at the time, since it inspired the rise of the naturalist movement. In the years that followed, Katai vigorously advocated the ideals of naturalism, at the same time writing numerous novels and short stories embodying his principles and pioneering on behalf of the new literary movement. Works such as the trilogy *Sei*, *Tsuma*, and *En*, and *Inaka kyōshi* won him increasing recognition and raised him to a position beside that of Shimazaki Tōson as one of the foremost writers of the naturalist school.

He employed a completely objective descriptive style that studiously avoided all philosophizing and personal comment while at the same time drawing material from the actual life around him and presenting it with a frankness that was considered daring at the time. As a result, his works had a profound impact upon the literary world of the period and played a large role in determining the character and direction of the naturalist movement in Japan. In his late years he produced a number of distinguished historical novels, such as *Minamoto no Yoshitomo*.

Toki Zemmaro (b. 1885)

Poet and student of Japanese literature. He was born in Asakusa, Tokyo. At one time he used the literary names Koyū and Aika. His father, well known as a priest-scholar, was the last of the official shogunate *renga* masters, and Zemmaro grew up under his influence. In 1908 he graduated from the Department of English Literature of Waseda University, where he was a classmate of Kitahara Hakushū and Wakayama Bokusui. He first began serious study of poetry during his days at middle school, when he joined the Shiragiku-kai, a group of poets, organized by Kaneko Kun'en, who selected poetry for *Shinsei* magazine. From then on until the birth of the naturalist movement he championed the cause of the *waka* as a poetic form concerned with everyday life and in 1910 published an unusual collection of *waka* in Roman script entitled *Nakiwarai*, becoming the first to write *tanka* in the three-line form. He was a close friend of Ishikawa Takuboku; after the latter's death Zemmaro published Takuboku's complete works. In 1913 he founded and became first editor of the magazine *Seikatsu to Geijutsu* ("Life and Art"), and the following year published a collection of verse, *Tatazumite*. In 1918 he joined the Tokyo *Asahi Shimbun*, and served successively as head of the social, arts, and research divisions of the newspaper. In 1927 he was sent to Europe and America, a trip that resulted in a collection of essays entitled *Gaiyū shinkyō*. His learned study *Tayasu Munetake*, to which he devoted himself during the war years, won him an Art Academy award in 1947 and a doctorate of literature in the following year. His other activities include his long-standing championship of the romanization of the writing of the Japanese language, and a great interest in the Nō, for which he himself wrote a number of new works. He made contributions in the general cultural field beyond those normal to a poet, an example being his "New Annotated Selection of the Poems of Tu Fu" (*Shinshaku Toho shisen*). His published works number about one hundred.

TOKUDA SHŪSEI (1871–1943)

Novelist. He was born in Ishikawa Prefecture, and after finishing Kanazawa Middle School studied for a time at a college in Ishikawa Prefecture. Around 1894 or 1895 he became a disciple of the novelist Ozaki Kōyō and began to gain recognition through the publication of such works as *Yabu-kōji* and *Kumo no yukue*. In time he came to be ranked beside Izumi Kyōka, Oguri Fūyō, and Yanagawa Shun'yō as one of the four outstanding followers of Ozaki Kōyō. But from the beginning his work differed in style from that of the other members of the Ken'yūsha, the group associated with Ozaki Kōyō, and as Shūsei matured as a writer, these differences became more pronounced. In 1908 he published serially in the *Kokumin Shimbun* a work entitled *Arajotai*, which attracted notice because of its humanism and naturalistic style. In 1910 he published *Ashiato*, and in the early years of the Taishō era (1912–1925) he followed it with *Tadare* and *Arakure*, all works of the highest order, which employ a purely objective style to convey the subtleties of feminine psychology and which rank among the finest achievements of Japanese naturalism.

In the Taishō era the naturalist movement in time found itself at an impasse, and Shūsei's work began to show signs of artistic stagnation, but by developing certain tendencies already apparent in *Arakure* and working to achieve greater technical mastery he was able to open up a way out of his difficulties. In the numerous works of his late years such as *Wakai* and *Kasō jimbutsu* he achieved greater psychological depth while continuing to employ a technique based upon minuteness of observation and absolute realism. His last work, *Shukuzu*, which was published serially during the Second World War, was for a time banned by the censorship authorities, but since the author's death it has come to be recognized as a masterpiece.

The naturalist movement in Japanese fiction was begun by Tayama Katai, but it was Tokuda Shūsei who was responsible for bringing it to true artistic maturity. The calm objectivity and seeming artlessness of his style impart to his works a flavor and sense of realism that are unique in the fiction of the Meiji, Taishō, and Shōwa eras. In addition, his works served as models for the *watakushi shōsetsu*, or "I" novel, a genre that has remained highly important in Japanese literature down to the present day, another indication of the deep and lasting influence of his work.

Tokutomi Roka (1868–1927)

Novelist and essayist. He was born in Kumamoto Prefecture in Kyushu, the younger brother of the famous historian and critic Tokutomi Sohō. In 1878 he and his brother entered Dōshisha, a Christian college in Kyoto, where he soon won recognition of his talents from Niijima Jō, the founder of the college. In 1885 he was baptized into the Methodist Church and for a time was active in the propagation of the Christian faith. In 1889, however, he went to Tokyo and became a proofreader for Min'yūsha, a publishing firm established and operated by his elder brother. He published a variety of translations and miscellaneous pieces at the time but did not gain any particular literary recognition.

It was the full-length novel entitled *Hototogisu*, published serially in 1898–99, which first established his reputation. This was followed by *Omoide no ki* and *Shizen to jinsei*, which further enlarged his fame and allowed him to become financially independent of his elder brother and to establish his own identity as an artist. In 1906 he traveled abroad to visit Tolstoy, whom he admired intensely, and later published an account of the meeting entitled *Junrei kikō*. Upon his return to Japan he abandoned city life and moved to the village of Chitose on the outskirts of Tokyo, where he lived in rustic retirement. His accounts of his life in the country were collected and published under the title *Mimizu no tawagoto*.

He later wrote *Yadorigi, Shi no kage ni*, and *Shinshun*, and in 1924 embarked upon the writing of *Fuji*, a work to which he devoted intense effort and which is a confession dealing with his earlier years, but he died before publication was completed, and the last section was published unrevised.

In a broad sense Roka was a writer who was nourished and brought up in the Christian faith, and at the same time may be called a poet of nature and a social critic. He possessed a passionate and sensitive nature characterized by strong likes and dislikes. He spent his life in the pursuit of the larger ideals of truth and love, and remained far removed from all the various literary and intellectual currents of the time. He maintained a position of lofty and solitary isolation, a unique figure in the literary world of the Meiji, Taishō and Shōwa eras. His complete works in 20 volumes were published in 1928 under the title *Roka zenshū*.

Tokutomi Sohō (1863–1957)

Critic. Born in Kumamoto Prefecture, he first studied at the Kumamoto Western School, but when the school was closed down he went to Tokyo, where he entered the school of English (later the First High School), then in winter of the same year, on his own initiative, entered Niijima Jō's Dōshisha (the present Dōshisha University). Following graduation, he devoted himself principally to teaching pupils at the Ōe Academy, which he founded at his home in the country, and to writing for local newspapers and magazines. In 1885 an article he wrote entitled *Daijūkyū seiki Nihon no seinen oyobi sono kyōiku* ("Youth and its Education in Nineteenth Century Japan"), later retitled *Shin-Nihon no seinen* ("The Youth of New Japan"), attracted the attention of the historical essayist Taguchi Ukichi; it was carried in the magazine *Tokyo Keizai Zasshi* and praised by the intelligentsia of the day. Another, longer piece entitled *Shōrai no Nihon* ("Japan of the Future") was published by the Keizai Zasshi company and was extremely favorably received, so that Sohō rapidly became well known. In 1886 he went to Tokyo and the following year started the Min'yūsha, which launched a magazine entitled *Kokumin no Tomo* ("The People's Friend"). His calls to young people to espouse the cause of democratic radicalism, made in a fresh, attractive kind of prose, proved immensely popular and won an enormous number of young readers. He next founded a newspaper, the *Kokumin Shimbun*, which also won a large readership. In the years that followed he waged a constant struggle with the government in the name of democracy and worked unceasingly in the cause of new ideas and new art. Active with him on the same newspaper were such later well-known names as Takekoshi Sansa, Kunikida Doppo, Miyazaki Koshoshi, and Tokutomi Roka.

Shortly before the Sino-Japanese War, Sohō's writing began to show leanings towards nationalism. In 1897, at the time of the Matsukata-Ōkuma coalition government, he was appointed counselor at the Ministry of Home Affairs. He was publicly criticized for an act contrary to his own long-proclaimed views, and his reputation declined drastically. Even his younger brother Roka broke with him, and *Kokumin no Tomo* was obliged to cease publication in 1898. From then on, he devoted most of his energies to the *Kokumin Shimbun*. During the Russo-Japanese War, he threw all his weight behind the policies of the Katsura government, and following the war his newspaper office was burned down by members of the public dissatisfied with the terms of the peace treaty. On the death of Katsura, he withdrew from political activity. In 1918, he began publication of his lifework, a voluminous history of modern Japan entitled *Kinsei Nihon kokumin shi*. During World War II, he served as president of the Nihon Bungaku Hōkoku-kai and Genron Hōkoku-kai, two patriotic organizations of writers and journalists respectively. In 1943 he received the Award of Cultural Merit, but following the war was banned from public life as a war criminal in the cultural field. During the postwar years he wrote almost nothing, living in retirement in the hotspring resort of Atami.

Sohō's activities in the field of mass communications extended for more than seventy years over the Meiji, Taishō and Shōwa eras; he was a born journalist in both the good and the bad senses, with far-ranging interests, a mind that could quickly grasp almost any subject, and an astonishingly fluent pen. His works comprise several hundred volumes, ranging from world politics to history and literature.

Tsubouchi Shōyō (1859–1935)

His varied activities included those of novelist, playwright, critic, translator, and teacher. He was born in Gifu Prefecture and in his youth read avidly in the works of such late Edo period fiction writers as Takizawa Bakin, Ryūtei Tanehiko, Shikitei Samba, and Jippensha Ikku, as well as frequenting the theater. As a result, the literature of late Edo times came to exert a powerful influence that remained with him throughout his lifetime and is evident even in his translations of Shakespeare. In 1883 he graduated from Tokyo Imperial University and immediately took a position with Waseda University, then known as Tokyo Semmon Gakkō, teaching Western history and the principles of constitutional government. At this time he also began making translations of works of English literature such as Shakespeare's *Julius Caesar* and Scott's *Lady of the Lake*. His real literary debut came in 1885 with the publication of *Shōsetsu shinzui* (*The Essence of the Novel*), which has been called the first work of modern Japanese literary criticism. In a manner highly advanced for the times, he laid down the principles that he believed should govern modern literature, rejecting the didacticism of earlier Japanese fiction in favor of realism, and stressing the importance of the novel form. His pronouncements and the challenge they presented to readers of the time were of epochal importance and in fact mark the starting point of modern Japanese literature. At the same time he published an original work of fiction entitled *Tōsei shosei katagi* (*The Character of Modern Students*), which was intended to illustrate his principles. In some ways it is a rather lightweight work and does not do justice to the author's literary ideals, though it had a certain value in providing concrete examples of how the reform of the novel might be carried out. His mastery of the techniques of realism in time improved, particularly through his association with other novelists such as Futabatei Shimei, but before long he abandoned fiction writing and turned his attention to the theater.

In 1890 he set up a department of literature in Waseda University, and the following year founded *Waseda Bungaku*, the official journal of the department. While working to promote the growth of literary talent through his role as a teacher, he also devoted great effort to the reform of the Japanese theater, writing such dramatic works as *Kiri hitoha*, *Maki no kata*, and *Hototogisu kojō no rakugetsu*. In 1905 he founded a literary association known as the Bungei Kyōkai, which, up until its disbandment in 1913, contributed greatly toward creating the foundation for a new movement in the theater. From it emerged such men as Shimamura Hōgetsu, who were to be the leaders of the new theater movement in the period to follow. At the same time Shōyō continued to devote much time to producing translations and critical essays, as well as to his teaching activities. He is particularly remembered for his complete translation of the works of Shakespeare, which he finished in 1928 at the age of sixty-nine. In commemoration of the occasion, the Shōyō Memorial Dramatic Museum was founded on the grounds of Waseda University.

For the role he played through his critical writings in establishing the principles of modern literature, the efforts he devoted to the training of persons of literary talent, and particularly for his work in reforming the ideals and practices of the Japanese theater and his masterful translations of Shakespeare, he deserves to be recognized as a figure of major importance in the history of modern Japanese literature.

TSUCHIYA BUMMEI (b. 1890)

Poet. He was born in Gumma Prefecture. On completing Takasaki Middle School in 1909, he came to Tokyo and stayed with the poet Itō Sachio, working in Itō's cowsheds while he attended the First High School. At the same time he became a disciple of Itō, who by this time was well along in years, contributing to the magazine *Araragi*, which Itō headed, and associating with such other promising young poets as Saitō Mokichi, Shimagi Akahiko, and Koizumi Chikashi, all of them students of Itō. He was the youngest member of the *Araragi* group and wrote works distinguished by freshness of style and lyricism. In 1913 he entered the philosophy course of Tokyo Imperial University, where he joined Akutagawa Ryūnosuke, Kume Masao and others in founding the third version of the magazine called *Shinshichō*, and he also wrote works of fiction. He completed college in 1916 and in 1918 was appointed instructor at Suwa Women's High School. In time he served as principal of the same school, then of Matsumoto Women's High School and of Kiso Middle School, and later became a professor of Hōsei and Meiji universities. While pursuing his teaching career, he continued to be active as a poet. His first collection of verse, entitled *Fuyukusa*, appeared in 1914 and was marked by intellectualism tinged with melancholy and a lyricism grounded upon realism. Later he replaced Saitō Mokichi as editor of *Araragi*. Perhaps partly as a result of the shock of Akutagawa's suicide in 1927, his poetry began to take on an increasing air of severe realism, concentrating upon the keen observation of the actual world. His later collections include *Ōkanshū*, *Sankokushū*, and two collections of poems written when he had evacuated Tokyo during the war, *Yamashita mizu* and *Jiryūsen*. The brooding pensiveness and realistic style of the works in these latter two collections exercised an important influence on the world of traditional Japanese poetry in the postwar years. He also has contributed to *Man'yōshū* studies, the long years of his research culminating in a work in twenty volumes entitled *Man'yōshū shichū*.

UEDA KAZUTOSHI (1867–1937)

Scholar of Japanese linguistics. He was born in Tokyo and in 1888 graduated from the Japanese literature course of Tokyo Imperial University. He studied under the British philologist Basil Hall Chamberlain and in 1890 went to Germany to continue his studies in philology, returning to Japan in 1894. He became a professor of Tokyo University, lecturing on linguistics and the Japanese language and playing a very active role in the promotion of modern and systematic studies of the nature and history of the Japanese language. His *Kokugo no tame* (1895) and *Kokugo no tame, dai-ni* (1903) are of particular historical significance because in them he propounds the theory that the syllables beginning with an "h" sound in modern Japanese had originally been pronounced with an initial "p," an assertion that aroused great controversy at the time but has long since been accepted as fact. He is thus one of the pioneers in the study of Japanese phonology; and in the history of the study of the Japanese language in general, may be said to have carried on the work of such great Edo period scholars as Arai Hakuseki, Keichū, and Motoori Norinaga. In conjunction with Matsui Kanji he compiled the important dictionary known as the *Dai-Nihon kokugo jiten*; with Hashimoto Shinkichi he wrote *Kohon setsuyōshū*; and with Higuchi Yoshi-chiyo, *Chikamatsu goi*. He cooperated with Haga Yaichi in working to lay the foundations for a scientific study of Japanese language and literature and exerted great effort in attempting to solve problems related to the inter-pretation and usage of the Japanese language. When the Committee for the Investigation of the Japanese Language was set up in 1902, he served as its chief member. He is the father of the woman novelist Enchi Fumiko.

WAKAYAMA BOKUSUI (1885–1928)

Poet. Born Wakayama Shigeru in Miyazaki Prefecture. While still at middle school he contributed poems and prose to *Shinsei* and other literary maga-zines. He went to Tokyo in 1904 and entered Waseda University, at the same time becoming a pupil of the poet Onoe Saishū. At university he was a classmate of Kitahara Hakushū and Toki Zemmaro. In 1905, when his teacher, Saishū, founded the Shazensōsha to publish a magazine of *waka* verse, Bokusui joined, along with Maeda Yūgure, Masatomi Ōyō, and others. In 1908 he graduated from Waseda University and published at his own expense his first collection of verse, entitled *Umi no koe*. Consisting for the most part of youthful, lyrical accounts of the tempestuous love affairs he had experienced during the preceding years, its romantic tone immediately won it a following among young people. Two of his most famous poems,

> I wonder if the white bird
> doesn't feel sad,
> through blue of the sky,
> blue of the sea
> drifting, but never taking on their hue.

> How many mountains,
> how many rivers must I cross
> to the land
> where loneliness ends?
> Today again I travel on.

are included in this collection. For a while after this he became a newspaper reporter, but did not continue at this for long.

In 1910 he published a second collection of verse, *Hitori utaeru*, then sponsored the magazine *Sōsaku* and devoted himself to its editing and publication. (Later *Sōsaku* was to appear only intermittently.) His third collection of verse, *Betsuri*, which also appeared in the same year, comprises the whole of the two earlier collections together with new work; its unique lyrics setting forth the sorrows of youth further enhanced his reputation, and with the publication of Maeda Yūgure's first collection of verse, *Shūkaku*, the two of them came virtually to dominate the world of poetry in Japan. Further collections followed for a total of fifteen volumes in all, the fifth collection, *Shi ka geijutsu ka* being notable for a new depth in his apprehension of life and art.

He married in 1912 and settled down to family life, yet still frequently set out on wanderings with only a saké bottle for companion, enjoying the beauties of nature and producing a large number of poems imbued with its essential secrets. His travel accounts, such as *Minakami kikō*, are unique in their harmony of style and feeling.

Wakayama Kishiko (b. 1888)

Poet. She was born in Nagano Prefecture. From an early age she took a deep interest in traditional and modern style poetry and gained recognition from Ōta Mizuho for her own ability as a poet. In 1912 she married the poet Wakayama Bokusui and, after her husband's death in 1928, became manager of the poetry magazine *Sōsaku*, which he had founded earlier. Her style is unassuming but tasteful, and her themes are drawn mainly from the events of everyday life, treated in such a way that the effect is both simple and profound. Her collections of poems include *Ichijiku, Hakubaishū, Chikumano,* and *Mefuki yanagi*. The following is typical of her work:

> From the dew
> that has clung to the taro leaf
> all day without falling

the light of the setting sun
is fading now.

YAMADA BIMYŌ (1868–1910)

Novelist, poet, and scholar of the Japanese language. Born in Kanda, Tokyo, he was still attending the First High School when he joined with Ozaki Kōyō and other former pupils of the school in founding the literary association Ken'yūsha, and published works such as *Tategoto zōshi* (1885), in the manner of Bakin and *Chokai shōsetsu tengu* in the modern colloquial style in *Garakuta Bunko*, the association's magazine. In 1887 he published the historical novel *Musashino* in the newspaper *Yomiuri Shimbun*, thereby acquiring an overnight reputation as a novelist. *Natsu kodachi*, published in 1888, was the work that finally established his position. In the same year he left the Ken'yūsha and became editor of the short-story magazine *Miyako no Hana*, in which he published such works as *Kochō* and *Ichigo hime*. He also published academic treatises such as *Nihon imbun ron*, on poetics; *Gembun itchi ron gairyaku*, an exposition of the merits of writing literature in the colloquial language; and *Nihon zokugo bumpō ron*, a study of the grammar of colloquial Japanese. His linguistic activities made an important contribution to the literary world—he was the earliest novelist to use the colloquial language in his creative work, he carried out the *wakachigaki*, writing in separate lines of the "new verse" (*shintaishi*), and in editing dictionaries he marked words with their accent in Tokyo speech. As literature his works lack depth, however, and he is represented by no major achievement, so that he died in comparative obscurity.

YAMAGUCHI SEISHI (b. 1901)

Haiku poet. He was born in Kyoto. While a student in the Third High School in Kyoto, he entered the Third High School and Kyoto University *Haiku* Association and contributed to the literary magazine *Hototogisu*. In 1922 he became acquainted with the poets Takahama Kyoshi and Mizuhara Shūōshi. He entered the Tokyo University *Haiku* Association and devoted himself entirely to poetry. In 1929 he became a member of the staff of *Hototogisu* and in 1932 brought out his first collection of poems, *Tōkō*. The freshness of his works and the new directions they explored exerted a considerable influence on the *haiku* world of the time, and he and Mizuhara Shūōshi soon became recognized as the leaders of the movement to instil new life into the *haiku* form. In 1935 he left the staff of *Hototogisu* and joined that of *Ashibi*, a magazine edited by Mizuhara Shūōshi. In 1940 he was stricken by illness and forced to undergo a long period of convalescence, but he continued to write *haiku* almost daily. In 1948 he published another collection of poems entitled *Tenrō*. In recognition of his work *Gendai haiku no kakushin*, which was published in 1924, he was awarded the Chū-Nichi Cultural Prize. Whereas earlier *haiku* had tended to confine themselves to descriptions of the natural scene or expressions of emotional states, Seishi's works display a breadth of subject matter and intellectual content that was quite unprecedented in this poetry form and that exercised a strong influence on its development.

Yamamoto Yūzō (b. 1887)

Playwright and novelist. He was born in Tochigi Prefecture. After finishing elementary school, he was sent to Tokyo as an apprentice, but he soon left and returned home, determined to further his education. In 1905 he went to Tokyo once more to continue his studies, entering Tokyo Imperial University, where he joined with Kikuchi Kan, Akutagawa Ryūnosuke, Kume Masao, and others in founding the third *Shinshichō*, a literary magazine that had been started twice before but had gone out of existence. After graduation, he was associated for a time with the Shimpa theater group headed by Inoue Masao, but left his position after a few months. For the following seven years he taught at Waseda University, but in 1923 he resigned and devoted his time wholly to writing. He began his literary career by writing plays, turning out some twenty works in the thirty-year period from 1914 to 1943. In 1920 the Shimpa group performed his *Seimei no kammuri*, and for the first time he gained recognition as a playwright. This work was followed by *Eijigoroshi*, *Sakazaki Dewa no kami*, *Dōshi no hitobito*, and other works that helped to confirm his position as an important dramatist. He endeavored to incorporate into his works the best elements of modern European drama and to work for the advancement of the Japanese theater, and the fact that most of his plays are still performed from time to time is proof of their merit and lasting appeal.

In 1926 he turned to fiction, publishing serially in the *Asahi Shimbun* a work entitled *Iki to shi ikeru mono*, which was never completed. He followed this with *Nami*, *Onna no isshō*, *Shinjitsu ichiro*, *Robō no ishi* (incomplete), and other works that won him a wide readership. In 1940 he wrote an article entitled *Pen wo oru* ("No More Writing") and remained silent during the war years, his next work being *Buji no hito* published in 1949. After the war he devoted his efforts to problems involved in the reform of the Japanese language and in 1947 he was elected to the House of Councilors. In 1941 he became a member of the Japan Art Academy, and in 1965 he received a Cultural Medal. He is not a prolific writer, generally producing only one work a year, but his works are invariably serious in tone and embued with a wealth of human feeling. Dealing with the struggle between idealism and reality and marked by an acute observation of human nature, they give expression to an intense longing for a world of spiritual harmony that has won the admiration and respect of a wide body of readers. In 1935 he began publication of a series of children's books entitled Shōkokumin Bunko, and is widely known for the lending library for children that he established in his own home, called Mitaka Shōkokumin Bunko.

YOKOMITSU RIICHI (1898–1947)

Novelist. Because his father was a surveying engineer and was constantly moving from place to place, Riichi was obliged to change schools a number of times. In 1916 he entered Waseda University but gradually lost interest in his studies and made up his mind to become a writer. The poverty and hardship he underwent during this period was to provide material for such later successful works as *Nichirin* and *Hae*. *Kanashimi no daika*, a work written during this period, is striking for its frankness, simplicity, and passion. He began to make many friends in the literary world and in 1920 became acquainted with Kikuchi Kan and enjoyed the latter's patronage. He joined the staff of the magazine *Bungei Shunjū* and in it published *Jidai wa hōtō suru*, an attack on the proletarian movement in literature that was coming to prominence at the time, and also published *Nichirin* and *Hae*, establishing himself as a young writer of promise. Around the time of the Kantō earthquake in 1923, a new literary movement led by Riichi and such other writers as Kawabata Yasunari and Kataoka Teppei began to take shape, and the group in 1924 founded a magazine called *Bungei Jidai*. Riichi's short story *Atama narabini hara* won for the group the appellation "Neo-Sensationalists," and he was looked upon, both in his creative works and his critical pronouncements, as the most active and pioneering of the members of the new movement.

In 1928, when the controversy over formalist literature broke out, he acted as the chief defender of art for art's sake against the attacks of the

Marxist writers, producing such critical essays as *Shin-kankaku-ha to Marukishizumu* and *Bungaku-teki yuibutsu-ron*. In 1928 he also published *Shanhai*, which was to be the last compilation of his works in the Neo-Sensationalist style; his next work, *Kikai*, showed a sudden shift to the techniques of the psychological novel. This was followed by such important works as *Monshō* and *Shin'en*, and in the period from 1937 to 1946 he was occupied with the writing of a lengthy novel entitled *Ryoshū*, which remained unfinished at the time of his death. It is an experimental work that deals with the confrontation between East and West and, in particular, attempts to gain recognition for the superiority of the Japanese spirit. Strongly colored by the ultra-nationalism characteristic of Japan during the war years and tending toward a kind of mystical dogmatism, it has been the target of bitter critical attack in the postwar period. Nevertheless, it is a work marked by deep sincerity of purpose and passionate lyricism and one that attempts to deal with the most important problems faced by the intellectuals of the time.

During his entire career as an artist, which began with Neo-Sensationalism and ended in *Ryoshū*, he devoted himself to opposing the realism that dominated the literature of the period just before him, to encouraging interest in new trends in European literature, to combating the proletarian writers and their view of literature, and to awakening a greater appreciation of Eastern culture, undertakings and problems that he was not always able to handle with complete artistic success. Nevertheless, he remains an outstanding representative of one type of writer typical of Shōwa literature, and many of the questions he raised in his works continue to be important themes in present-day literature.

Yosano Akiko (1878–1942)

Poet. She was born in Sakai just south of Osaka, the third daughter of a merchant named Hō Sōshichi. At an early age she acquired a thorough knowledge of the classics of Japanese literature, and through such magazines as *Shigaramisōshi* and *Bungakkai* became acquainted with the new literary movement that was beginning to appear on the scene. In 1900 she submitted some of her poems in *tanka* form to *Myōjō*, the literary magazine headed by Yosano Hiroshi, and met the latter when he came to Osaka on a visit. The acquaintance grew into a romance, and the following year she ran away from home, went to Tokyo, and married Hiroshi, who had earlier divorced his first wife. Around this period she was extremely active in the pages of *Myōjō*, and the publication of her first collection of poems, entitled *Midare-*

gami, attracted rapid and widespread attention. Her poems, characterized by vivid imagination and an outpouring of intense passion, opened the way for the modernization of the *tanka* form and signaled a new era in Meiji period romanticism. The following poems are typical of her work at this time:

> At twenty,
> proud of the black hair
> that flows
> through the comb—
> the beauty of her spring!

> Not even trying to feel
> the hot blood that flows
> beneath this soft skin,
> are you not lonely,
> you who preach the Way?

In the works *Koōgi, Dokusō, Koigoromo,* and *Maihime,* published from 1904 to 1906, she continued to develop and bring to maturity her own special literary talent. In the very midst of the Russo-Japanese War she published an antiwar poem entitled *Kimi shinitamou koto nakare,* which begins "Ah, little brother, I weep for you!" an action that aroused widespread public criticism at the time.

At about the time when advocates of the naturalist school were beginning to gain a hearing, her poetic style began to show signs of stagnation and her work for the first time became separated from the mainstream of literary development. She turned her attention to fiction, producing modern language versions of such early classics as *The Tale of Genji.* During the Taishō era, which lasted from 1912 to 1925, she was active as a critic, involving herself particularly with questions relating to women, but her thinking did not display any great originality. She was responsible for the founding of a women's college called the Bunka Gakuin, which laid emphasis upon education in the arts, and taught there for a time herself. In 1912 she revived the magazine *Myōjō,* which had earlier gone out of existence, and attempted to restore life to the romantic movement, but her efforts failed to receive the kind of popular response that she had hoped for. The collection of poems entitled *Hakuōshū,* published posthumously, deals with her emotional life in the years following the death of her husband in 1935 and contains a number of poems that move the reader with their simplicity of statement and pervading tone of melancholy beauty. The following is an example; in Japanese thought, west represents the direction of death:

From that western direction
that holds you,
streaming down
as though in pity—
the hour when the setting sun shines.

Yosano Hiroshi (1873–1935)

Poet. He is often referred to by his literary name Tekkan. His father was a priest of the Nishi Hongan-ji branch of the Jōdo Shinshū sect of Buddhism and a poet. From a very early age he was taught by his parents to read Buddhist texts and works of Chinese and Japanese literature, and he learned to compose poetry in Chinese. In 1892, at the age of nineteen, he went to Tokyo and became a disciple of the poet and scholar of Japanese literature Ochiai Naobumi. He joined with Ōmachi Keigetsu in initiating a new movement in the writing of *tanka* or traditional Japanese poetry, publishing a violent attack on the conservative school entitled *Bōkoku no on* ("The Voice of a Doomed Nation") and leading the way to reform. In 1896 he published his first collection of verses entitled *Tōzai namboku*, which is marked by a youthful romanticism and refusal to be fettered by form. The *tanka* included in the volume hold a place of particular importance in the history of modern Japanese literature as the first fruits of the new movement to reform the writing of poetry in traditional form. In 1900 he founded a magazine called *Myōjō* and worked to transfer the techniques of European literature to Japanese poetry, to open the way for freer expression of emotion in poetry, and to create a new literature dominated by romanticism. He fell in love with Hō Akiko, also a writer of poetry, and they were married, the two of them making of *Myōjō* a brilliant vehicle for the display of the new romantic movement. The movement fostered such outstanding poets as Takamura Kōtarō, Ishikawa Takuboku, Yoshii Isamu, Kinoshita Mokutarō, and Kitahara Hakushū, but in time its principles were challenged by other movements that came to the fore, such as naturalism and aestheticism. In 1908 Yosano discontinued publication of *Myōjō* with the one hundredth issue and started a magazine called *Subaru*. He visited France in 1911 and in 1914 published a collection of translations of mostly French poetry entitled *Rira no hana* as one of the outcomes of the trip. In his late years he devoted most of his time to a study of the etymology of the Japanese language entitled *Nihon gogengaku no kenkyū*.

Major Schools of Literature

Waka Poets

I

Minamoto no Tsunenobu

Minamoto no Toshiyori

Shun'e

Kamo no Chōmei

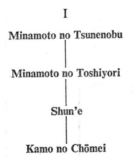

II

Fujiwara no Akisuke

Fujiwara no Kiyosuke   **Kenshō**

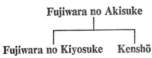

III

Keichū

Imai Jikan   Kaihoku Jakuchū   Andō Tameakira

Waka Poets

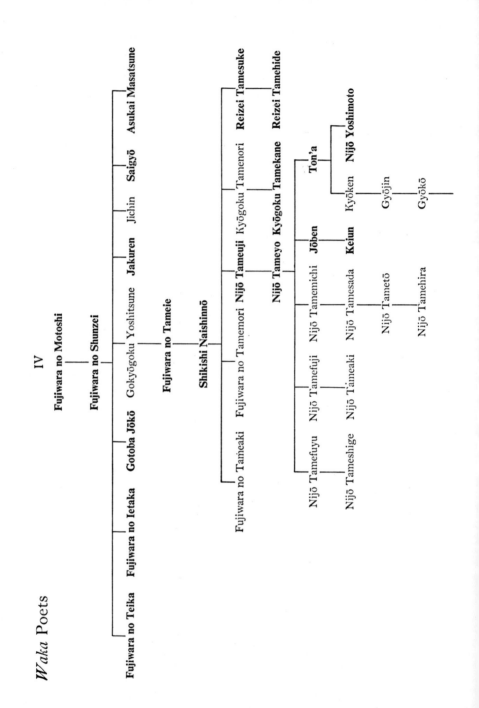

IV

Fujiwara no Motoshi

Fujiwara no Shunzei

Fujiwara no Teika — Fujiwara no Ietaka — Gotoba Jōkō — Gokyōgoku Yoshitsune — Jakuren — Jichin — Saigyō — Asukai Masatsune

Fujiwara no Tameie

Shikishi Naishinnō

Fujiwara no Tameaki — Fujiwara no Tamemori — Nijō Tameuji — Kyōgoku Tamenori — Reizei Tamesuke

Nijō Tameyo — Kyōgoku Tamekane — Reizei Tamehide

Nijō Tamefuyu — Nijō Tamefuji — Nijō Tamemichi — Jōben — Ton'a

Nijō Tameshige — Nijō Tameaki — Nijō Tamesada — Keiun — Nijō Yoshimoto

Nijō Tametō — Kyōken

Nijō Tamehira — Gyōjin

Gyōkō

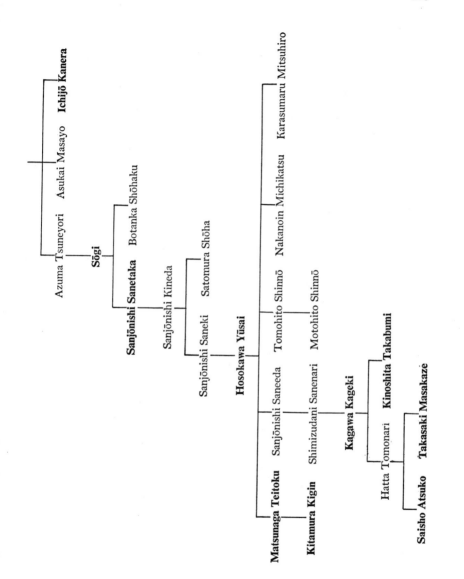

Waka Poets

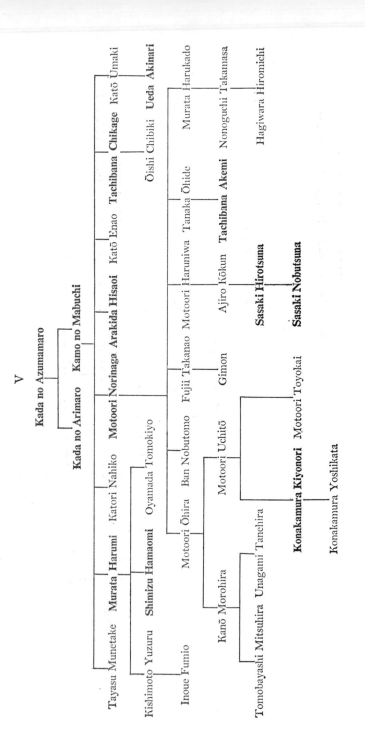

V

Kada no Azumamaro

Kada no Arimaro Kamo no Mabuchi

Tayasu Munetake **Murata Harumi** Katori Nahiko

Kishimoto Yuzuru **Shimizu Hamaomi** Oyamada Tomokiyo

Inoue Fumio Motoori Ōhira Ban Nobutomo

Kanō Morohira Motoori Uchitō

Tomobayashi Mitsuhira Unagami Tanehira

Konakamura Yoshikata

Konakamura Kiyonori Motoori Toyokai

Motoori Norinaga Arakida Hisaoi Katō Enao **Tachibana Chikage** Katō Umaki

Ōishi Chibiki **Ueda Akinari**

Fujii Takanao Motoori Haruniwa Tanaka Ōhide Murata Harukado

Gimon Ajiro Kōkun **Tachibana Akemi** Nonoguchi Takamasa

Sasaki Hirotsuna Hagiwara Hiromichi

Sasaki Nobutsuna

Waka Poets

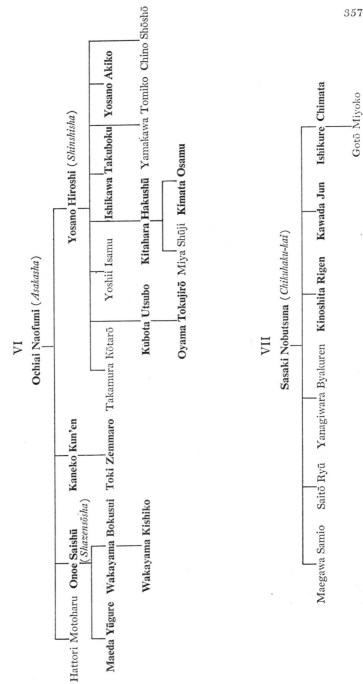

VI
Ochiai Naofumi (*Asakasha*)

Hattori Motoharu **Onoe Saishū**
(*Shazensōsha*)

Kaneko Kun'en

Maeda Yūgure Wakayama Bokusui Toki Zemmaro Takamura Kōtarō

Wakayama Kishiko

Yosano Hiroshi (*Shinshisha*)

Ishikawa Takuboku Yosano Akiko

Yamakawa Tomiko Chino Shōshō

Yoshii Isamu

Kubota Utsubo Kitahara Hakushū Kimata Osamu

Oyama Tokujirō Miya Shūji **Kimata Osamu**

VII
Sasaki Nobutsuna (*Chikuhaku-kai*)

Maegawa Samio Saitō Ryū Yanagiwara Byakuren **Kinoshita Rigen Kawada Jun Ishikure Chimata**

Gotō Miyoko

Waka Poets

VIII

Masaoka Shiki (*Negishi Tanka-kai*)

Katori Hozuma · **Nagatsuka Takashi**

Itō Sachio (*Araragi; Ashibi*) · Oka Fumoto

Nakamura Kenkichi · Hirafuku Hyakusui · Ishihara Jun

Tsuchiya Bummei · **Saitō Mokichi** · **Shimagi Akahiko**

Takayasu Kuniyo · **Kondō Yoshimi** · Satō Satarō · Morimoto Jikichi · Imai Kuniko

Haiku Poets

TEIMON SCHOOL
Matsunaga Teitoku

Nonoguchi Ryūho · Matsue Shigeyori · Yasuhara Teishitsu · **Kitamura Kigin**

Sumi Taigi · Ikenishi Gonsui · **Kamijima Onitsura** · Kitamura Koshun · **Matsuo Bashō** · Nakarai Bokuyō

Yamaguchi Sodō · Yamaoka Genrin

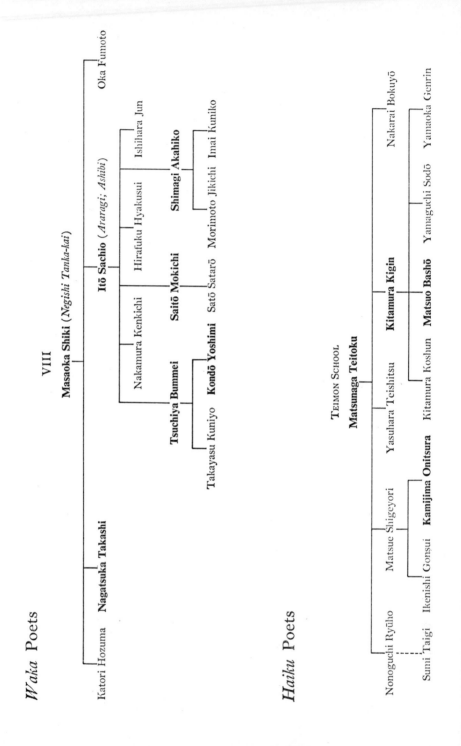

Haiku Poets

DANRIN SCHOOL

Nishiyama Sōin

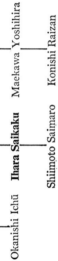

Okanishi Ichū   **Ihara Saikaku**   Maekawa Yoshihira

Shiimoto Saimaro   Konishi Raizan

SHŌMON SCHOOL

Matsuo Bashō

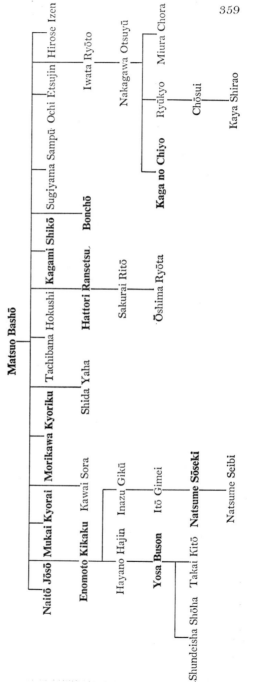

Naitō Jōsō   **Mukai Kyorai**   **Morikawa Kyoriku**   Tachibana Hokushi   **Kagami Shikō**   Sugiyama Sampū   Ochi Etsujin   Hirose Izen

Enomoto Kikaku   Kawai Sora   Shida Yaha   **Hattori Ransetsu**   **Bonchō**   Iwata Ryōto

Hayano Hajin   Inazu Gikū   Sakurai Ritō   Nakagawa Otsuyū

Yosa Buson   Itō Gimei   Ōshima Ryōta   **Kaga no Chiyo**   Ryūkyo   Miura Chora

Shundeisha Shōha   Takai Kitō   **Natsume Sōseki**   Chōsui

Natsume Seibi   Kaya Shirao

Haiku Poets

NIHON SCHOOL; *Hototogisu*
Masaoka Shiki

- **Takahama Kyoshi**
- **Naitō Meisetsu** — Matsuse Seisei
  - **Kawahigashi Hekigodō**
- Sakamoto Shihōda — Murakami Seigetsu
- Ishii Rogetsu
- **Natsume Sōseki**
- Ōtani Gyōseki — Nakagawa Shimei
- Samukawa Sokotsu — Aoki Getto

Tsukuba-kai
Fujii Shiei
Kubo Tenzui
Ōmachi Keigetsu
Ōno Shachiku
Sassa Seisetsu
Sasakawa Rimpū
Taoka Reiun

Shinkeikō-ha
Kawahigashi Hekigodō
Ogiwara Seisensui
Ōsuga Otsuji
Usuda Arō

Shūsei-kai
Itō Shōu
Iwaya Sazanami
Okano Chijū
Ozaki Kōyō
Tsunoda Chikurei

Chu Hsi Neo-Confucianism

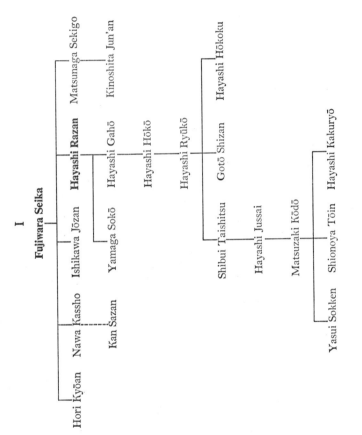

I

Fujiwara Seika

- Hori Kyōan
- Nawa Kassho
  - Kan Sazan
- Ishikawa Jōzan
- **Hayashi Razan**
  - Yamaga Sokō
  - Hayashi Gahō
    - Hayashi Hōkō
    - Hayashi Ryūkō
      - Shibui Taishitsu
      - Gotō Shizan
        - Hayashi Jussai
        - Matsuzaki Kōdō
          - Yasui Sokken
          - Shionoya Tōin
          - Hayashi Kakuryō
      - Hayashi Hōkoku
- Matsunaga Sekigo
  - Kinoshita Jun'an

Chu Hsi Neo-Confucianism

School of Ancient Learning

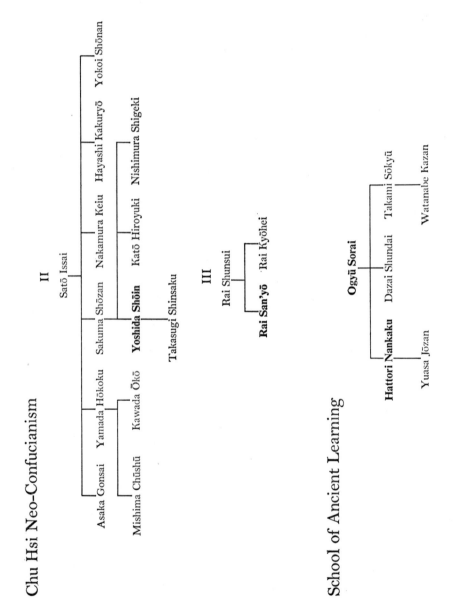

Chu Hsi Neo-Confucianism

II

Satō Issai

Asaka Gonsai Yamada Hōkoku Sakuma Shōzan Nakamura Keiu Hayashi Kakuryō Yokoi Shōnan

Mishima Chūshū Kawada Ōkō Yoshida Shōin Katō Hiroyuki Nishimura Shigeki

Takasugi Shinsaku

III

Rai Shunsui

Rai San'yō Rai Kyōhei

School of Ancient Learning

Ogyū Sorai

Hattori Nankaku Dazai Shundai Takami Sōkyū

Yuasa Jōzan Watanabe Kazan

Selected Glossary

bugyō

Literally, "to honor and carry out," a term originally designating the carrying out of orders or the person who does so. From the time of the founding of the Kamakura shogunate on, however, it was used as a title for a military official. The number and importance of persons with this title varied considerably in different periods. Under the Edo shogunate, there were twenty or thirty some persons with this title who performed various functions in the central and local governments. Among them, the Sambugyō (Three Bugyō) were the most important. These were:

1. The Machi-bugyō (Town Bugyō), officials appointed to such important cities as Edo, Osaka, Kyoto, and Sumpu and charged with the supervision of administrative and legal matters and the policing of the areas. They were particularly important as the supervisors of the *chōnin*, the townsmen. Their headquarters were known as *bugyōsho*, with the name of the city prefixed.

2. The Kanjō-bugyō (Accounting Bugyō), chief fiscal officials for the Edo shogunate who supervised the collection of taxes from the lands under the direct control of the shogunate.

3. Jisha-bugyō (Temple and Shrine Bugyō), officials who supervised matters pertaining to temples and shrines and their lands and to religious matters in general.

chōka

Long poetic form consisting of alternating lines of five and seven syllables and concluding with an extra seven-syllable line. Many examples are found in the *Man'yōshū* anthology compiled in the Nara period, but in the following Heian period it declined rapidly in use and was seldom employed thereafter.

chōnin

Term for the merchants and craftsmen living in the towns during the Edo period. Already in Kamakura times there were merchants and artisans living in the towns, but from the sixteenth century on, with the growth of numerous castle towns, the *chōnin*, or townsman class, became of particular importance. In theory the *chōnin* were at the bottom of the social scale, inferior to both the samurai and farmer classes. But because of the economic power created by their commercial activities, they were able to live in relative affluence and to develop a distinctive culture of their own.

COURT RANKS: ikai

A system of court ranks established under the *ritsuryō* type of government in ancient Japan and assigned to the officials and members of the aristrocracy. It consisted of thirty stages grouped under ten major ranks. The first, second, and third ranks, called *ichi-i*, *ni-i*, and *san-i* respectively, were subdivided into *shō* (senior) and *ju* (junior) divisions, making a total of six stages for these three ranks. The fourth to the eighth ranks carried not only the *shō* and *ju* divisions, but to these were added the further divisions of *jō* (upper) and *ge* (lower), thus making a total of twenty stages for these five ranks. The ninth rank was subdivided into the two stages of *dai-so-i-jō* (major beginning rank upper grade) and *dai-so-i-ge* (major beginning rank lower grade), while the tenth, or lowest, rank was similarly divided into *shō-so-i-jō* (minor beginning rank upper grade) and *shō-so-i-ge* (minor beginning rank lower grade). See table below.

Each rank corresponded to certain official positions. Thus the highest rank, that of *shō-ichi-i*, or senior first rank, corresponded to the highest government position, that of *dajōdaijin*, or prime minister, while the second ranks corresponded to the ministers of the left and right, etc. Similarly, a member of the court nobility holding the rank of *ju-san-i* (junior third rank) would be entitled to appointment as a *chūnagon* (middle counselor in the council of state), a *konoe-no-taishō* (general of the imperial guard), or a *Dazai-no-sochi* (commander of the Dazaifu government office in Kyushu). These correspondences differed somewhat in different periods, however, and the rank and official position of a given individual did not always match exactly.

Table of *ikai* or court ranks

1st rank	senior first rank	(*shō-ichi-i*)
	junior first rank	(*jū-ichi-i*)

2nd rank	senior second rank	*(shō-ni-i)*
	junior second rank	*(ju-ni-i)*
3rd rank	senior third rank	*(shō-san-i)*
	junior third rank	*(ju-san-i)*
4th rank	senior fourth rank upper grade	*(shō-shi-i-jō)*
	senior fourth rank lower grade	*(shō-shi-i-ge)*
	junior fourth rank upper grade	*(ju-shi-i-jo)*
	junior fourth rank lower grade	*(ju-shi-i-ge)*
5th rank	senior fifth rank upper grade	*(shō-go-i-jō)*
	senior fifth rank lower grade	*(shō-go-i-ge)*
	junior fifth rank upper grade	*(ju-go-i-jō)*
	junior fifth rank lower grade	*(ju-go-i-ge)*
6th rank	senior sixth rank upper grade	*(shō-roku-i-jō)*
	senior sixth rank lower grade	*(sho-roku-i-ge)*
	junior sixth rank upper grade	*(ju-roku-i-jō)*
	junior sixth rank lower grade	*(ju-roku-i-ge)*
7th rank	senior seventh rank upper grade	*(shō-shichi-i-jō)*
	senior seventh rank lower grade	*(shō-shichi-i-ge)*
	junior seventh rank upper grade	*(ju-shichi-i-jō)*
	junior seventh rank lower grade	*(ju-shichi-i-ge)*
8th rank	senior eighth rank upper grade	*(shō-hachi-i-jō)*
	senior eighth rank lower grade	*(sho-hachi-i-ge)*
	junior eighth rank upper grade	*(ju-hachi-i-jō)*
	junior eighth rank lower grade	*(ju-hachi-i-ge)*
9th rank	major beginning rank upper grade	*(dai-so-i-jō)*
	major beginning rank lower grade	*(dai-so-i-ge)*
10th rank	minor beginning rank upper grade	*(shō-so-i-jō)*
	minor beginning rank lower grade	*(shō-so-i-ge)*

Genji Monogatari

Novel in fity-four *chō*, or chapters, written by Murasaki Shikibu, lady-in-waiting to the empress of Emperor Ichijō, and completed early in the eleventh century. Written in a beautiful and elegant style and interspersed with *waka*, it portrays the aristocracy of the period and is rich in descriptions of nature and delineations of the lives and personalities of its numerous characters. It has had an incalculable influence on the literature and other arts of later periods and is generally regarded as the supreme masterpiece of Japanese letters.

gesaku

General term for the popular literature of the Edo period, in contrast to the traditional and more refined types of literature such as poetry and prose in Chinese, *waka*, etc. It includes a number of different kinds of fictional works such as *yomihon*, *sharebon*, *kokkeibon*, *ninjōbon*, *kibyōshi* (q.v.), etc. Writers of such works are known as *gesakusha*.

gidayū

Abbreviation for *gidayū-bushi*, the distinctive type of chanted narration developed for the *jōruri* (q.v.), or puppet drama, by the famous chanter Takemoto Gidayū (1651–1714) and still in use today. The term *gidayū* has also come to be used as a designation for the *jōruri* itself. During the Meiji era a type of *gidayū-bushi* performed by young women and known as *musume gidayū* enjoyed great popularity for a time.

Gozan

Literally"Five Mountains," a term used to refer to the most important and powerful Zen temples of the Kamakura and Muromachi periods. The term customarily designated the five most important temples of Kyoto, such as the Nanzen-ji, Shōkoku-ji, etc., and the five most important temples of Kamakura, such as the Kenchō-ji, Engaku-ji, etc., though the particular temples included in such lists varied somewhat from period to period. The term *Gozan bungaku*, or "Literature of the Five Mountains," is used to designate the important body of poetry and prose composed in Chinese by the monks of the major Zen temples, particularly during the Muromachi period.

gunki monogatari

A general term for the narrative works written in the Kamakura and Muromachi periods that center about the activities of the newly powerful warrior class, focusing in particular on scenes of battle. In addition to the term *gunki monogatari*, or "military tales," they are also called *senki monogratari*, or "war tales." In style they employ a large number of constructions and terms borrowed from Chinese, which give the language an economy and vigor appropriate to the scenes described. Among the outstanding examples of the genre, which is unknown in Japanese literature before the middle ages, are the *Heike monogatari* and the *Taiheiki*.

hon'i

A system of honorary ranks bestowed upon the *shinnō*, the sons and daughters of an emperor. There were four ranks, designated *ippon*, *nihon*, *sampon*, and *shihon*, each of which carried with it a fixed amount of land and tax revenue. Not every offspring of an emperor, however, necessarily recieved such a rank. The system was laid down in the *Yōrōryō*, the code of laws promulgated in the early Nara period.

jōruri

A type of puppet drama developed during the Edo period. It had its origins in the particular type of chanting employed in the Muromachi period for recitations of a popular love tale called the *Jōruri monogatari* from the name of its heroine, Princess Jōruri. In the early Edo period, a samisen accompaniment was added to the recitation, and in time puppets were employed to depict the action of the story. Still later, a performer named Takemoto Gidayū (1651–1714) developed the distinctive type of chanted narration that has ever since been associated with the puppet drama, and the distinguished playwright Chikamatsu Monzaemon (1653–1724) cooperated with him in producing new plays of great beauty and subtlety. The *jōruri*, through the efforts of Chikamatsu and other talented writers, reached the height of its development during the Genroku era (1688–1704), but thereafter it was replaced in popularity by the kabuki and fell into gradual decline. As a form of classical drama, however, it continues to be performed even today. In the beginning of the Meiji period, Osaka, where the *jōruri* had earlier reached the peak of its development, boasted two *jōruri* theaters, the Toyotake-za and the Bunraku-za. From the great popularity of the latter, the *jōruri* came to be referred to as *bunraku*, a designation that continues in use today.

kabuki

Form of drama that evolved during the Edo period. It is said to have begun in the early Edo period when a woman named Izumo no Okuni performed popular songs of the time and improvised dances to accompany them. These early performances, presented entirely by women, came to be known as *Okuni kabuki*. The shogunate, considering them injurious to public morals, placed a ban on them, whereupon young boys, known as *wakashū*, were substituted for the women performers. When the boys in turn were banned, adult men were substituted, leading to the type of *kabuki* known today. With its prime emphasis upon performance, the *kabuki* continued to develop and grow in complexity, and although it was for a time overshadowed by the *ningyō jōruri,* or puppet drama, it reached the height of its growth and popularity during the period from around 1781 to 1830. At this time, first-rate actors and playwrights, borrowing elements from the puppet drama and adding *nagauta* and other types of singing as musical accompaniment, succeeded in creating a highly colorful and appealing dramatic form. Though the *kabuki* is essentially formalistic and observes conventions very different from those of realistic drama, it continues to enjoy popularity with the Japanese public.

kasen

1. Originally a term for a person of particularly outstanding talent in the composition of *waka*. Later, the term came to be used to designate the outstanding poets of a particular period, as in the Rokkasen (Six Poetic Geniuses of the early Heian period), or the Sanjūrokkasen (Thirty-six Poetic Geniuses of the middle Heian period).

2. Because of the fame of the Thirty-six Poetic Geniuses, the term *kasen* came in much later times to designate a group of *renga* or *haiku* that contained a total of thirty-six lines.

katauta

A simple poetic form consisting of seventeen syllables arranged in three lines in the pattern of 5-7-5 syllables. As the name *katauta,* or "part-of-a-poem," indicates, it was looked upon as only part of a longer form and seldom as a poetic form in its own right. The form was often employed in very early times for poems addressed to a lover, and exchanges of such poems were called *mondōka,* or "question-and-answer poems." After Nara times the form was seldom used. Because the arrangement of syllables and lines is the same as that of the *haiku* form, the eighteenth century scholar Takebe Ayatari attempted to treat the *haiku* as identical with the *katauta.*

kiki no kayō

Term used to refer to the songs recorded in the two earliest works of Japanese history, the *Kojiki* (some 110 songs) and the *Nihon Shoki* (some 130 songs). They are marked by great simplicity and directness of expression and powerful rhythms. Some are irregular in form, while others employ the five-syllable and seven-syllable line lengths characteristic of the forms such as the *chōka* and *tanka* found later in the *Man'yōshū.*

Kojiki

The oldest extant Japanese historical text, it is in three *kan* (chapters) and was completed in 712. According to the account in the preface, it was written down by Ō no Yasumaro on the basis of recitations conducted for him by Hieda no Are. Arranged in chronological form, it deals with the successive emperors of Japan and also contains numerous myths and legends pertaining to the early period. Though intended as a work of history, it is rich in literary interest and value.

Kokinshū (Kokin wakashū)

The oldest officially sponsored anthology of Japanese poetry, it is in twenty *kan* (chapters). Work on it was begun in 905 on imperial order, and it was probably completed around 913 or 914. The work of compilation was carried out by the poet and official Ki no Tsurayuki (d. 946) and four other editors. It contains over eleven hundred poems, nearly all in the *tanka* form. The form of the anthology became the model for the numerous imperially sponsored anthologies compiled in later ages.

The poems in the *Kokinshū* are characterized by elegance of tone, highly polished expression, frequent use of rhetorical devices, and a rather intellectualized type of thought and feeling. These qualities came to be recognized as the marks of the so-called *Kokin* style, which exercised a profound influence upon the Japanese poetry of later periods.

kyōka

Literally, "crazy poem," a type of poem that uses the same 5-7-5-7-7 line pattern as the *tanka* but is humorous or satirical in nature. It is much more colloquial in diction than the *tanka* and unrestrained, even vulgar, in choice of subject and manner of expression. It originated as a kind of diversion indulged in by the *waka* and linked-verse poets of the late middle ages, but during the Edo period, when it enjoyed great popularity, it became established as a separate literary form in its own right. Specialists in the *kyōka* form such as Ōta Shokusanjin and Yadoya Meshimori appeared, and during the period from around 1781 to 1830 it was one of the most flourishing literary forms among the townsman class. Thereafter, however, it declined into increasing vulgarness and triviality.

makurakotoba

A type of rhetorical device used in prose and poetry of ancient times. It consists of an epithet or descriptive term used to precede and modify a certain noun and to lend rhythm to the passage. The term *makurakotoba*, or "pillow word," derives from the fact that it serves as a "pillow" for the noun to rest upon. Such words or phrases are most often five syllables in length and are employed frequently in poetry, where they comprise a single line of verse. Examples are the phrases *ashihiki no* to describe mountains, or *hisakata no* to describe the sky. In earliest times they appear to have had a definite meaning, though this gradually became lost and the terms retained only a decorative function. Thus the meaning of the terms *ashihiki no* and *hisakata no* is a matter of doubt and conjecture. *Makurakotoba* were used most frequently in the Nara period, after which their use declined steadily. The total number of such phrases is very large.

Man'yōgana

A system devised in early times to transcribe the sounds of the Japanese language. Since ancient Japanese had no writing system of its own, Chinese characters were borrowed and used purely for their sound value to form a syllabary. Because the syllabary is used to a large extent in the Nara period anthology of poetry entitled the *Man'yōshū*, the syllabary is known as *Man'yōgana*; it is also called *magana*, or "true syllabary." In Heian times, two more types of syllabary known as *hiragana* and *katakana* were developed from abbreviated writings of various Chinese characters and, being easier and more convenient to use, soon replaced the *Man'yōgana*. The latter remained in use only for the writing of certain place names, family and personal names, etc.

Man'yōshū

The oldest extant anthology of Japanese poetry, in twenty *kan* (chapters). It is not known who the compiler or compilers may have been, though it is clear that the poet and official Ōtomo no Yakamochi (718–785) played a major role in its production. It appears to have been completed sometime late in the Nara period, which ended in 784. It contains some forty-five hundred poems composed over a period of 450 years by all types of persons from emperors and empresses down to anonymous commoners. The poetic forms employed are the *chōka*, *tanka*, and *sedōka* (q.v.), and the style for the most part is direct and realistic and filled with an emotional sincerity and vitality seldom known in later ages. The anthology is counted among the greatest masterpieces of Japanese literature.

michiyuki

Term designating a rhymed passage in a tale or drama that describes the sights encountered on a journey and the emotions aroused. It is found in the *gunki monogatari* (q.v.), or military tales, and the *Nō*, *jōruri*, and *kabuki* (q.v.) dramas. Also called a *michiyuki-bun*. In the *jōruri* and *kabuki* dramas, it customarily deals with a journey carried out by a pair of lovers. Particularly famous are the *michiyuki* of this type in the dramas *Sonezaki shinjū*, *Shinjū Ten no amijima*, and the fourth act of *Kanadehon chūshingura*.

monjō hakase

Officials who in the Nara and Heian periods gave instruction in history and Chinese prose and poetry at the *daigakuryō* (imperial university). Sons of the aristocracy entered the *daigakuryō*, where they received the kind of instruction needed to qualify them to become officials of the central government. The university offered four courses of instruction, of which the *monjōdō*, or history and Chinese literature course, was one; the others were the *myōbōdō* (law course), the *myōgyōdō* (Confucian course), and the *sandō* (mathematics course). From late Nara times on, the *monjōdō* came to be looked on with special importance, and the *monjō hakase* (one man during most periods, though at certain periods two men held the post simultaneously) was regarded as the most outstanding scholar of the time.

Leaving aside those sons of the higher aristocracy who by birth were assured of important posts in the government, the ordinary student in the *monjōdō* course underwent periodic examinations that, when passed, allowed him to advance to the levels of *mojōshō*, *monjō tokugyōshō*, and *shūsai* in that order, after which he was appointed to an official post.

monogatari

General term for works of fiction, particularly those written during the time from the Heian to the Muromachi periods. Depending upon the nature of the work, the genre is subdivided into various particular forms such as the *denki monogatari* (wonder tale), of which the *Taketori monogatari* is the principal example; the *uta monogatari* (poem tale) such as the *Ise monogatari*; the *shajitsu monogatari* (realistic table) such as the *Genji monogatari*; the *rekishi monogatari* (historical tale), represented by the *Ōkagami*; the *setsuwa monogatari* (didactic tale), represented by the *Konjaku monogatari*; the *gunki monogatari* (military tale), represented by the *Heike monogatari*, etc.

The form began in the Heian period with such works as the *Taketori monogatari* and *Ise monogatari* and reached its highest peak of development in the eleventh century with the *Genji monogatari*. The works of this period, which are almost entirely fictional and deal with the society of the aristocracy, are known as *tsukuri monogatari* (invented tales). When this type of "invented" or fictional tale had fallen into decline, it was replaced by such works as the historical tale, military tale, or didactic tale, which are often at least partially factual in nature and which represent a new type of prose writing evolved from the old *monogatari* form.

NAMES: azana, gō

Upon the occasion of the capping ceremony that represented a boy's entry into manhood, a Chinese youth would customarily be given a *tzu*, or polite name, by which he was thereafter known to his friends and other persons of society in general. This custom was imitated in Japan mainly by scholars of Chinese learning, the *tzu*, or polite name, being known in Japanese as an *azana*.

It was customary for Chinese, particularly when writing poetry or engaging in other artistic activities, to adopt a *go* or *hao*, an artistic or literary name that they employed in addition to their usual given names. The custom was imitated by scholars, painters, writers, and other similar types of men in Japan. Sometimes the *gō* was written immediately after the family name, sometimes only the *gō* alone was used. The *gō* is also referred to at times as a *gagō*.

Nihon Shoki

The oldest officially sponsored history of Japan, it is in thirty *kan* (chapters) and was completed in 720, eight years after the completion of the *Kojiki* (q.v.). Like the *Kojiki*, it deals with the history of Japan from mythical times down to the seventh century, concentrating upon the activities of the successive rulers but also including a wide variety of other material. It was compiled by a large group of scholars headed by Imperial Prince Toneri, and is written almost entirely in classical Chinese.

norito

Words of prayer addressed to deities in Shinto worship ceremonies. Fragmentary examples are found in the *Kojiki* and *Nihon Shoki*, but the oldest examples that employ a regular form are the twenty-seven pieces recorded in the *Engishiki* compiled in 927.

otogizōshi

A general term for the short popular tales written in the Muromachi period. Several hundred such tales are extant, but their authorship and exact date of composition are unknown. Naive in content and artless in style, they are in the nature of fairy tales, often with a didactic element. They are particularly valuable for the picture they convey of life among the common people of the period.

renga

The term *renga*, or linked verse, originally designated two types of poems: 1. *tanrenga* (short linked verse), a single *tanka* in which the first three lines are composed by one person and the last two by another; 2. *chōrenga* or (long linked verse), composed by two or more persons who take turns supplying units of three lines in 5-7-5 syllable pattern alternating with units of two lines in 7-7 pattern. The *tanrenga* form was used in Heian times along with the regular *tanka*, but from early Kamakura times the *chōrenga* gained increasing popularity, until the term *renga* became a virtual synonym for *chōrenga*. The *renga*, as already stated, was commonly the product of several poets, though occasionally a single poet produced works in the form. The *renga* in time became highly regularized, the number of lines conforming to certain fixed patterns such as *kasen* (thirty-six-lined), hundred-lined, thousand-lined, or even ten-thousand-lined. In content, *renga* fall into two general categories, those of a light or humorous nature, and those elgant and refined in sentiment in the manner of the *waka*, with the latter type predominating. *Renga* were composed not only by members of the court aristocracy, but by priests, warriors, and common people as well, the form reaching the height of its popularity during the Muromachi period. With the Edo period, it began to decline, and since Meiji times has all but gone out of existence. The most outstanding *renga* poet is Iio Sōgi (1421–1502), and the *Shinsen tsukubashū*, a collection of *renga* that he helped to edit, is considered to contain the finest examples of works in the form.

sedōka

A poetic form consisting of thirty-eight syllables arranged in six lines of 5-7-7-5-7-7 syllables respectively. The name *sedōka*, or "head-repeated poem," derives from the fact that the syllable pattern of the first tercet is repeated in the second one. The Nara period anthology *Man'yōshū* contains some sixty examples, but they date mainly from the early period represented in the anthology, and the form was seldom used in the middle period or thereafter.

senryū

Verse form that uses the same 5-7-5 syllable pattern as the *haiku* (q.v.) but employs colloquial diction and is devoted to the treatment of humorous or satirical themes. Unlike the *haiku*, it does not demand the inclusion of a *kigo*, a word indicative of the season, and is much freer in its choice of subject. It evolved from the *haiku* form and enjoyed great popularity during the Edo period, particularly among the common people, when experts in composing or selecting *senryū* appeared and *senryū* anthologies were compiled and published. By far the most popular of such experts was Karai Senryū, and the form in time came to be known by his name. As a vehicle for lighthearted literary expression it has continued to be popular to the present day.

sewamono

Literally, "everyday piece," a term for a type of drama in the *jōruri* and kabuki (q.v.) theaters that deals with events contemporary with the playwright, depicting the lives and characters of the townsman society of Edo times. It stands in contrast to the *jidaimono*, which deals with events drawn from history or legend, and is far more complex and large-scale in construction. Particularly noted among the *sewamono* are those written for the *jōruri* theater by Chikamatsu Monzaemon (1653–1724), which typically deal with the conflict between duty and desire faced by ill-fated lovers, and those of Furukawa Mokuami (1816–1893), which were written for the kabuki and reflect the changing social conditions of the late Edo and Meiji periods.

sui, iki

Terms appearing in the arts of the *chōnin* (townsmen) of the Edo period that designate the townsmen's own distinctive ideals of beauty. The terms are found particularly in the *ukiyo zōshi* and other types of literature of the Kyoto and Osaka areas, designating a person who knows his way around the world of entertainment and the licensed quarters and who in general understands the ins and outs of the world and of human behavior. Only a person with such understanding, a possessor of *sui* or *iki*, was thought worthy of being regarded as a true townsman. The same concept remains alive today in the Japanese concept of the ideal common man.

Both *sui* and *iki* represent a kind of composite of high class and low class beauty, refined and vulgar beauty, gaudy and restrained beauty. *Sui* reflects the taste and society of the Genroku era (1688–1704) and tends toward a rather flamboyant type of beauty, while *iki* reflectes those of the Bunka and Bunsei eras (1804–1830) and is more subdued.

tanka

Poetic form consisting of thirty-one syllables arranged in five lines according to the syllable pattern 5-7-5-7-7. Also referred to as *waka* (q.v.). From early times it has been the most popular of poetic forms, and many of the masterpieces of Japanese poetry are cast in it.

utaawase

A competition in which a group of persons compose poems on a fixed theme and the results are submitted to the verdict of a *hanja*, or judge. The contestants are arranged in two groups, designated "left" and "right" respectively. One contestant from each group submits a poem on the assigned theme, and the judge, a person chosen for his superior knowledge of poetry and ability as a poet, decides which of the poems is superior. At the conclusion of the match, the wins are totaled to determine which side has won. One pair of competing poems is known as a *ban*, and a single match or contest may consist of anywhere from a few *ban* to as many as fifteen hundred. The verdicts or critical remarks of the judge are termed *hanji*. The custom of holding such poetry contests began in the early Heian period and gained great popularity among the court and aristocracy, but from the middle ages on gradually declined. Many of the most famous poems in the language are the products of such contests.

utamakura

A famous historical or scenic site that has often been referred to in Japanese poetry in the past. The term originally designated a kind of manual for use in the composition of Japanese poetry that gave explanations of poetic expressions and listed the conventional epithets associated with famous places, but later it came to refer to the famous places themselves.

waka

General term for Japanese poems that employ a fixed form such as the *chōka*, *tanka*, *sedōka*, or *katauta* (q.v.). The term means literally a *Yamato uta*, or Japanese poem, as opposed to a *Kara uta*, or Chinese poem. In later ages, as the *tanka* form gained overwhelming popularity, the term *waka* in practice became synonymous with *tanka*.

Bibliography

APOLOGY: All bibliographic material supplied by the compilers of this dictionary was researched in the Japanese National Diet Library. A number of titles seem to be of unpublished theses and papers; such material, even without the necessary publication data, has been retained here in the hope that it might be of some help to the researcher.

Abutsu-ni
Tamai, Kosuke. *Abutsu-ni zakkō.*
Ishida, Yoshisada. *Izayoi nikki.* Nihon koten zensho. Tokyo: Asahi Shimbunsha, 1954.

Akazome Emon
Igarashi, Chikara. *Heianchō bungakushi,* vol. 1. Tokyo: Tokyodō, 1949.
Hisamatsu, Sen'ichi. *Wakashi: Sōron kodaihen.* Tokyo: Tokyodō, 1948.

Akutagawa Ryūnosuke
Nakamura, Kiichirō. *Akutagawa Ryūnosuke.* Tokyo: Kaname Shobō, 1954.
Shindō, Junko. *Akutagawa Ryūnosuke.* Tokyo: Kawade Shobō Shinsha, 1964.

Arai Hakuseki
Yamaji, Aizan. *Arai Hakuseki.*
Ueda Mannen. *Arai Hakuseki.*
———. *Gengogakusha to shite no Arai Hakuseki.*
Yoshino, Sakuzō. *Arai Hakuseki to Yowan Shirōte.*
Tani, Yoshihiko. *Arai Hakuseki to sono rekishi kenkyū.*
Izu, Kimio. *Arai Hakuseki.*
Arai Hakuseki zenshū. Tokyo: Tosho Kankōkai, 1905–07.

Arakida Hisaoi
Ōkawa, Shigeo, and Minami, Shigeki. *Kokugakusha denki shūsei.* Tokyo: Dai Nihon Tosho, 1904.
Sasaki, Nobutsuna. *Wakashi no kenkyū.* Tokyo: Dai Nihon Gakujutsu Kyōkai, 1915.

Ariga Nagao
Hisamatu, Sen'ichi. *Kinsei kindai-hen.* Nihon bungaku hyōronshi, vol. 2. Tokyo: Shibundō, 1952.

Arishima Takeo
Kōno, Toshirō. *Arishima Takeo.* Gendai Nihon bugaku kōza, shōsetsu, vol. 4. Tokyo: Sanseidō, 1962.
Senuma, Shigeki. "Arishima Takeo den." *Bungei,* 1962–63.

Ariwara no Narihira
Hisamatsu, Sen'ichi. *Wakashi: Sōron kodaihen.* Tokyo: Tokyodō, 1948.

Imaizumi, Tadayoshi. *Ariwara no Narihira*. Nihon bugaku kōza, vol. 1. Tokyo: Kawade Shobō, 1950.

Asukai Masatsune
Kubota, Utsubo. *Shinkokin wakashū hyōshaku*. Tokyo: Tokyodō, 1964–65.
Ishida Yoshisada. *Shinkokin wakashū zenchūkai*. Tokyo: Yūseidō Shuppan, 1960.

Awano Seiho
Ishida, Hakyō. *Awano Seiho*. Haiku kōza, vol. 6. Tokyo: Kaizōsha, 1932–33.
Mizuhara, Shūōshi. *Awano Seiho*. Haiku kōza, vol. 8. Tokyo: Kaizōsha, 1932–33.

Ben no Naishi
Ikeda, Kikan. *Kyūtei joryū nikki bungaku*. Tokyo: Shibundō, 1965.
Shimada, Taizō. *Chūsei no nikki kikō bungaku*. Kaizōsha Nihon bungaku kōza, zuihitsu nikki-hen. Tokyo: Kaizōsha, 1933–35.
Tamai, Kosuke. *Ben no Naishi nikki shinchū*. Tokyo: Taishūkan Shoten, 1958.

Bonchō
Morikawa, Kyoriku. *Fūzoku monzen*. Tokyo: Iwanami Shoten, 1949.
Imoto, Noichi. *Bonchō: Shomon wo meguru hitobito*. Tokyo: Shikyū Kokyōsha, 1953.
———. *Bonchō*. Haiku kōza, vol. 2. Tokyo: Meiji Shoin, 1958.

Chikako (Shinshi)
Yokoyama, Seiga. *Nihon josei kajinshi*.
Hisamatsu, Sen'ichi. *Chūsei waka shiron*. Tokyo: Hanawa Shobō, 1959.

Chikamatsu Hanji
Shuzui, Kenji. *Chikamatsu Hanji shū*. Nihon koten zensho. Tokyo: Asahi Shimbunsha, 1949.

Chikamatsu Monzaemon
Kuroki, Kanzō. *Chikamatsu Monzaemon*. Tokyo: Daitō Shuppansha, 1942.
Shuzui, Kenji. *Kinsei gikyoku kenkyū*. Chūkōkan, 1932.
Kawatake, Shigetoshi. *Chikamatsu Monzaemon*. Tokyo: Yoshikawa Kōbunkan, 1958.
Mori, Osamu. *Chikamatsu Monzaemon*. Tokyo: San'ichi Shobō, 1959.

Dōgen
Washio, Junkyō. *Dōgen zenji*.
Watsuji, Tetsurō. *Nihon seishinshi kenkyū*, 2 vols. Tokyo: Iwanami Shoten, 1935.
Tsuji, Zennosuke. *Nihon bukkyōshi*.
Nishio, Minoru. *Dōgen to Zeami*. Tokyo: Iwanami Shoten, 1965.

Eifuku (Yōfuku) Mon-in
Sasaki, Harutsuna. *Eifuku Mon-in*. Tokyo Seikatsusha, 1943.

Ejima Kiseki
Suzuki, Toshiya. *Nihon kinsei shōsetsushi*. Tokyo: Meguro Shoten, 1920, 1922.
Mizutani, Futō, *Hachimonjiya-mono kenkyū*. Tokyo: Shun'yōdō.
Hisamatsu, Sen'ichi, et al, ed. *Shimpan Nihon bungakushi, kinsei*. Tokyo: Shibundō, 1964.

Enchi Fumiko
Yoshida, Seiichi. *Koten to gendai bungaku*. 1955.

Enomoto Kikaku
Shida, Yoshihide. *Shōmon jittetsu*. Iwanami kōza, Nihon bungaku. Tokyo: Iwanami Shoten, 1933.
Imaizumi, Jun'ichi. *Genroku haijin Takarai Kikaku*. Tokyo: Ōfūsha, 1969.

Fujioka Sakutarō
Kazamaki, Keijirō. "Haga Yaichi to Fujioka Sakutarō." *Bungaku*, 1955.

Fujiwara no Akisue
Inoue, Muneo. "Rokujō Tōke no seisui." *Kokubungaku Kenkyū*, vol. 15, 1957.
Totani, Mitsue. "Rokujō Akisue no uta." *Gakuen*, 1960.

Fujiwara no Akisuke
Inoue, Muneo. "Fujiwara no Akisuke den no kōsatsu." *Kokugo to Kokubungaku*, 1959.

Fujiwara no Ietaka
Kubota, Jun. *Fujiwara no Ietaka kashū to sono kenkyū*. Tokyo: Miyai Shoten, 1968.
Kazamaki, Keijirō. *Shinkokin jidai*. Tokyo: Jimbun Shoin, 1936.
Taniyama, Shigeru. *Shinkokin no kajin*.

Fujiwara no Kintō
Hisamatsu, Sen'ichi. *Kintō karonshū*. Tokyo: Kotenbunko, 1951.
Nomura, Hachirō, *Kokubungaku kenkyūshi*. Tokyo: Genkō Shoten, 1926.

Fujiwara no Kiyosuke
Nose, Asaji. "Rokujōke no kajin to sono kagaku shisō." *Kokugo Kokubun no Kenkyū*, 1928.
Sasaki, Nobutsuna. *Nihon kagakushi*. Tokyo: Hakubunkan, 1910.

Fujiwara no Michitoshi
Inoue, Muneo. *Fujiwara no Michitoshi nempu. Heianchō bungaku kenkyū*. 1957.

Fujiwara no Mototoshi
Hashimoto, Fumio. *Mototoshi: sono ningenzō—rufubon Mototoshi shū o megutte*. 1958.
————. "Minamoto no Toshiyori, Fujiwara no Mototoshi no karon—sono tairitsu no kiban," *Kokubungaku*, 1958.

Fujiwara no Shunzei
Hisamatsu, Sen'ichi. *Kodai chūsei hen*. Nihon bungaku hyōronshi, vol. 1. Tokyo: Shibundō, 1949.
Taniyama, Shigeru. *Yūgen no kenkyū*. Tokyo: Kyōiku Tosho, 1943.

Fujiwara no Tameie
Yasui, Hisayoshi, ed. *Fujiwara Tameie zen kashū*. Tokyo: Musashino Shoin, 1962.

Fujiwara no (Kyōgoku) Tamekane
Toki, Zemmaro. *Yakuchū Tamekane-kyō wakashō*. Kyoto: Fukuin Shobō, 1963.
Hisamatsu, Sen'ichi. *Chūsei waka shiron*. Tokyo: Hanawa Shobō, 1959.

Fujiwara no (Nijō) Tameuji
Nishishita, Kyōichi. *Waka shiron*. Tokyo: Shibundō, 1944.
Waka bungaku daijiten. Tokyo: Meiji Shoin, 1962.

Fujiwara no (Nijō) Tameyo
Hisamatsu, Sen'ichi. "Chūsei wakashi ron." *Waka sakusha burui*. Tokyo: Hanawa Shobō, 1959.
Taniyama, Shigeru. *Wakashi: chūsei*. Waka bungaku kōza. Tokyo: Ōfūsha, 1969.

Fujiwara no Teika
Ishida, Yoshisada. *Fujiwara no Teika no kenkyū*. Tokyo: Bungadō Shoten, 1957.
Kazamaki, Keijirō. *Shinkokin jidai*. Tokyo: Jimbun Shoin, 1936.

Fujiwara Seika
Hara, Sōkei, and Tōjō, Kindō. *Sentetsu sōdan*. Tokyo: Shōeidō Shoten, 1892.
Inoue, Tetsujirō. *Nihon Shushigakuha no tetsugaku*. Tokyo: Tomiyamabō, 1937.
Fujiwara Seika shū. Kokumin seishin bunka kenkyūsho. Tokyo: Kokumin Seishin Bunka Kenkyūjo, 1938–39.

Funahashi Seiichi
Kawakami, Tetsutarō. "Funahashi Seiichi." *Gunzō*, July, 1951.

Uramatsu, Samitarō. *Funahashi Seiichi no sakka seishin.* Shinsei gendai Nihon bungaku zenshū, vol. 14. Tokyo: Chikuma Shobō, 1958.

Funya no Yasuhide
Tsukahara, Tetsuo. "Rokkasen." *Heian bungaku kenkyū.* 1935.
Sayama, Sei. "Rokkasen no mondai." *Waka bungaku kenkyū.* 1956.

Fushimi Tennō
Sasaki, Harutsuna. *Fushimi Tennō gyosei no kenkyū.* Tokyo: Jimbun Shoin, 1943.

Futabatei Shimei
Tsubouchi, Shōyō, and Uchida, Roan, eds. *Futabatei Annai.* Futabatei Shimei zenshū, bekkan. Tokyo: Iwanami Shoten, 1954.
Inagaki, Tatsuo. *Bungaku kakumeiki to Futabatei Shimei.* Iwanami kōza, Bungaku, vol. 4. Tokyo: Iwanami Shoten.

Gion Nankai
Matsushita, Tadashi. *Edo jidai no shifū shiron.* Tokyo: Meiji Shoin, 1969.

Godaigo Tennō
Kuroita, Katsumi. *Godaigo Tennō onjiseki.* Nara: Yoshino Jingū Hōsankai, 1932.

Gomurakami Tennō
Ōnogi, Katsutoyo. *Shinyō wakashū.* Nihon bungaku. Tokyo: Iwanami Shoten, 1932.

Goshirakawa Tennō
Niima, Shin'ichi. *Kayōshi no kenkyū.* Tokyo: Shibundō, 1947.

Gotoba Jōkō
Sasaki, Nobutsuna. *Nihon kagakushi.* Tokyo: Hakubunkan, 1910, 1942.

Gusai
Kaneko, Kinjirō. *Tsukubashū no kenkyū.* Tokyo: Kazama Shobō, 1965.

Hachimonjiya Jishō
Hachimonjiya-mono kenkyū. Nihon bungaku kōza, vol. 8. Tokyo: Shinchōsha, 1926–28.
Fujimura, Tsukuru. *Ukiyo-zōshi no kenkyū.* Nihon bungaku kōza, kinsei no bungaku. Tokyo: Kaizōsha, 1933–35.

Haga Yaichi
"Haga hakase tsuitōgō." *Kokugo to Kokubungaku,* 1927.
Kazamaki, Keijirō. "Haga Yaichi to Fujioka Sakutarō." *Bungaku,* 1955.
Haga Yaichi shū. Meiji bungaku zenshū, vol. 44. 1968.

Hagiwara Sakutarō
Itō, Hitoshi, ed. *Hagiwara Sakutarō.* Kindai bungaku kanshō kōza, vol. 15, Tokyo: Kadokawa Shoten, 1958–67.
Miyoshi, Tatsuji, *Hagiwara Sakutarō.* Tokyo: Chikuma Shobō, 1963.

Hanazono Tennō
Iwahashi, Koyata. *Hanazono Tennō.* Tokyo: Yoshikawa Kōbunkan.

Hasegawa Nyozekan
Muramatsu, Sadataka. "Hasegawa Nyozekan." *Kokubungaku,* 1961.
Hasegawa Nyozekan: shakai hihan no genron. Nihon no shisōka, vol. 3. Asahi Shimbunsha, 1963.

Hattori Nankaku
Haga, Yaichi. *Nihon kambungakushi.*
Edo jidai no kanshi kambun. Shinchō Nihon bungaku kōza, vols. 13, 14. Tokyo: Shinchōsha, 1927, 1928.

Hattori Ransetsu
Shida, Yoshihide. *Shōmon jittetsu.* Iwanami kōza, Nihon bungaku. Tokyo: Iwanami Shoten.
Higuchi Kō, *Bashō, Kikaku, Ransetsu.* Haiku kōza, vol. 2. Tokyo: Kaizōsha, 1932.

Hayashi Razan
Naramoto, Tatsuya, ed. *Nippon no shisōka.* Tokyo: Mainichi Shimbunsha, 1954.
Imanaka, Kanji. *Hayashi Razan no kyōgaku-shisō.* Kokumin seikatsushi kenkyū, vol. 3. Tokyo: Yoshikawa Kōbunkan, 1958.
Hori, Isao. *Hayashi Razan.* Jimbutsu sōsho. Tokyo: Yoshikawa Kōbunkan, 1964.

Hieda no Are
Hisamatsu, Sen'ichi, et al. *Kojiki taisei.* Tokyo: Heibonsha, 1958.
Kurano, Kenji. *Kojiki.* Tokyo: Kōbundō, 1955.

Higuchi Ichiyō
Yoshida, Seiichi. *Higuchi Ichiyō kenkyū.* Tokyo: Shinchōsha, 1956.
Shioda, Ryōhei. *Higuchi Ichiyō kenkyū.*

Hirabayashi Taiko
Hirano, Ken. *Hirabayashi Taiko.* Gendai no sakka. Tokyo: Kadokawa Shoten, 1957.

Hiraga Gennai
Teruoka, Yasutaka. *Kinsei bungaku no tembō.* Tokyo: Meiji Shoin, 1953.
Noda, Hisao. *Hiraga Gennai no hito to shōgai.* Tokyo: Kōseikaku, 1944.
Nakamura, Yukihiko. *Fūraisanjinshū.* Nihon koten bungaku taikei. Tokyo: Iwanami Shoten, 1961.

Hirano Kuniomi
Miyabe, Temmin. *Hirano Kuniomi.*
Sasaki, Nobutsuna. *Kinsei wakashi.* Tokyo: Hakubunkan, 1923.

Hōnen
Mochizuki, Shintei, ed. *Hōnen shōnin zenshū.* Kyoto: Sōsuisha, 1906.
Tamura, Enchō. *Hōnen.* Jimbutsu Sōsho. Tokyo: Yoshikawa Kōbunkan, 1959.
Ikawa, Teikei, ed. *Hōnen shōnin den zenshū.* Osaka: Hōnen Shōninden Zenshū Kankōkai, 1952.

Hori Bakusui
Temmei meika kusen. Nihon haisho taikei. Tokyo: Nihon Haisho Taikei, 1926–28.
Ōkawa, Ryōryō. *Bakusui.* Haiku kōza, vol. 3. Tokyo: Meiji Shoin, 1959.
Shimizu, Takayuki. *Chūkōki no hairon.* Haiku kōza, vol. 5. Tokyo: Meiji Shoin, 1900–01.

Hori Tatsuo
Maruoka, Akira, ed. *Hori Tatsuo kenkyū.* Tokyo: Shinchōsha, 1958.
Kokubo, Minoru. *Hori Tatsuo ron.* Tokyo: Mugi Shobō, 1965.

Hosokawa Yūsai
Kuwada, Tadachika. *Hosokawa Yūsai.* Tokyo: Nihon Shoin, 1948.
Hisamatsu, Sen'ichi, ed. *Nihon bungakushi, kinsei.* Tokyo: Shibundō, 1956.

Hozumi no Miko
Oyama, Tokujirō. *Man'yōshū-kogi jimbutsuden.*
Kawasaki, Yasuyuki. *Temmu Tennō no shoōji, shoōjo.* Man'yōshū taisei, vol. 9. Tokyo: Heibonsha, 1953.

Ichijō Kanera
Fukui, Kyūzō. *Ichijō Kanera.* Kōseikaku, 1943.

Igarashi Chikara
Oka, Kazuo. *Koten shōyō*. Tokyo: Kasama Shoin, 1971.

Ihara Saikaku
Kataoka, Ryōichi. *Ihara Saikaku*. Tokyo: Iwanami Shoten, 1948.
Teruoka, Yasutaka. *Saikaku: Hyōron to kenkyū*. Tokyo: Chūō Kōrosha, 1948, 1950.
Nihon bungakushi, kinsei. Tokyo: Shibundō, 1956.

Iida Dakotsu
Yamamoto, Kenkichi. *Gendai haiku*, vol. 1. Tokyo: Kadokawa Shoten, 1951.
"Dakotsu tsuitō tokushū." *Kirara*, 1963.

Iketani Shinzaburō
Funabashi, Seiichi. "Iketani Shinzaburō tsuitō tokushū." *Sakuhin*, 1934.
Takami, Jun. *Shōwa bungaku seisuishi*, vol. 1. Tokyo: Bungei Shunjūsha, 1958.

Ikkyū Sōjun
Kuwata, Tadachika. *Ikkyū zenji*. Sekai ijinden zenshū, vol. 43. Tokyo: Kaiseisha, 1964.
Mushanokōji, Saneatsu. *Ikkyū, Sorori, Ryōkan*. Tokyo: Kōdansha, 1937.
Furuta Shōkin, *Ikkyū*. Tokyo: Yūzankaku, 1944.

Ikuta Chōkō
Ino, Kenji. "Ikuta Chōkō no shōgai to shisō." *Nihon bungaku no kindai to gendai*. Tokyo: Miraisha, 1958.

Imagawa Ryōshun
Koyama, Keiichi. *Imagawa Ryōshun*. Tokyo: Sanseidō, 1944.

Inawashiro Kensai
Kaneko, Kinjirō. *Rengashi Kensai denkō*. Tokyo: Nan'undō Ōfūsha, 1962.

Ise
Usuda, Jingorō. *Heian joryū kajin, Ise den*. Seigodō, 1943.

Ishibashi Ningetsu
Yamamoto, Kenkichi, ed. *Ishibashi Nigetsu hyōronshū*. Tokyo: Iwanami Shoten, 1939.

Ishida Hakyō
Kusumoto, Kenkichi. *Ishida Hakyō*. Tokyo: Nan'undō Ōfūsha 1962.

Ishikawa Masamochi
Kyōka kenkyū. Iwanami bungaku kōza. Tokyo: Iwanami Shoten, 1933.
Suga, Chikuho. *Kinsei kyōkashi*. Tokyo: Nakanishi Shobō, 1936.

Ishikawa no Iratsume
Takagi, Ichinosuke, et al, eds. *Man'yōshū*. Nihon koten bungaku taikei, vol. 4. Tokyo: Iwanami Shoten, 1957.
Takeda, Yukichi. *Man'yōshū zenchūshaku*. Tokyo: Kadokawa Shoten, 1956–57.
Omodaka, Hisataka. *Man'yōshū chūshaku*. Tokyo: Chūō Kōronsha, 1968.

Ishikawa Takuboku
Kindaichi, Kyōsuke. *Teihon Ishikawa Takuboku*. Tokyo: Kadokawa Shoten, 1949, 1951.
Iwaki, Yukinori. *Ishikawa Takuboku*. Tokyo: Meiji Shoin 1965.

Ishikawa Tatsuzō
Nakajima, Kenzō. "Ishikawa Tatsuzō." *Gendai sakka ron*. Tokyo: Eihōsha, 1955.
Nakano, Yoshio, ed. "Ishikawa Tatsuzō." *Gendai no sakka*. Tokyo: Iwanami Shoten, 1955.

Ishikure Chimata
"Ishikure Chimata tsuitōgō." *Kokoro no Hana*, 1944.

"Nobutsuna-kei kajin tokushū." *Tanka Kenkyū*, 1963.

Ishizaka Yōjirō
Ōi, Kōsuke. *Ishizaka Yōjirō ron*. Shōwa sakka ron, vol. 2. Tokyo: Shōgakkan, 1943.
Togaeri, Hajime. *Ishizaka Yōjirō ron*. Shōwa no sakkatachi, vol. 2. Tokyo: Eihōsha, 1955.

Itō Hitoshi
Hirano, Ken. "Itō Hitoshi." *Gendai no sakka*. Tokyo: Kadokawa Shoten, 1957.
Nakamura, Mitsuo. *Itō Hitoshi ron*. 1958.

Itō Jinsai
Ishida, Ichirō. *Itō Jinsai*. Tokyo: Yoshikawa Kōbunkan, 1960.
Nihon bungaku daijiten. Tokyo: Shinchōsha, 1950.

Itō Sachio
Saitō, Mokichi. *Itō Sachio*. Tokyo: Chūō Kōronsha, 1947.

Izumi Shikibu
Fujioka, Tadazane. *Izumi Shikibu*. Nihon bungaku kōza, vol. 2. Tokyo: Kawade Shobō, 1950.
Yoshida, Kōichi. *Izumi Shikibu no kenkyū*, vols. 1, 2. Tokyo: Koten Bunko, 1964, 1967.

Jakuren
Kazamaki, Keijirō. *Shin kokin jidai*. Tokyo: Jimbun Shoin, 1936.

Jien
Manaka, Fujiko. *Jien oshō no kenkyū*. Tokyo: Morikita Shoten, 1943.

Jimmu Tennō
Takagi, Ichinosuke. "Nihon bungaku ni okeru jojishi jidai." *Yoshino no ayu*. Tokyo: Iwanami Shoten, 1943.
Ishimoda, Tadashi. "Kodai kizoku no eiyū jidai." *Shigaku*. 1948.

Jippensha Ikku
Fujimura, Saku. *Ikku kenkyū*. Nihon bungaku kōza, vol. 10. Tokyo: Shinchōsha, 1931–32.

Jitō Tennō
Takeda, Yukichi. *Kōshitsu kajin*. Sakusha-betsu Man'yōshū hyōshaku, vol. 1. Tokyo: Hibonkaku, 1935.
Tsugita, Masaki. *Man'yōshū no kōshitsu kajin*. Man'yōshū kōza, sakka-hen, vol. 4. Tokyo: Sōgensha, 1952.

Jōben
Koyama, Shin'ichi. *Shinkō wakashi*. Daimeidō, 1932.

Jōjin Azari no Haha
Tamai, Kōsuke. "Jōjin Azari no kakei." *Bungaku*, 1943.
Usuda, Jingorō. "Jōjin Azari no haha." *Kokubungaku*, 1959.

Jomei Tennō
Saigo, Nobutsuna. *Man'yō shiki daiichibu*. Tokyo: University of Tokyo Press, 1958.
Tanabe, Yukio. *Shoki Man'yō no sekai*. Tokyo: Hanawa Shobō, 1957.

Jōō
Toda, Katsuhisa. *Takeno Jōō*. Tokyo: Chūō Kōron Bijutsu Shuppan, 1969.

Juntoku-in
Kyūsonjin, Noboru. *Yakumomishō to sono kenkyū*. Tokyo: Kōseikaku, 1939.
Hisamatsu, Sen'ichi. *Chūsei wakashi*. Tokyo: Tokyodō, 1961.

Kada no Arimaro
Ōnuki, Shimpo. *Kada Azumamaro-ō*. 1911.

Haga, Yaichi. *Kokugakushi gairon.* Tokyo: Kokugo Denshūjo, 1900.
Hisamatsu, Sen'ichi, ed. *Kinsei.* Nihon bungakushi, vol. 4. Tokyo: Shibundō, 1956.

Kada no Azumamaro
Okawa, Shigeo, and Minami, Shigeki. *Kokugakusha denki shūsei.* Tokyo: Dai Nihon Tosho, 1904.
Kōno, Shōzō. *Kokugaku no kenkyū.* Tokyo: Ōokayama Shoten, 1934.

Kada Tamiko
Onuki, Maura. *Kada Azuma-ō.* 1911.

Kagami Shikō
Morikawa, Kyoriku, and Mukai, Kyorai, eds. *Haikai modō.* Tokyo: Iwanami Shoten, 1954.
Ebara, Taizō. "Shikō." *Shōmon no hitobito.* Daiyasu Shuppan, 1946.
Kagami, Torao. *Shikō.* Haiku kōza, vol. 3. Tokyo: Meiji Shoin, 1959.

Kaga no Chiyo
Hegi, Hekiken. "Chiyo ni jiseki zakkō." *Gekka,* vol. 2.
Kawashima, Tsuyu. *Joryūhaijin.* Tokyo: Meiji Shoin, 1957.

Kagawa Kageki
Yamamoto, Kashō. *Kagawa Kageki ron.* 1942.
Kuroiwa, Ichirō. *Kagawa Kageki no kenkyū.* Kobe: Bunkyō Shoin, 1957.

Kakimon-in
Tanimori, Yoshiomi. *Kakimon-in onuta no maki shōchū.*
Murata, Masashi. "Maedake-hon Kakimon-in gyoshū no kachi." *Nambokuchō shiron.* Tokyo: Chūō Kōronsha, 1949.

Kakinomoto no Hitomaro
Saitō, Mokichi. *Kakinomoto no Hitomaro.* Tokyo: Iwanami Shoten, 1934–1940.
Takeda, Yukichi. *Kakinomoto no Hitomaro hyōden.* Man'yōshū taisei, sakusha kenkyū-hen, vol. 1. Tokyo: Heibonsha, 1953.
Morimoto, Jikichi. *Hitomaro no sekai.*

Kambara Ariake
Yano, Hojin. *Kambara Ariake,* rev. ed. Tokyo: Tōkō Shoin, 1959.
Matsumura, Midori. *Kambara Ariake ronkō.* Tokyo: Meiji Shoin, 1965.

Kamijima (Uejima) Onitsura
Yamazaki, Kiyoshi. *Onitsura ron.* Tokyo: Chikuma Shobō, 1944.
Suzuki, Shigemasa. *Haijin Onitsura no kenkyū.* Tokyo: Kyōritsusha, 1926.
Okada, Rihei, ed. *Onitsura zenshū.* Tokyo: Kadokawa Shoten, 1968.

Kamo no Chōmei
Yanase, Kazuo. *Kamo no Chōmei no shin kenkyū.* 1963.

Kamo no Mabuchi
Motoori, Norinaga. *Tamakatsuma.* Tokyo: Iwanami Shoten, 1958.
Sasaki, Nobutsuna. *Kamo no Mabuchi to Motoori Norinaga.* Tokyo: Kōbundō, 1917.
Nomura, Hachirō. *Kokugaku zenshi.* Tokyo: Seki Shoin, 1928, 1929.
Hisamatsu, Sen'ichi. *Kokugaku: sono seiritsu to kokubungaku no kankei.* Tokyo: Shibundō, 1941.
———. "Kamo no Mabuchi, Kagawa Kageki." *Rekidai kajin kenkyū.* 1938.

Kan'ami
Nonomura, Kaizō. *Zeami jūrokubushū.*
———. *Kan'ami, Zeami jiseki kō.*
Nogami, Toyoichirō. *Kan'ami Kiyotsugu.* Tokyo: Kaname Shobō, 1949.

Kaneko Kun'en
Onoe, Saishū. "Kaneko Kun'en-kun." *Shumi*, 1910.
"Kaneko Kun'en no tanka hyōshaku." *Kokubungaku*, 1958.

Karai Senryū
Unga, Hentetsu. *Nihon bungaku yūgi taizen.*

Karu no Hitsugi-no-miko
Nakajima, Junji. "Karu no Hitsugi-no-miko no hiren." *Kaishaku to Kanshō*, 1954.
Aoki, Seiko. "Kinashi no Karu no Hitsugi-no-miko to Karu no Ōiratsume no uta."
Nihon jojōshi-ron. Tokyo: Kōbundō, 1957.

Karu no Ōiratsume
Tsuchihashi, Kan. *Kodai kayō-shū.* Nihon koten bungaku taikei, vol. 3, Tokyo: Iwanami
Shoten, 1957.

Kasa no Iratsume (Otome)
Hisamatsu, Sen'ichi. "Kasa no Iratsume." *Man'yōshū to jidai bungaku.* Tokyo: Kasama
Shoin, 1973.

Kasa no Kanamura
Sasaki, Nobutsuna. *Kasa no Kanamura.* Man'yōshū hyōshaku, vol. 2. Tokyo: Rokko
Shuppan.
Inukai, Takashi. *Kasa no Kanamura.* Nihon bungakusha hyōden zensho.
Takasaki, Masahide. *Kasa no Kanamura.* Man'yōshū taisei, sakka kenkyū-hen, vol. 2.
Tokyo: Heibonsha, 1954.

Katō Shūson
"Shūson-ron tokushū-gō." *Kanrai*, 1950.
Tagawa, Hiroko. *Katō Shūson.*

Kawabata Bōsha
Kawabata Bōsha tokushū. *Haiku*, 1957.
"Kawabata Bōsha ron." *Haiku*, 1958.

Kawabata Yasunari
Saigusa, Yasutaka. *Kawabata Yasunari.* Tokyo: Yushindō, 1961.
Hasegawa, Izumi. *Kawabata Yasunari ronkō.* Tokyo: Meiji Shoin, 1965.
Kawabata bungaku kenkyū-kai, ed. *Kawabata Yasunari no hito to geijutsu.* Tokyo: Kyōiku
Sentā, 1971.

Kawada Jun
Kimata, Osamu. "Kawada Jun." *Kindai tanka no kanshō to hihyō.* Tokyo: Meiji Shoin,
1964.

Kawahigashi Hekigotō
Uryū, Toshiichi. *Kawahigashi Hekigotō.* Haiku kōza, vol. 8. Tokyo: Meiji Shoin, 1900.
Abe, Kimio. *Kawahigashi Hekigotō.* Tokyo: Nan'undō, 1964.

Kawai Suimei
Iwasa, Tōichirō. "Kawai Suimei." *Gendaishi kanshō.*
Furukawa, Kiyohiko. "Kawai Suimei hyōden." *Nihon Bungaku Kenkyū.* May, 1951.

Kawaji Ryūkō
Ishimaru, Hisashi. *Kawaji Ryūkō: Hito to sakuhin.* Gendai bungaku kōza, vol. 4. Tokyo:
Meiji Shoin, 1961.
Hitomi, Tōmei. "Kōgoshi no seiritsu to katei." *Gakuen.* Tokyo: Shōwa Women's Univer-
sity.

Kawatake Mokuami
Kawatake, Shigetoshi. *Kawatake Mokuami*. Tokyo: Yoshikawa Kōbunkan, 1961.
Okamoto, Kidō. *Mokuami kenkyū*. Tokyo: Shinchōsha, 1926–28.

Keichū
Nakagawa, Masafusa. *Keichū jisekikō*.
Ōmachi, Keigetsu. "Keichū ajari." *Kokubungaku taikō*, vol. 1.
Hisamatsu, Sen'ichi. *Keichū*. Tokyo: Yoshikawa Kōbunkan, 1963.

Keikai
Takeda, Yūkichi. *Nihon reiiki*. Tokyo: Asahi Shimbunsha, 1950.
Matsuura, Sadatoshi. *Nihon reiiki*. Tokyo: Kōbundō, 1956.

Keiun (Kyōun)
Dai Nihonshi, ch. 221. Tokyo: Yoshikawa Kōbunkan, 1911.
Ishida, Yoshisada. *Ton'a, Kyōun*. Tokyo: Sanseidō, 1943.

Kenreimon-in no Ukyō-no-daibu
Tomikura, Tokujirō. *Ukyō-no-daibu, Kojijū*.
Hon'iden, Shigemi. *Kenreimon-in Ukyō-no-daibu shū zenshaku*. 1950.

Kenshō
Fukui, Kyūzō. *Dai Nihon kagakushi*. Tokyo: Fujishobō, 1926.
Nomura, Hachirō. *Kokubungaku kenkyūshi*. Tokyo: Hara Shoten, 1926.
Kyūsojin, Noboru. *Kenshō, Jakuren*. Tokyo: Sanseidō, 1942.

Kikuchi Kan
Kobayashi, Hideyo. *Kikuchi Kan ron*. Kikuchi Kan zenshū, vol. 4.
Asami, Jun. "Kikuchi Kan ron." *Meiji-Taishō bungaku kenkyū*. Tokyo: Tōkyōdō Shuppan, 1949–58.

Kimata Osamu
Yashiro, Tōson. "Kimata Osamu ron." *Yakumo*, 1947.
Kagawa, Susumu. *Kimata Osamu*. Gendai kajin ron, vol. 1. Tokyo: Ōfūsha, 1963.

Ki no Iratsume
Morimoto, Jikichi. "Man'yōshū sakka kōshō." *Araragi*, 1929.

Ki no Kaion
Mizutani, Futō. *Ki no Kaion jōrurishū kaidai; Eiri jōrurishi*. Tokyo: Taiyōsha, 1929.
Shuzui, Kenji. *Kaion, Izumo, Hanji*.
Jōruri kenkyū bunken shūsei. Nihon engeki kenkyūkai.
Kuroki, Kanzō. *Ki no Kaion kenkyū*. Nihon bungaku kōza, vol. 10. Tokyo: Shinchōsha.
———. *Jōrurishi*. Tokyo: Seijisha, 1948.

Kinoshita Chōshōshi
Motoori, Norinaga. *Tamakatsuma*. Tokyo: Iwanami Shoten, 1958.
Sasaki, Nobutsuna. *Kinsei wakashi*. Tokyo: Hakubunkan, 1923.
Usami, Kisohachi. *Wakashi ni kansuru kenkyū*. Wakatake Shuppan.
Yoshida, Kōichi, ed. *Zenkashū*, and *Wabunshū*. Chōshōshi zenshū, vols. 1, 2. Tokyo: Koten Bunko, 1972.

Kinoshita Rigen
Kimata, Osamu. "Kinoshita Rigen." *Kindai tanka no kanshō to hihyō*. Tokyo: Meiji Shoin, 1964.
Kagawa, Susumu. "Kinoshita Rigen ron." *Gendai kajin ron*. Tokyo: Ōfūsha, 1961–64.

Kinoshita Takabumi
Sasaki, Nobutsuna. *Kinsei wakashi*. Tokyo: Hakubunkan, 1923.

Hisamatsu, Sen'ichi. *Nihon bungaku hyōronshi.* Tokyo: Shibundō, 1952.

Ki no Tomonori
Fujioka, Sakutarō. *Kokubungaku zenshi, Heianchō hen.* Tokyo: Iwanami Shoten, 1923.
Saeki, Umetomo. *Kokin wakashū.* Tokyo: Iwanami Shoten, 1958.

Ki no Tsurayuki
Nishishita, Kyōichi. *Ki no Tsurayuki.* Nihon bungaku kōza, vol. 2. Tokyo: Kawade Shobō, 1950.
Kazamaki, Keijirō. "Ki no Tsurayuki." *Kokugo to Kokubungaku,* Oct., 1952.
Hagitani, Sunao. "Ki no Tsurayuki." *Kokubungaku,* 1957.

Kisen Hōshi
Ishida, Yoshisada. *Hyakunin isshu.* Tokyo: Yūseidō Shuppan, 1956; Kyoto: Tankōsha, 1971.

Kitabatake Chikafusa
Yamada, Yoshio. *Jinnō shōtōki jutsugi.* Tokyo: Min'yūsha, 1932.

Kitahara Hakushū
Nishimoto, Akio. *Kitahara Hakushū.* Shinseisha, 1965.
Kimata, Osamu; Kawazoe, Kunimoto; and Hasegawa Izumi, eds. *Kitahara Hakushū Gendai bungaku kōza,* vol. 4. Tokyo: Meiji Shoin, 1961.

Kitamura Kigin
Ishikura, Shigetsugu. *Kitamura Kigin den,* 1898.
Kigin, Haiku kōza, vol. 2. Tokyo: Meiji Shoin, 1958.

Kobayashi Hideo
Symposium: "Kobayashi Hideo to sakuhin." *Kaishaku to Kanshō,* 1961.
Etō, Jun. *Kobayashi Hideo.* Tokyo: Kōdansha, 1965.

Kobayashi Issa
Iijima, Kyoshin. *Haikaiji Issa.*
Itō, Masao. *Kobayashi Issa.* Nihon koten zensho. Tokyo: Asahi Shimbunsha, 1953.
Kobayashi, Keiichirō. "Kobayashi Issa." *Jimbutsu sōsho.* Tokyo: Yoshikawa Kōbunkan, 1961.

Kōda Rohan
"Kōda Rohan tokushūgō." *Bungaku,* 1947.
Yanagida, Izumi. *Kōda Rohan.* Tokyo: Chūō Kōronsha, 1942.
Saitō, Mokichi. *Kōda Rohan.* Tokyo: Senshin Shorin, 1949.

Koizumi Yakumo
Tanabe, Ryūji. *Koizumi Yakumo kenkyū.* Nihon bungaku kōza, vol. 14. Tokyo: Shinchōsha, 1932.

Komparu Zenchiku
Yoshida, Tōgo. *Nōgaku koten, Zenchiku-shū.* Nōgakukai, 1915.
Nonomura, Kaizō. *Komparu Jūshichibu-shū.* Shun'yōdō, 1932.

Konakamura Kiyonori
Hisamatsu, Sen'ichi. *Konakamura Kiyonori no gakumon.* Nihon bungaku hyōronshi, vol. 2. Tokyo: Shibundō, 1936–50.

Kondō Yoshimi
Taya, Toshi. "Kondō Yoshimi." *Kaishaku to Kanshō,* 1964.

Kōun (Nagachika)
Iwabashi, Koyata. "Kazan-in Nagachika." *Kokugo to Kokubungaku,* Nov., 1953.

Kubota Utsubo
"Kubota Utsubo kenkyū." *Tanka*, Dec., 1955.
Kubota, Shin'ichirō. *Kubota Utsubo*. Tokyo: Ōfūsha Shuppan, 1962.

Kūkai
Naitō, Torajirō. *Nihon bunkashi kenkyū*. Tokyo: Kadokawa Shoten, 1955.
Konishi, Jin'ichi. *Bunkyō hifuron kō*. Kenkyū hen, vol. 1. Daiyasu Shuppan, 1948; Kenkyū hen, vol. 2., Kōbun hen. Tokyo: Kōdansha, 1951, 1953.

Kumagai Naoyoshi
Sasaki, Nobutsuna. *Nihon kagakushi*. Tokyo: Hakubunkan, 1910.
————. *Kinsei wakashi*. Tokyo: Hakubunkan, 1923.
Fukui, Kyūzō. *Dai Nihon kagaku shi*.
Kanekawa, Shōtoku. *Kumagai Naoyoshi den*.

Kunikida Doppo
Sakamoto, Hiroshi, *Kunikida Doppo*. Tokyo: Seijō Kokubun Gakkai, 1948.
Yoshida, Seiichi. "Kunikida Doppo." *Shizen shugi no kenkyū*. Tokyo: Tokyodō, 1955, 1958.

Kyokutei (Takizawa) Bakin
Asō, Isoji. *Takizawa Bakin*. Tokyo: Yoshikawa Kōbunkan, 1959.

Maeda Yūgure
Kimata, Osamu. *Maeda Yūgure*. Nihon kajin kōza, kindai no kajin, vol. 2. Tokyo: Kōbundō, 1961.
Maeda, Tōru. "Yūgure kenkyū." *Shiika*, 1955.

Masaoka Shiki
Takahama, Kyoshi. *Shiki ni tsuite*. Tokyo: Sōgensha, 1953.
"Tokushū Masaoka Shiki." *Haiku*, Sep., 1962.

Matsunaga Teitoku
Fujii, Otsuo. *Edo bungaku kenkyū*. Tokyo: Naigai Shuppan, 1921.
Odaka, Toshio. *Matsunaga Teitoku no kenkyū*. Tokyo: Shibundō, 1956.

Matsuo Bashō
Yamazaki, Tōkichi. *Bashō-san Tōsei*.
Kobayashi, Ichirō. *Bashōō no isshō*.
Higuchi, Isao. *Bashō kenkyū*. Bunken Shoin, 1923.
Hagiwara, Seisensui. *Tabibi to Bashō*.
Sōma, Gyofū. *Issa to Ryōkan to Bashō*.
Okumura, Kenzō. *Bashō denkikō*. 1963.
Hagiwara, Ragetsu. *Bashō no zembō*.
Sugiura, Shōichirō. *Bashō no kenkyū*. Tokyo: Iwanami Shoten, 1958.
Yamamoto, Kenkichi. *Bashō: Sono kaishaku to hihyō*, 3 vols. Tokyo: Shinchōsha, 1955–56.

Mibu no Tadamine
Yamada, Takao. *Nihon kagaku no genryū*. Tokyo: Nihon Shoin, 1952.
Ogami, Hachirō. *Kokin wakashū kenkyū*. Nihon bungaku kōza, vol. 5. Tokyo: Shinchōsha, 1932–32.
Hisamatsu, Sen'ichi. *Kodai chūsei hen*. Nihon bungaku hyōronshi, vol. 1. Tokyo: Shibundō, 1949.

Michitsuna no Haha
Ikeda, Kikan. *Kyūtei joryū nikki bungaku*. Tokyo: Shibundō, 1927.
Kawaguchi, Hisao. *Kagerō nikki*. Nihon koten bungaku taikei, vol. 20. Tokyo: Iwanami Shoten, 1957.

Uemura, Etsuko. *Kagerō nikki no kenkyū.* Tokyo: Meiji Shoin, 1972.

Minamoto no Shitagou
Okada, Mareo. *Minamoto no Shitagou kō.* Ritsumeikan daigaku ronsō, vol. 4.

Minamoto no Takakuni
Hisamatsu, Sen'ichi. *Nihon bungakushi chūko,* vol. 2. Tokyo: Shibundō, 1955.

Minamoto no Toshiyori
Usami, Kimihachi. "Minamoto no Toshiyori den no kenkyū." *Wakashi ni kansuru kenkyū.* Tokyo: Wakatake Shuppan, 1953.
Sekine, Keiko. *Samboku kikashū no kenkyū to kōhon.* Tokyo: Meiji Tosho Shuppan, 1952.

Minamoto no Tsunenobu
Hisamatsu, Sen'ichi. *Kodai chūsei hen.* Nihon bungaku hyōronshi, vol. 1. Tokyo: Shibundō, 1949.
Sekine, Keiko. *Shikashū no kenkyū.* Tokyo: Kazama Shoten, 1967.

Mishima Yukio
Terada, Tōru. "Mishima Yukio ron." *Gunzō,* 1953.
Isoda, Kōichi. "Junkyō no bigaku—Mishima Yukio ron." *Bungakukai,* 1964.

Mitomi Kyūyō
Kubota, Hanya. "Kindai shishi ni okeru Mitomi Kyūyō." *Meiji-Taishō bungaku kenkyū.* Tokyo: Tokyodō, 1949–59.
Muramatsu, Takeshi. "Nihon no shōchō shugi—Mitomi Kyūyō." *Bungaku,* 1962.

Miyake Setsurei
Yanagida, Izumi. *Tetsujin Miyake Setsurei sensei.* Tokyo: Jitsugyō no Nihonsha, 1956.
Sakata, Yoshio, ed. *Meiji zenhanki no nashonarizumu.* Tokyo: Miraisha, 1958.

Miyamoto Yuriko
"Miyamoto Yuriko tokushū." *Kindai Bungaku,* 1951.
Honda, Shūgo, ed. *Miyamoto Yuriko kenkyū.* Tokyo: Shinchōsha, 1957.

Miyazaki Koshoshi
Rai, Michiko. "Miyazaki Koshoshi shiron." *Kokubun,* 1960.

Miyazaki Sammai
"Miyazaki Sammai." *Kindai bungaku kenkyū sōsho.* Tokyo: Shōwa Women's University, 1962.

Mizuhara Shūōshi
Yamamoto, Kenkichi. "Mizuhara Shūōshi." *Gendai Haiku,* vol. 1.
"Shūōshi tokushūgō." *Haiku,* 1952.

Morikawa Kyoriku (Kyoroku)
Kinsei haiku haibun-shū. Nihon koten bungaku taikei, vol. 92. Tokyo: Iwanami Shoten, 1964.

Mori Ōgai
Takahashi, Yoshitaka. *Mori Ōgai.* Tokyo: Shinchōsha, 1954.
Hasegawa, Izumi. *Mori Ōgai ronkō.* Tokyo: Meiji Shoin, 1965.
Mori, Oto. *Mori Ōgai.* Nara: Yōtokusha, 1949.

Motoori Norinaga
Ban, Nobutomo. *Suzunoyaō ryakunempu.*
Muraoka, Noritsugu. *Motoori Norinaga.* Keiseisha, 1911.
Hisamatsu, Sen'ichi. "Norinaga no mono no aware to kaminagara michi." *Jōdai Nihon bungaku no kenkyū.*
Sasatsuki, Kiyomi. *Motoori Norinaga no kenkyū.* Tokyo: Iwanami Shoten, 1944.

Mujū
Nishio, Kōichi. *Chūsei no setsuwa*. Nihon bungaku kōza, vol. 3. Tokyo: Kawade Shobō, 1951.

Mukai Kyorai
Nakanishi, Kei. *Mukai Kyorai*. Haiku kōza, vol. 2. Tokyo: Meiji Shoin.
Ehara, Taizō. *Kyorai-shō, Sanzōshi, Tabine ron*. Tokyo: Iwanami Shoten.

Munenaga Shinnō
Kawada, Jun. *Yoshino-chō no hika*. Tokyo: Daiichi Shobō, 1938.

Murai Gensai
Ebihara, Hachirō. *Murai Gensai shōron*.

Murakami Kijō
Urano, Yoshio. "Murakami Kijō no shōgai to haidō." *Shuntō*, 1948-50.
Tajima, Takeo. "Murakami Kijō." *Haiku*, 1957.

Murakami Namiroku
Murakami, Namiroku. *Waga gojūnen*.
Nihon bungaku daijiten. Tokyo: Shinchōsha.

Murasaki Shikibu
Oka, Kazuo. *Genji monogatari no kiso-teki kenkyū*.
Shimazu, Hisamoto. *Murasaki Shikibu*. Tokyo: Seigodō, 1943.
Abe, Akio. *Murasaki Shikibu nikki zenshaku*. Tokyo: Shino Kokyōsha, 1949.
Imai, Gen'e. *Murasaki Shikibu*. Tokyo: Yoshikawa Kōbunkan, 1966.

Murata Harumi
Hisamatsu, Sen'ichi. *Nihon bungaku hyōronshi*. Tokyo: Shibundō, 1952.
Sasaki, Nobutsuna. *Wakashi no kenkyū*. Tokyo: Dai Nihon Gakujutsu Kyōkai, 1915.

Muro Kyūsō
Ishikawa, Matsutarō. *Kaibara Ekiken, Muro Kyūsō shū*. Sekai kyōiku hōten, Nihon hen. Tokyo: Tamagawa University Press, 1968.

Mushanokōji Saneatsu
Kamei, Katsuichirō. *Mushakōji Saneatsu ron*. Gendai Nihon bungaku zenshū, vol. 19. "Shirakaba-ha no bungaku." *Kaishaku to Kanshō*, tokushū, 1957.

Musō Soseki
Tamamura, Takeji. *Musō kokushi*. Kyoto: Heigakuji Shoin, 1958.

Myōe
Tanaka, Hisao. *Myōe*. Yoshikawa kōbundō jimbutsu sōsho. Tokyo: Yoshikawa Kōbunkan, 1961.
Shirasu, Masako. *Myōe shōnin*. Tokyo: Kōdansha.

Myōkū
Yoshida, Tōgo, et al. *Enkyoku zenshū, furoku rombun*.
Takano, Tatsuyuki. *Nihon kayōshi*. Tokyo: Shunjūsha, 1926.

Nagai Kafū
Nakamura, Shin'ichirō, ed. *Nagai Kafū kenkyū*. Tokyo: Shinchōsha, 1956.
"Nagai Kafū tsuitō tokushū-gō." *Chūō Kōron*, 1959.

Nagatsuka Takashi
Saitō, Mokichi, ed. "Nagatsuka Takashi kashū." *Kaisetsu*, 1933.
Fujikawa, Chūji. "Nagatsuka Takashi no geijutsu-ron." *Kokugo to Kokubungaku*, vol. 8, nos. 1-3.

Naitō Jōsō
Morikawa, Kyoriku. *Fūzoku monzen*. Tokyo: Iwanami Shoten, 1949.
——, and Mukai, Kyorai, eds. *Haikai mondō*. Tokyo: Iwanami Shoten, 1954.
Ichihashi, Taku. *Jōsō denki kōsetsu*. Nagoya: Aichi Kenritsu Daigaku Kokubun Gakkai, 1964.

Naitō Meisetsu
Masaoka, Shiki. "Naitō Meisetsu." *Hototogisu*, 1897.
Shibata, Shokyoku. *Shiki o meguru hitobito*. Haiku kōza, vol. 8. Tokyo: Meiji Shoin, 1958.

Nakae Chōmin
Kōtoku, Shūsui. *Chōmin sensei*. Kōtoku Shūsui senshū, vol. 1.
Hijikata, Kazuo. *Nakae Chōmin*. Tokyo: Tokyo University Press, 1958.

Nakamura Kusatao
"Nakamura Kusatao tokushū." *Haiku*, 1958.
Kasai, Teruo. *Nakamura Kusatao*. Gendai bungaku kōza, vol. 9. Tokyo: Meiji Shoin, 1962.

Nakatomi no Yakamori
Ishii, Shoji. *Nakatomi no Ason Yakamori to Sano no Chigami no Otome*. Man'yōshū taisei, vol. 9. Tokyo: Heibonsha, 1953.

Nakatsukasa
Sayama, Sei. "Heianchō utaawase taisei, Ise to Nakatsukasa." *Bungaku*, 1959.

Nakatsukasa no Naishi
Tamai, Kōsuke. *Nakatsukasa no Naishi nikki shinchū*.
Ikeda, Kikan. *Kyūtei joryū nikki bungaku*. Tokyo: Shibundō, 1927.

Nakazawa Rinsen
Nakazawa Rinsen. Kindai bungaku kenkyū sōsho, vol. 19. Tokyo: Shōwa Women's University, 1962.

Namiki Gohei
Hanabusa, Yoshizane. *Engeki tsūshi*.
Ihara, Seiseien. *Namiki Gohei kenkyū*. Nihon bungaku kōza, vol. 10. Tokyo: Shinchōsha, 1931–32.
Ihara, Toshio. *Kinsei Nihon engekishi*. Tokyo: Waseda University, 1913.

Natsume Sōseki
Senuma, Shigeki. *Natsume Sōseki*. Tokyo: University of Tokyo Press, 1970.
Eto, Jun. *Natsume Sōseki*. Tokyo: Shinchōsha, 1974.

Nichiren
Nichirenshū. Nihon koten bungaku taikei, vol. 82. Tokyo: Iwanami Shoten.

Nijō Yoshimoto
Fukui, Kyūzō. *Nijō Yoshimoto*. Seigodō, 1943.

Niwa Fumio
Terada, Tōru. "Niwa Fumio ron." *Tembō*, 1950.
"Niwa Fumio: hito to sakuhin." *Bungakukai*, 1953.

Nogami Yaeko
Senuma, Shigeki. "Nogami Yaeko ron." *Taishō no sakkatachi*. Tokyo: Eihōsha, 1955.
Tanikawa, Tetsuzō. *Nogami Yaeko*. Gendai Nihon bungaku zenshū, vol. 28. Tokyo: Chikuma Shobō, 1955.

Nomura Bōtō-ni
Kubo, Onokichi. "Nomura Bōtō-ni to sono shūi." *Kokugo to Kokubungaku*, vol. 4, no. 10.

Nukada no Ōkimi
Tani, Kaoru, *Nukada no Ōkimi*. Tokyo, Waseda Daigaku Shuppan, 1960.
Tanabe, Yukio. *Nukada no Ōkimi*. Shoki Man'yō no sekai. Tokyo: Hanawa Shobō, 1957.
Oyama, Tokujirō. *Nukada no Ōkimi kō*. Man'yōshū taisei, sakka kenkyū-hen. Tokyo: Heibonsha, 1953.

Ochiai Naofumi
Koyama, Shin'ichi. "Ochiai Naobumi ron." *Seiju*, Meiji tanka kenkyūgō, June, 1925.
Kaneko, Kun'en. "Ochiai Naobumi no kokubun shiika shin'undō." *Waseda Bungaku*, June, 1924.
Katagiri, Akitomo. *Ochiai Naobumi ron; Ochiai Naobumi shū*. Meiji bungaku zenshū. Tokyo: Chikuma Shobō, 1968.

Ōe no Masafusa
Yamanaka, Yutaka. "Ōe no Masafusa." *Kokugo to Kokubungaku*, Oct., 1957.
Totani, Mitsue. "Ōe no Masafusa no uta." *Bungaku Gogaku*, vol. 19.

Ōe no Masahira
Manabe, Noriko. "Akazome Emon no shūhen." *Bungaku Gogaku*.
Okada, Masayuki. *Nihon kambungakushi*. Tokyo: Kyōritsusha Shoten, 1929; Tokyo: Yoshikawa Kōbunkan, 1954.

Ogyū Sorai
Iwahashi, Junsei. *Sorai kenkyū*. Tokyo: Seki Shoin, 1934.
Imanaka, Hiroshi. *Soraigaku no kisoteki kenkyū*. Tokyo: Yoshikawa Kōbunkan, 1966.
Nihon bungakushi, kinsei. Tokyo: Shibundō, 1964.
Nihon bungaku daijiten. Tokyo: Shinchōsha, 1950.

Okamoto Kidō
Hata, Kōichi. "Okamato Kidō ron." *Engei gahō*. 1923.
Okamoto Kidō shū. Gendai Nihon bungaku zenshū.

Ōkuma Kotomichi
Ueda, Hideo. *Ōkuma Kotomichi*. Nihon kajin kōza, Kinsei no kajin, vol. 5. Tokyo: Kōbundō, 1962.

Ōku no Himemiko
Kawasaki, Yasuyuki. *Temmu tennō no shoōji, shoōjo*. Man'yōshū taisei, vol. 9. Tokyo: Heibonsha, 1953.
Tsugita, Masaki. *Man'yōshū no kōshitsu kajin*. Man'yōshū kōza. Tokyo: Sōgensha, 1952.

Ōmachi Keigetsu
Hinatsu, Kōnosuke. *Meiji Taishō shishi*, vol. 1. Tokyo: Sōgensha, 1951.

Onoe Saishū
"Onoe Saishū tsuitōgō." *Mizugame*, 1957.
Kubota, Utsubo, et al, eds. *Meiji tankashi*. Kindai tankashi, vol. 1. Tokyo: Shunjūsha, 1958.

Ono no Komachi
Kuroiwa, Ruikō. *Ono no Komachi ron*.
Nishishita, Kyōichi. "Densetsuka sareta Ono no Komachi," *Kokugo to Kokubungaku*, 1929.
Takasaki, Masahide. *Rokkasen zengo*. Takasaki Masahide chosakushū, vol. 4. Tokyo: Ōfūsha, 1971.

Ono no Takamura
Haga, Yaichi. *Nihon kambungakushi*.
Hisamatsu, Sen'ichi. *Nihon bungakushi, chūko*. Tokyo: Shibundō, 1955.

Ō no Yasumaro
Kurano, Kenji. *Kojiki ronkō.* Kyoto: Kyoto In Shoten, 1944.
Yamada, Takao. *Kojiki gaisetsu.* Tokyo: Chūō Kōronsha, 1941.
Watsuji, Tetsurō. *Nihon kodai bunka.* Tokyo: Iwanami Shoten, 1951.

Origuchi Shinobu
"Origuchi Shinobu tsuitōgō." *Tanka,* 1954.
Chikatsu, Shigeji, and Okano, Hirohiko. *Shakuchōkū.* Kindai tanka, vol. 4. Tokyo: Ōfūsha Shuppan, 1961.

Ōshikōchi no Mitsune
Minegishi, Yoshiaki. *Ōshikōchi no Mitsune.* Nihon kajin kōza, Chūko kajin. Sendai: Bunritosho Shuppansha, 1961.
Matsuda, Takeo. *Ōchō wakashū no kenkyū.* Tokyo: Ganshōdō Shoten, 1936.

Ōtagaki Rengetsu
Murakami, Sodō. *Rengetsu-ni zenshū.* Kyoto: Rengetsu-ni Zenshū Hampukai, 1927.

Ōta Mizuho
Shiga, Mitsuko, and Kimata, Osamu. "Ōta Mizuho to sono nagare." *Tanka,* 1958.
Ōta, Seikyū. *Ōta Mizuho.* Tokyo: Ōfūsha Shuppan, 1961.

Ōta Nampo
Tsurumi, Tokō. *Ōta Nampo.*
Suga, Chikuho. *Kinsei kyōkashi.* Tokyo: Nakanishi Shobō, 1936.

Ōtomo no Ikenushi
Man'yōshū taisei. Tokyo: Heibonsha, 1953–56.

Ōtomo no Kuronushi
Fujiwara no Kensho. *Kokinshū mokuroku.*
Fujimura, Tsukuru. *Nihon bungaku daijiten.* Tokyo: Shinchōsha, 1932–35.
Kubota, Utsubo. *Kokin wakashū hyōshaku,* 2 vols. Tokyo: Tokyodō, 1935, 1937.

Ōtomo no Tabito
Takeda, Yukichi. *Ōtomo no Tabito.* Man'yōshū kōza, ch. 1. Tokyo: Sōgensha, 1952.
Tsuchiya, Bummei. *Tabito to Okura.*
Gomi, Chiei. *Ōtomo no Tabito josetsu.* Man'yōshū taisei, vol. 10. Tokyo: Heibonsha, 1954.

Ōtomo no Yakamochi
Oyama, Tokujirō. *Ōtomo no Yakamochi no kenkyū.* Tokyo: Heibonsha, 1956.
Hisamatsu, Sen'ichi. *Ōtomo no Yakamochi.* Man'yōshū kōza, sakusha kenkyū-hen, vol. 1. Tokyo: Shun'yōdō, 1933.
Kawasaki, Yasuyuki. *Ōtomo no Yakamochi.* Kiki Man'yō no sekai. Tokyo: Ochanomizu Shobō, 1952.

Ōtsu no Miko
Kawasaki, Yasuyuki. *Temmu tennō no shoōji, shoōjo.* Man'yōshū taisei, vol. 9. Tokyo: Heibonsha, 1953.
Tsugita, Masaki. *Man'yōshū no kōshitsu kajin.* Man'yōshū kōza. Tokyo: Sōgensha, 1952.

Oyama Tokujirō
"Oyama Tokujirō tsuitō tokushū." *Tanka,* Aug., 1963.

Ozaki Kōyō
Tokuda, Shūsei. *Ozaki Kōyō kenkyū.* Nihon bugaku kōza, vol. 13. Tokyo: Shinchōsha, 1931–32.

Fukuda, Kiyoto. *Ozaki Kōyō.* Kindai bungaku kanshō kōza, vol. 2. Tokyo: Kadokawa Shoten, 1959.

Ozawa Roan
Sasaki, Nobutsuna. *Nihon kagakushi.* Tokyo: Hakubunkan, 1910.
Hisamatsu, Sen'ichi, ed. *Kinsei.* Nihon bungakushi, vol. 4. Tokyo: Shibundō, 1956.
Sasaki, Nobutsuna. *Kinsei wakashi.* Tokyo: Hakubunkan, 1923.
Kinsei wakashū. Nihon koten bugaku taikei, vol. 93. Tokyo: Iwanami Shoten, 1966.

Rai San'yō
Tokutomi, Iichirō. *Rai San'yō.* Tokyo: Min'yūsha, 1926.
Ichishima, Kenkichi. *Zuihitsu Rai San'yō.*

Reizei Tamehide
Sasaki, Nobutsuna. *Nihon kagakushi.* Tokyo: Hakubunkan, 1910, 1942.
Fukui, Kyūzō. *Dai Nihon kagakushi.* Tokyo: Fuji Shobō, 1926.
Inoue, Muneo. *Nambokuchōki.* Chūsei kadanshi no kenkyū. Tokyo: Meiji Shoin, 1965.

Reizei Tamesuke
Hisamatsu, Sen'ichi. "Tamesuke to Reizeike kagaku no tanjō." *Bungaku,* Aug., 1934.

Ryōkan
Yoshino, Hideo. *Ryōkan oshō no hito to uta.* Tokyo: Yayoi Shobō, 1971.
Takagi, Ichinosuke, and Hisamatsu, Sen'ichi. *Ryōkan.* Nihon koten bungaku taikei, vol. 93. Tokyo: Iwanami Shoten, 1966.

Ryūtei Rijō
Asō, Isoji. *Kokkeibon no kenkyū.* Nihon bungaku kōza, vol. 4. Tokyo: Kaizōsha, 1933–35.
Mizuno, Minoru. *Edo chōnin bungaku.* Iwanami kōza, Nihon bungakushi. Tokyo: Iwanami Shoten.

Ryūtei Tanehiko
Mizutani, Futō. *Retsudentai shōsetsushi.* Tokyo: Shun'yōdō, 1897.
Yamaguchi, Gō. *Tanehiko kessakushū kaidai.* Shinteikoku Bunko.
Ishida, Motosue. *Kusazōshi no iroiro.* Tokyo: Nansō Shoin, 1928.
Nihon bungakushi, kinsei. Tokyo: Shibundō, 1955–60.

Saganoya Omuro
Sasabuchi, Tomoichi. *Rōman shugi bungaku no tanjō.* Tokyo: Meiji Shoin, 1958.

Saga Tennō
Ozawa, Masao. "Heian jidai shoki ni okeru kanshi to waka no shōchō." *Kokugo to Kokubun,* 1948.
Matsuura, Sadatoshi. "Ryōunshū kenkyū oboegaki." *Bungaku ronsō.* 1952.

Saigyō
Kubota, Shōichirō. *Saigyō no kenkyū.* Tokyo: Yagumo Shorin, 1943.

Saimei Tennō
Sawagata, Hisataka. *Man'yō kajin no tanjō.* Tokyo: Heibonsha, 1956.
Tanabe, Yukio. *Shoki Man'yō no sekai.* Tokyo: Hanawa Shobō, 1957.

Saisho Atsuko
Sasaki, Nobutsuna. *Saisho Atsukoshū fuki.* Gendai tanka zenshū, vol. 2. Tokyo: Sōgensha, 1953.

Saitō Mokichi
"Saitō Mokichi tsuitōgō." *Araragi,* Oct., 1953.
Satō, Satarō. *Saitō Mokichi kenkyū.* Tokyo: Hōbunkan, 1957.

Sakanoue no Iratsume
Gomi, Yasuyoshi. *Ōtomo Sakanoue no Iratsume.* Man'yōshū taisei, sakka kenkyū-hen, vol. 2. Tokyo: Heibonsha, 1954.
Goto, Miyoko. *Ōtomo Sakanoue no Iratsume.* Man'yōshū kōza, sakka-hen. Tokyo: Sōgensha, 1952.

Sanjōnishi Sanetaka
Hara, Katsuo. *Higashiyama jidai no ichi-shinshin no seikatsu.* Tokyo: Chikuma Shobō, 1967.

Sano no Chigami no Otome
Ishii, Shōji. *Nakatomi no Ason Yakamori to Sano no Chigami no Otome.* Man'yōshū taisei, vol. 9. Tokyo: Heibonsha, 1953.

Santō Kyōden
Miyatake, Gaikotsu. *Santō Kyōden.*
Koike, Tōgorō. *Santō Kyōden no kenkyū.* Tokyo: Iwanami Shoten, 1935.
Mizuno, Minoru. *Kyōden, Bakin.*
Kōki Edo chōnin bungaku. Iwanami kōza, Nihon bungakushi. Tokyo: Iwanami Shoten
Hisamatsu, Sen'ichi. *Kinsei.* Nihon bungakushi, vol. 4. Tokyo: Shibundō, 1956.

Sanuki no Suke
Ozaki, Tomomitsu. *Sanuki no suke nikki.* Tokyo: Ōfūsha, 1960.
Tamai, Kōsuke. *Sanuki no suke nikki.* Tokyo: Asahi Shimbunsha, 1953.

Sasakawa Rimpū
Hisamatsu, Sen'ichi, ed. *Sasakawa Rimpū shū,* Meiji bungaku zenshū, vol. 41. 1971.

Sasaki Nobutsuna
"Sasaki Nobutsuna tsuitōgō." *Kokoro no Hana,* April, 1964.

Sassa Seisetsu
Sassa Seisetsu. Kindai bungaku kenkyū sōsho, vol. 17. Tokyo: Kōyōkai, Shōwa Women's University, 1961.

Satomi Ton
Miyoshi, Yukio. *Satomi Ton ron.* Taishō no sakka tachi. Tokyo: Eihōsha, 1955.
Muramatsu, Sadataka. "Satomi Ton to Shirakaba-ha: Shiga Naoya kara dasshutsu wo chūshin to shite." *Meiji Taishō Bungaku Kenkyū,* Jan., 1956.

Sei Shōnagon
Kishigami, Shinji. *Sei Shōnagon denkikō.* Tokyo: Shinseisha, 1958.
Ikeda, Kikan. *Chūko kokubungaku sōkō.*
Tanaka, Jūtarō. *Sei Shōnagon.* Asahi koten zensho. Tokyo: Asahi Shimbunsha, 1957.

Shiga Mitsuko
Gendai tanka taikei, vol. 3. Tokyo: Kawade Shobō, 1952.
Shiga Mitsuko zenkashū. Tokyo: Shunjūsha, 1961.

Shiga Naoya
Kobayashi, Hideo. "Shiga Naoya ron." *Kaizō,* 1939.
Nakamura, Mitsuo. *Shiga Naoya ron.* Tokyo: Bungei Shunjūsha, 1954.

Shiki no Miko
Takeda, Yukichi. *Sakusha-betsu Man'yōshū hyōshaku,* vol. 1. Tokyo: Hibonkaku, 1935.
Saitō, Mokichi. *Man'yō shūka.* Tokyo: Iwanami Shoten, 1949.

Shikishi Naishinnō
Kunishima, Akie. "Shikishi Naishinnō ron." *Kaishaku to Kanshō,* 1949.
Yasuda, Ayao. *Shin kokinshū kajin ron.* Tokyo: Ōfūsha, 1960.

Shikitei Samba
Fujii, Otsuo. *Shikitei Samba*. Edo bungaku kenkyū. Tokyo: Naigai Shuppan, 1921.

Shimagi Akahiko
Saitō, Mokichi. *Shimagi Akahiko*. Tokyo: Kadokawa Shoten, 1949.

Shimamura Hōgetsu
Kawafuku, Kunimoto. *Shimamura Hōgetsu*. Tokyo: Waseda University, 1953.
Ozaki, Hirotsugu. *Shimamura Hōgetsu*. Tokyo: Miraisha, 1965.

Shimazaki Tōson
Hirano, Ken. *Shimazaki Tōson*. Tokyo: Kawade Shobō, 1953.
Shibukawa, Gyō. *Shimazaki Tōson*. Tokyo: Chikuma Shobō, 1964.

Shimizu Hamaomi
Hisamatsu, Sen'ichi, ed. *Nihon bungakushi*. Tokyo: Shibundō, 1956.

Shimokōbe Chōryū
Sasaki, Nobutsuna. *Nihon kagakushi*. Tokyo: Hakubunkan, 1910.
———. *Kinsei wakashi*. Tokyo: Hakubunkan, 1923.
Hisamatsu, Sen'ichi. *Keichū no shōgai*. Osaka: Sōgensha, 1942.

Shinkei
Araki, Yoshio. *Shinkei*. Tokyo: Sōgensha, 1948.

Shinran
Jūkaku. *Mattoshū*.
Uien. *Tannishō*.
Nakata, Ōjun, et al. *Shinranshū; Nichirenshū*. Nihon koten bungaku taikei, vol. 82. Tokyo: Iwanami Shoten, 1964.

Shioi Ukō
Shioi Ukō. Kindai bungaku kenkyū sōsho, vol. 13. Tokyo: Kōyōkai, Shōwa Women's University, 1959.
Shioi Ukō shū. Meiji bungaku zenshū, vol. 41. Tokyo: Chikuma Shobō, 1971.

Shōmu Tennō
Takeda, Yukichi. *Kōshitsu kajin*. Sakusha-betsu Man'yōshū hyōshaku, vol. 1. Tokyo: Hibonkaku, 1935.
Hisamatsu, Sen'ichi. *Shōmu Tennō to Man'yōshū*. Man'yōshū to sono zengo. Tokyo: Tōkō Shoin, 1958.

Shōtoku Taishi
Kimoto, Michifusa. *Jōdai kayō shōkai*.
Kawamura, Etsumaro. *Man'yōshū densetsu kakō*. Tokyo: Kōshisha Shobō, 1936.
Hisamatsu, Sen'ichi. *Shōtoku Taishi no waka*. Man'yōshū to sono zengo. Tokyo: Tōkō Shoin, 1958.

Shūa
Fukui, Kyūzō. *Renga no shi-teki kenkyū*, 2 vols. Tokyo: Seibidō Shoten, 1930, 1931.
Kitō, Saizō. *Rengashi ronkō*. Tokyo: Meiji Shoin, 1973.

Shun'e
Shimazu, Tadao. "Shun'e hōshi o megutte—sono wakashiteki kōsatsu." *Kokugo Kokubun*, 1953.
Yanase, Kazuo. *Shun'e hōshi zenkashū*.

Sōgi
Kaneko, Kinjirō. *Shinsen Tsukuba shū no kenkyū*. Tokyo: Kazama Shobō, 1969.
Etō, Yasusada. *Sōgi no kenkyū*.

Sōjō Henjō
Hisamatsu, Sen'ichi. *Wakashi sōron, kodaihen,* vol. 1. Tokyo: Tokyodō, 1948.
Hon'iden, Shigemi. "Rokkasen zengo, Sōjō Henjō." *Kokubungaku,* 1957.

Sone no Yoshitada
Kubota, Toshi. *Sone no Yoshitada.* Nihon kajin kōza, vol. 2. Tokyo: Kōbundō, 1960.
Ikeda, Yasaburō. *Nihon bungakushi nōto II, Sone no Yoshitada.* Nihon bugaku kōza, vol. 2. Tokyo: Kawade Shobō, 1950.

Sugawara no Michizane
Kawaguchi, Hisao. *Heianchō Nihon kambungakushi no kenkyū,* vols. 1, 2. Tokyo: Meiji Shoin, 1959, 1961.

Susukida Kyūkin
Hinatsu, Kōnosuke. *Susukida Kyūkin.* Meiji Taishō shijin. Tokyo: Kaname Shobō, 1950.
Matsumura, Midori. *Susukida Kyūkin.* Tokyo: Kadokawa Shoten, 1959.

Tachibana Akemi
Tsujimori, Shūei. *Tachibana Akemi.* Yūkōsha, 1943.

Tachibana Chikage
Sasaki, Nobutsuna. *Wakashi no kenkyū.* Tokyo: Dai Nihon Gakujutsu Kyōkai, 1915.
Nomura, Hachirō. *Kokugaku zenshi,* vol. 2. Tokyo: Seki Shoin, 1929.
Sekine, Masanao. "Katō Chikage to sono jisei." *Karasukago.*

Taira no Kanemori
Fujioka, Sakutarō. *Kokubungaku zenshi, Heianchō-hen.* Tokyo: Kaiseikan, 1906.

Tajima no Himemiko
Morimoto, Kenkichi, *Man'yō kōshitsu kajin.* Nihon bungakusha hyōden zensho.
Tsugita, Masaki. *Man'yōshū no kōshitsu kajin.* Man'yōshū kōza, sakka-hen, vol. 4. Tokyo: Sōgensha, 1952–54.

Takahama Kyoshi
Mizuhara, Shūōshi. *Takahama Kyoshi.* Tokyo: Bungei Shunjūsha, 1952.
Yamamoto, Kenkichi. "Takahama Kyoshi." *Shōwa haiku.* Tokyo: Kadokawa Shoten, 1958.

Takami Jun
Nakamura, Shin'ichirō. "Takami Jun." *Gunzō.*
Yamamoto, Kenkichi. "Tokyo no hedo o haku sakka: Takami Jun no hito to sakuhin." *Bungei Shunjū,* bessatsu, 1953.

Takasaki Masakaze
Koizumi, Tōzō. *Outadokoro-ha.* Kindai tankashi, Meiji-hen. Tokyo: Hakuyōsha, 1955.
Kimata, Osamu. *Takasaki Masakaze.* Meiji tanka kōza, vol. 1.

Takasue no Musume
Ikeda, Kikan. *Joryū nikki bungaku.* Tokyo: Shibundō, 1927.
Tamai, Kōsuke. *Sarashina nikki sakukkan-kō.* Ikuei Shoin, 1925.
Nishishita, Keiichi. *Sarashina nikki.* Nihon koten bungaku taikei.

Takayama Chogyū
Okazaki, Yoshie. *Takayama Chogyū ron.* Meiji Taishō bungaku kenkyū.
Naruse, Masakatsu. "Chogyū, Niichie, Sōshi." *Hon,* 1964.

Takayama Sōzei
Shimazu, Tadao. "Sōzei no sakufū," *Kokugo Kokubun,* 1957.

Takebe Ayatari
Maeda, Toshiharu. "Takebe Ayatari ron." *Kaishaku,* June, 1962.

Hamadate, Sadakichi. *Kanyōsai Takebe Ayatari.* 1929.

Takechi no Miko
Tsugita, Masaki. *Man'yōshū no kōshitsu kajin.* Man'yōshū kōza, sakka-hen. Tokyo: Sōgensha, 1952.
Kawasaki, Yasuyuki. *Temmu tennō no shoōji, shoōjo.* Man'yōshū taisei, vol. 9. Tokyo: Heibonsha, 1953.

Takeda Izumo
Tamenaga, Itchō. *Kabuki kotohajime.*
Shuzui, Kenji. *Kaion, Izumo, Hanji.* Iwanami kōza, Nihon bungaku.
Hisamatsu, Sen'ichi, ed. *Nihon bungakushi: kinsei.* Tokyo, Shibundō, 1956.

Takeshima Hagoromo
Iwaki, Juntarō. *Meiji bungakushi.* Tokyo: Shūbunkan Shoten, 1929.
Hinatsu, Kōnosuke. *Meiji Taishō shishi,* vol. 1. Tokyo: Sōgensha, 1948.
Takeshima Hagoromo shū. Meiji bungaku zenshū. Tokyo: Chikuma Shobō, 1971.

Tameko
Toki, Zemmaro. *Fujiwara Tameko, Kamakura Muromachi shūka.* Waka bungaku jiten. Tokyo: Meiji Shoin, 1962.

Tamenaga Shunsui
Fujioka, Sakutarō. *Kindai shōsetsushi.* Tokyo: Ōkura Shoten, 1917.
Yamaguchi, Gō. *Tamenaga Shunsui kenkyū.* Shinchōsha Nihon bungaku kōza, vol. 10. Tokyo: Shinchōsha, 1931–32.
Jimbo, Kazuya. *Tamenaga Shunsui no kenkyū.* Tokyo: Hakujitsusha, 1964.

Tanabe no Sakimaro
Hisamatsu, Sen'ichi. *Tanabe no Sakimaro.* Man'yōshū nyūmon.
Okabe, Masahiro. *Takahashi no Mushimaro to Tanabe no Sakimaro.* Man'yōshū taisei, vol. 10. Tokyo: Heibonsha, 1954.

Tanizaki Jun'ichirō
Nakamura, Mitsuo. *Tanizaki Jun'ichirō.* Tokyo: Kawade Shobō, 1952.
Kazamaki, Keijirō, and Yoshida, Seiichi, eds. *Tanizaki Jun'ichirō no bungaku.* Tokyo: Hanawa Shobō, 1954.

Tayama Katai
Masamune, Hakuchō. "Tayama Katai." *Sakkaron.* Tokyo: Sōgensha 1951.
Kobayashi, Ichirō. *Tayama Katai.* Tokyo: Asahisha, 1963.

Temmu Tennō
Omodaka, Hisataka. *Temmu Tennō.* Man'yō kajin no tanjō. Tokyo: Heibonsha, 1956.
Tanabe, Yukio. *Ōama no Miko.* Shoki Man'yō no sekai. Tokyo: Hanawa Shobō, 1957.

Tenji Tennō
Omodaka, Hisataka. *Tenji Tennō no gyosei* Man'yō kajin no tanjō. Tokyo: Heibonsha, 1956.
Tanabe, Yukio. *Tenji Tennō.* Shoki Man'yō no sekai. Tokyo: Hanawa Shobō, 1957.

Toda Mosui
Santō, Kyōzan. *Mosui kō.* 1908.
Sasaki, Nobutsuna. *Kagaku ronsō.* Tokyo: Hakubunkan, 1908.
———. *Toda Mosui ron.* Tokyo: Chikuhakukai, 1913.

Toki Zemmaro
Hyōden Toki Zemmaro. Hashi tankakai, 1964.

Tokuda Shūsei
Hirotsu, Kazuo. "Tokuda Shūsei ron." *Yagumo*, 1944.
Hirano, Ken. "Tokuda Shūsei." *Geijutsu to Jisseikatsu*, 1958.
Noguchi, Fujio. *Tokuda Shūsei den.* Tokyo: Chikuma Shobō, 1965.

Tokugawa Mitsukuni
Takasu, Yoshijirō. *Mito gikō o kataru.* Tokyo: Ida Shoten, 1942.
Okuda, Genzō. *Tokugawa Mitsukuni.* Tokyo: Fukyūsha, 1952.
Saitō, Shin'ichirō, ed. *Gikō kojitsu.* Mito: Mitogaku Shinkōkai, 1954.
Ōkubo, Ryō. *Mito Mitsukuni to Mitogaku.* Tokyo: Daidōkan, 1935.

Tokutomi Roka
"Tokutomi Roka kenkyū." *Meiji-Taishō bungaku kenkyū.* 1957.

Tokutomi Sohō
Masamune, Hakuchō. "Sohō to Roka." *Bundan jimbutsu hyōron.* Tokyo: Chūō Kōronsha, 1932.
Kokuminteki shimeikan no rekishiteki hensen. Kindai Nihon shisōshi kōza, vol. 8, 1961.

Ton'a
Ishida, Yoshisada. *Ton'a, Keiun.* Tokyo: Sanseidō, 1943.
Tsuboi, Shigeji. *Senke Motomaro ron.* Gendaishi kanshō, vol. 2.
Bundo, Junsaku. "Senke Motomaro." *Kokubungaku*, 1960.

Tsubouchi Shōyō
Kawatake, Shigetoshi, and Yanagida, Izumi. *Tsubouchi Shōyō.* Tokyo: Tomiyamabō, 1939.
Tsubouchi, Shikō. *Tsubouchi Shōyō kenkyū.* Tokyo: Waseda Daigaku Shuppan, 1953.

Tsuchii (Doi) Bansui
Hinatsu, Kōnosuke. *Kaitei zōho Meiji Taishō shishi*, vol. 1. Tokyo: Sōgensha, 1951.
Okazaki, Yoshie. *Bansui no shifū.*

Tsuchiya Bummei
Yoneda, Toshiaki. *Tsuchiya Bummei.* Tokyo: Keisō Shobō, 1966.

Tsunenobu no Haha
Sekine, Keiko. *Tsunenobu Haha-no-shū.* Tokyo: Koten Bunko, 1951.

Tsuruya Namboku
Tsubouchi, Shōyō. *Tsuruya Namboku den.*
Kawatake, Shigetoshi. *Kabuki sakusha no kenkyū.* Tokyo: Tokyodō, 1940.

Ueda Akinari
Fujii, Otsuo. *Ayatari to Akinari.* Edo bungaku kenkyū. Kyoto: Naigai Shuppan, 1921.
————, ed. *Akinari ibun.* Kyoto: Naigai Shuppan, 1921.
Moriyama, Shigeo. *Hōken shomin bungaku no kenkyū.* Tokyo: San'ichi Shobō, 1960.
Nakamura, Sachihiko. *Kinsei sakka kenkyū.* Tokyo: San'ichi Shobō, 1971.

Ueda Kazutoshi
"Ueda Kazutoshi tokushūgō." *Kokugo to Kokubungaku.*
Ueda Kazutoshi shū. Meiji bungaku zenshū, vol. 44. 1968.

Wakayama Bokusui
"Saishū, Kun'en, Bokusui, Yūgure-kei kajin tokushū." *Tanka Kenkyū*, Nov., 1963.
Kimata, Osamu. "Wakayama Bokusui." *Kindai tanka no kanshō to hihyō.* Tokyo: Meiji Shoin, 1964.

Wakayama Kishiko
Daigoho, Toshio. *Wakayama Bokusui: denkihen.* Tokyo: Futami Shobō, 1944.

Moriwaki, Kazuo. *Wakayama Bokusui*. Tokyo: Ōfūsha, 1961.

Yamabe no Akahito
Kazamaki, Keijirō. *Yamabe no Akahito*. Man'yōshū taisei, sakka kenkyū-hen, vols. 9, 10. Tokyo: Heibonsha, 1954.
Gomi, Chiei. *Yamabe no Akahito*. Man'yōshū taisei, sakka kenkyū-hen, vol. 9. Tokyo: Heibonsha, 1954.
Ozaki, Nobuo. *Yamabe no Akahito*. Waka bungaku kōza, vol. 5. Tokyo: Ōfūsha, 1969.

Yamada Bimyō
Shioda, Ryōhei. *Yamada Bimyō kenkyū*. Kyoto: Jimbun Shoin, 1938.
Homma, Hisao. *Meiji bungaku sakka ron*. Tokyo: Waseda Daigaku Shuppan, 1951.

Yamaguchi Seishi
Yamamoto, Kenkichi. *Yamaguchi Seishi*. Gendai haiku, vol. 2. Tokyo: Kadokawa Shoten, 1952.
"Seishi tokushū-gō." *Haiku*, 1953.

Yamamoto Yūzō
Kawakami, Tetsutarō. *Yamamoto Yūzō ron*. Nihon bungaku kōza, vol. 13. Tokyo: Kaizōsha, 1933–35.
Masamune, Hakuchō. *Yamamoto Yūzō, sakka ron*. Tokyo: Sōgensha, 1951.

Yamanoue no Okura
Takagi, Ichinosuke. *Okura to Tabito*. Iwanami kōza, Nihon bungaku taisei. Tokyo: Iwanami Shoten.
Tsugita, Masaki. *Yamanoue no Okura*. Man'yōshū taisei, sakka kenkyū-hen. Tokyo: Heibonsha, 1953.

Yamato Takeru no Mikoto
Takagi, Ichinosuke. *Yoshino no ayu*. Tokyo: Iwanami Shoten, 1943.
Toma, Seita. *Yamato Takeru no Mikoto*. Tokyo: Sōgensha, 1953.

Yokoi Yayū
Fujii, Otsuo. *Edo bungaku kenkyū*. Tokyo: Naigai Shuppan, 1921.
Iwata, Kurō. *Yayū*. Haiku kōza, vol. 3. Tokyo: Meiji Shoin, 1957–58.
Ishida, Motosue. "Yayū kenkyū; Yayū-ō nempu." *Haibungaku ronkō*. Yōtokusha, 1944.

Yokomitsu Riichi
Itō, Hitoshi. *Yokomitsu Riichi to shin-kankaku-ha*. Nihon no kindai bungaku. Tokyo: Kōdansha, 1961.

Yosa (Taniguchi) Buson
Teruoka, Yasutaka. *Buson: shōgai to geijutsu*. Tokyo: Meiji Shoin, 1954.
Morimoto, Tetsurō. *Shijin Yosa Buson no sekai*. Tokyo: Shibundō.
Hagiwara, Sakutarō. *Kyōshū no shijin Yosa Buson*. Tokyo: Shinchōsha, 1951.

Yosano Akiko
Shioda, Ryōhei. *Yosano Akiko*.
Kimata, Osamu. *Yosano Akiko*. Gendai bungaku kōza, Hito to sakuhin. Tokyo: Meiji Shoin, 1962.

Yosano Hiroshi
Jimbo, Kōtarō. *Yosano Tekkan ron*. Gendai Nihon shijin ron.
Kimata, Osamu. *Yosano Hiroshi*. Kindai tanka no kanshō to hihyō. Tokyo: Meiji Shoin, 1964.

Yoshida Kenkō
Sano, Yasutarō. *Tsurezuregusa kōgi*. Tokyo: Fukumura Shoten, 1953.

————. "Tsurezuregusa to chosha no seikatsu." *Kaishaku to Kanshō*, March, 1953.
Nishio, Minoru. *Sakuhin kenkyū Tsurezuregusa.* Tokyo: Gakuseisha, 1955.

Yoshida Shōin
Matsumoto, Sannosuke. "Yoshida Shōin." Nihon no meicho, vol. 31. Tokyo: Chūō Kōronsha, 1973.

Yuhara no Ōkimi
Abe, Toshiko. "Yuhara no Ōkimi." *Kokubungaku*, 1958.

Zeami
Nose, Chōji. *Zeami jūrokubushū hyōshaku.*
Nonomura, Kaizō. *Kan'ami Zeami jiseki kō.*
Nishio, Minoru. *Dōgen to Zeami.* Tokyo: Iwanami Shoten, 1965.

Index